Western Civilization

A Brief Survey

Volume II: From the 1400s

Houghton Mifflin Company   **Boston**

Dallas   Geneva, Illinois   Palo Alto   Princeton, New Jersey

S0-AIE-470

8-91

Cover credit: August Macke, *Promenade,* 1913. Oil on canvas. Städtische
Galerie im Lenbachhaus, Munich.

Library of Congress Catalog Card Number: 89-80955
ISBN: 0-395-52990-5

BCDEFGHIJ-A-9543210

Contents

Part IV
The Modern West: From the French Revolution to the Industrial Age 1789–1914

Chapter 11
The Era of the French Revolution: The Affirmation of Liberty and Equality   300

Chapter 12
Ferment of Ideas: Romanticism, Conservatism, Liberalism, Nationalism 328

Chapter 15
Europe in the Industrial Age: Modernization and Imperialism

Chapter 18
The Soviet Union: Modernization and Totalitarianism

Part VI
The Contemporary World: The Global Age
Since 1945

Chapter 21
Europe After 1945: Recovery, Realignment,
Division   562

List of Maps

Preface

Western civilization is a grand but tragic drama. The West has forged the instruments of reason that make possible a rational comprehension of physical nature and human culture, conceived the idea of political liberty, and recognized the intrinsic worth of the individual. But the modern West, though it has unravelled nature's mysteries, has been less successful at finding rational solutions to social ills and conflicts between nations. Science, the great achievement of the Western intellect, while improving conditions of life, has also produced weapons of mass destruction. Though the West has pioneered in the protection of human rights, it has also produced totalitarian regimes that have trampled on individual freedom and human dignity. And although the West has demonstrated a commitment to human equality, it has also practiced brutal racism.

Despite the value that Westerners have given to reason and freedom, they have shown a frightening capacity for irrational behavior and a fascination for violence and irrational ideologies, and they have willingly sacrificed liberty for security or national grandeur. The world wars and totalitarian movements of the twentieth century have demonstrated that Western civilization, despite its extraordinary achievements, is fragile and perishable.

Western Civilization: A Brief Survey is an abridged version of *Western Civilization: Ideas, Politics, and Society*. Like the longer text, this volume examines the Western tradition—those unique patterns of thought and systems of values that constitute the Western heritage. While focusing on key ideas and broad themes, the text also provides economic, political, and social history for students in Western civilization courses.

The text is written with the conviction that history is not a meaningless tale. Without a knowledge of history, men and women cannot fully know themselves, for all human beings have been shaped by institutions and values inherited from the past. Without an awareness of the historical evolution of reason and freedom, the dominant ideals of Western civilization, commitment to these ideals will diminish. Without a knowledge of history, the West cannot fully comprehend or adequately cope with the problems that burden its civilization and the world.

In attempting to make sense out of the past, the author has been careful to avoid superficial generalizations that oversimplify historical events and forces and arrange history into too neat a structure. But the text does strive to interpret and synthesize in order to provide students with a frame of reference with which to comprehend the principal events and eras in Western history.

Distinctive Features

This brief edition was prepared for Western Civilization courses that run for one term only, for instructors who like to supplement the main text with primary-source readers, novels, or monographs, and for humanities courses in which additional works on literature and art will be assigned. In abbreviating the longer text by about a third, the number of chapters has been reduced from 37 to 22. The emphasis on the history of ideas and culture has been retained, but the amount of detail has of necessity been reduced.

The text contains several pedagogical features. Chapter introductions provide comprehensive overviews of key themes and give a sense of direction and coherence to the flow of history. Many chapters contain concluding essays that treat the larger meaning of the material. Facts have been carefully selected to illustrate key relationships and concepts and to avoid overwhelming students with unrelated and disconnected data. Each chapter concludes with an annotated bibliography and review questions. The questions refer students to principal points and aim at eliciting thoughtful answers. In addition to the many illustrations and 32 maps, there is a color art insert. The art captions include questions that call on students to draw historical inferences from what they see.

This text is published in both single-volume and two-volume editions. Volume I treats the period from the first civilizations in the Near East through the Age of Enlightenment in the eighteenth century (Chapters 1–10). Volume II covers the period from the Renaissance and the Reformation to the contemporary age (Chapters 8–22), and incorporates the last three chapters in Volume I: "Transition to the Modern Age: Renaissance and Reformation," "Political and Economic Transformation: National States, Overseas Expansion, Commercial Revolution," and "Intellectual Transformation: The Scientific Revolution and the Age of Enlightenment." Volume II also contains a comprehensive introduction that surveys the ancient world and the Middle Ages; the introduction is designed particularly for students who have not taken the first half of the course.

Ancillaries

Learning and teaching ancillaries, including a *Study Guide, Instructor's Manual with Test Items,* and *Map Transparencies* also contribute to the text's usefulness. The *Study Guide* has been prepared by Professor Lyle E. Linville of Prince George's Community College. For each text chapter, the *Study Guide* contains an introduction, learning objectives, words to know, identifications, a map study exercise, chronological/relational exercises, multiple-choice and essay questions, and a "transition," which reflects back on the chapter and looks forward to the next chapter's topic. The map study has outline maps, and students are asked to locate geographical features on them. A duplicate set of maps appears at the back of the book and may be removed for use in class quizzes. In the chronological/relational exercises, students are asked to put a list of items in their chronological order; then in an exercise that develops critical thinking skills, students are asked to write a paragraph indicating the relationship of the items to one another, along with their historical significance.

The *Instructor's Manual with Test Items* was also prepared for the brief edition by Professor Linville. The *Manual* contains chapter outlines, learning objectives, lecture topics, a film/video bibliography, essay and discussion questions, multiple-choice questions, and identifications. In addition, a set of 30 map transparencies is available on adoption.

Acknowledgments

In preparing this abridgement, I have made extensive use of the chapters written by my colleagues for *Western Civilization: Ideas, Politics, and Society*. Chapter 8, "Transition to the Modern Age: Renaissance and Reformation," and Chapter 9, "Political and Economic Transformation: National States, Overseas Expansion, Commercial Revolution," are based largely on James R. Jacob's and Margaret C. Jacob's chapters in the longer volume. Chapter 10, "Intellectual Transformation: The Scientific Revolution and the Age of Enlightenment," is drawn largely from Margaret C. Jacob's material. Much of Chapter 14, "The Industrial Revolution: The Transformation of Society," and Chapter 15, "Europe in the Industrial Age: Modernization and Imperialism," is drawn from Myrna Chase's chapters. Chapter 18, "The Soviet Union: Modernization and Totalitarianism," and the two concluding chapters—"Europe After 1945: Recovery, Realignment, Division" and "The New Globalism: Problems and Prospects"—are an abridgement of Theodore H. Von Laue's chapters. To a lesser or greater extent, my colleagues' material has been abridged, restructured, and rewritten to meet the needs of this volume. Therefore, I alone am responsible for all interpretations and any errors. I wish to thank my colleagues for their gracious permission to use their words and thoughts.

Also, I would like to thank the following instructors for their critical reading of sections of the manuscript:

John W. Arnot, *West Los Angeles College*

Achilles Avraamides, *Iowa State University*

Stuart T. Cooke, *College of San Mateo*

Roger P. Davis, *Kearney State College*

Donald S. Gochberg, *Michigan State University*
William E. Gohlman, *State University College of New York at Geneseo*
Robert W. Roetger, *Emerson College*

Many of their suggestions were incorporated into the final version. I am also grateful to the staff at Houghton Mifflin Company who lent their considerable talents to the project. I would like to express my gratitude to George Bock who assisted in the planning of the text from its inception and who read the manuscript with an eye for major concepts and essential relationships. As ever, I am grateful to my wife, Phyllis G. Perry, for her encouragement.

M.P.

Introduction

The Foundations of
Western Civilization

Western civilization is a blending of two traditions that emerged in the ancient world: the Judeo-Christian and the Greco-Roman. Before these traditions took shape, the drama of civilization was well advanced, having arisen some five thousand years ago in Mesopotamia and Egypt.

Religion was the central force in these first civilizations in the Near East. Religion provided explanations for the operations of nature, justified traditional rules of morality, and helped people to deal with their fear of death. Law was considered sacred, a commandment of the gods. Religion united people in the common enterprises needed for survival, such as the construction of irrigation works. Religion also promoted creative achievement in art, literature, and science. In addition, the power of rulers, who were regarded as gods or as agents of the gods, derived from religious traditions. The many achievements of the Egyptians and the Mesopotamians were inherited and assimilated by both the Greeks and the Hebrews, the spiritual ancestors of Western civilization. But Greeks and Hebrews also rejected and transformed elements of the older Near Eastern traditions and conceived a new view of God, nature, and the individual.

The Hebrews

By asserting that God was one, sovereign, transcendent, and good, the Hebrews effected a religious revolution that separated them forever from the world-views of the Mesopotamians and Egyptians. This new conception of God led to a new awareness of the individual. In confronting God, the Hebrews developed an awareness of *self,* or *I.* The individual became conscious of his or her moral autonomy and personal worth. The Hebrews believed that God had bestowed on his people the capacity for moral freedom—they could choose between good and evil. Fundamental to Hebrew belief was the insistence that God had created human beings to be free moral agents. God did not want people to grovel before him, but to fulfill their moral potential by freely making the choice to follow, or not to follow, God's law. Thus, the Hebrews originated the idea of moral freedom—that each individual is responsible for his or her own actions. Inherited by Christianity, this idea of moral autonomy is central to the Western tradition.

The Hebrew conception of ethical monotheism, with its stress on human dignity, is one source of the Western tradition. The other source derives from the ancient Greeks; they originated scientific and philosophic thought and conceived both the idea and the practice of political freedom.

The Greeks

In the Near East, religion dominated political activity, and following the mandates of the gods was a ruler's first responsibility. What made Greek political life different from that of earlier civilizations—and gives it enduring significance—was the Greek's gradual realization that community problems were caused by human beings and required human solutions. The Greeks came to understand law as an achievement of the rational mind, rather than as an edict imposed by the gods. In the process, they also originated the idea of political freedom and created democratic institutions.

Greece comprised small, independent city-states. In the fifth century B.C., the city-state (*polis*) was in its maturity. A self-governing community, it expressed the will of free citizens, not the desires of gods, hereditary kings, or priests. The democratic orientation of the city-states was best exemplified by Athens, which was also the leading cultural center of Greece. In the Assembly, which was open to all adult male citizens, Athenians debated and voted on key issues of state.

In addition to the idea of political freedom, the Greeks conceived a new way of viewing nature and human society. The first speculative philosophers emerged during the sixth century B.C. in Greek cities located in Ionia in Asia Minor. Curious about the basic composition of nature and dissatisfied with earlier legends about creation, the Ionians sought physical, rather than mythico-religious, explanations for natural occurrences.

During this search, these philosophers arrived at a new concept of nature and a new method of inquiry. They maintained that nature was not manipulated by arbitrary and willful gods and that it was not governed by blind chance. The Ionians said that underlying the seeming chaos of nature were principles of order, that is, general rules that could be ascertained by human minds. This discovery marks the beginning of scientific thought. It made possible theoretical thinking and the systematization of knowledge. This is distinct from the mere observation and collection of data. Greek mathematicians, for example, organized the Egyptians' practical experience with land measurements into the logical and coherent science of geometry. In another instance, the Greeks used the data collected by Babylonian priests, who observed the heavens because they believed that the stars revealed their gods' wishes. The

Greeks' purpose was not religious—they sought to discover the geometrical laws underlying the motion of heavenly bodies. At the same time, Greek physicians drew a distinction between medicine and magic, and began to examine human illness in an empirical and rational way. By the fifth century the Greek mind had applied reason to the physical world and to all human activities. This emphasis on reason marks a turning point for human civilization.

In their effort to understand the external world, early Greek thinkers had created the tools of reason. Greek thinkers now began a rational investigation of the human being and the human community. The key figure in this development was Socrates.

Socrates' central concern was the perfection of individual human character, the achievement of moral excellence. Excellence of character was achieved, said Socrates, when individuals regulated their lives according to objective standards arrived at through rational reflection, that is, when reason became the formative, guiding, and ruling agency of the soul. Socrates wanted to subject all human beliefs and behavior to the clear light of reason and in this way to remove ethics from the realm of authority, tradition, dogma, superstition, and myth. He believed that reason was the only proper guide to the most crucial problem of human existence—the question of good and evil.

Plato, Socrates' most important disciple, used his master's teachings to create a comprehensive system of philosophy that embraced the world of nature and the social world. Socrates had taught that there were universal standards of right and justice and that these were arrived at through thought. Building on the insights of his teacher, Plato insisted on the existence of a higher world of reality, independent of the world of things experienced every day. This higher reality, he said, is the realm of Ideas or Forms—unchanging, eternal, absolute, and universal standards of beauty, goodness, justice, and so forth. Truth resides in this world of Forms and not in the world revealed through the human senses.

Aristotle, Plato's student, was the leading expert of his time in every field of knowledge, with the possible exception of mathematics. Aristotle objected to Plato's devaluing of the material world. Possessing a scientist's curiosity to understand the facts of nature, Aristotle appreciated the world of phenomena, of concrete things, and respected knowledge obtained through the senses. Like Plato, Aristotle believed that understanding universal principles is the ultimate aim of knowledge. But unlike Plato, Aristotle held that to obtain such knowledge, the individual must study the world of facts and objects revealed through sight, hearing, and touch. Aristotle adapted Plato's stress on universal principles to the requirements of natural science.

By discovering theoretical reason, by defining political freedom, and by affirming the worth and potential of human personality, the Greeks broke with the past and founded the rational and humanist tradition of the West. "Had Greek civilization never existed," said poet W. H. Auden, "we would never have become fully conscious, which is to say that we would never have become, for better or worse, fully human."[1]

The Hellenistic Age

By 338 B.C., Philip of Macedonia (a kingdom to the north of Greece) had extended his dominion over the Greek city-states. After the assassination of Philip in 336 B.C., his twenty-year-old son Alexander succeeded to the throne. Fiery, proud, and ambitious, Alexander sought to conquer the vast Persian Empire. Winning every battle, Alexander's army carved an empire that stretched from Greece to India. In 323 B.C., Alexander not yet thirty-three years of age, died of a fever. His generals engaged in a long and bitter struggle to succeed him. As none of the generals or their heirs could predominate, Alexander's empire was fractured into separate states.

The period from the early city-states that emerged in 800 B.C. until the death of Alexander the Great in 323 B.C. is called the *Hellenic Age*. The next stage in the evolution of Greek civilization (*Hellenism*) is called the *Hellenistic Age*. It ended in 30 B.C. when Egypt, the last major Hellenistic state, fell to Rome.

Although the Hellenistic Age had absorbed the heritage of classical (Hellenic) Greece, its style of civilization changed. During the first phase of Hellenism, the polis had been the center of political life. The polis had given the individual identity, and it was believed that only within the polis could a Greek live a good and civilized life. During the Hellenistic Age, this situation changed. The city-state was eclipsed in power and importance by kingdoms. While cities retained a large measure of autonomy in domestic affairs, they had lost their freedom of action in foreign affairs. No longer were they the self-sufficient and independent communities of the Hellenic period.

Hellenistic society was characterized by a mingling of peoples and an interchange of cultures. As a result of Alexander's conquests, tens of thousands of Greek soldiers, merchants, and administrators settled in eastern lands. Greek traditions spread to the Near East, and Mesopotamian, Hebrew, and Persian traditions—particularly religious beliefs—moved westward. Cities were founded in the east patterned after the city-states of Greece. The ruling class in each Hellenistic city was united by a common Hellenism that overcame national, linguistic, and racial distinctions.

During the Hellenistic Age, Greek scientific achievement reached its height. Hellenistic scientists attempted a rational analysis of nature, engaged in research, organized knowledge in logical fashion, devised procedures for mathematical proof, separated medicine from magic, grasped the theory of experiment, and applied scientific principles to mechanical devices. Hellenistic science, says historian Benjamin Farrington, stood "on the threshold of the modern world. When modern science began in the sixteenth century, it took up where the Greeks left off."[2]

Hellenistic philosophers preserved the rational tradition of Greek philosophy. Like their Hellenic predecessors, they regarded the cosmos as governed by universal principles intelligible to the rational mind. The most important philosophy in the Hellenistic world was Stoicism. By teaching that the world constituted a single society, Stoicism gave theoretical expression to the world-mindedness of the age. Stoicism with its concept of a world-state offered an answer to the problems of the loss of community and the alienation caused by the decline of the city-state. By stressing inner strength in dealing with life's misfortunes, Stoicism offered an avenue to individual happiness in a world fraught with uncertainty.

At the core of Stoicism was the belief that the universe contained a principle of order: the *logos* (reason). This ruling principle permeated all things; it accounted for the orderliness of nature. Because people were part of the universe, said the Stoics, they also shared in the logos that operated throughout the cosmos. Since reason was common to all, human beings were essentially brothers and fundamentally equal.

Stoicism had an enduring impact on the Western mind. To some Roman political theorists, their Empire fulfilled the Stoic ideal of a world community in which people of different nationalities held citizenship and were governed by a worldwide law that accorded with the law of reason and by natural law that operated throughout the universe. Stoic beliefs—such as all human beings are members of one family; each person is significant; distinctions of rank are of no account; and human law should not conflict with natural law—were incorporated into Roman jurisprudence, Christian thought, and modern liberalism. There is continuity between Stoic thought and the principle of inalienable rights stated in the American Declaration of Independence.

Rome

Rome, conqueror of the Mediterranean world and transmitter of Hellenism, inherited the universalist tendencies of the Hellenistic Age and embodied them in its law and institutions. Roman history falls into two periods: the Republic, which began in 509 B.C. with the overthrow of the Etruscan monarchy; and the Empire, which started in 27 B.C. when Octavian became, in effect, the first Roman emperor.

The Roman Republic

The history of the Roman Republic was marked by three principal developments: the struggle between patricians and plebeians, the conquest of Italy and the Mediterranean world, and the civil wars. At the beginning of the fifth century B.C., Rome was dominated by *patricians* (the landowning aristocrats). The *plebeians* (commoners) had many grievances; these included enslavement for debt, discrimination in the courts, prevention of intermarriage with patricians, lack of political representation, and the absence of a written code of laws.

Resentful of their inferior status, the plebeians organized and waged a struggle for political, legal, and social equality. They were resisted every step of the way by the patricians, who wanted to preserve their dominance. The plebeians had one decisive weapon: their threat to secede from Rome, that is, not to pay taxes, work, nor serve in the army. Realizing that Rome, which was constantly involved in warfare on the Italian peninsula, could not endure without plebeian help, the pragmatic patricians begrudgingly made concessions. Thus the plebeians slowly gained legal equality.

Although many plebeian grievances were resolved and the plebeians gained the right to sit in the Senate, the principal organ of government, Rome was still ruled by an upper class. Power was concentrated in a ruling oligarchy consisting of patricians and influential plebeians who had joined forces with the old nobility.

By 146 B.C., Rome had become the dominant power in the Mediterranean world. Roman expansion occurred in three main stages: the uniting of the Italian peninsula, which gave Rome the manpower that transformed it from a city-state into a great power; the struggle with Carthage, from which Rome emerged as ruler of the western Mediterranean; and the subjugation of the Hellenistic states of the eastern Mediterranean, which brought Romans into close contact with Greek civilization.

A crucial consequence of expansion was Roman contact with the legal experience of other peoples. Roman jurists, demonstrating the Roman virtues of pragmatism and common sense, selectively incorporated elements of the legal codes and traditions of these nations into Roman law. Thus Roman jurists gradually and empirically fashioned the *jus gentium,* the law of nations or peoples.

Roman jurists then identified the jus gentium with the natural law (*jus naturale*) of the Stoics. The jurists said that law should accord with rational principles inherent in nature—universal norms capable of being discerned by rational people. The law of nations—Roman civil law (the law of the Roman state) combined with principles drawn from Greek and other sources— eventually replaced much of the local law in the Empire. This evolution of a universal code of law that gave expression to the Stoic principles of common rationality and humanity was the great achievement of Roman rule.

Another consequence of expansion was increased contact with Greek culture. Gradually the Romans acquired knowledge about scientific thought, philosophy, medicine, and geography from Greece. Adopting the humanist outlook of the Greeks, the Romans came to value human intelligence and eloquent and graceful prose and oratory. Rome creatively assimilated the Greek achievement and transmitted it to others, thereby extending the orbit of Hellenism.

During Rome's march to empire, all its classes had demonstrated a magnificent spirit in fighting foreign wars. With Carthage and Macedonia no longer threats to Rome, this cooperation deteriorated. Rome became torn apart by internal dissension during the first century B.C.

Julius Caesar, a popular military commander, gained control of the government. Caesar believed that only strong and enlightened leadership could permanently end the civil warfare destroying Rome. Rome's ruling class feared that Caesar would destroy the Republic and turn Rome into a monarchy.

Regarding themselves as defenders of republican liberties and senatorial leadership, aristocratic conspirators assassinated Caesar in 44 B.C. The murder of
Caesar plunged Rome into renewed civil war. Finally, in 31 B.C., Octavian,
Caesar's adopted son, defeated his rivals and emerged as master of Rome. Four
years later, Octavian, now called Augustus, became in effect the first Roman
emperor.

The Roman Empire

The rule of Augustus signified the end of the Roman Republic and the beginning of the Roman Empire, the termination of aristocratic politics and the
emergence of one-man rule. Under Augustus the power of the ruler was dis-
guised; in ensuing generations, however, emperors would wield absolute
power openly.

Augustus was by no means a self-seeking tyrant, but a creative statesman.
His reforms rescued a dying Roman world and inaugurated Rome's greatest
age. For the next two hundred years the Mediterranean world enjoyed the
blessings of the *pax Romana,* the Roman peace.

The ancient world had never experienced such a long period of peace, order,
efficient administration, and prosperity. The Romans called the pax Romana a
"Time of Happiness." It was the fulfillment of Rome's mission—the creation
of a world-state that provided peace, security, ordered civilization, and the rule
of law. The cities of the Roman Empire served as centers of Greco-Roman
civilization, which spread to the furthest reaches of the Mediterranean. Roman
citizenship, gradually granted, was finally extended to virtually all free men by
an edict in A.D. 212.

In the third century, the ordered civilization of the pax Romana ended. The
Roman Empire was plunged into military anarchy, as generals supported by
their soldiers fought for the throne. Germanic tribesmen broke through the
deteriorating border defenses to raid, loot, and destroy. Economic problems
caused cities, the centers of civilization, to decay. Increasingly people turned
away from the humanist values of Greco-Roman civilization and embraced
Near Eastern religions that offered a sense of belonging, a promise of immor-
tality, and relief from earthly misery.

The emperors Diocletian (285–305) and Constantine (306–337) tried to
contain the forces of disintegration by tightening the reins of government and
squeezing more taxes out of the citizens. In the process they divided the Empire
into eastern and western halves, and transformed Rome into a bureaucratic,
regimented, and militarized state.

Diocletian and Constantine had given Rome a reprieve, but in the last part
of the fourth century, the problem of guarding the frontier grew more acute.
At the end of 406, the borders finally collapsed; numerous German tribes
overran the Empire's western provinces. In 410 and again in 455, Rome was
sacked by Germanic invaders. German soldiers in the pay of Rome gained
control of the government and dictated the choice of emperor. In 476, German

officers overthrew the Roman Emperor Romulus and placed a fellow German on the throne. This act is traditionally regarded as the end of the Roman Empire in the West.

Early Christianity

When the Roman Empire was in decline, a new religion, Christianity, was sweeping across the Mediterranean world. Christianity was based on the life, death, and teachings of Jesus, a Palestinian Jew who was executed by the Roman authorities. Jesus was heir to the ethical monotheism of the Hebrew prophets. He also taught the imminent coming of the reign of God and the need for people to repent their sins—to transform themselves morally in order to enter God's kingdom. People must love God and their fellow human beings.

In the time immediately following the crucifixion of Jesus, his followers were almost exclusively Jews, who could more appropriately be called Jewish-Christians. To the first members of the Christian movement, Jesus was both a prophet who proclaimed God's power and purpose and the Messiah whose coming heralded a new age. To Paul, another Jewish-Christian, Jesus was the redeemer who held out the promise of salvation to the entire world and the savior-god who took on human flesh and atoned for the sins of humanity by suffering death upon the cross. And Saint Paul carried this message to Jews and especially to non-Jews (Gentiles).

The Christian message of a divine Savior, a concerned Father, and brotherly love inspired men and women who were dissatisfied with the world of here-and-now, who felt no attachment to city or Empire, who derived no inspiration from philosophy, and who suffered from a profound sense of loneliness. Christianity offered the individual what the city and the Roman world-state could not: a personal relationship with God, a promise of eternal life, and membership in a community of the faithful (the church) who cared for each other.

Unable to crush Christianity by persecution, Roman emperors decided to gain the support of the growing number of Christians within the Empire. By A.D. 392, Theodosius I had made Christianity the state religion of the Empire and declared the worship of pagan gods illegal.

The Judeo-Christian and Greco-Roman traditions are the two principal components of Western civilization. Both traditions valued the individual. For classical humanism, individual worth derived from the human capacity to reason, to shape character and life according to rational standards. Christianity also places great stress on the individual. It teaches that God cares for each person and wants people to behave righteously, and that He made them morally autonomous.

Despite their common emphasis on the individual, the Judeo-Christian and

Greco-Roman traditions essentially have different world-views. With the victory of Christianity, the ultimate goal of life shifted away from achieving excellence in this world through the full and creative development of human talent, toward attaining salvation in a heavenly city. For Christians, a person's worldly accomplishments counted very little if he or she did not accept God and his revelation. Greek classicism held that there was no authority higher than reason; Christianity taught that without God as the starting point, knowledge is formless, purposeless, and error-prone.

But Christian thinkers did not seek to eradicate the rational tradition of Greece. Rather, they sought to fit Greek philosophy into a Christian framework. In doing so, Christians performed a task of immense historical significance—the preservation of Greek philosophy.

The Middle Ages

The triumph of Christianity and the establishment of Germanic kingdoms on once-Roman lands constituted a new phase in Western history: the end of the ancient world and the beginning of the Middle Ages. In the ancient world the locus of Greco-Roman civilization was the Mediterranean Sea. The heartland of medieval civilization shifted to the north, to regions of Europe that Greco-Roman civilization had barely penetrated.

The Early Middle Ages

During the Early Middle Ages (500–1050), a common civilization evolved with Christianity at the center, Rome as the spiritual capital, and Latin as the language of intellectual life. The opening centuries of the Middle Ages were marked by a decline in trade, town life, central authority, and learning. The Germans were culturally unprepared to breathe new life into classical civilization. A new civilization with its own distinctive style was taking root, however. It consisted of Greco-Roman survivals, the native traditions of the Germans, and the Christian outlook.

Christianity was the integrating principle of the Middle Ages, and the church its dominant institution. People came to see themselves as participants in a great drama of salvation. There was only one truth—God's revelation to humanity. There was only one avenue to heaven—the church. To the medieval mind, society without the church was as inconceivable as life without the Christian view of God. By teaching a higher morality, the church tamed the warrior habits of the Germanic peoples. By copying and preserving ancient texts, monks kept alive elements of the high civilization of Greece and Rome.

One German people, the Franks, built a viable kingdom with major centers in France and the Rhine Valley of Germany. Under Charlemagne, who ruled from 768 to 814, the Frankish empire reached its height. On Christmas day in the year 800, Pope Leo crowned Charlemagne as "Emperor of the Romans." The title signified that the tradition of a world empire still survived, despite the demise of the Roman Empire three hundred years earlier. Because the pope crowned Charlemagne, this act meant that the emperor had a spiritual responsibility to spread and defend the faith.

The crowning of a German ruler as emperor of the Romans by the head of the church represented the merging of German, Christian, and Roman elements—the essential characteristic of medieval civilization. This blending of traditions was also evident on a cultural plane, for Charlemagne, a German warrior-king, showed respect for classical learning and Christianity, both non-Germanic traditions. During his reign, a distinct European civilization took root, but it was centuries away from fruition.

Charlemagne's successors could not hold the empire together, and it disintegrated. As central authority waned, large landowners began to exercise authority over their own regions. Furthering this movement toward localism and decentralization were simultaneous invasions by Muslims, Vikings from Scandinavia, and Magyars originally from Western Asia. They devastated villages, destroyed ports, and killed many people. Trade was at a standstill, coins no longer circulated, and untended farms became wastelands. The European economy collapsed, the political authority of kings disappeared, and cultural life and learning withered.

During these times, large landowners, or lords, wielded power formerly held by kings over their subjects, an arrangement called *feudalism.* Arising during a period of collapsing central authority, invasion, scanty public revenues, and declining commerce and town life, feudalism attempted to provide some order and security. A principal feature of feudalism was the practice of *vassalage,* in which a man in a solemn ceremony pledged loyalty to a lord. The lord received military service from his vassal, and the vassal obtained land, called a *fief,* from his lord.

Feudalism was built on an economic foundation known as *manorialism.* A village community (manor), consisting of serfs bound to the land, became the essential agricultural arrangement in medieval society. In return for protection and the right to cultivate fields, serfs owed obligations to their lords, and their personal freedom was restricted in a variety of ways.

Manorialism and feudalism presupposed an unchanging social order with a rigid system of estates, or orders—clergy who prayed, lords who fought, and peasants who toiled. The revival of an urban economy and the re-emergence of the king's authority in the High Middle Ages (about 1050 to 1270) would undermine feudal and manorial relationships.

The High Middle Ages

By the end of the eleventh century, Europe showed many signs of recovery and vitality. The invasions of Magyars and Vikings had ended, and kings and powerful lords imposed greater order in their territories. Improvements in technology and the clearing of new lands increased agricultural production. More food, the fortunate absence of plagues, and the limited nature of feudal warfare contributed to a population increase.

Expanding agricultural production, the end of Viking attacks, greater political stability, and a larger population revived commerce. In the twelfth and thirteenth centuries, local, regional, and long-distance trade gained such a momentum that some historians describe the period as a commercial revolution that surpassed commerce in the Roman Empire during the pax Romana.

In the eleventh century, towns re-emerged throughout Europe, and in the next century became active centers of commerce and intellectual life. Socially, economically, and culturally, towns were a new and revolutionary force. Towns contributed to the decline of manorialism because they provided new opportunities for commoners, apart from food-producing.

A new class (the middle class) of merchants and artisans appeared; unlike the lords and serfs, the members of this class were not affiliated with the land. Townspeople possessed a value system different from that of lords, serfs, or clerics. Whereas the clergy prepared people for heaven, the feudal lords fought and hunted, and the serfs toiled in small villages, townspeople engaged in business and had money and freedom. Townspeople were freeing themselves from the prejudices of both feudal aristocrats, who considered trade and manual work degrading, and the clergy, who cursed the pursuit of riches as an obstacle to salvation. Townspeople were critical, dynamic, and progressive—a force for change.

Other signs of growing vitality in Latin Christendom (western and central Europe) were the greater order and security provided by the emergence of states. While feudalism fostered a Europe that was split into many local regions, each ruled by a lord, the church envisioned a vast Christian commonwealth, *Respublica Christiana,* guided by the pope. During the High Middle Ages, the ideal of a universal Christian community seemed close to fruition. Never again would Europe possess such spiritual unity.

But forces were propelling Europe into a different direction. Aided by educated and trained officials who enforced royal law, tried people in royal courts, and collected royal taxes, kings enlarged their territories and slowly fashioned strong central governments. Gradually, subjects began to transfer their prime loyalty away from the church and their lords to the person of the king. In the process the foundations of European states were laid. Not all areas followed the same pattern. England and France achieved a large measure of unity during the Middle Ages; Germany and Italy remained divided into numerous independent territories.

Accompanying economic recovery and political stability in the High Middle Ages was a growing spiritual vitality. This vigor was marked by several developments. The common people showed greater devotion to the church. Within the church, reform movements attacked clerical abuses, and the papacy grew more powerful. Holy wars against the Muslims drew the Christian community closer together. During this period, the church with great determination tried to make society follow divine standards, that is, to shape all institutions according to a comprehensive Christian outlook.

European economic and religious vitality was paralleled by a cultural flowering in philosophy, literature, and the visual arts. Creative intellects achieved on a cultural level what the papacy accomplished on an institutional level—the integration of society around a Christian viewpoint. The High Middle Ages saw the restoration of some learning of the ancient world, the rise of universities, the emergence of an original form of architecture (the Gothic), and the creation of an imposing system of thought (scholasticism).

Medieval theologian-philosophers called *scholastics* fashioned Christian teachings into an all-embracing philosophy that represented the spiritual essence of medieval civilization. They achieved what Christian thinkers in the Roman Empire had initiated and what learned men of the Early Middle Ages were groping for: a synthesis of Greek philosophy and Christian revelation.

The Late Middle Ages

By the opening of the fourteenth century, Latin Christendom had experienced more than 250 years of growth, but during the late Middle Ages, roughly the fourteenth and early fifteenth centuries, medieval civilization declined. The fourteenth century, an age of adversity, was marked by crop failures, famine, population decline, plagues, stagnating production, unemployment, inflation, devastating warfare, abandoned villages, and violent rebellions by the poor and weak of towns and countryside, who were ruthlessly suppressed by the upper classes. This century witnessed flights into mysticism, outbreaks of mass hysteria, and massacres of Jews; it was an age of pessimism and general insecurity. The papacy declined in power, heresy proliferated, and the synthesis of faith and reason erected by the Christian thinkers during the High Middle Ages began to disintegrate. All these developments were signs that the stable and coherent civilization of the thirteenth century was drawing to a close.

But the decline of medieval civilization in the fourteenth century brought no new dark age to Europe. Its economic and political institutions and technological skills had grown too strong. Instead, the waning of the Middle Ages opened up possibilities for another stage in Western civilization—the modern age.

In innumerable ways the modern world is linked to the Middle Ages. European cities, the middle class, the state system, English common law, universities—all had their origins in the Middle Ages. During the Middle Ages, important advances were made in business practices, such as double-entry bookkeeping and the growth of credit and banking facilities. By translating and commenting on the writings of Greek philosophers and scientists, medieval scholars preserved a priceless intellectual heritage without which the modern mind could never have evolved. During the Middle Ages, Europeans began to lead the rest of the world in the development of technology.

Medieval philosophers, believing that God's law was superior to the decrees of states, provided a theoretical basis for opposing tyrannical kings who violated Christian principles. The idea that both the ruler and the ruled are bound by a higher law would become a principal element of modern liberal thought. The Christian stress on the sacred worth of the individual and on the higher law of God has never ceased to influence Western civilization. The Christian commandment to "love thy neighbor" has permeated modern reform movements.

Feudalism contributed to the history of liberty. The idea evolved that law should not be imposed by an absolute monarch, but requires the collaboration of king and subjects; that a king too should be bound by the law; and that lords should have the right to resist a monarch who violates agreements. Related to this development was the emergence of representative institutions, notably the English Parliament. The king was expected to consult its members on matters concerning the realm's affairs.

Despite these concrete elements of continuity, the characteristic outlook of the Middle Ages is much different from that of the modern world. Religion was the integrating feature of the Middle Ages, whereas science and secularism determine the modern outlook. Medieval thought began with the existence of God and the truth of his revelation as interpreted by the church, which set the standards and defined the purposes for human endeavor.

The medieval mind rejected the fundamental principle of Greek philosophy and modern thought—the autonomy of reason. Without the guidance of revealed truth, reason was seen as feeble. Unlike either ancient or modern thinkers, medieval scholars believed ultimately that reason alone could not provide a unified view of nature or society. To understand nature, law, morality, or the state, it was necessary to know its relationship to a supernatural order, a higher world.

In the modern view, both nature and the human intellect are self-sufficient. Nature is a mathematical system that operates without miracles or any other form of divine intervention. To comprehend nature and society, the mind needs no divine assistance; it accepts no authority above reason. The modern mind finds it unacceptable to reject conclusions of science on the basis of clerical authority and revelation, or to base politics, law, and economics on religion; it rejects the medieval division of the universe into a heavenly realm of perfection and a lower earthly realm. Scientific and secular attitudes have driven Christianity and faith from their central position to the periphery of human concerns.

The transformation of the medieval worldview based on religion into the modern view based on science and reason occurred over a span of four centuries. We shall now examine the movements that helped shape the modern world: the Renaissance, the Reformation, the Commercial Revolution, the growth of national states, the Scientific Revolution, the Enlightenment, and the Industrial Revolution.

Notes

1. W. H. Auden, ed., *The Portable Greek Reader* (New York: Viking, 1952), p. 38.

2. Benjamin Farrington, *Greek Science* (Baltimore: Penguin Books, 1961), p. 301.

Foundation of the Academy of Sciences in 1666, by Testelin. The commemorative painting shows Louis XIV (seated) with Colbert at his side. (*Versailles/Cliché des Musées Nationaux*)

III ❡ The Rise of Modernity: From the Renaissance to the Enlightenment

1350–1789

Chapter ⚋ 8

Transition to the Modern Age: Renaissance and Reformation

From the Italian Renaissance of the fifteenth century through the Age of Enlightenment of the eighteenth century, the outlook and institutions of the Middle Ages disintegrated and distinctly modern forms emerged. The radical change in European civilization could be seen on every level of society. On the economic level, commerce and industry expanded greatly, and capitalism largely replaced medieval forms of economic organization. On the political level, central government grew stronger at the expense of feudalism. On the religious level, the rise of Protestantism fragmented the unity of Christendom. On the social level, middle-class townspeople increasing in number and wealth, began to play a more important role in economic and cultural life. On the cultural level, the clergy lost its monopoly over learning, and the other-worldly orientation of the Middle Ages gave way to a secular outlook in literature and the arts. Theology, the queen of knowledge in the Middle Ages, surrendered its crown to science. Reason, which in the Middle Ages had been subordinate to revelation, asserted its independence.

Many of these tendencies manifested themselves dramatically during the Renaissance. The word *renaissance* means "rebirth," and it is used to refer to the attempt by artists and thinkers to recover and apply the ancient learning and standards of Greece and Rome. In historical terms, the Renaissance is both a cultural movement and a period. As a movement it was born in the city-states of northern Italy and spread to the rest of Europe. As a period it runs from about 1350 to 1600. Until the late fifteenth century the Renaissance was restricted to Italy. What happened there in the fourteenth and fifteenth centuries sharply contrasts with civilization in the rest of Europe, which until the end of the fifteenth century still belonged to the Late Middle Ages.

The nineteenth-century historian Jacob Burckhardt in his classic study, *The Civilization of the Renaissance in Italy* (1860), held that the Renaissance is the point of departure for the modern world. During the Renaissance, said Burckhardt, individuals showed an increasing concern for worldly life and self-consciously aspired to shape their destinies, an attitude that is the key to modernity.

Burckhardt's thesis has been challenged, particularly by medievalists who view the Renaissance as an extension of the Middle Ages, not as a sudden break with the past. These critics argue that Burckhardt neglected important links between medieval and Renaissance culture. A distinguishing feature of the Renaissance, the revival of classical learning, had already emerged in the High Middle Ages to such an extent that historians speak of "the renaissance of the twelfth century." The Renaissance owes much to the legal and scholastic studies that flourished in the Italian universities of Padua and Bologna before 1300. Town life and trade, hallmarks of Renaissance society, were also a heritage from the Middle Ages.

To be sure, the Renaissance was not a complete and sudden break with the Middle Ages. Many medieval ways and attitudes persisted. Nevertheless, Burckhardt's thesis that the Renaissance represents the birth of modernity has much to recommend it. Renaissance writers and artists themselves were aware of their age's novelty. They looked back on the medieval centuries as a "Dark Age" that followed the grandeur of ancient Greece and Rome, and they believed that they were experiencing a rebirth of cultural greatness. Renaissance artists and writers were fascinated with the cultural forms of Greece and Rome; they sought to imitate classical style and to capture the secular spirit of antiquity. In the process they broke with medieval artistic and literary forms. They valued the full development of human talent and expressed a new excitement about the possibilities of life in this world. This outlook represents a break from the Middle Ages and the emergence of modernity.

The Renaissance, then, was an age of transition that saw the rejection of certain elements of the medieval outlook, the revival of classical cultural forms, and the emergence of distinctly modern attitudes.

This rebirth began in Italy during the fourteenth century and gradually spread north and west to Germany, France, England, and Spain during the late fifteenth and the sixteenth centuries.

The Renaissance was one avenue to modernity; another was the Reformation. By dividing Europe into Catholic and Protestant, the Reformation ended medieval religious unity. It also accentuated the importance of the individual person, a distinctive feature of the modern outlook. It stressed individual conscience rather than clerical authority, called for a personal relationship between each man or woman and God, and called attention to the individual's inner religious capacities. ✌

Italy: Birthplace of the Renaissance

The city-states of northern Italy that spawned the Renaissance were developed urban centers where people had the wealth, freedom, and inclination to cultivate the arts and to enjoy the fruits of worldly life. In Italy, moreover, reminders of ancient Rome's grandeur were visible everywhere; Roman roads, monuments, and manuscripts intensified the Italians' links to their Roman past. Northern Italian city-states had developed as flourishing commercial and banking centers and had monopolized trade in the Mediterranean during the twelfth and thirteenth centuries. The predominance of business and commerce within these city-states meant that the feudal nobility, who held the land beyond the city walls, played a much less important part in government than they did elsewhere in Europe. By the end of the twelfth century, the city-states had adopted a fairly uniform pattern of republican self-government built around the office of a chief magistrate.

However, this republicanism proved precarious. During the fourteenth and early fifteenth centuries, republican institutions in one city after another toppled, giving way to rule by despots. The city-states had come to rely on mercenary troops, whose leaders, the notorious *condottieri*—unschooled in and owing no loyalty to the republican tradition—simply seized power during emergencies.

Florence, the leading city of the Renaissance, held out against the trend toward despotism for a long time. But by the mid-fifteenth century, even Florentine republicanism was giving way before the intrigues of a rich banking family, the Medici. They had installed themselves in power in the 1430s with the return of Cosimo de' Medici from exile. Cosimo's grandson, Lorenzo the Magnificent, completed the destruction of the republican constitution in 1480, when he managed to set up a government staffed by his supporters.

Lorenzo de' Medici. The Medici preferred to wield power behind the scenes through secret alliances and intrigue. Lorenzo, who became head of the family in his teens, fostered the notion of the good citizen; this portrait of him is by Agnolo Bronzino. (*Scala/Art Resource*)

LAVRENTIVS MEDICES   PETRI FILIVS.

Dramatically new ways of life emerged within the Italian city-states. Prosperous business people played a leading role in the political and cultural life of the city. With the expansion of commerce and industry, the feudal values of birth, military prowess, and a fixed hierarchy of lords and vassals decayed in favor of ambition and individual achievement, whether at court, in the counting house, or inside the artist's studio.

Art served as a focus of civic pride and patriotism. Members of the urban upper class became patrons of the arts, providing funds to support promising artists and writers. Just as rulers contended on the battlefield, they competed for art and artists to bolster their prestige. The popes, too, heaped wealth on artists to enhance their flagging prestige. They became the most lavish patrons of all, as the works of Michelangelo and Raphael testify.

The result of this new patronage by popes and patricians was an explosion of artistic creativity. The amount and especially the nature of this patronage also helped to shape both art and the artist. Portraiture became a separate genre for the first time since antiquity and was developed much further than ever before. Patrician rivalry and insecurity of status, fed by the Renaissance ethic of individual achievement and reward, produced a scramble for honor and reputation. This pursuit fostered the desire to be memorialized in a painting, if not in a sculpture. A painter like Titian was in great demand.

The great artists emerged as famous men by virtue of their exercise of brush and chisel. In the Middle Ages, artists had been regarded as craftsmen who did lowly (manual) labor and who, as a result, were to be accorded little, if any, status. Indeed, they remained anonymous for the most part. But the unparalleled Renaissance demand for art brought artists public recognition.

Renaissance society was also marked by a growing secular outlook. Intrigued by the active life of the city and eager to enjoy the worldly pleasures that their money could obtain, wealthy merchants and bankers moved away from the medieval preoccupation with salvation. To be sure, they were neither nonbelievers nor atheists, but increasingly religion had to compete with worldly concerns. Consequently, members of the urban upper class paid religion less heed, or at least did not allow it to interfere with their quest for the full life. The challenge and pleasure of living well in this world seemed more exciting than the promise of heaven. This outlook found concrete expression in Renaissance art and literature.

Individualism was another hallmark of Renaissance society. Urban life released people of wealth and talent from the old constraints of manor and church. The urban elite sought to assert their own personalities, to discover and to express their own particular feelings, to demonstrate their unique talents, to win fame and glory, and to fulfill their ambitions. This Renaissance ideal was explicitly elitist. It applied only to the few, entirely disregarding the masses; it valued what was distinctive and superior in an individual, not what was common to all; it was concerned with the distinctions of the few, not the needs or rights of the many. Individualism became deeply embedded in the Western soul and was expressed by artists who sought to capture individual character, by explorers who ventured into uncharted seas, by conquerors who carved out empires in the New World, and by merchant-capitalists who amassed fortunes.

The Renaissance Outlook: Humanism and Secular Politics

Humanism

The most characteristic intellectual movement of the Renaissance was *humanism,* an educational and cultural program based on the study of ancient Greek and Roman literature. The humanist attitude toward antiquity differed from that of medieval scholars. Medieval scholars sought to fit classical learning into a Christian world-view. Renaissance humanists, in contrast, did not subordinate the classics to the requirements of Christian doctrines; rather, they valued ancient literature for its own sake—for its clear and graceful style, for its insights into human nature. From the ancient classics, humanists expected to learn much that could not be provided by medieval writings—how to live well in this world and how to perform one's civic duties, for example. For the humanists the classics were a guide to the good life, the active life. To achieve self-cultivation, to write well, to speak well, and to live well, it was necessary to know the classics. In contrast to scholastic philosophers who used Greek philosophy to prove the truth of Christian doctrines, Italian humanists used classical learning to nourish their new interest in a worldly life. Whereas medieval scholars were familiar with only some ancient Latin writers, Renaissance humanists restored to circulation every Roman work that could be found. Similarly, whereas knowledge of Greek was very rare in Latin Christendom during the Middle Ages, Renaissance humanists increasingly cultivated the study of Greek in order to read Homer, Demosthenes, Plato, and other ancients in the original.

Although predominantly a secular movement, Italian humanism was not un-Christian. True, humanists often treated moral problems in a purely secular manner, but when they did deal with religious and theological questions, they did not challenge Christian belief or question the validity of the Bible. They did, however, attack scholasticism for its hairsplitting arguments and preoccupation with trivial questions. They stressed instead a purer form of Christianity based on the direct study of the Bible and writings by the church fathers.

An early humanist, sometimes called the father of humanism, was Petrarch (1304–1374). Petrarch and his followers carried the recovery of the classics further by making a systematic attempt to discover the classical roots of medieval Italian rhetoric. Petrarch's own efforts to learn Greek were largely unsuccessful, but by encouraging his students to master the ancient tongue, he advanced humanist learning. Petrarch was particularly drawn to Cicero, the ancient Roman orator. Following the example of Cicero, he insisted that education should consist not only of learning and knowing things, but also of learning how to communicate one's knowledge and how to use it for the public good. Therefore, the emphasis in education should be on rhetoric and moral philosophy, wisdom combined with eloquence. This was the key to virtue in the ruler, the citizen, and the republic. Petrarch helped to make Ciceronian values dominant among the humanists. His followers set up schools to inculcate the new Ciceronian educational ideal.

Implicit in the humanist educational ideal was a radical transformation of the Christian idea of human beings. According to the medieval (Augustinian) view, men and women, because of their sinful nature, were incapable of attaining excellence through their own efforts. They were completely subject to divine will. In contrast, the humanists, recalling the classical Greek concept of human beings, made the achievement of excellence through individual striving the end not only of education, but of life itself. Because individuals were capable of this goal, moreover, it was their duty to pursue it as the end of life. The pursuit was not effortless; indeed, it took extraordinary energy and skill.

People, then, were capable of excellence in every sphere and duty-bound to make the effort. This emphasis on human creative powers was one of the most characteristic and influential doctrines of the Renaissance. A classic expression of it is found in the *Oration on the Dignity of Man* (1486) by Giovanni Pico della Mirandola (1463–1494). Man, said Pico, has the freedom to shape his own life. Pico has God say to man: "We have made you a creature" such that "you may, as the free and proud shaper of your own being, fashion yourself in the form you may prefer."[1]

An attack on the medieval scholastics was implicit in the humanist educational ideal. From the humanist perspective, scholasticism failed not only because its terms and Latin usage were barbarous, but also because it did not provide useful knowledge. This humanist emphasis on the uses of knowledge also offered a stimulus to science and art.

So hostile were the humanists to all things scholastic and medieval that they reversed the prevailing view of history. The Christian view saw history as a simple unfolding of God's will and providence. The humanists stressed the importance of human actions and human wills in history—of people as active participants in the shaping of events. They characterized the epoch preceding their own as a period of declension from classical heights, and saw their own time as a period of rebirth, representing the recovery of classical wisdom and ideals. Thus, the humanists invented the notion of the Middle Ages as that period separating the ancient world from their own by a gulf of darkness. To the humanists, then, we owe the current periodization of history into ancient, medieval, and modern. There was also an element in the humanist view of today's idea of progress: they dared to think that they, "the moderns," might even surpass the ancient glories of Greece and Rome.

The humanist emphasis on historical scholarship yielded a method of critical inquiry that could help to undermine traditional loyalties and institutions. The work of Lorenzo Valla (c. 1407–1457) provides the clearest example of this trend. Educated as a classicist, Valla trained the guns of critical scholarship on the papacy in his most famous work, *Declamation Concerning the False Decretals of Constantine.* The papal claim to temporal authority rested on a document that purported to verify the so-called Donation of Constantine, whereby when the Emperor Constantine moved the capital to Constantinople in the fourth century, he had bestowed on the pope dominion over the entire western Empire. But Valla proved that the document was based on an eighth-century forgery because the language at certain points was unknown in Constantine's own time and did not come into use until much later.

Also embedded in the humanist re-evaluation of individual potential was a new appreciation of the moral significance of work. For the humanist the honor, fame, and even glory bestowed by one's city or patron for meritorious deeds was the ultimate reward for effort. The humanist pursuit of praise and reputation became something of a Renaissance cult.

A Revolution in Political Thought

Renaissance humanists turned away from the religious orientation of the Middle Ages and discussed the human condition in secular terms. In this way they opened up new possibilities for thinking about political and moral problems. Niccolo Machiavelli (1469–1527), a keen observer of Italian politics, regarded the Italian city-states, ruled by men whose authority rested solely on their cunning and effective use of force, as a new phenomenon that traditional political theory, concerned with ideal Christian ends, could not adequately explain. Italian princes made no effort to justify their policies on religious grounds; war was endemic, and powerful cities took over weaker ones; diplomacy was riddled with intrigue, betrayal, and bribery. In such a tooth-and-claw world, where political survival depended on alertness, cleverness, and strength, medieval theorists, who wanted the earthly realm to accord with standards revealed by God, seemed utterly irrelevant. Machiavelli simply wanted rulers to understand how to prepare and expand the state's power. In his book *The Prince,* he expounded a new political theory, one that had no place for Christian morality but that coincided with the emerging modern secular state. He himself was aware that his study of statecraft in the cold light of reason, free of religious and moral illusions, represented a new departure.

Machiavelli held that survival was the state's overriding aim; this consideration transcends any concern with moral or religious values and the interests of individual subjects. Removing questions of good and evil from the realm of political consideration, Machiavelli maintained that all means are permitted the prince when the state's survival is at stake. Successful princes, contended Machiavelli, have always been indifferent to moral and religious considerations—a lesson of history that rulers ignore at their peril. Thus, if the situation warrants it, the prince violates agreements with other rulers, goes back on his word with his subjects, and resorts to cruelty and terror.

Machiavelli broke with the distinguishing feature of medieval thought—the division of the universe into the higher world of the heavens and a lower earthly realm. To this extent, he did for politics what Galileo did a century

Giotto (c. 1276–1337): The Epiphany. Whether or not Giotto is classified as a Late Gothic or Early Renaissance painter, he was a revolutionary innovator. His choice of eye-level perspective and his habit of capturing dramatic gesture brought viewers directly into his pictorial space. (*The Metropolitan Museum of Art, John Stewart Kennedy Fund, 1911. 11.126.1*)

later for physics. Medieval thinkers held that rulers derived their power from God and had a religious obligation to govern in accord with God's commands. Rejecting completely this otherworldly, theocentric orientation, Machiavelli ascribed no divine origin or purpose to the state, but saw it as a natural entity; politics had nothing to do with God's intent or with moral precepts originating in a higher world. Machiavelli's significance as a political thinker consists in the fact that he removed political thought from a religious frame of reference and viewed the state and political behavior in the detached and dispassionate manner of a scientist. In secularizing and rationalizing political philosphy, he initiated a trend of thought that we recognize as distinctly modern.

Renaissance Art

The essential meaning of the Renaissance is conveyed through its art, particularly architecture, sculpture, and painting. Renaissance examples of all three art forms reflect a style that stressed proportion, balance, and harmony. These artistic values were achieved through a new, revolutionary conceptualization of space and spatial relations. Renaissance art also reflects to a considerable extent the values of Renaissance humanism, a return to classical models in architecture, to the rendering of the nude figure, and to a heroic vision of human beings.

Medieval art served a religious function and sought to represent spiritual aspiration; the world was a veil merely hinting at the other perfect and eternal world. Renaissance art did not stop expressing spiritual aspiration, but its setting and character differ altogether. This world is no longer a shroud, but becomes the *place* where people live, act, and worship. The reference is less to the other world and more to this world, and people are treated as creatures who find their spiritual destiny as they fulfill their human one. Renaissance art at its most distinctive represents a conscious revolt against the art of the Middle Ages. This revolt produced revolutionary discoveries that served as the foundation of Western art up to this century.

In art, as in philosophy, the Florentines played a leading role in this esthetic transformation. They, more than anyone else, were responsible for the way artists saw and drew for centuries and for the way most Western people still see or want to see. The first major contributor to Renaissance painting was the Florentine painter Giotto (c. 1276–1337). Borrowing from Byzantine painting, he created figures modeled by alterations in light and shade. He also developed several techniques of perspective, representing three-dimensional figures and objects on two-dimensional surfaces, so that they appear to stand in space. Giotto's figures also look remarkably alive. They are drawn and arranged in space to tell a story, and the expressions they wear and the illusion of movement they convey heighten the dramatic effect. Giotto's best works were *frescoes,* wall paintings painted while the plaster was still wet or *fresh.* Lionized in

Botticelli (1444–1510): The Birth of Venus. Botticelli was a member of the Florentine group of Neo-Platonists. They tried to harmonize Greco-Roman ideals with those
of Christianity. The nude goddess is Venus, but the modest tilt of the head is the
traditional pose of the Virgin Mary. To Botticelli the beauty of Venus and the purity
of Mary were identical. (*Alinari/Art Resource*)

his own day, Giotto had no immediate successors, and his ideas were not taken
up and developed further for almost a century.

By the early fifteenth century the revival of classical learning had begun in
earnest. In Florence it had its artistic counterpart among a circle of architects,
painters, and sculptors who sought to revive classical art. The leader of this
group was an architect, Filippo Brunelleschi (1377–1446). He designed
churches (Florence Cathedral, for instance) reflecting classical models. To him,
we also owe a scientific discovery of the first importance in the history of art:
the rules of perspective. Giotto had revived the ancient technique of foreshort-
ening; Brunelleschi completed the discovery by rendering perspective in mathematical terms. Brunelleschi's devotion to ancient models and his new tool of
mathematical perspective set the stage for the further development of Renaissance painting. Brunelleschi's young Florentine friend Masaccio (1401–1428)
took up the challenge. Faithful to the new rules of perspective, Masaccio was
also concerned with painting statuesque figures and endowing his paintings
with a grandeur and simplicity whose inspiration is classical. Perspective came
with all the force of religious revelation.

In his work *On Painting,* Leon Battista Alberti (1404–1472), a humanist, scholar, and art theoretician, brought the Renaissance trend toward perspectival art to a summation by advancing the first mathematical theory of artistic perspective. By defining visual space and the relationship between the object and the observer in mathematical terms, Renaissance art and artistic theory paved the way for the development of the modern scientific approach to nature, which later found expression in the astronomy of Copernicus and the physics of Galileo.

Renaissance artists were dedicated to representing things as they are, or at least as they are seen to be. Part of the inspiration for this was also classical. The ancient ideal of beauty was the beautiful nude. Renaissance admiration for ancient art meant that artists for the first time since the fall of Rome studied anatomy; they learned to draw the human form by having models pose for them, a practice fundamental to artistic training to this day. Another member of Brunelleschi's circle, the Florentine sculptor Donatello (1386–1466), also showed renewed interest in the human form.

Among the great Renaissance artists were Leonardo da Vinci (1452–1519), Michelangelo Buonarroti (1475–1564), and Raphael Santi (1483–1520). All of them were closely associated with Florence, and all of them were contemporaries. Leonardo was a scientist and engineer as well as a great artist. He was an expert at fortifications and gunnery, an inventor, an anatomist, and a naturalist. He brought this close observation of nature to his paintings and combined it with powerful psychological insight to produce works that, although few in number, were of unsurpassed genius. Among the most important of these are *The Last Supper* and *La Gioconda* (the Mona Lisa). The Mona Lisa is an example of an artistic invention of Leonardo's—what the Italians call *sfumato*. Leonardo left the outlines of the face a little vague and shadowy; this freed it of any wooden quality, which more exact drawing would impart, and thus made it more lifelike and mysterious.

Michelangelo's creation of artistic harmony derived from a mastery of anatomy and drawing. His model in painting came from sculpture; his paintings are sculpted drawings. He was of course a sculptor of the highest genius, whose approach to his art was poetic and visionary. Instead of trying to impose form on marble, he thought of sculpting as releasing the form from the rock. Among his greatest sculptures are *David, Moses,* and *The Dying Slave.* Michelangelo was also an architect and, patronized by the pope, he designed the dome of the new St. Peter's basilica in Rome. But perhaps his most stupendous work was the ceiling of the Sistine Chapel in the Vatican, commissioned by Pope Julius II. In four years, working with little assistance, Michelangelo covered the empty space with the most monumental sculpted pictures ever painted, pictures that summarize the Old Testament story. The *Creation of Adam* is the most famous of these superlative frescoes.

Raphael, the last of these three artistic giants, is especially famous for the sweetness of his Madonnas. But he was capable of painting other subjects and conveying other moods, as he did in the portrait of his patron, *Pope Leo X with Two Cardinals.*

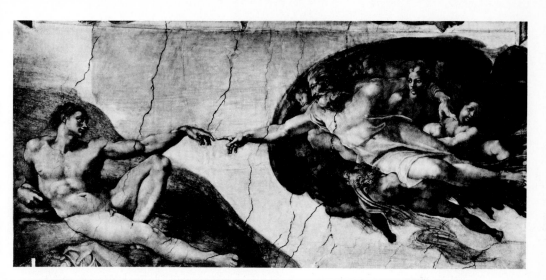

Michelangelo Buonarroti (1475–1564): Creation of Adam.   The art of Michelangelo relies on the human figure for expressive power, using virtually no background. In this painting, God propels himself effortlessly through the air, bringing the energy that will give life to the listless shell of Adam's recumbent body. The fresco is one of a series commissioned by Pope Julius II to decorate the ceiling of the Sistine Chapel in the Vatican in Rome. (*Scala/Art Resource*)

The Spread of the Renaissance

Aided by the invention of printing, the Renaissance spread to Germany, France, England, and Spain in the late fifteenth and the sixteenth centuries. In its migration northward, Renaissance culture adapted itself to conditions different from those in Italy, particularly the strength of lay piety. For example, the Brethren of the Common Life was a lay movement emphasizing education and practical piety. Intensely Christian and at the same time anticlerical, the people in such lay movements found in Renaissance culture tools for sharpening their wits against the clergy—not to undermine the faith, but rather to restore it to its Apostolic purity.

Thus, northern humanists were profoundly devoted to ancient learning, just as the humanists in Italy had been. But nothing in northern humanism compares to the paganizing trend associated with the Italian Renaissance. The northerners were chiefly interested in the question of what constituted original Christianity. They sought a model by which they might reform the corrupted church of their own time.

Humanism outside Italy was less concerned with the revival of classical values than with the reform of Christianity and society through a program of Christian humanism. The Christian humanists cultivated the new arts of rhetoric and history, as well as the classical languages—Latin, Greek, and

Hebrew. But the ultimate purpose of these pursuits was more religious than it had been in Italy, where secular interests predominated. Northern humanists used humanist scholarship and language to satirize and vilify medieval scholastic Christianity and to build a purer, more Scriptural Christianity. The discovery of accurate biblical texts, it was hoped, would lead to a great religious awakening. Protestant reformers, including Martin Luther, relied on humanist scholarship.

Erasmian Humanism

To Erasmus (c. 1466–1536) belongs the credit for making Renaissance humanism an international movement. He was educated in the Netherlands by the Brethren of the Common Life, which was one of the most advanced religious movements of the age, combining mystical piety with rigorous humanist pedagogy. Erasmus traveled throughout Europe as a humanist educator and biblical scholar. Like other Christian humanists, he trusted the power of words and used his pen to attack scholastic theology and clerical abuses and to promote his philosophy of Christ. His weapon was satire, and his *Praise of Folly* and *Colloquies* won him a reputation for acid wit vented at the expense of conventional religion.

True religion, Erasmus argued, does not depend on dogma, ritual, or clerical power. Rather it is revealed clearly and simply in the Bible and therefore is directly accessible to all people, from the wise and great to the poor and humble. Erasmian humanism stressed toleration, kindness, and respect for human rationality.

This clear but quiet voice was drowned out by the storms of the Reformation, and the Erasmian emphasis on the individual's natural capacities fell down before a renewed emphasis on human sinfulness and dogmatic theology. Erasmus was caught in the middle and condemned on all sides; for him, the Reformation was both a personal and historical tragedy. He had worked for peace and unity only to experience a spectacle of war and fragmentation. Erasmian humanism, however, survived these horrors as an ideal, and during the next two centuries, whenever thinkers sought toleration and rational religion, they looked back to Erasmus for inspiration.

French and English Humanism

Exemplifying the humanist spirit in France was François Rabelais (c. 1495–c. 1553), a former monk. In response to religious dogmatism, Rabelais asserted the essential goodness of the individual and the right to enjoy the world rather than be bound by the fear of a punishing God. In his folk epic, *Gargantua and Pantagruel,* he celebrated earthly life and earthly enjoyments, expressed an appreciation for secular learning and a confidence in human nature, and attacked monastic orders and clerical education for stifling the human spirit. Rabelais said that once freed from theology with its irrelevant concerns, and from narrow-minded clergy who deprived them of life's joys, people could by

Erasmus by Hans Holbein the Younger (c. 1497–1543). The brilliance and honesty of Erasmus's philosophical treatises endeared him to both conservative Catholic and Protestant reformers. As a humanist and in his pursuit of truth, he travelled freely throughout Europe. (*Louvre/Cliché des Musées Nationaux*)

virtue of their native goodness, build a paradise on earth and disregard the one dreamed up by theologians. In *Gargantua and Pantagruel,* he imagined a monastery where men and women spend their lives "not in laws, statutes, or rules, but according to their own free will and pleasure." They slept and ate when they desired and learned to "read, write, sing, play upon several musical instruments, and speak five or six . . . languages and compose in them all very quaintly." Only one rule did they observe: "DO WHAT THOU WILT."[2]

The most influential humanist of the early English Renaissance was Sir Thomas More (1478–1535), who studied at Oxford. His impact arose from both his writing and his career. Trained as a lawyer, he became a successful civil servant and member of Parliament. His most famous book is *Utopia,* the major utopian treatise to be written in the West since Plato's *Republic* and one of the most original works of the entire Renaissance. Many humanists had attacked private wealth as the principal source of pride, greed, and human cruelty. But More was the only one to carry this insight to its logical conclusion: in *Utopia,* he called for the elimination of private property. He had too keen a sense of human weakness to think that people could become perfect, but he used *Utopia* to call attention to contemporary abuses and to suggest radical reforms. He exploited the satirical and ironical potential of recent overseas discoveries by setting *Utopia* among a non-Christian people, which made his criticism more caustic and pointed. More succeeded Cardinal Wolsey as Lord Chancellor under Henry VIII. But when the king broke with the Roman Catholic church, More resigned, unable to reconcile his conscience with the king's rejection of papal supremacy. Three years later, in July 1535, More was executed for treason for refusing to swear an oath acknowledging the king's ecclesiastical supremacy.

William Shakespeare (1564–1616), widely considered the greatest playwright the world has ever produced, gave expression to Renaissance values—honor, heroism, and the struggle against fate and fortune. But there is nothing conventional about Shakespeare's treatment of characters possessed of these virtues. His greatest plays, the tragedies (*King Lear, Julius Caesar,* and others), explore a common theme: men, even heroic men, despite virtue, are able only with the greatest difficulty, if at all, to overcome their human weaknesses. What fascinates Shakespeare is the contradiction between the Renaissance image of nobility, which is often the self-image of Shakespeare's heroes, and man's capacity for evil and self-destruction. The plays are thus intensely human, but so much so that humanism fades into the background. Thus, art transcends doctrine to represent life itself.

The Renaissance and the Modern Age

The Renaissance, then, marks the birth of modernity—in art, in the idea of the individual's role in history and in nature, and in society, politics, war, and diplomacy. Central to this birth is a bold new view of human nature: individuals in all endeavors are free of a given destiny imposed by God from the outside—free to make their own destiny, guided only by the example of the past, the force of present circumstances, and the drives of their own inner nature. Individuals, set free from theology, are seen to be the products, and in turn the shapers, of history. Their future is not wholly determined by providence, but is partly the work of their own free will.

Within the Italian city-states where the Renaissance was born, rich merchants were at least as important as the church hierarchy and the old nobility. Commercial wealth and a new politics produced a new culture that relied heavily on ancient Greece and Rome. This return to antiquity also entailed a rejection of the Middle Ages as dark, barbarous, and rude. The humanists clearly preferred the secular learning of ancient Greece and Rome to the clerical learning of the more recent past. The reason for this was obvious: the ancients had the same worldly concerns as the humanists; the scholastics did not.

The revival of antiquity by the humanists did not mean, however, that they identified completely with it. The revival itself was done too self-consciously for that. In the very act of looking back, the humanists differentiated themselves from the past and recognized that they were different. They were in this sense the first modern historians, because they could study and appreciate the past for its own sake and to some degree on its own terms.

In the works of Renaissance artists and thinkers, the world was to a large extent depicted and explained without reference to a higher supernatural realm of meaning and authority. This is clearly seen in Machiavelli's analysis of politics. Renaissance humanism exuded a deep confidence in the capacities of able people, instructed in the wisdom of the ancients, to understand and change the world. Renaissance realism, then, was mixed with idealism, and this potent combination departed sharply from the medieval outlook. In place of Christian resignation there grew a willingness to confront life directly and a belief that human beings can succeed even against great odds.

This new confidence is closely related to another distinctive feature of the Renaissance—the cult of the individual. Both prince and painter were motivated in part by the desire to display their talents and to satisfy their ambitions. This individual striving was rewarded and encouraged by the larger society of rich patrons and calculating princes who valued ability. Gone was the medieval Christian emphasis upon the virtue of self-denial and the sin of pride. Instead, the Renaissance placed the highest value on self-expression and self-fulfillment, on the realization of individual potential, especially of the gifted few. The Renaissance fostered an atmosphere in which talent, even genius, was allowed to flourish.

To be sure, the Renaissance image of the individual and the world, bold and novel, was the exclusive prerogative of a small, well-educated urban elite and did not reach down to include the masses. Nevertheless, the Renaissance set an example of what people might achieve in art and architecture, taste and refinement, education and urban culture. In many fields the Renaissance set the cultural standards of the modern age.

Background to the Reformation:
The Medieval Church in Crisis

The Renaissance had revitalized European intellectual life and in the process discarded the medieval preoccupation with theology. Similarly, the Reformation marked the beginning of a new religious outlook. The Protestant Reformation, however, did not originate in the elite circles of humanistic scholars. Rather, it was sparked by Martin Luther (1483–1546), an obscure German monk and brilliant theologian. Luther instituted a rebellion against the church's authority that in less than one decade shattered irrevocably the religious unity of Christendom. The Reformation, begun in 1517, dominated European history throughout much of the sixteenth century.

The Roman Catholic church, centered in Rome, was the one European institution that transcended geographic, ethnic, linguistic, and national boundaries. For centuries it had extended its influence into every aspect of European society and culture. As a result, its massive wealth and power appeared to take predominance over its commitment to the search for holiness in this world and salvation in the next. Encumbered by wealth, addicted to international power, and protective of their own interests, the clergy, from the pope on down, became the center of a storm of criticism, starting in the Late Middle Ages.

In the fourteenth century, as kings increased their power and as urban centers with their sophisticated laity grew in size and numbers, people began to question the authority of the international church and its clergy. Political theorists rejected the pope's claim to supremacy over kings. The central idea of medieval Christendom—a Christian commonwealth led by the papacy— increasingly fell into disrepute. Theorists were arguing that the church was only a spiritual body, and therefore its power did not extend to the political realm. They said that the pope had no authority over kings, that the state needed no guidance from the papacy, and that the clergy were not above secular law. During the late fourteenth century Latin Christendom witnessed the first systematic attacks ever launched against the church. Church corruption—such as the selling of indulgences (see page 221), nepotism (the practice of appointing one's relatives to offices), the holding of many bishoprics, and the sexual indulgence of the clergy—was nothing new. What was new and startling was the willingness of educated and uneducated Christians to attack these practices publicly.

Thus, the Englishman John Wycliffe and the Bohemian John Huss (see page 192), both learned theologians, denounced the wealth of the clergy as a violation of Christ's precepts and attacked the church's authority at its root by arguing that the church did not control an individual's destiny. They maintained that salvation depends not on participating in the church's rituals nor on receiving its sacraments, but on accepting God's gift of faith.

Wycliffe's and Huss's efforts to initiate reform coincided with a powerful resurgence of religious feeling in the form of mysticism. Late medieval mystics sought an immediate and personal communication with God; such experiences inspired them to advocate concrete reforms for the purpose of renewing the church's spirituality. The church hierarchy inevitably regarded mysticism with some suspicion, for if individuals could experience God directly, they would seemingly have little need for the church and its rituals. In the fourteenth century, these mystical movements seldom became heretical. But in the sixteenth and seventeenth centuries, radical reformers often found in Christian mysticism a powerful alternative to institutional control and even to the necessity of a priesthood.

With the advent of Lutheranism, personal faith, rather than adherence to the practices of the church, became central to the religious life of European Protestants. Renaissance humanists had sought to reinstitute the wisdom of ancient times; Protestant reformers wanted to restore the spirit of early Christianity, in which faith seemed purer, believers more sincere, and clergy uncorrupted by luxury and power. By the 1540s, the Roman Catholic church had initiated its own internal reformation, but it came too late to stop the movement toward Protestantism in northern and western Europe.

The Lutheran Revolt

The Reformation was initiated by Martin Luther, who had experienced the personal agony of doubting the church's power to give salvation and who had the will and talent to convey that agony to all Christians and to win the support of powerful princes. As a young student, Luther fulfilled his father's wish and studied law, but at the age of twenty-one, he suddenly abandoned his legal studies to enter the Augustinian monastery at Erfurt. Luther began his search for spiritual and personal identity, and therefore for salvation, within the strict confinement and discipline of the monastery. He pursued his theological studies there and prepared for ordination into the priesthood.

The Break with Catholicism

As he studied and prayed, Luther grew increasingly terrified about the possibility of his damnation. As a monk he sought union with God, and he understood the church's teaching that salvation depended on faith, works (meaning acts of charity, prayer, fasting, and so on), and grace. He participated in the sacraments of the church, which according to its teaching were intended to give grace. Indeed, after his ordination, Luther administered the sacraments. Yet he still felt the weight of his sins, and nothing the church could offer seemed to relieve that burden. Seeking solace and salvation, Luther increasingly turned to reading the Bible. Two passages seemed to speak directly to him: "For in it the righteousness of God is revealed through faith for faith: as it is written, 'He who through faith is righteous shall live' " (Romans 1:17); and "They are justified by his grace as a gift, through the redemption which is in Christ Jesus" (Romans 3:24). In these two passages, Luther found, for the first time in his adult life, some hope for his own salvation. Faith, freely given by God through Christ, enables the recipient to receive salvation.

The concept of salvation by faith alone provided an answer to Luther's spiritual quest. Practicing such good works as prayer, fasting, pilgrimages, participation in the Mass and the other sacraments had never brought Luther peace of mind. He concluded that no amount of good works, however necessary for maintaining the Christian community, would bring salvation. Through reading the Bible and through faith alone, the Christian could find the meaning of earthly existence. For Luther, the true Christian was a courageous figure who faced the terrifying quest for salvation armed only with the hope that God had granted the gift of faith. The new Christian served others not to trade good works for salvation but solely to fulfill the demands of Christian love.

The starting point for the Reformation was Luther's attack in 1517 on the church's practice of selling indulgences. The church taught that some individuals go directly to heaven or hell, while others go to heaven only after spending time in purgatory; this waiting period is necessary for those who have sinned excessively in this life but who have had the good fortune to repent before death. To die in a state of mortal sin meant to suffer in hell eternally. Naturally people worried about how long they might have to spend in purgatory. Indulgences were intended to remit portions of that time and were granted to individuals by the church for their prayers, attendance at Mass, and almost any acts of charity—including monetary offerings to the church. This last good work was the most controversial, since it could easily appear that people were buying their way into heaven.

In the autumn of 1517 a monk named Tetzel was selling indulgences in the area near Wittenberg. Luther launched his attack on Tetzel and the selling of indulgences by tacking on the door of the Wittenberg castle church his ninety-five theses. Luther's theses (propositions) challenged the entire notion of selling indulgences, not only as a corrupt practice but also as a theologically unsound assumption—namely, that salvation can be earned by good works.

At the heart of Luther's argument in the ninety-five theses and in his later writings was the belief that the individual achieves salvation through inner religious feeling, a sense of contrition for sins, and trusting God's mercy. Luther also believed that church attendance, fasting, pilgrimages, charity, and other good works did not earn salvation. The church, in contrast, held that *both* faith and good works were necessary for salvation. Luther further insisted that every individual could discover the meaning of the Bible unaided by the clergy; the church, however, maintained that only the clergy could read and interpret the Bible properly. Luther argued that in matters of faith there was no difference between the clergy and the laity. Each person could receive faith directly and freely from God. But the church held that the clergy were intermediaries between individuals and God and that in effect Christians reached eternal salvation through the clergy. For Luther, no priest, no ceremony, no sacrament could bridge the gulf between the Creator and his creatures. Hope lay only in a personal relationship between the individual and God, as expressed through faith in God's mercy and grace. By holding that clergy and church rituals do not hold the key to salvation, Luther rejected the church's claim that it alone offered men and women the way to eternal life.

Recognizing that his life might be in danger if he continued to preach without a protector, Luther appealed for support to the prince of his district, Frederick, the elector of Saxony. The elector was a powerful man in international politics—one of seven lay and ecclesiastical princes who chose the Holy Roman emperor. Frederick's support convinced church officials, including the pope, that this monk would have to be dealt with cautiously. When in 1520 the pope finally acted against Luther, it was too late; Luther had been given the needed time to promote his views. He proclaimed that the pope was Antichrist and that the church was the "most lawless den of robbers, the most shameless of all brothels, the very kingdom of sin, death and Hell." When the papal bull excommunicating him was delivered, Luther burned it.

No longer members of the church, Luther and his followers established congregations for the purpose of Christian worship. Christians without the church needed protection, and in 1520 Luther published the *Address to the Christian Nobility of the German Nation*. In it, he appealed to the emperor and the German princes to reform the church and to cast off their allegiance to

**Martin Luther (left) and the Witten-
berg Reformers (Frederick of Saxony
and Ulrich Zwingli in center) by
Lucas Cranach the Younger.**
Luther benefited from his powerful
protector, Frederick, who wielded
influence in the church due to his
office as elector of popes. Zwingli, a
Swiss from Zurich, practiced a form
of Christianity very close to that of
Luther and claimed to have developed his ideas independently of
Luther. (*The Toledo Museum of
Art, Gift of Edward Drummond
Libbey*)

the pope, who he argued had used taxes and political power to exploit them
for centuries. His appeal produced some success; the Reformation flourished
on the resentment against foreign papal intervention that had long festered in
Germany. In this and other treatises, Luther made it clear that he wanted to
present no threat to legitimate political authority, that is, to the power of the
German princes.

In 1521, Charles V, the Holy Roman emperor, who was a devout Catholic,
summoned Luther to Worms, giving him a pass of safe conduct. There Luther
was to answer to the charge of heresy, both an ecclesiastical and a civil offense.
When asked to recant, Luther replied: "Unless I am convinced of error by the
testimony of Scripture or by clear reason . . . I cannot and will not recant
anything, for it is neither safe nor honest to act against one's conscience. God
help me. Amen." Shortly after this confrontation with the emperor, Luther
went into hiding to escape arrest. During that one-year period he translated the
New Testament into German. His followers, or Lutherans, were eventually
called *Protestants,* those who protested against the established church, and the
term became generic for all followers of the Reformation.

Print Shop, Sixteenth-Century Print.   Neither the Renaissance nor the Reformation would have been so widespread without printing, which was invented in Nuremberg in the 1450s. The printed word was the medium for the rapid transmission of Luther's and Calvin's revolutionary treatises, first in Germany and Switzerland and then elsewhere in Europe. (*The Bettmann Archive/BBC Hulton*)

The Appeal and Spread of Lutheranism

Spread rapidly by the new printing press, the tenets of Protestantism offered the hope of revitalization and renewal to its adherents. Lutheranism appealed to the devout, who resented the worldliness and lack of piety of many clergy. But the movement found its greatest following among German townspeople who objected to money flowing from their country to Rome in the form of church taxes and payment for church offices. In addition, the Reformation provided the nobility with the unprecedented opportunity to confiscate church lands, to eliminate church taxes, and to gain the support of their subjects by serving as leaders of a popular and dynamic religious movement. The Reformation also gave the nobles a way of resisting the Catholic Holy Roman emperor, Charles V, who wanted to extend his authority over the German princes. Resenting the Italian domination of the church, many other Germans who supported Martin Luther believed that they were freeing German Christians from foreign control.

Lutheranism also drew support from the peasants, who saw Luther as their champion against their oppressors—both lay and ecclesiastical lords and the townspeople. Indeed, in his writings and sermons, Luther often attacked the greed of the princes and bemoaned the plight of the poor. Undoubtedly,

Luther's successful confrontation with the authorities served to inspire the peasants. In 1524, these long-suffering people openly rebelled against their lords. The Peasants' Revolt spread to over one-third of Germany; some 300,000 people took up arms against their masters.

But Luther had no intention of associating his movement with a peasant uprising at the risk of alienating the nobility who supported him. Luther was a political conservative who hesitated to challenge secular authority. To him, the good Christian was an obedient subject. He virulently attacked the rebellious peasants, urging the nobility to become "both judge and executioner" and to "knock down, strangle, and stab" the insurgents. By 1525 the peasants had been put down by the sword. The failure of the Peasant's Revolt meant that the German peasantry remained among the most backward and oppressed until well into the nineteenth century.

Initially the Holy Roman emperor, who was at war with France over parts of Italy and whose eastern territories were threatened by the Ottoman Turks, hesitated to intervene militarily in the strife between Lutheran and Catholic princes, a delay that proved crucial. The religious conflict was settled by the Peace of Augsburg (1555), which decreed that each territorial prince should determine the religion of his subjects. Broadly speaking, northern Germany became largely Protestant while Bavaria and other southern territories remained in the Roman Catholic church. The Holy Roman emperor, who had been successfully challenged by the Lutheran princes, saw his power diminished. The decentralization of the empire and its division into Catholic and Protestant regions would block German unity until the last part of the nineteenth century.

The Spread of the Reformation

Nothing better illustrates people's dissatisfaction with the church in the early sixteenth century than the rapid spread of Protestantism. There was a pattern to this phenomenon. Protestantism grew strong in northern Europe—northern Germany, Scandinavia, the Netherlands, and England; it failed in the Latin countries, although not without a struggle in France. In general, Protestantism was an urban phenomenon, and it prospered where local magistrates supported it and where the distance from Rome was greatest.

Calvinism

The success of the Reformation outside Germany and Scandinavia derived largely from the work of John Calvin (1509–1564), a French scholar and theologian. Sometime in 1533 or 1534, Calvin met French followers of Luther and became convinced of the truth of the new theology. He began to spread its beliefs immediately after his conversion, and within a year he and his friends were in trouble with the civil and ecclesiastical authorities.

Calvin soon abandoned his humanistic and literary studies to become a preacher of the Reformation. From early in his religious experience, he emphasized the power of God over sinful and corrupt humanity. Calvin's God thundered and demanded obedience, and the terrible distance between God and the individual was mediated only by Christ. Calvin embraced a stern theology, holding that God's laws must be rigorously obeyed, that social and moral righteousness must be earnestly pursued, that political life must be carefully regulated, and that human emotions must be strictly controlled.

Even more than Luther, Calvin explained salvation in terms of uncertain predestination—that God, who grants grace for his own inscrutable reasons, knows in advance who will earn salvation and who will be condemned to hell. Calvin argued that although people are predestined to salvation or damnation, they can never know with certainty their fate in advance. This terrible decree could and did lead some people to despair. For others—in a paradox difficult for the modern mind to comprehend—Calvinism gave a sense of self-assurance and righteousness that made the saint, that is, the truly predestined man or woman, into a new kind of European. Most of Calvin's followers seemed to believe that in having comprehended the fact of predestination, they had received a bold insight into their unique relationship with God.

Calvinists were individuals who assumed that only unfailing dedication to God's law could be seen as a sign of salvation; thus, Calvinism made for stern men and women, active in their congregations and willing to suppress vice in themselves and others. Calvinism could also produce revolutionaries willing to defy any temporal authorities that were perceived to be in violation of God's laws. For Calvinists, obedience to Christian law became the dominating principle of life.

Forced to flee France, Calvin finally sought safety in Geneva, a small, prosperous Swiss city near the French border. There he eventually established a Protestant church that closely regulated the citizens' personal and social lives. Elders of the Calvinist church governed the city and imposed strict discipline in dress, sexual mores, church attendance, and business affairs; they severely punished irreligious and sinful behavior. Prosperous merchants as well as small shopkeepers saw in Calvinism a series of doctrines that justified the self-discipline they already exercised in their own lives and wished to impose on the unruly masses. They particularly approved of Calvin's economic views, for he saw nothing sinful about commercial activities, unlike many Catholic clergy.

Geneva became the center of international Protestantism. Calvin trained a new generation of Protestant reformers of many nationalities, who carried his message back to their homelands. Calvin's *Institutes of the Christian Religion* (1536), in its many editions, became (after the Bible) the leading textbook of the new theology. In the second half of the sixteenth century, Calvin's theology of predestination spread into France, England, the Netherlands, and parts of the Holy Roman Empire.

Map 8.1   The Protestant and the Catholic Reformations ▶

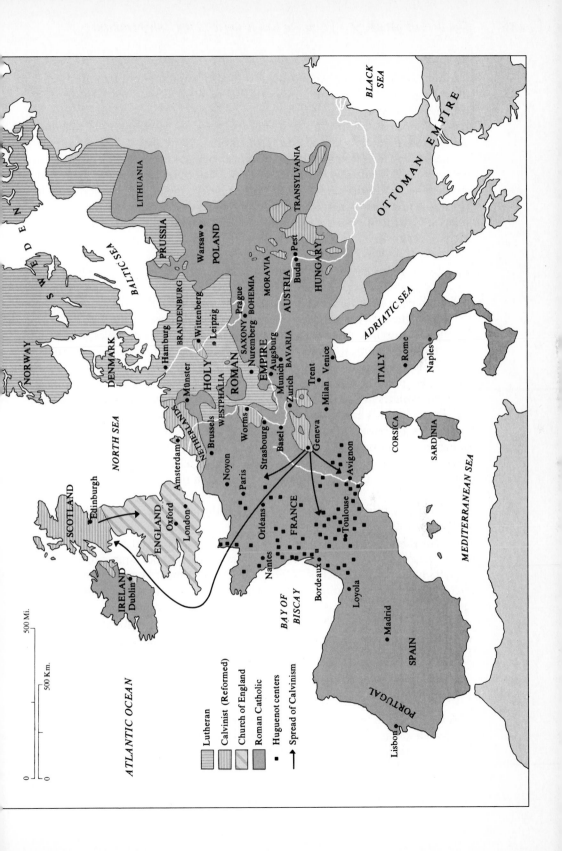

ATLANTIC OCEAN

NORWAY

SWEDEN

DENMARK

NORTH SEA

BALTIC SEA

LITHUANIA

PRUSSIA

BRANDENBURG

POLAND

• Warsaw

• Hamburg

Münster •

HOLY

ROMAN

WESTPHALIA

Amsterdam •

NETHERLANDS

Brussels •

• Wittenberg

• Leipzig

SAXONY

Prague •

BOHEMIA

MORAVIA

Nuremberg • EMPIRE

Augsburg •

Worms •

Munich •

BAVARIA

Zurich •

Basel •

Strasbourg •

AUSTRIA

Buda • • Pest

HUNGARY

TRANSYLVANIA

Trent •

Venice •

Milan •

ADRIATIC SEA

ITALY

Rome •

Naples •

SCOTLAND

Edinburgh •

ENGLAND

Oxford •

London •

IRELAND

Dublin •

• Noyon

Paris •

Orleans •

FRANCE

Nantes •

Bordeaux •

BAY OF
BISCAY

Geneva •

Avignon •

Toulouse •

Loyola •

CORSICA

SARDINIA

MEDITERRANEAN SEA

SPAIN

• Madrid

PORTUGAL

Lisbon •

BLACK
SEA

OTTOMAN EMPIRE

500 Mi.

500 Km.

0

0

Lutheran

Calvinist (Reformed)

Church of England

Roman Catholic

■ Huguenot centers

→ Spread of Calvinism

Calvin always opposed any recourse to violence and supported the authority of magistrates. Yet when monarchy became their persecutor, his followers felt compelled to resist. Calvinist theologians became the first political theoreticians of modern times to publish cogent arguments for opposition to monarchy, and eventually for political revolution. In France and later in the Netherlands, Calvinism became a revolutionary ideology, complete with an underground organization composed of dedicated followers who challenged monarchical authority. In the seventeenth century, the English version of Calvinism—Puritanism—performed the same function. Thus, in certain circumstances, Calvinism possessed the moral force to undermine the claims of the monarchical state over the individual.

France

Although Protestantism was illegal in France after 1534, the Protestant minority, the Huguenots, grew, becoming a well-organized underground movement. Huguenot churches, often under the protection of powerful nobles, assumed an increasingly political character in response to monarchy-sponsored persecution. French Protestants became sufficiently organized and militant to challenge their persecutors, King Henry II and the Guise—one of the foremost Catholic families in Europe—and in 1562 civil war erupted between Catholics and Protestants. What followed was one of the most brutal religious wars in the history of Europe. In 1572, on Saint Bartholomew's Day, the gruesome slaughter of thousands of Protestant men, women, and children stained the streets with blood. So intense was the religious hatred at the time that the massacre inspired the pope to have a Mass said in thanksgiving for a Catholic "victory."

After nearly thirty years of brutal fighting throughout France, victory went to the Catholic side—but barely. Henry of Navarre, a Protestant leader, became King Henry IV, but only after he agreed to reconvert to Catholicism. Henry established a tentative peace by granting Protestants limited toleration. In 1598 he issued the Edict of Nantes, the first document in any national state that attempted to institutionalize a degree of religious toleration. In the seventeenth century the successors of Henry IV (who was assassinated in 1610) gradually weakened and then in 1685 revoked the edict. The theoretical foundations of toleration, as well as its practice, remained tenuous in early modern Europe.

England

The Reformation was initiated in England not by religious reformers but by the king himself. Henry VIII (1509–1547) removed the English church from the jurisdiction of the papacy because the pope refused to grant him an annulment of his marriage to his first wife. The English Reformation thus began as a political act on the part of a self-confident Renaissance king. But the Reformation's origins stretched back into the Middle Ages, for there was a long tradition of heresy as well as anticlericalism in England that had its roots in Wycliffe's actions in the fourteenth century.

When Henry VIII decided that he wanted a divorce from the Spanish princess Catherine of Aragon, in 1527–28, the pope in effect ignored his request. As the pope stalled, Henry grew more desperate—he needed a male heir and presumed that the failure to produce one lay with his wife. At the same time, he desired the shrewd and tempting Anne Boleyn. Henry VIII arranged to grant himself a divorce by severing England from the church. In 1534, with Parliament's approval he had himself declared supreme head of the Church of England. In 1536 he dissolved the monasteries and seized their property, which was distributed or sold to his loyal supporters. In most cases, it went to the lesser nobility and landed gentry. By involving Parliament and the gentry, Henry VIII turned the Reformation into a national movement.

In the eleven years following Henry's death in 1547, there were three monarchs. Henry VIII was succeeded by his son, Edward VI, a Protestant, who reigned from 1547 to 1553. On his death, he was succeeded by Mary (1553–1558), the daughter of Henry VIII and Catherine of Aragon. Mary, a devout Catholic, severely persecuted Protestants. By the 1558 succession of Elizabeth I, Henry's second daughter (by Anne Boleyn), England was a Protestant country again. Elizabeth's reign was characterized by a heightened sense of national identity and the persecution of Catholics, who were seen as a threat to national security. Fear of invasion by Spain, which was intent on returning England to the papacy, contributed to English anti-Catholicism.

The English, or Anglican, church as it developed in the sixteenth century differed to only a limited degree in its customs and ceremonies from the Roman Catholicism it replaced. The exact nature of England's Protestantism became a subject of growing dispute. Was the Anglican church to be truly Protestant? Were its services and churches to be simple, lacking in "popish" rites and rituals and centered on Scripture and sermon? Obviously, the powerful Anglican bishops would accept no form of Protestantism that might limit their privileges, ceremonial functions, and power. These issues contributed to the English Revolution of the seventeenth century (see pages 249–251).

The Radical Reformation

The leading Protestant reformers generally supported established political authorities, whether they were territorial princes or urban magistrates. For the reformers, human freedom was a spiritual, not a social, concept. Yet the Reformation did help trigger revolts among the artisan and peasant classes of central and then western Europe. By the 1520s, several radical reformers arose, often from the lower classes of European society, and attempted to channel popular religion and folk beliefs into a new version of reformed Christianity that spoke directly to the temporal and spiritual needs of the oppressed.

Radical reformers proclaimed that God's will was known by his saints—those predestined for salvation. They said that the poor would inherit the earth, which at present was ruled by the Antichrist; the saint's task was to purge this earth of evil to make it ready for Christ's Second Coming. For the radicals, the Scriptures, which spoke of God's love for the wretched and lowly, became an inspiration for social revolution. Luther, Calvin, and other reformers vigorously condemned the social doctrines that were preached by the radical reformers.

The largest group in the Radical Reformation prior to 1550 has the general name of *Anabaptists*. Having received the inner light—the message of salvation—Anabaptists felt born anew and yearned to be rebaptized. Anabaptists were new Christians, new persons led by the light of conscience to seek reform and renewal of all institutions in preparation for Christ's Second Coming.

In 1534, Anabaptists captured the city of Münster in Westphalia, near the western border of Germany. They seized the property of nonbelievers, burned all books except the Bible, and in a mood of jubilation and sexual excess, openly practiced polygamy. All the while the Anabaptists proclaimed that the Day of Judgment was close at hand. Provoked by their actions, Lutheran Prince Philip of Hesse and his army crushed the Anabaptists.

Because of this Anabaptist revolt, *Münster* became a byword for dangerous revolution in early modern Europe. Determined to prevent these wild enthusiasts from gaining strength in their own territories, princes attacked them with ferocity. In Münster today, the cages still hang from the church steeple where the Anabaptist leaders were tortured and left to die as a warning to all would-be imitators.

By the late sixteenth century, many radical movements had either gone underground or grown quiet. But a century later, during the English Revolution (1640–1660), the beliefs and political goals of the Radical Reformation again surfaced, threatening to push the revolution in a direction that its gentry leaders desperately feared. Although the radicals failed in England too, they left a tradition of democratic and antihierarchical thought. The radical assertion that saints, who have received the inner light, are the equal of anyone, regardless of social status, helped shape modern democratic thought.

The Catholic Response

The Protestant threat impelled the Roman Catholic church to institute reforms. In the first instance, the energy for reform came from ordinary clergy as well as lay people such as Ignatius Loyola (1491–1556). Trained as a soldier, this pious Spanish reformer sought to create a new religious order fusing the intellectual excellence of humanism with a reformed Catholicism that would appeal to powerful economic and political groups. Founded in 1534, the Society of Jesus, more commonly known as the Jesuits, became the backbone of the Catholic Reformation in southern and western Europe. The Jesuits combined traditional monastic discipline with a dedication to teaching and an emphasis on the power of preaching, and they sought to use both to win converts back to the church.

El Greco (1541–1614): Portrait of a Cardinal (probably Don Fernando Niño de Guevara).   The Spanish church fiercely opposed the Reformation. The Inquisition persecuted Protestants relentlessly. The tenseness of the sitter captures the wary militancy of Spanish Catholicism. The cardinal's cool glance is belied by his claw-like hand. (*The Metropolitan Museum of Art, Bequest of Mrs. H. O. Havemeyer, 1929. The H. O. Havemeyer Collection. 29.100.5*)

The Jesuits offered hope—a religious revival based on ceremony, tradition, and the power of the priest to offer forgiveness. In addition, they opened some of the finest schools in Europe. Just as the Lutherans in Germany sought to bring literacy to the masses so that they might read the Bible, the Jesuits sought to bring intellectual enhancement to the laity, especially to the rich and powerful. The Jesuits pursued positions as confessors to princes and urged them to press their efforts to strengthen the church in their territories.

By the 1540s the Counter Reformation was well under way. The leaders of this Catholic movement attacked many of the same abuses that had impelled Luther to speak out, but they avoided a break with the doctrinal and spiritual authority of the clergy.

The Counter Reformation also took aggressive and hostile measures against Protestantism. The church tried to counter the popular appeal of Protestantism by offering dramatic, emotional, even sentimental piety to the faithful. For individuals who were unmoved by this appeal to sentiment or by the church's more traditional spirituality and who allied with Protestant heresy, the church resorted to sterner measures. The Inquisition—the church court dealing with heretics—expanded its activities, and wherever Catholic jurisdiction prevailed, unrepentant heretics were subject to death or imprisonment. Catholics did not hold a monopoly on persecution: wherever Protestantism obtained official status—in England, Scotland, and Geneva, for instance—Catholics or religious radicals also sometimes faced persecution.

One of the Catholic church's main tools was censorship. By the 1520s the impulse to censor and burn dangerous books intensified dramatically as the church tried to prevent the spread of Protestant ideas. In the rush to eliminate heretical literature, the church condemned the works of reforming Catholic humanists as well as those by Protestants. The Index of Prohibited Books became an institutional part of the church's life. Over the centuries the works of many leading thinkers were placed on the Index, which was not abolished until 1966.

The Counter Reformation policies of enlightened education, vigorous preaching, church building, persecution, and censorship did succeed in bringing thousands of people, Germans and Bohemians in particular, back into the church. In addition, the church implemented some concrete changes in policy and doctrine. In 1545, the Council of Trent met to reform the church and to strengthen it to face the Protestant challenge. Over the many years that it was convened (until 1563), the council modified and unified church doctrine; abolished many corrupt practices, such as the selling of indulgences; and vested final authority in the papacy, thereby ending the long and bitter struggle within the church over papal authority. The Council of Trent purged the church and gave it doctrinal clarity on such matters as the roles of faith and good works in attaining salvation. It passed a decree that the church shall be the final arbiter of the Bible. All compromise with Protestantism was rejected (not that Protestants were anxious for it). The Reformation had split western Christendom irrevocably.

The Reformation and the Modern Age

At first glance, the Reformation would seem to have renewed the medieval stress on otherworldliness and reversed the direction toward a secularism that had been taken by the Renaissance. Yet the Reformation contributed substantially to the shaping of the modern world. It shattered the religious unity of Europe, the chief characteristic of the Middle Ages, and further weakened the church, the principal institution of medieval society, whose moral authority and political power waned considerably. To this day Europe remains a continent of Catholics and Protestants.

By strengthening the power of monarchs and magistrates at the expense of religious bodies, the Reformation furthered the growth of the modern state. Protestant rulers totally repudiated the pope's claim to temporal power and extended their authority over Protestant churches in their lands. In Catholic lands, the church reacted to the onslaught of Protestantism by supporting rather than challenging monarchs. Protestantism did not create the modern secular state; it did, however, help to free the state from subordination to religious authority. Such autonomy is an essential feature of modern political life.

Very indirectly, Protestantism contributed to the growth of political liberty—another ideal in the modern West. To be sure, neither Luther nor Calvin championed political freedom. Luther said that subjects should obey the commands of their rulers, and Calvinists created a theocracy in Geneva that closely regulated its citizens. Nevertheless, the Reformation provided a basis for challenging monarchical authority. During the religious wars, some Protestant theorists supported resistance to monarchs whose edicts, they believed, defied God's law as expressed in the Bible. This religious justification for rebelling against tyrannical authority helped fuel the English Revolution of the seventeenth century and the American Revolution a century later. Both revolutions were instrumental in creating the modern constitutional state. Moreover, the Protestant view that all believers—laity, clergy, lords, kings—were masters of their own spiritual destiny eroded hierarchical authority and accorded with emerging constitutional government.

The Reformation also contributed to the creation of an individualistic ethic that is characteristic of the modern world. Protestants sought a direct and personal relationship with God and interpreted the Bible for themselves. Facing the prospect of salvation or damnation entirely on their own, without the church to provide aid and security, and believing that God had chosen them to be saved, Protestants developed an inner confidence and assertiveness. This religious individualism was the counterpart of the intellectual individualism of the Renaissance humanists.

In 1904, the German sociologist Max Weber argued that Protestantism encouraged the growth of capitalism. Weber acknowledged that capitalism existed in Europe before the Reformation; merchant bankers in medieval Italian and German towns, for example, engaged in capitalist practices. But, he argued, Protestantism (particularly Calvinism) gave to capitalism a particular dynamism. Protestant businessmen believed that they had a religious obligation to make money, and their religion gave them the self-discipline to do it. According to Calvin's doctrine of predestination, salvation could not be attained through any worldly actions, but Calvin's followers came to believe that certain activities were signs that God was working through them, that they had indeed been elected. Thus Calvinists held that hard work, diligence, dutifulness, efficiency, frugality, and a disdain for hedonism—all virtues that contribute to rational and orderly business procedures and to business success—were signs of election. In effect, argued Weber, Protestantism gave religious approval, which Catholicism did not, to money-making and the businessman's way of life.

The tradition of individual striving for material gain, so much a part of Western culture today, developed out of what had once been a religious quest

Chronology 8.1 ✦ The Renaissance and the Reformation

1304–1374	Petrarch, "father of humanism"
c. 1445	Johann Gutenberg invents movable metal type
1513	Machiavelli writes *The Prince*
1517	Martin Luther writes his ninety-five theses and the Reformation begins
1520	Pope Leo X excommunicates Luther
1524–1526	The German peasants revolt
1529	The English Parliament accepts Henry VIII's Reformation
1534	Henry VIII is declared head of the Church of England; King Francis I of France declares Protestants heretics; Ignatius Loyola founds the Society of Jesus; Anabaptists, radical reformers, capture Münster in Westphalia
1535	Sir Thomas More, English humanist and author of *Utopia,* is executed for treason
1536–1564	Calvin leads the Reformation in Geneva with Guillaume (William) Farel
1545–1563	The Council of Trent
1555	The Peace of Augsburg

for salvation, made urgent in this world by the theology of the Protestant Reformation. Sixteenth-century Protestantism created a new, highly individual, spirituality. Survival in this world and salvation in the next came to depend on inner faith and self-discipline; for the prosperous, both eventually became useful in a highly competitive world where individuals rule their own lives and the labor of others and represent themselves and others in government.

Notes

1. Giovanni Pico della Mirandola, *Oration on the Dignity of Man,* trans. by A. Robert Caponigri (Chicago: Henry Regnery, 1956), p. 7.

2. François Rabelais, *Gargantua and Pantagruel,* trans. by Sir Thomas Urquhart (1883), I. 57.

Suggested Reading

Brucker, Gene A., *Renaissance Florence* (rev. ed., 1983). An excellent analysis of the city's physical character, its economic and social structure, its political and religious life, and its cultural achievements.

Burckhardt, Jacob, *The Civilization of the Renaissance in Italy* (1860). 2 vols. (1958). The first major interpretative synthesis of the Renaissance; still an essential resource.

Burke, Peter, *Popular Culture in Early Modern Europe* (1978). A fascinating account of the social underside from the Renaissance to the French Revolution.

Grimm, Harold J., *The Reformation Era,* 1500–1650, 2nd ed. (1973). The best and most complete narrative available.

Koenigsberger, H. G., and George L. Mosse, *Europe in the Sixteenth Century* (1968). Some very good chapters on the Reformation.

Ozment, Steven E., *The Reformation in the Cities* (1975). A good survey of the Reformation in Germany.

Pullan, Brian S., *A History of Early Renaissance Italy* (1973). A solid, brief account.

Skinner, Quentin, *The Foundations of Modern Political Thought,* 2 vols. (1978). The first volume covers the Renaissance; highly informed.

Review Questions

1. What is the connection between the Renaissance and the Middle Ages? What special conditions gave rise to the Italian Renaissance?
2. What is humanism and how did it begin? What did the humanists contribute to education and the writing of history?
3. How can it be said that Machiavelli invented a new politics?
4. What are the general features of Renaissance art?
5. What factors encouraged the spread of the Renaissance into the western European monarchies and the Rhineland?
6. Why is the Renaissance considered the departure from the Middle Ages and the beginning of modernity?
7. What were the medieval roots of the Reformation?
8. How did Luther's theology mark a break with the church? Why did many Germans become followers of Luther?
9. In what ways did the radical reformers differ from the other Protestants?
10. What role did the Jesuits and the Inquisition play in the Counter Reformation? What did the Counter Reformation accomplish?
11. How did the Reformation weaken medieval institutions and traditions?

Chapter ⚮ 9

Political and Economic Transformation: National States, Overseas Expansion, Commercial Revolution

From the thirteenth to the seventeenth century a new and unique form of political organization emerged in the West: the dynastic or national state, which harnessed the material resources of its territory, directed the energies of the nobility into national service, and increasingly centralized political authority. The national state is the essential political institution of the modern West.

During the Middle Ages, some kings began to forge national states. However, medieval political forms differed considerably from those that developed later, in the early modern period. In the Middle Ages, feudal lords gave homage to their kings but retained power in their local territories, resisting the centralizing efforts of monarchs. Local and even national representative assemblies, which met frequently to give advice to kings, at times acted as a brake on the king's power. The clergy supported the monarch, but governed their congregations or monasteries as separate spiritual realms. The papacy challenged the authority of monarchs when it believed they did not fulfill their duty to rule in accordance with Christian teachings as interpreted by the church.

In early modern times, powerful monarchs subdued these competing systems of political authority and created a bureaucracy that coordinated and administered the activities of the central government.

Thus kings were the central figures in the creation of the national state. Strong dynastic states were formed wherever monarchs succeeded in subduing local aristocratic and ecclesiastical power systems. Where the monarchs failed, as they did in Germany and Italy, no viable states evolved until well into the nineteenth century.

By the early seventeenth century, Europeans had developed the concept of the state—an autonomous political entity to which its subjects owed duties and obligations. The essential prerequisite of the western concept of the state, as it emerged in the early modern period, was the idea of *sovereignty:* within its borders the state was supreme; all other institutions, both secular and religious, had to recognize the state's authority. The art of governing entailed molding the ambitions and strength of the powerful and wealthy into the state's service. The state, its power growing through war and taxation, had become the basic unit of political authority in the West.

In the sixteenth and seventeenth centuries, the idea of liberty, now so basic to western political life and thought, was only rarely discussed and generally only by Calvinist opponents of absolutism. Not until the mid-seventeenth century in England was there a body of political thought contending that human liberty was compatible with the new modern state. In general, despite the English (and Dutch) developments, absolutism dominated the political development of early modern Europe. It was not until the late eighteenth and nineteenth centuries that absolutism was widely challenged by advocates of liberty.

The principle of balance of power, an integral part of modern international relations, also emerged during early modern times. When one state threatened to dominate Europe, as did Spain under Philip II and France under Louis XIV, other states joined forces and resisted. The fear that one state would upset the balance of power and achieve European domination pervaded international relations in future centuries.

Seeking to enrich their treasuries and to extend their power, states promoted commercial growth and overseas expansion. The extension of European hegemony over much of the world was well under way by the eighteenth century. ❡

Hapsburg Spain

The Spanish political experience of the sixteenth century stands as one of the most extraordinary in the history of modern Europe. Spanish kings built a dynastic state that burst through its frontiers and encompassed Portugal, part of Italy, the Netherlands, and enormous areas in the New World. Spain became an intercontinental empire—the first in the West since Roman times.

In the eighth and ninth centuries, the Muslims controlled all of Spain except for some tiny Christian kingdoms in the far north. In the ninth century, these Christian states began a 500-year struggle—the Reconquest—to drive the Muslims from the Iberian Peninsula. By the middle of the thirteenth century, Granada in the south was all that remained of Muslim lands in Spain.

The 500-year struggle for Christian hegemony in the Iberian Peninsula left the Spanish fiercely religious and strongly suspicious of foreigners. Despite centuries of intermarriage with non-Christians, by the early sixteenth century, purity of blood and orthodoxy of faith became necessary for and synonymous with Spanish identity. In 1492 the Jews and the Muslims were physically expelled from Spain or forced to convert. This process of detection and conversion was supervised by the church, or more precisely, by the Inquisition. Run by clerics but responsive to state policies, the Inquisition existed to enforce religious uniformity and to ferret out the increasing numbers of Muslims and Jews who ostensibly converted to Catholicism but who remained secretly loyal to their own religions. Using its legal right to torture as well as burn heretics, the Inquisition represented the dark side of Spanish genius at conquest and administration, and its shadow stretched down through the centuries well into the twentieth.

Ferdinand and Isabella

In 1469, Ferdinand, heir to the throne of Aragon, married Isabella, heir to the throne of Castile. Although Ferdinand and Isabella did not give Spain a single legal and tax system or a common currency, their policies did contribute decisively to Spanish unity and power. They broke the power of aristocrats who had operated from their fortified castles in effect like kings, waging their private wars at will; they brought the Spanish church into alliance with the state; and in 1492 they drove the Muslims from Granada, their last territory in Spain. The crusade against the Muslim infidels accorded with the aims of the militant Spanish church. With a superior army, with the great aristocrats pacified, and with the church and the Inquisition under monarchical control, the Catholic kings expanded their interests and embarked on an imperialist foreign policy that made Spain dominant in the New World.

Isabella and Ferdinand.   With the marriage of Ferdinand of Aragon to Isabella of Castile, Spain came into being as a nation. At the battle of Granada, they defeated the last of the Islamic forces on the Spanish mainland. Columbus courted and won the patronage of Isabella. Monies that had previously been used to fight Islam were diverted to exploration. The wealth of the New World would repay her patronage beyond all expectation. (*Copyright reserved to H.M. The Queen*)

The Reign of Charles V: King of Spain and Holy Roman Emperor

Dynastic marriage constituted another crucial part of Ferdinand and Isabella's foreign policy. They strengthened their ties with the Austrian Hapsburg kings by marrying one of their children, Juana (called "the Mad" for her insanity), to Philip the Fair, son of Maximilian of Austria, the head of the ruling Hapsburg family. Philip and Juana's son Charles (1516–1556) inherited the kingdom of Ferdinand and Isabella; through his other grandparents, he also inherited the Netherlands, Austria, Sardinia, Sicily, the kingdom of Naples, and Franche Comté. In 1519, he was also elected Charles V, Holy Roman emperor. Charles became the most powerful ruler in Europe, but his reign also saw the emergence of political, economic, and social problems that eventually led to Spain's decline.

Charles's inheritance was simply too vast to be governed effectively, but that was only dimly perceived at the time. The Lutheran Reformation proved to be the first successful challenge to Hapsburg power. It was the first phase of a religious and political struggle between Catholic Spain and Protestant Europe that would dominate the last half of the sixteenth century.

The achievements of Charles V's reign rested on the twin instruments of army and bureaucracy. The Hapsburg empire in the New World was vastly extended and, on the whole, effectively administered and policed. Out of this sprawling empire with its exploited native populations came the greatest flow of gold and silver ever witnessed by Europeans. Constant warfare in Europe, coupled with the immensity of the Spanish administrative network, required a steady intake of capital. However, this easy access to capital appears to have been detrimental in the long run to the Spanish economy. There was no incentive for the development of domestic industry, bourgeois entrepreneurship, or international commerce. Moreover, constant war engendered and perpetuated a social order geared to the aggrandizement of a military class, rather than to the development of a commercial class. And although war expanded Spain's power in the sixteenth century, it sowed the seeds for the financial crises of the 1590s and beyond, and for the eventual decline of Spain as a world power.

Philip II

Philip II inherited the throne from his father, Charles V, who abdicated in 1556. Charles left his son with a vast empire in both the Old and New Worlds that had been administered competently enough, yet was also burdened by the specters of bankruptcy and heresy. A zeal for Catholicism ruled Philip's private conduct and infused his foreign policy. In the 1560s Philip sent the largest land army ever assembled in Europe into the Netherlands, with the intention of crushing Protestant-inspired opposition to Spanish authority. The ensuing revolt of the Netherlands lasted until 1609, and the Spanish lost their industrial heartland as a result of it.

The Dutch established a republic governed by the prosperous and progressive bourgeoisie. Rich from the fruits of manufacture and trade in everything from tulip bulbs to ships and slaves, the Dutch merchants ruled their cities and provinces with fierce pride. By the early seventeenth century, this new nation of only 1.5 million practiced the most innovative commercial and financial techniques in Europe.

Philip's disastrous attempt to invade England was also born of religious zeal. Philip regarded an assault on England, the main Protestant power, as a holy crusade against the "heretic and bastard," Queen Elizabeth; he particularly resented English assistance to the Protestant Dutch rebels. Sailing from Lisbon in May 1588, the Spanish Armada, carrying 22,000 seamen and soldiers, met with defeat. Its ships were too large and cumbersome to negotiate the treacherous English Channel, where the English ships easily outmaneuvered them and broke their formation with fire ships. Moreover, strong winds, typical for this time of year, drove the Armada out of striking position. The defeat had an enormous psychological effect on the Spanish, who saw it as divine punishment and openly pondered what they had done to incur God's displeasure.

The End of the Spanish Hapsburgs

After the defeat of the Armada, Spain gradually and reluctantly abandoned its imperial ambitions in northern Europe. The administrative structure built by Charles V and Philip II did remain strong throughout the seventeenth century; nevertheless, by the first quarter of the century, enormous weaknesses had surfaced in Spanish economic and social life. In 1596, Philip II was bankrupt, his vast wealth overextended by the cost of foreign wars. Bankruptcy reappeared at various times in the seventeenth century, while the agricultural economy, at the heart of any early modern nation, stagnated. The Spanish in their golden age had never devoted enough attention to increasing domestic production.

Despite setbacks, Spain was still capable of taking a very aggressive posture during the Thirty Years' War (1618–1648). The Austrian branch of the Hapsburg family joined forces with their Spanish cousins, and neither the Swedes and Germans nor the Dutch could stop them. Only French participation in the Thirty Years' War on the Protestant side tipped the balance decisively against the Hapsburgs. Spanish aggression brought no victories, and with the Peace of Westphalia (1648), Spain officially recognized the independence of the Netherlands and severed its diplomatic ties with the Austrian branch of the family.

By 1660, the imperial age of the Spanish Hapsburgs had come to an end. The rule of the Protestant princes had been secured in the Holy Roman Empire; the Protestant and Dutch Republic flourished; Portugal and its colony of Brazil were independent of Spain; and dominance over European affairs had passed to France. The quality of material life in Spain deteriorated rapidly, and the ever-present gap between rich and poor widened even more drastically. The traditional aristocracy and the church retained their land and power but failed conspicuously to produce effective leadership.

The Spanish experience illustrates two observations in the history of the European state. First, the state as empire could only survive and prosper if the domestic economic base remained sound. The Spanish reliance on bullion from its colonies and its failure to cultivate industry and to reform the taxation system spelled disaster. Second, states with a vital and aggressive bourgeoisie flourished at the expense of regions where aristocracy and church dominated and controlled society and its mores—Spain's situation. The latter social groups tended to despise manual labor, profit taking, and technological progress. Although kings and dynastic families originally created them, after 1700 the major dynastic states were increasingly nurtured by the economic activities of merchants and traders—by the bourgeoisie. Yet the bureaucracy of the dynastic states continued to be dominated by men drawn from the lesser aristocracy. This was nowhere truer than in France, where once again monarchs created the national state.

The Growth of French Power

Although both England and France effectively consolidated the power of their central governments, each became a model of a different form of statehood. The English model was a constitutional monarchy in which the king's power was limited by Parliament and the rights of the English people were protected by law and tradition. The French model emphasized at every turn the glory of the king and, by implication, the sovereignty of the state and its right to stand above the interests of its subjects. France's monarchy became absolute, and French kings emphasized that they had been selected by God to rule, a theory known as the divine right of kings. This theory gave monarchy a sanctity that various French kings used to enforce their commands over the population, including rebellious feudal lords.

The evolution of the French state was a very gradual process, one not completed until the late seventeenth century. In the Middle Ages the French monarchs recognized the rights of, and consulted with, representative assemblies called *Estates*. These assemblies (whether regional or national) were composed of deputies drawn from the various elites: the clergy, the nobility, and, significantly, the leaders of cities and towns in a given region. Early modern French kings increasingly wrested power from the nobility, reduced the significance of the Estates, and eliminated interference from the church.

Religion and the French State

In every emergent state, tension existed between the monarch and the papacy. At issue was control over the church within that territory—over its personnel, wealth, and, of course, its pulpits, from which an illiterate majority learned what their leaders believed they should know, not only in matters of religion but also about submission to civil authority. The monarch's power to make church appointments could ensure a complacent church, one that would preach obedience to royal authority and was compliant on matters of taxes.

For the French monarchs, centuries of tough bargaining with the papacy paid off in 1516, when Francis I (1515–1547) concluded the Concordat of Bologna. Under this agreement Pope Leo X permitted the French king to nominate, and therefore effectively to appoint, men of his choice to all the highest offices in the French church. The Concordat of Bologna laid the foundation for what became known as the *Gallican church*, a term signifying that

Map 9.1   Europe, 1648 ▶

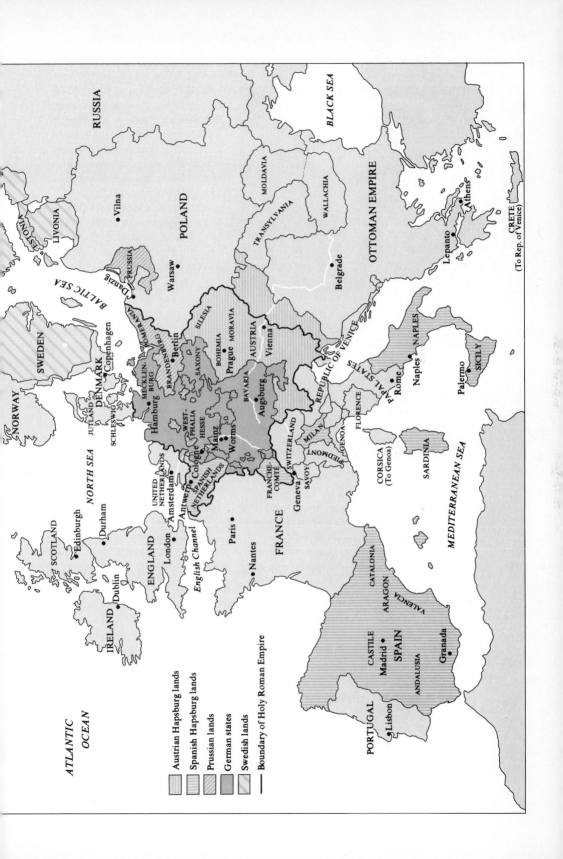

ATLANTIC
OCEAN

NORWAY

SWEDEN

RUSSIA

ESTONIA

LIVONIA

• Vilna

POLAND

BLACK SEA

MOLDAVIA

TRANSYLVANIA

WALLACHIA

Belgrade •

OTTOMAN EMPIRE

CRETE
(To Rep. of Venice)

Athens •

Lepanto •

BALTIC SEA

Danzig

PRUSSIA

POMERANIA

Warsaw •

SILESIA

BOHEMIA

MORAVIA

Prague •

AUSTRIA

Vienna •

REPUBLIC OF VENICE

PAPAL STATES

NAPLES

SICILY

Palermo •

Naples •

Rome •

SARDINIA

CORSICA
(To Genoa)

MEDITERRANEAN SEA

DENMARK

JUTLAND

SCHLESWIG

Copenhagen •

MECKLEN-
BURG

BRANDENBURG

Berlin •

SAXONY

Hamburg •

WEST-
PHALIA

HESSE

Mainz •

Worms •

Augsburg •

BAVARIA

SWITZERLAND

MILAN

Geneva •

SAVOY

PIEDMONT

GENOA

FLORENCE

FRANCHE-
COMTÉ

NORTH SEA

SCOTLAND

Edinburgh •

Durham •

ENGLAND

London •

IRELAND

Dublin •

English Channel

UNITED
NETHERLANDS

Amsterdam •

Antwerp •

Cologne •

SPANISH
NETHERLANDS

Paris •

Nantes •

FRANCE

PORTUGAL

Lisbon •

SPAIN

Madrid •

CASTILE

ANDALUSIA

Granada •

VALENCIA

ARAGON

CATALONIA

Austrian Hapsburg lands
Spanish Hapsburg lands
Prussian lands
German states
Swedish lands
Boundary of Holy Roman Empire

Francis I of France by Jean Clouet (1486–1541). Francis I was a true Renaissance prince, power hungry and a patron of the arts. The aged Leonardo da Vinci ended his days at Francis's court at Amboise as guest of the French king. Francis was also a brilliant politician; through his concordat of Bologna with Pope Leo X, French monarchs could appoint men of their choice to high church offices in France. (*Louvre/Cliché des Musées Nationaux*)

the Catholic church in France was sanctioned and overseen by the French kings. By the early sixteenth century, the central government had been strengthened at the expense of papal authority and of traditional privileges enjoyed by local aristocracy.

The Protestant Reformation, however, challenged royal authority and threatened the very survival of France as a unified state. Francis I, fearful that Protestantism would undermine his authority, declared Protestant beliefs and practices illegal and punishable by fine, imprisonment, and even execution. However, the Protestant minority (the Huguenots) grew in strength. From 1562 to 1598, France experienced waves of religious wars that cost the king control over vast areas of the kingdom. The great aristocratic families, the Guise for the Catholics and the Bourbons for the Protestants, drew up armies that scourged the land, killing and maiming their religious opponents and dismantling the authority of the central government.

In 1579, extreme Huguenot theorists published the *Vindiciae contra Tyrannos*. This theoretical statement, combined with a call to action, was the first of its kind in early modern times. It justified rebellion against, and even the execution of, an unjust king. European monarchs might claim power and divinely sanctioned authority, but by the late sixteenth century, their subjects had available the moral justification to oppose by force, if necessary, their monarch's will, and this justification rested on Scripture and religious conviction. Significantly, this same treatise was translated into English in 1648, a year before Parliament publicly executed Charles I, king of England.

The Valois kings floundered in the face of this kind of political and religious opposition. The era of royal supremacy instituted by Francis I came to an abrupt end during the reign of his successor, Henry II (1547–1559). Wed to Catherine de' Medici, a member of the powerful Italian banking family, Henry occupied himself not with the concerns of government but with the pleasures of the hunt. The sons who succeeded Henry—Francis II (1559–1560), Charles IX (1560–1574), and Henry III (1574–1589)—were uniformly weak. Their mother, Catherine, who was the virtual ruler, ordered the execution of thousands of Protestants by royal troops in Paris—the infamous St. Bartholomew's Day Massacre (1572) which, with the bloodbath that followed, became a symbol of the excesses of religious zeal.

The civil wars begun in 1562 were renewed in the massacre's aftermath. They dragged on until the death of the last Valois king in 1589. The Valois failure to produce a male heir to the throne placed Henry, duke of Bourbon and a Protestant, in line to succeed to the French throne. Realizing that the overwhelmingly Catholic population would not accept a Protestant king, Henry (apparently without much regret) renounced his adopted religion and embraced the church. Henry IV (1589–1610) granted to his Protestant subjects and former followers a degree of religious toleration through the Edict of Nantes (1598), but they were never welcomed in significant numbers into the royal bureaucracy. Throughout the seventeenth century, every French king attempted to undermine the Protestants' regional power bases and ultimately to destroy their religious liberties.

The Consolidation of French Monarchical Power

The defeat of Protestantism as a national force set the stage for the final consolidation of the French state in the seventeenth century under the great Bourbon kings, Louis XIII and Louis XIV. Louis XIII (1610–1643) realized that his rule depended on an efficient and trustworthy bureaucracy, an ever-replenishable treasury, and constant vigilance against the localized claims to power made by the great aristocracy and by the Protestant cities and towns. Cardinal Richelieu, who served as Louis XIII's chief minister from 1624 to 1642, became the great architect of French absolutism.

Richelieu's morality rested on one sacred principle embodied in a phrase he invented: *raison d'état,* reason of state. Richelieu sought to serve the state by bringing under the king's control the disruptive and antimonarchical elements within French society. He increased the power of the central bureaucracy, attacked the power of independent, and often Protestant, towns and cities, and persecuted the Huguenots. Above all, he humbled the great nobles by limiting their effectiveness as councilors to the king and by prohibiting their traditional privileges, such as using a duel rather than court action to settle grievances. Reason of state also guided Richelieu's foreign policy. It necessitated France's

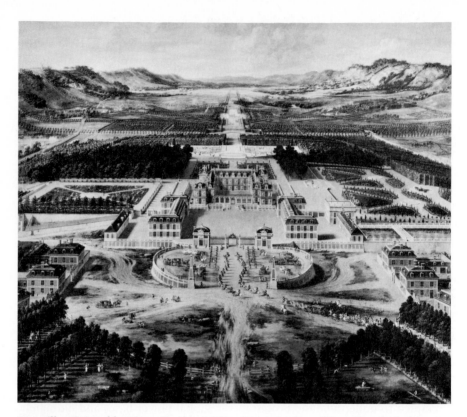

Versailles, Painted by Pierre Patel in 1668.   The splendor of Versailles, both the buildings and the extensive grounds, were widely imitated by European monarchs, and epitomized the power and wealth of the king. (*Versailles/Cliché des Musées Nationaux*)

turning against Catholic Spain and entering on the Protestant and hence anti-Spanish side in the war that was raging at the time in the Holy Roman Empire. The outcome of France's entry into the Thirty Years' War (1618–1648) produced a decided victory for French power on the Continent.

Richelieu died in 1642 and Louis XIII the following year. Cardinal Mazarin, who took charge during the minority of Louis XIV (who was five years old when Louis XIII died), continued Richelieu's policies. Mazarin's heavy-handed actions produced a rebellious reaction, the *Fronde*—a series of street riots that eventually cost the government control over Paris and lasted from 1648 to 1653. Centered in Paris and supported by the great aristocracy, the courts, and Paris's poorer classes, the Fronde threatened to develop into a full-scale uprising. It might have done so, but for one crucial factor: its leadership was fundamentally divided. Court judges (lesser nobles who had often just risen from the ranks of the bourgeoisie) deeply distrusted the great aristocrats and refused in the end to make common cause with them. And both groups feared disorders among the urban masses.

When Louis XIV finally assumed responsibility for governing in 1661, he vowed that the events he had witnessed as a child during the Fronde would never be repeated. In the course of his reign, he achieved the greatest degree of monarchical power held during the early modern period. No absolute monarch in Western Europe, before or at that time, had so much personal authority or commanded such a vast and effective military and administrative machine. Louis XIV's reign represents the culmination of a process of increasing monarchical authority that had been under way for centuries. Intelligent, cunning, and possessing a unique understanding of the requirements of his office, Louis XIV worked long hours at being king, and he never undertook a venture without an eye to his personal grandeur. The sumptuous royal palace at Versailles was built for that reason; similarly, etiquette and style were cultivated there on a scale never before seen in any European court.

When Mazarin died, Louis XIV did away with the office of first minister; he would rule France alone. The great nobles, "princes of the blood," enjoyed great social prestige but exercised decreasing political influence. Louis XIV treated the aristocrats to elaborate rituals, feasts, processions, displays, and banquets; but amid all the clamor, their political power dwindled.

Louis XIV's domestic policies centered around his incessant search for new revenues. Not only the building of Versailles but also wars cost money, and Louis XIV waged them to excess. To raise capital, he used the services of Jean Baptiste Colbert, a brilliant administrator who improved methods of tax collecting, promoted new industries, and encouraged international trade. Operating with a total bureaucracy of about a thousand officials and no longer bothering even to consult the parlements or Estates, Louis XIV ruled absolutely in accordance with the principle of divine right—that the monarch is selected to rule by God.

Yet Louis XIV's system was fatally flawed. Without any effective check on his power and dreams of international conquest, there was no limit imposed on the state's capacity to make war or on the ensuing national debt. Louis XIV coveted vast sections of the Holy Roman Empire; he also sought to check Dutch commercial prosperity and had designs on the Spanish Netherlands. By the 1680s, his domestic and foreign policies took on a violently aggressive posture. In 1685, he revoked the Edict of Nantes, forcing many of the country's remaining Protestants to flee. In 1689, he embarked on a military campaign to secure territory from the Holy Roman Empire. And in 1701, he tried to bring Spain under the control of the Bourbon dynasty. Louis XIV, however, underestimated the power of his northern rivals, England and the Netherlands. The combined power of England and the Netherlands in alliance with the Holy Roman Empire and the Austrians brought defeat to Louis XIV's ambitions.

Louis XIV's participation in these long wars emptied the royal treasury. By the late seventeenth century taxes had risen intolerably, and they were essentially levied on those least able to pay—the peasants. Thus, for the great majority of French people, absolutism meant a decline in living standards and a significant increase in mortality rates. Absolutism also meant increased surveillance over the population: royal authorities censored books; spied on heretics, Protestants, and freethinkers; and even tortured and executed opponents of state policy.

In the France of Louis XIV, the dynastic state had reached maturity and had begun to display some of its classic characteristics: centralized bureaucracy; royal patronage to enforce allegiance; a system of taxation universally but inequitably applied; and suppression of political opposition either through the use of patronage or, if necessary, through force. Another important feature was the state's cultivation of the arts and sciences as a means of increasing national power and prestige. Together, these policies enabled the French monarchy to achieve political stability, to enforce a uniform system of law, and to channel the country's wealth and resources into the service of the state as a whole.

Yet at his death in 1715, Louis XIV left his successors a system of bureaucracy and taxation that was vastly in need of overhaul but was still locked into the traditional social privileges of the church and nobility to an extent that made reform virtually impossible. The pattern of war, excessive taxation of the lower classes, and expenditure in excess of revenues had severely damaged French finances. Failure to reform the system led to the French Revolution of 1789.

The Growth of Limited Monarchy and Constitutionalism in England

In 1066, William, duke of Normandy and vassal to the French king, had invaded and conquered England, acquiring at a stroke the entire kingdom. In succeeding centuries, English monarchs continued to strengthen central authority and to tighten the bonds of national unity. At the same time, however, certain institutions and traditions evolved—common law, Magna Carta, and Parliament—that checked royal power and protected the rights of the English people.

Central government in England was threatened after the Hundred Years' War (1337–1453) when English aristocrats brought back from France a taste for warfare. In the ensuing civil war—the War of the Roses (1455–1485)—gangs of noblemen with retainers roamed the English countryside, and lawlessness prevailed for a generation. Only in 1485 did the Tudor family emerge triumphant.

The Tudor Achievement

Victory in the civil wars allowed Henry VII (1485–1509) to begin the Tudor dynasty. Henry VII's goal was to bring an unruly nobility into check. Toward this end, he brought commoners into the government; these commoners, unlike the great magnates, could be channeled into royal service because they craved what the king offered—financial rewards and elevated social status.

Although they did not fully displace the aristocracy, commoners were brought into Henry VII's inner circle, into the Privy Council, into the courts. The strength and efficiency of Tudor government were shown during the Reformation, when Henry VIII (1509–1547) made himself head of the English church.

The Protestant Reformation in England was a revolution in royal as well as ecclesiastical government. It attacked and defeated a main obstacle to monarchical authority—the power of the papacy. No change in religious practice could be instituted by the monarchy alone. Parliament's participation in the Reformation gave it a greater role and sense of importance than it had ever possessed in the past.

At Henry VIII's death, the Tudor bureaucracy and centralized government was strained to its utmost, yet it survived. The government weathered the reign of Henry's sickly son Edward VI (1547–1553) and the extreme Protestantism of some of his advisers, and it survived the brief and deeply troubled reign of Henry's first daughter, Mary (1553–1558), who attempted to return England to Catholicism. At Mary's death, England had come dangerously close to the religious instability and sectarian tension that undermined the French kings during the final decades of the sixteenth century.

Henry's second daughter, Elizabeth I, became queen in 1558. The Elizabethan period was characterized by a heightened sense of national identity. The English Reformation enhanced that sense, as did the increasing fear of foreign invasion by Spain. The fear was abated only by the defeat of the Spanish Armada in 1588. In the seventeenth century, the English would look back on Elizabeth's reign as a golden age. It was the calm before the storm, a time when a new commercial class was formed that, in the seventeenth century, would demand a greater say in government operations.

Religion played a vital role in this realignment of political interests and forces. Many of the old aristocracy clung to the Anglicanism of the Henrican Reformation, and in some cases to Catholicism. The newly risen gentry found in the Protestant Reformation of Switzerland and Germany a form of religious worship more suited to their independent and entrepreneurial spirit. Many of them embraced Puritanism, the English version of Calvinism.

The English Revolution, 1640–1689

The forces threatening established authority were dealt with ineffectively by the first two Stuart kings—James I (1603–1625) and Charles I (1625–1649). Both believed, as did their Continental counterparts, in royal absolutism, and both preached, through the established church, the doctrine of the divine right of kings. James I, an effective and shrewd administrator, conducted foreign policy without consulting Parliament, and Charles disbanded Parliament and attempted to collect taxes without its consent. These policies ended in disaster.

The English Revolution broke out in 1640 because Charles I needed new taxes to defend the realm against a Scottish invasion. Parliament, finally called after an eleven-year absence, refused his request unless he granted certain basic rights: Parliament to be consulted in matters of taxation, trial by jury, *habeas corpus,* and a truly Protestant church responsive to the beliefs and interests of its laity. Charles refused, for he saw these demands as an assault on royal authority. The ensuing civil war was directed by Parliament, financed by taxes and the merchants, and fought by the New Model Army led by Oliver Cromwell (1599–1658), a Puritan squire who gradually realized his potential for leadership.

The New Model Army was unmatched by any ever seen before in Europe. Parliament's rich supporters financed it, gentleman farmers led it, and religious zealots filled its ranks, along with the usual cross-section of poor artisans and day laborers. This army brought defeat to the king, his aristocratic followers, and the Anglican church's hierarchy.

In January 1649, Charles I was publicly executed by order of Parliament. During the interregnum (time between kings) of the next eleven years, one Parliament after another joined with the army to govern the country as a republic. In the distribution of power between the army and the Parliament, Cromwell proved to be a key element. He had the support of the army's officers and some of its rank and file, and he had been a member of Parliament for many years. His control over the army was secured, however, only after its rank and file was purged of radicals drawn largely from the poor. Some of these radicals wanted to level society, that is, to redistribute property and to give the vote to all male citizens.

After Cromwell died in 1658, the country was without effective leadership. Parliament, having secured the economic interests of its constituency (gentry, merchants, and some small landowners), chose to restore court and crown and invited the exiled son of the executed king to return to the kingship. Having learned the lesson his father had spurned, Charles II (1660–1685) never instituted royal absolutism.

But Charles's brother, James II (1685–1688), was a foolishly fearless Catholic and admirer of French absolutism. James gathered at his court a coterie of Catholic advisers and supporters of royal prerogative and attempted to bend Parliament and local government to the royal will. James's Catholicism was the crucial element in his failure. The Anglican church would not back him, and political forces similar to those that had gathered against his father, Charles I, in 1640 descended on him. The ruling elites, however, had learned their lesson back in the 1650s: civil war would produce social discontent among the masses. The upper classes wanted to avoid open warfare and preserve the monarchy as a constitutional authority, but not as an absolute one. Puritanism, with its sectarian fervor and its dangerous association with republicanism, was allowed to play no part in this second and last phase of the English Revolution.

In early 1688, Anglicans, some aristocrats, and opponents of royal prerogative formed a conspiracy against James II. Their purpose was to invite his son-in-law, William of Orange, *stadholder* (head) of the Netherlands and husband of James's Protestant daughter Mary, to invade England and rescue its government from James's control. James, who had lost the loyalty of key men in the army, powerful gentlemen in the counties, and the Anglican church, fled the country, and William and Mary were declared king and queen by act of Parliament.

This bloodless revolution—sometimes called the Glorious Revolution—created a new political and constitutional reality. Parliament secured its rights to assemble regularly and to vote on all matters of taxation; the rights of *habeas corpus* and trial by jury (for men of property and social status) were also secured. These rights were in turn legitimated in a constitutionally binding document, the Bill of Rights (1689). All Protestants, regardless of their sectarian bias, were granted toleration.

The English Revolution, in both its 1640 and its 1688 phases, secured English parliamentary government and the rule of law. Gradually the monarchical element in that system would yield to the power and authority of parliamentary ministers and state officials. The Revolution of 1688–89 was England's last revolution. In the nineteenth and twentieth centuries, parliamentary institutions would be gradually and peacefully reformed to express a more democratic social reality. The events of 1688–89 have rightly been described as "the year one," in that they fashioned a system of government that operated effectively in Britain and was also capable of being adopted with modification elsewhere. The British system became a model for other forms of bourgeois representative government adopted in France and former British colonies, beginning with the United States.

The Holy Roman Empire: The Failure to Unify Germany

In contrast to the French, English, Spanish, and Dutch experiences in the early modern period, the Germans failed to achieve national unity. This failure is tied to the history of the Holy Roman Empire. That union of various distinct central European territories was created in the tenth century when Otto I, in a deliberate attempt to revive Charlemagne's empire, was crowned emperor of the Romans. Later the title was changed to Holy Roman emperor, with the kingdom consisting of mostly German-speaking principalities.

Most medieval emperors busied themselves not with administering their territories but with attempting to secure control of the rich Italian peninsula and with challenging the rival authority of various popes. In the meantime, the German nobility extended and consolidated their rule over their peasants and over various towns and cities. Their aristocratic power remained a constant obstacle to German unity.

In the medieval and early modern periods the Holy Roman emperors were dependent on their most powerful noble lords—including an archbishop or two—because the office of emperor was an elected one, not the result of hereditary succession. German princes, some of whom were electors—such as the archbishops of Cologne and Mainz, the Hohenzollern elector of Brandenburg, the landgrave of Hesse, and the duke of Saxony—were fiercely independent. All belonged to the empire, yet all regarded themselves as autonomous powers. These decentralizing tendencies were highly developed by the fifteenth century. The Hapsburgs maneuvered themselves into a position from which they could monopolize the imperial elections. The empire became increasingly German and Hapsburg, with Worms as the seat of imperial power.

The centralizing efforts of the Hapsburg Holy Roman Emperors Maximillian I (1493–1519) and Charles V (1519–1556) were impeded by the Reformation, which bolstered the Germans' already well-developed tendencies toward local independence. The German nobility were all too ready to use the Reformation as a vindication of their local power, and indeed Luther made just such an appeal to their interests. War raged in Germany between the Hapsburgs and the Protestant princes, united for mutual protection in the Schmalkadic League. The Treaty of Augsburg (1555) conferred on every German prince the right to determine the religion of his subjects. The princes retained their power; a unified German state was never constructed by the Hapsburgs.

When an exhausted Emperor Charles V abdicated in 1556, he gave his kingdom to his son Philip and his brother Ferdinand. Philip inherited Spain and its colonies as well as the Netherlands, and Ferdinand acquired the Austrian territories. Two branches of the Hapsburg family were thus created. Throughout the sixteenth century the Austrian Hapsburgs barely managed to control these sprawling and deeply divided German territories. Religious disunity and the particularism and provinciality of the German nobility continued to prevent the creation of a German state.

The Austrian Hapsburg emperors, however, never missed an opportunity to further the cause of Catholicism and to strike at the power of the German nobility. No Hapsburg was ever more fervid in that regard than the Jesuit-trained Archduke Ferdinand II, who ascended to the throne in Vienna in 1619. His policies provoked a war within the empire that engulfed the whole of Europe. The Thirty Years' War (1618–1648) began when the Bohemians, whose anti-Catholic tendencies went back to fourteenth-century heretic John Huss, attempted to put a Protestant king on their throne. Austrian and Spanish Hapsburgs reacted by sending an army into the kingdom of Bohemia, and suddenly the whole empire was forced to take sides along religious lines. Bohemia suffered an almost unimaginable devastation; the ravaging Catholic army sacked and burned three-fourths of the kingdom's towns and practically exterminated its aristocracy.

Until the 1630s, it looked as if the Hapsburgs would be able to use the war to enhance their power and to promote centralization. But the intervention of Protestant Sweden, led by Gustavus Adolphus and encouraged by France, wrecked Hapsburg ambitions. The ensuing military conflict devastated vast areas of northern and central Europe. The civilian population suffered untold hardships. Partly because the French finally intervened directly, the Spanish Hapsburgs emerged from the Thirty Years' War with no benefits. At the Treaty of Westphalia (1648), the Austrian Hapsburgs gained firm control of the eastern states of the kingdom, with Vienna as their capital. Austria took shape as a dynastic state, while the German territories in the empire remained fragmented by the independent interests of the feudal nobility.

European Expansion

During the period from 1450 to 1750, western Europe entered an era of overseas exploration and economic expansion that transformed society. European adventurers discovered a new way to reach the rich trading centers of India by sailing around Africa. They also conquered, colonized, and exploited a new world across the Atlantic. These discoveries and conquests brought about an extraordinary increase in business activity and the supply of money, which stimulated the growth of capitalism. People's values changed in ways that were alien and hostile to the medieval outlook. By 1750, the model Christian in northwestern Europe was no longer the selfless saint but the enterprising businessman. The era of secluded manors and walled towns was drawing to a close. A world economy was emerging in which European economic life depended on the market in Eastern spices, African slaves, and American silver. During this age of exploration and commercial expansion, Europe generated a peculiar dynamism unmatched by any other civilization. A process was initiated that by 1900 would give Europe mastery over most of the globe and wide-ranging influence over other civilizations.

Forces Behind Expansion

Combined forces propelled Europeans outward and enabled them to dominate Asians, Africans, and American Indians. European monarchs, merchants, and aristocrats fostered expansion for power and profit; religion and technology played their part. As the numbers of the landed classes exceeded the supply of available land, the sons of the aristocracy looked beyond Europe for the lands and fortunes denied them at home. Nor was it unnatural for them to do so by plunder and conquest—their ancestors had done the same thing for centuries.

Merchants and shippers also had reason to look abroad. Trade between Europe, Africa, and the Orient had gone on for centuries, but always through intermediaries who increased the costs and decreased the profits on the European end. Gold had been transported by Arab nomads across the Sahara from the riverbeds of West Africa. Spices had been shipped from India and the East Indies by way of Muslim and Venetian merchants. Western European merchants now sought to break those monopolies by going directly to the source— to West Africa for gold, slaves, and pepper, and to India for pepper, spices, and silks.

The centralizing monarchical state also played its part in expansion. Monarchs who had successfully established royal hegemony at home, like Ferdinand and Isabella of Spain, looked for opportunities to extend their control overseas. From overseas empires came gold, silver, and commerce that paid for ever-more expensive royal government at home and for war against rival dynasties abroad.

Religion, too, helped in expansion. The crusading tradition was well established, especially on the Iberian Peninsula, where a 500-year struggle known as the Reconquest had taken place to drive out the Muslims. Cortés, the Spanish conqueror of Mexico, for example, saw himself as following in the footsteps of Paladin Roland, the great medieval military hero who had fought to drive back Muslims and pagans. Prince Henry the Navigator hoped that the Portuguese expansion into Africa would serve two purposes: the discovery of gold and the extension of Christianity at the expense of Islam.

Not only did the West have the will to expand, it also possessed the technology needed for successful expansion—in the form of armed sailing vessels. This factor distinguished the West from China and the lands of Islam and helps explain why the West, not the oriental civilizations, launched an age of conquest resulting in global mastery. Not only were sailing ships more maneuverable and faster in the open seas than galleys (ships propelled by oars), but the addition of guns below deck that could fire and cripple or sink distant enemy ships gave them another tactical advantage. The galleys of the Arabs in the Indian Ocean and the junks of the Chinese were not armed with such guns. In battle they relied instead on the ancient tactic of coming up alongside the enemy vessel, shearing off its oars, and boarding to fight on deck.

The gunned ship gave the West naval superiority from the beginning. The Portuguese, for example, made short work of the Muslim fleet sent to drive them out of the Indian Ocean in 1509. That victory at Diu, off the western coast of India, indicated that the West not only had found an all-water route to the Orient but was there to stay.

The Portuguese Empire

In the first half of the fifteenth century, a younger son of the king of Portugal, named Prince Henry the Navigator (1394–1460) by English writers, sponsored voyages of exploration and the nautical studies needed to undertake them. The Portuguese first expanded into islands in the Atlantic Ocean. In 1420 they began to settle Madeira and raise corn there, and in the 1430s they pushed into the Canaries and the Azores in search of new farmlands and slaves for their colonies. In the middle decades of the century they moved down the west African coast to the mouth of the Congo River and beyond, establishing trading posts as they went.

By the end of the fifteenth century, the Portuguese had developed a viable imperial economy among the ports of West Africa, their Atlantic islands, and western Europe—an economy based on sugar, black slaves, and gold. Africans panned gold in the riverbeds of central and western Africa, and the Portuguese purchased it at its source.

Map 9.2   Overseas Exploration and Conquest, c. 1400–1600 ▶

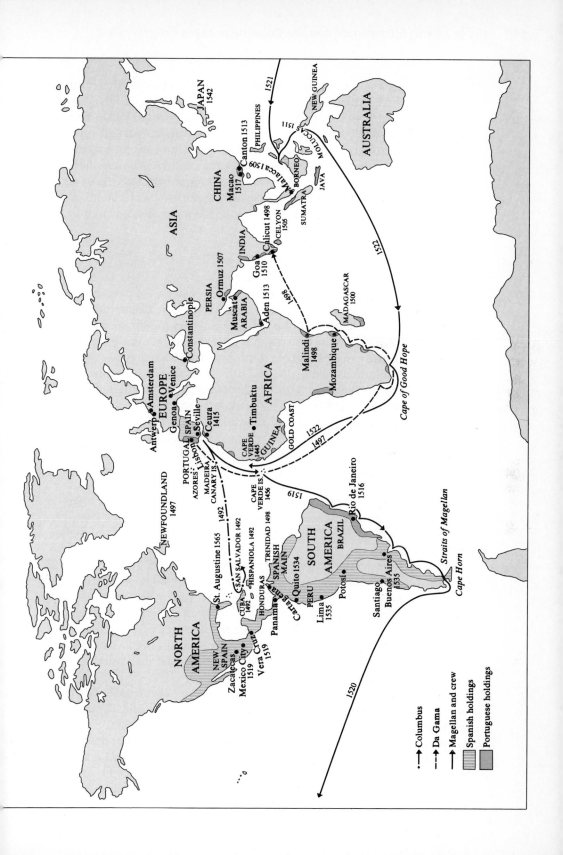

NORTH AMERICA

NEW SPAIN

Zacatecas
Mexico City 1519
Vera Cruz 1519

St. Augustine 1565

SAN SALVADOR 1492
CUBA 1492
HONDURAS
HISPANIOLA 1492
Panama
Caracas
TRINIDAD 1498
SPANISH MAIN

Quito 1534
PERU
Lima 1535
Potosí
Santiago
Buenos Aires 1535

SOUTH AMERICA

BRAZIL

Rio de Janeiro 1516

Straits of Magellan

Cape Horn

1520

1519

NEWFOUNDLAND 1497

PORTUGAL
AZORES
Lisbon
MADEIRA
CANARY IS.
1492
CAPE VERDE IS. 1456

EUROPE
Amsterdam
Antwerp
Genoa
Venice
SPAIN
Seville
Ceuta 1415
Constantinople

CAPE VERDE 1445
GUINEA
GOLD COAST

AFRICA

Timbuktu

Malindi 1498

Mozambique

Cape of Good Hope

MADAGASCAR 1500

1522

1497

1522

1498

ASIA

PERSIA
Ormuz 1507
Muscat
ARABIA
Aden 1513

INDIA
Goa 1510
Calicut 1498
CELYON 1505

CHINA
Macao 1517
Canton 1513

JAPAN 1542

MALACCA 1509
SUMATRA
BORNEO
JAVA
PHILIPPINES
MOLUCCAS 1511

1521

1511

1522

NEW GUINEA

AUSTRALIA

• Columbus
→ Da Gama
→ Magellan and crew
▨ Spanish holdings
▧ Portuguese holdings

The Portuguese did not stop in western Africa. By 1488, Bartholomeu Dias had reached the southern tip of the African continent; a decade later Vasco da Gama sailed around the Cape of Good Hope and across the Indian Ocean to India. By discovering an all-water route to the Orient, Portugal broke the commercial monopoly of Eastern goods that Genoa and Venice had enjoyed. With this route to India and the East Indies, the Portuguese found the source of the spices needed to make dried and tough meat palatable. As along the African coast, they established fortified trading posts—most notably at Goa on the western coast of India (Malabar) and at Malacca (now Singapore) in the Malay Peninsula.

The Spanish Empire

Spain stumbled onto its overseas empire, which nonetheless proved to be the biggest and richest of any until the eighteenth century. Columbus, who believed that he could reach India by sailing west, won the support of Isabella, queen of Castile. But on his first voyage (1492) he landed on the large Caribbean island that he named Española (Little Spain). Within decades, two events revealed that Columbus had discovered not a new route to the East but new continents: Vasco Nuñez de Balboa's discovery of the Pacific Ocean at the Isthmus of Panama in 1513, and the circumnavigation of the globe (1519–1522) by the expedition led by Ferdinand Magellan, which sailed through the strait at the tip of South America that now bears his name.

Stories of the existence of large quantities of gold and silver to the west lured the Spaniards from their initial settlements in the Caribbean to Mexico. In 1519, Hernando Cortés landed on the Mexican coast with a small army; during two years of campaigning he managed to defeat the native rulers, the Aztecs, and to conquer Mexico for the Spanish crown. A decade later, Francisco Pizarro achieved a similar victory over the mountain empire of the Incas in Peru.

For good reasons, the Mexican and Peruvian conquests became the centers of the Spanish overseas empire. First, there were the gold hoards accumulated over the centuries by the rulers for religious and ceremonial purposes. When these supplies were exhausted, the Spanish discovered silver at Potosí in Upper Peru in 1545 and at Zacatecas in Mexico a few years later. From the middle of the century, the annual treasure fleets sailing to Spain became the financial bedrock of Philip II's war against the Muslim Turks and the Protestant Dutch and English.

Not only gold and silver lured Spaniards to the New World. The will to conquer and convert the pagan peoples of the New World continued the crusading spirit used against the Muslims during the five previous centuries of Spanish history. The rewards were what they had always been: the propagation of the true faith, service to the Crown, and handsome land grants. The land was especially attractive in the sixteenth century because the number of hidalgos (lesser nobility) was increasing with the general rise in population, and as a result the amount of land available to them at home was shrinking.

The opportunity for profit drove some farmers to work harder and manage their land better.

All over Europe, landlords held their properties in the form of manors. A particular type of rural society and economy had evolved on these manors in the Late Middle Ages. By the fifteenth century, much manor land was held by peasant-tenants according to the terms of a tenure known in England as *copyhold*. The tenants had certain hereditary rights to the land in return for the performance of certain services and the payment of certain fees to the landlord. Principal among these rights was the use of the commons—the pasture, woods, and pond. For the copyholder, access to the commons often made the difference between subsistence and real want, because the land tilled on the manor might not produce enough to keep a family. Arable land was worked according to ancient custom. The land was divided into strips, and each peasant of the manor was assigned a certain number of strips. This whole pattern of peasant tillage and rights in the commons was known as the *open-field system*. After changing little for centuries, it was met head-on by the incentives generated by the price revolution.

In England, landlords aggressively pursued the possibilities for profit resulting from the inflation of farm prices. This pursuit required far-reaching changes in ancient manorial agriculture, changes that are called *enclosure*. The open-field system was geared to providing subsistence for the local village and, as such, prevented large-scale farming for a distant market. In the open-field system, the commons could not be diverted to the production of crops for sale. Moreover, the division of the arable land into strips reserved for each peasant made it difficult to engage in profitable commercial agriculture.

English landlords in the sixteenth century fought a two-pronged attack against the open-field system in their attempt to transform their holdings into market-oriented, commercial ventures. First they deprived their tenant peasantry of the use of the commons; then they changed the conditions of tenure from copyhold to leasehold. Whereas copyhold was heritable and fixed, leasehold was not. When a lease came up for renewal, the landlord could raise the rent beyond the tenant's capacity to pay. Restriction of rights to the commons deprived the poor tenant of critically needed produce. Both acts of the landlord forced peasants off the manor or into the landlord's employ as farm laborers. With tenants gone, fields could be incorporated into larger, more productive units. Landlords could hire labor at bargain prices because of the swelling population and the large supply of peasants forced off the land by enclosure. Subsistence farming gave way to commercial agriculture—the growing of a surplus for the marketplace. But rural poverty increased because of the mass evictions of tenant farmers.

In the fifteenth and sixteenth centuries, the Dutch developed a new kind of farming, known as *convertible husbandry*. This farming system employed a series of innovations that replaced the old three-field system of crop rotation, which had left one-third of the land unused at any given time. The new techniques used all the land every year and provided a more diversified agriculture.

The Expansion of Trade and Industry

The conditions of the price revolution also caused trade and industry to expand. Population growth exceeding the capacity of local food supplies stimulated commerce in basic foodstuffs—for example, the Baltic trade with western Europe. Equally important as a stimulus to trade and industry was the growing income of landlords, merchants, and in some instances, peasants. This income created a rising demand for consumer goods. Another factor in commercial and industrial expansion was the growth of the state. With increasing amounts of tax revenue to spend, the expanding monarchies of the sixteenth and seventeenth centuries bought more and more supplies—ships, weapons, uniforms, paper—and so spurred economic expansion.

Innovations in Business

Markets tended to shift from local to regional or even to international, a condition that gave rise to the merchant-capitalist. Unlike local producers, the merchant-capitalists' operations extended across local and national boundaries. An essential feature of merchant capitalism was the *putting-out system* of production. The manufacture of woolen textiles is a good example of how the system worked. The merchant-capitalist would buy the raw wool from English landlords who had enclosed their manors to take advantage of the rising price of wool. The merchant's agents collected the wool and took it (put it out) to nearby villages for spinning, dyeing, and weaving. The work was done in the cottages of peasants, many of whom had been evicted from the surrounding manors as a result of enclosure and therefore had to take what work they could get at the lowest possible wages. When the wool was processed into cloth, it was picked up and shipped to market.

Accompanying the emergence of the merchant-capitalist and the putting-out system was a cluster of other innovations in business life. Some of them had roots in the Middle Ages and were important in the evolution of the modern capitalist economy. Banking operations grew more sophisticated, making it possible for depositors to pay their debts by issuing written orders to their banks to make transfers to their creditors' accounts—the origins of the modern check. Accounting methods also improved. The widespread use of double-entry bookkeeping made errors immediately evident and gave a clear picture of the financial position of a commercial enterprise. Very important to overseas expansion was the form of business enterprise known as the joint-stock company, which allowed small investors to buy shares in a venture. These companies made possible the accumulation of the large amounts of capital needed for large-scale operations, like the building and deployment of merchant fleets, which were quite beyond the resources of one person.

Different Patterns of Commercial Development

England and the Netherlands   In both England and the United Provinces the favorable conditions led to large-scale commercial expansion. In the 1590s the

Inside the Amsterdam Stock Exchange by J. Berckheyde.   Seventeenth-century Holland saw the rise of a solid bourgeosie and produced an economic system that looked toward twentieth-century capitalism. Every available commodity was sold, from spices and slaves to tulips. (*Amsterdams Historisch Museum*)

Dutch devised a new ship, the *fluit,* or flyboat, to handle bulky grain shipments at the lowest possible cost. This innovation allowed them to capture the Baltic trade, which became a principal source of their phenomenal commercial expansion between 1560 and 1660. Equally dramatic was their commercial penetration of the Orient. Profits from the European carrying trade built ships that allowed the Dutch first to challenge and then to displace the Portuguese in the spice trade with the East Indies during the early seventeenth century. The Dutch chartered the United East India Company in 1602 and established trading posts in the islands, which were the beginnings of a Dutch empire that lasted until World War II.

The English traded throughout Europe in the sixteenth and seventeenth centuries, especially with Spain and the Netherlands. The seventeenth century saw the foundation of a British colonial empire along the Atlantic seaboard in North America from Maine to the Carolinas and in the West Indies, where the English managed to dislodge the Spanish in some places.

In both England and the United Provinces, government promoted the interests of business. In the late sixteenth and early seventeenth centuries the northern provinces of the Spanish Netherlands, centered on Holland, won their independence from Spain in a protracted struggle. Political power in these so-called United Provinces passed increasingly into the hands of an urban patriciate of merchants and manufacturers based in cities like Delft, Haarlem, and especially Amsterdam. There urban interests pursued public policies that served their pocketbooks. In England, because of the revolutionary transfer of power from the king to Parliament, economic policies more closely reflected the interests of big business, whether agricultural or commercial. Enclosure, for example, was abetted by parliamentary enactment. The Bank of England, founded in 1694, expanded credit and increased business confidence. The Navigation Acts, which proved troublesome to American colonists, required that all goods traded between England and its colonies be carried in English ships.

France and Spain   France benefited from commercial and industrial expansion, but not to the same degree as England. A principal reason for this was the aristocratic structure of French society. Family ties and social intercourse between aristocracy and merchants, such as existed in England, were largely absent in France. Consequently, the French aristocracy remained contemptuous of commerce. Also inhibiting economic expansion were the guilds— remnants of the Middle Ages that restricted competition and production. In France there was relatively less room than in England for the merchant-capitalist operating outside the guild structures.

Spain presents an even clearer example of failure to grasp the opportunities afforded by the price revolution. By the third quarter of the sixteenth century, Spain possessed the makings of economic expansion: unrivaled amounts of capital in the form of silver, a large and growing population, rising consumer demand, and a vast overseas empire. These factors did not bear fruit because the Spanish value system regarded business as a form of social heresy. The Spanish held in high esteem those gentlemen who possessed land gained through military service and crusading ardor, which enabled them to live on rents and privileges. So commerce and industry remained contemptible pursuits.

Numerous wars in the sixteenth century (with France, the Lutheran princes, the Ottoman Turks, the Dutch, and the English) put an increasing strain on the Spanish treasury, even with the annual shipments of silver from the New World. Spain spent its resources on maintaining and extending its imperial power and Catholicism, rather than on investing in economic expansion. In the end, the wars cost even more than Spain could handle. The Dutch for a time, and the English and the French more permanently, displaced Spain as the great power. The English and the Dutch had taken advantage of the opportunities presented by the price revolution; the Spanish had not.

The Fostering of Mercantile Capitalism

The changes described—especially in England and the Netherlands—represent a crucial stage in the development of the modern economic system known as *capitalism.* This is a system of *private enterprise:* the main economic decisions (what, how much, where, and at what price to produce, buy, and sell) are made by private individuals in their capacity as owners, workers, or consumers.

From 1450 to 1600, several conditions fostered a sustained incentive to invest and reinvest—a basic factor in the emergence of modern capitalism. One was the price revolution stemming from a supply of basic commodities that could not keep pace with rising demand. Prices continued to climb, creating the most powerful incentive of all to invest rather than to consume. Why spend now, those with surplus wealth must have asked, when investment in commercial farming, mining, shipping, and publishing (to name a few important outlets) is almost certain to yield greater wealth in the future?

Another stimulus for investment came from government—and this occurred in two ways. First, governments acted as giant consumers whose appetites throughout the early modern period were expanding. Merchants who supplied governments with everything from guns to frescoes not only prospered but were led to reinvest because of the constancy and growth of government demand. Governments also sponsored new forms of investment, whether to supply the debauched taste for new luxuries at the king's court or to meet the requirements of the military. Private investors also reaped incalculable advantages from overseas empires. Colonies supplied cheap raw materials and cheap (slave) labor and served as markets for exports. They greatly stimulated the construction of both ships and harbor facilities and the sale of insurance.

The second government stimulus was state policies, known as mercantilism, meant to augment national wealth and power. According to mercantilist theory, wealth from trade was measured in gold and silver, of which there was believed to be a more or less fixed quantity. The state's goal in international trade became to sell more abroad than it bought, that is, to establish a favorable balance of payments. When the amount received for sales abroad was greater than that spent for purchases, the difference would be an influx of precious metal into the state. By this logic, mercantilists were led to argue for the goal of national sufficiency: a country should try to supply most of its own needs to keep imports to a minimum.

To stimulate the national economy, governments subsidized new industries, chartered companies to engage in overseas trade, and broke down local trade barriers, such as guild regulations and internal tariffs. The price revolution, the concentration of wealth in private hands, and government activity combined to provide the foundation for sustained investment and for the emergence of mercantile capitalism. This new force in the world should not be confused with industrial capitalism. The latter evolved with the Industrial Revolution in eighteenth-century England, but mercantile capitalism paved the way for it.

Toward a Global Economy

The transformations considered in this chapter were among the most momentous in the world's history. In an unprecedented development, one small part of

Chronology 9.1 ❧ Economic and Political Transformations

1394–1460	Henry the Navigator, prince of Portugal, encourages expansion into Africa for gold and his anti-Muslim crusade
1469	Ferdinand and Isabella begin their rule of Castile and Aragon
1485	Henry VII begins the reign of the Tudor dynasty in England
1488	Bartholomeu Dias reaches the tip of Africa
1492	Christopher Columbus reaches the Caribbean island of Española on his first voyage; the Jews are expelled from Spain; Granada, the last Muslim kingdom in Spain, is conquered, ending the Reconquest
1497	Vasco da Gama sails around Cape of Good Hope (Africa) to India
1519	Charles V of Spain becomes Hapsburg emperor of the Holy Roman Empire
1519–1521	Hernando Cortés conquers the Aztecs in Mexico
1531–1533	Francisco Pizarro conquers the Incas in Peru
1552	Silver from the New World flows into Europe via Spain, contributing to a price revolution
1556–1598	Philip II of Spain persecutes Jews and Muslims
1562–1598	Religious wars in France

the world, western Europe, had become the lord of the sea lanes, the master of many lands throughout the globe, and the banker and profit-taker in an emerging world economy. Western Europe's global hegemony was to last well into this century. In conquering and settling new lands, Europeans exported Western culture around the globe, a process that accelerated in the twentieth century.

The effects of overseas expansion were profound. The native populations of the New World were decimated. As a result of the labor shortage, millions of blacks were imported from Africa to work as slaves on plantations and in mines. Black slavery would produce large-scale effects on culture, politics, and society that have lasted to the present day.

The widespread circulation of plant and animal life also had great consequences. Horses and cattle were introduced to the New World. (So amazed were the Aztecs to see man on horseback that at first they thought horse and

Chronology 9.1 continued

1572	The St. Bartholomew's Day Massacre—Queen Catherine of France orders thousands of Protestants executed
1588	The Spanish Armada is defeated by the English fleet
1598	French Protestants are granted religious toleration by the Edict of Nantes
1624–1642	Cardinal Richelieu, Louis XIII's chief minister, determines royal policies
1640–1660	The English Revolution
1648	The Treaty of Westphalia ends the Thirty Years' War
1649	Charles I, Stuart king of England, is executed by an act of Parliament
1649–1660	England is co-ruled by Parliament and the army under Oliver Cromwell
1660	Charles II returns from exile and becomes king of England
1685	Louis XIV of France revokes the Edict of Nantes
1688–1689	Revolution in England; end of absolutism
1694	The Bank of England is founded
1701	Louis XIV tries to bring Spain under French control

rider were one demonic creature.) In return the Old World was introduced to corn, the tomato, and most important, the potato, which was to become a staple of the northern European diet. Manioc, from which tapioca is made, was transplanted from the New World to Africa, where it helped sustain the population.

Western Europe was wrenched out of the subsistence economy of the Middle Ages and launched on a course of sustained economic growth. This transformation resulted from the grafting of traditional forms, like primogeniture and holy war, onto new forces, like global exploration, price revolution, and convertible husbandry. Out of this change emerged the beginnings of a new economic system, mercantile capitalism, which in large measure provided the economic thrust for European world predominance and paved the way for the Industrial Revolution of the eighteenth and nineteenth centuries.

Suggested Reading

Anderson, Perry, *Lineages of the Absolutist State* (1974). An excellent survey, written from a Marxist perspective.

Cipolla, Carlo M., *Guns, Sails and Empires* (1965). Connections between technological innovation and overseas expansion, 1400 to 1700.

Davis, David Brion, *The Problem of Slavery in Western Culture* (1966). Authoritative and highly suggestive.

Davis, Ralph, *The Rise of the Atlantic Economies* (1973). A reliable recent survey of early modern economic history.

Elliott, J. H., *Imperial Spain, 1469–1716* (1963). An excellent survey of the major European power of the early modern period.

Koenigsberger, H. G., *Early Modern Europe, 1500–1789* (1987). The best survey of the period, by a master historian.

Parry, J. H., *The Age of Reconnaissance* (1963). A short survey of exploration.

Plumb, J. H., *The Growth of Political Stability in England, 1675–1725* (1967). A basic book, clear and readable.

Shennan, J. H., *The Origins of the Modern European State* (1974). An excellent brief introduction.

Review Questions

1. In what ways did early modern kings increase their power, and what relationship did they have to the commercial bourgeoisie in their countries?

2. What were the strengths and weaknesses of the Spanish state?

3. Why did England move in the direction of parliamentary government, while most countries on the Continent embraced absolutism? Describe the main factors.

4. What were the new forces for expansion operating in early modern Europe?

5. What is the connection between the price revolution and overseas expansion? What was the principal cause of the price revolution? Why?

6. What was enclosure? How did the price revolution encourage it?

7. What is mercantile capitalism? What three patterns of the distribution of wealth fostered its development?

Chapter ✿ 10

Intellectual Transformation:
The Scientific Revolution and the
Age of Enlightenment

Starting in the late fourteenth century, the cohesive medieval world began to disintegrate, a process that lasted to the late seventeenth century. Not only did basic medieval institutions like feudalism and the church weaken, but the medieval view of the universe, or world-view, faded and was gradually replaced by the modern, scientific understanding of nature. This transformation occurred within the particular historical context created by the Renaissance and the Reformation, as well as by the growth in commercial prosperity and state power.

The unique contribution of the seventeenth-century Scientific Revolution to the making of the modern world-view lay in its new mechanical conception of nature, which enabled Westerners to discover and explain the laws of nature mathematically. They came to see nature as composed solely of matter whose motion, occurring in space and measurable by time, was governed by laws of force. This philosophically elegant construction renders the physical world knowable, and even possibly manageable.

The Scientific Revolution also entailed the discovery of a new scientific methodology of observation and experimentation. By the late seventeenth century, no one could entertain a serious interest in any aspect of the physical order without actually doing experiments or without observing, in a rigorous and systematic way, the behavior of physical phenomena. A new scientific culture had been born. During the eighteenth century, this method of inquiry became of vital importance as a model for progress in the human sciences as well as the natural sciences.

The eighteenth century is called the Age of Enlightenment, or Age of Reason, for during this period an educated elite, expressing supreme confidence in the power of reason, attempted a rational analysis of European institutions and beliefs. The Enlightenment was heavily indebted to the experimental method and the mechanical picture of the universe that were formed during the Scientific Revolution. Scientific research seemed to show that order and mathematically demonstrable laws were at work in the physical universe. The thinkers of the Enlightenment, called *philosophes,* argued that it should be possible to examine *human* institutions with the intention of imposing a comparable order and rationality. ✌

Medieval Cosmology

The unique character of the modern scientific outlook is most understandable in contrast with what went before it—the medieval understanding of the natural world and its physical properties. That understanding rested on a blend of Christian thought with theories derived from ancient Greek writers like Aristotle and Ptolemy.

The explanations given by Aristotle (384–322 B.C.) for the motion of heavy bodies permeated medieval scientific literature. In trying to understand motion, Aristotle had argued simply that it was in the nature of things to move in certain ways. A stone falls because it is absolutely heavy; fire rises because it is absolutely light. Weight is an absolute property of a physical thing; therefore, motion results from the properties of bodies, and not from the forces or laws of motion at work in nature.

Aristotle's physics fitted neatly into his *cosmology,* or world picture. The earth, being the heaviest object, lay stationary and suspended at the center of the universe. The sun, the planets, and the moon revolved in circles around the earth. Aristotle presumed that the planets were made of a kind of fine, luminous ether and were held in their circular orbits by luminous spheres, or "tracks." These spheres possessed a certain reality, although invisible to human beings, and hence they came to be known as the crystalline spheres.

Ptolemy of Alexandria produced the *Almagest* (A.D. 150), a handbook of Greek astronomy based on the theories of Aristotle. Central to that work was the assumption that a motionless earth stood at the center of the universe (although some Greeks had disputed the notion) and that the planets move about it in a series of circular orbits interrupted by smaller circular orbits called epicycles.* By the Late Middle Ages, Ptolemy's handbook, because of the support it lent to Aristotelian cosmology, had come to embody standard astronomical wisdom.

Medieval thinkers integrated the cosmology of Aristotle and Ptolemy into a Christian framework that drew a sharp distinction between the world beyond the moon and an earthly realm. Celestial bodies were composed of the divine ether, a substance too pure, too spiritual to be found on earth; heavenly bodies, unlike those on earth, were immune to all change and obeyed different laws of motion than earthly bodies did. The universe was not homogeneous but divided into a higher world of the heavens and a lower world of earth. Earth could not compare with the heavens in spiritual dignity, but God had nevertheless situated it in the center of the universe. Earth deserved this position of importance, for only here was the drama of salvation performed. This vision of the universe was to be shattered by the Scientific Revolution.

A New View of Nature

Renaissance Background

With the advent of the Renaissance, which began in Italy in the late fourteenth century, a new breed of intellectuals began to challenge medieval assumptions about human beings and nature, armed with a collection of newly discovered ancient Greek and Roman texts. The philosophy of Plato was seized on as an alternative to medieval scholasticism. The great strength of Plato's philosophy lay in his belief that one must look beyond the appearance of things to an invisible reality that is simple, rational, and mathematically explainable. Plato's search for this fundamental reality thus influenced thinkers of the Scientific Revolution, who found inspiration in the Platonic tradition that nature's truths apply universally and possess the elegance and simplicity of mathematics. With this impulse to mathematicize nature came the desire to describe it accurately. Thus, in addition to the humanists, Renaissance art, which aspired to depict the human body and the natural world as exactly as possible, is an antecedent of the Scientific Revolution.

The Copernican Revolution

The geocentric view of the universe postulated by Aristotle and Ptolemy was challenged by Nicolaus Copernicus (1473–1543), a Polish churchman, astronomer, and mathematician. As a young man, Copernicus enrolled in the

---

* Since, in reality, the path of a planet is not a circle, but an ellipse, Ptolemy used epicycles to save the appearance of circular motion. A planet revolved uniformly around a small circle, an epicycle, which in turn revolved around the earth on a large circle. By ascribing a sufficient number of epicycles to a given planet, thus creating a system of "wheels on wheels," astronomers could retain their commitment to the perfect circular motion of planets.

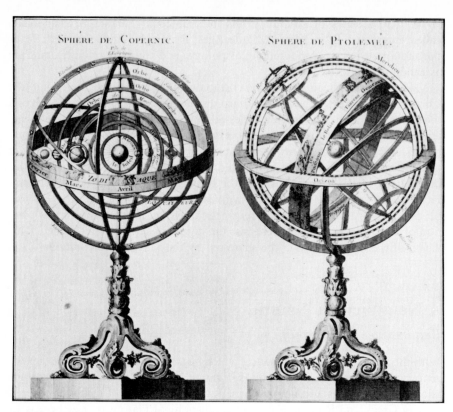

Armillary Spheres According to Copernicus and Ptolemy.   Copernicus overturned thirteen hundred years of cosmology with the appearance of his treatise on heavenly motion. The idea of a heliocentric universe supported by mathematical evidence brought the medieval mind-set to an irrefutable end. (*Smithsonian Institution Photo No. 65,420*)

University of Krakow, where he may have come under the influence of Renaissance Platonism, which was spreading outward from the Italian city-states. He also journeyed to Italy, and in Bologna and Padua he may have become aware of ancient Greek texts containing arguments for the sun being the center of the universe. The mathematical complexity of the Ptolemaic system troubled Copernicus, who believed that truth was the product of elegance and simplicity. Toward the end of his stay in Italy, he became convinced that the sun lay at the center of the universe, so he set out on a lifelong task to work out mathematical explanations of how a heliocentric universe operated. Because he did not want to engage in controversy with the followers of Aristotle, Copernicus did not publish his findings until 1543, in a work entitled *On the Revolutions of the Heavenly Spheres.* Legend says his book, which in effect began the Scientific Revolution, was brought to him on his deathbed.

His treatise on the universe retained some elements of the Aristotelian-Ptolemaic system. Copernicus never doubted Aristotle's basic notion of the perfect circular motion of the planets or the existence of crystalline spheres within which the stars revolved, and he retained many of Ptolemy's epicycles. But Copernicus proposed a heliocentric model of the universe that was mathematically simpler than Ptolemy's earth-centered universe. Thus, he eliminated some of Ptolemy's epicycles and cleared up various problems that had troubled astronomers who had based their work on an earth-centered universe. By removing the earth from its central position and by giving it motion—that is, by making the earth just another planet—Copernicus undermined the system of medieval cosmology and made the birth of modern astronomy possible. Because they were committed to the Aristotelian-Ptolemaic system and to biblical statements that supported it, most thinkers rejected Copernicus's conclusions.

Tycho and Kepler: The Laws of Planetary Motion

The most gifted astronomer in the generation after Copernicus, Tycho Brahe (1546–1601), never accepted the Copernican system. He did, however, realize more fully than any contemporaries the necessity for new observations. Aided by the king of Denmark, Tycho built the finest observatory in Europe to use in his work. Tycho's fame ultimately rests on his skill as a practicing astronomer.

Tycho Brahe and His Observatory's Interior.   Although Tycho Brahe remained a staunch Aristotelian, his observation of a new star in 1572 and a comet in 1577 challenged these traditional views. His precise scientific approach to astronomy and careful mathematical calculations were to be his greatest legacy. (*The British Library*)

He bequeathed to future generations precise calculations about the movements of heavenly bodies, which proved invaluable.

These calculations were put to greatest use by Johannes Kepler (1571–1630), a German who collaborated with Tycho during the latter's final years. Tycho bequeathed his astronomical papers to Kepler, who brought to this data a scientific vision that was both experimental and mystical. Kepler searched persistently for harmonious laws of planetary motion. He did so because he believed profoundly in the Platonic ideal: a spiritual force infuses the physical order; beneath appearances are harmony and unity; and the human mind can begin to comprehend that unity only through *gnosis*—a direct and mystical realization of unity—and through mathematics. Kepler believed that both approaches were compatible, and he managed to combine them. He believed in and practiced astrology (as did Tycho), and throughout his lifetime he tried to contact an ancient but lost and secret wisdom.

In the course of his studies and observations of the heavens, Kepler discovered the three basic laws of planetary motion. First, the orbits of the planets are elliptical, not circular as Aristotle and Ptolemy had assumed, and the sun is one focus of the ellipse. Unlike Tycho, Kepler accepted Copernicus's theory and provided proof for it. Kepler's second law demonstrated that the velocity of a planet is not uniform, as had been believed, but increases as its distance from the sun decreases. Kepler's third law—that the squares of the times taken by any two planets in their revolutions around the sun are in the same ratio as the cubes of their average distances from the sun—brought the planets together into a unified mathematical system.

The significance of Kepler's work was immense. He gave sound mathematical proof to Copernicus's theory, eliminated forever the use of epicycles that had saved the appearance of circular motion, and demonstrated that mathematical relationships can describe the planetary system. But Kepler left an important question unresolved: what kept the planets in their orbits? Why did they not fly out into space or crash into the sun? The answer would be supplied by Isaac Newton, who synthesized the astronomy of Copernicus and Kepler with the new physics developed by Galileo.

Galileo: Experimental Physics

At the same time that Kepler was developing a new astronomy, his contemporary, Galileo Galilei (1564–1642), was breaking with the older physics of Aristotle. A Pisan by birth, Galileo lived for many years in Padua, where he conducted some of his first experiments on the motion of bodies. Guided by the dominant philosophy of the Italian Renaissance—the revived doctrines of Plato—Galileo believed that beyond the visible world lay universal truths, subject to mathematical verification. Galileo insisted that the study of motion be based on mathematics. For this Late Renaissance natural philosopher, mathematics became the language of nature. Galileo also believed that only after experimenting can one discern the harmonious laws of the universe and give them mathematical expression.

Galileo established a fundamental principle of modern science—the order and uniformity of nature. There are no distinctions in rank or quality between the heavens and earth; heavenly bodies are not perfect and changeless as Aristotle had believed. In 1609, Galileo built a telescope through which he viewed the surface of the moon. The next year, in a treatise called *The Starry Messenger,* he proclaimed to the world that the moon "is not smooth, uniform, and precisely spherical as a great number of philosophers believe it and the other heavenly bodies to be, but is uneven, rough, and full of cavities . . . being not unlike the face of the earth, relieved by chains of mountains and deep valleys."[1] In addition, Galileo observed spots on the sun, providing further evidence that heavenly objects, like earthly objects, undergo change. There are no higher and lower worlds; nature is the same throughout.

Through his telescope Galileo also saw moons around Jupiter, a discovery that served to support the Copernican hypothesis. If Jupiter had moons, then all heavenly bodies did not orbit the earth. The moons of Jupiter removed a fundamental criticism leveled against Copernicus and opened up the possibility that indeed the earth, with its own moon, might be just like the planet Jupiter, and both might in turn revolve around a central point—the sun.

With Galileo, the science of Copernicus and the assault on Aristotle entered a new phase. Backed by teachers within the academic community who routinely taught the old astronomy, priests in Florence preached against Galileo, using Aristotle's writings and the Bible to back their attacks. In 1633, Galileo's teachings were condemned and he was placed under house arrest. Science as preached by Galileo was not, as he knew perfectly well, inherently dangerous to Catholicism. But the clergy and their academic allies saw it as a challenge to their power, and they could enlist the papacy and the Inquisition in their support. As a result, students of the new science in Catholic countries looked to Protestant countries as places to live or publish their books. Censorship worked to stifle intellectual inquiry, and by the middle of the seventeenth century science had become, because of historical circumstance, an increasingly Protestant and northern European phenomenon.

The Newtonian Synthesis

By the middle of the seventeenth century, largely because of the work of Copernicus, Kepler, and Galileo, Aristotle and Ptolemy had been dethroned. A new philosophy of nature and a new science had come into being whose essence lay in the mathematical expression of physical laws that describe matter in motion. Yet what was missing was an overriding law that could explain the motion observed in the heavens and on earth. This law was supplied by Isaac Newton (1642–1727).

In the *Principia Mathematica* of 1687, Newton not only formulated universal mathematical laws but offered a philosophy of nature that sought to explain the essential structure of the universe: matter is atomic in structure and is acted upon by immaterial forces that are placed in the universe by God. Newton said that the motion of matter could be explained by three laws: inertia, that a body remains in a state of rest or continues its motion in a straight line unless impelled to change by forces impressed on it; acceleration, that the change in the motion of a body is proportional to the force acting on it; and that for every action there is an equal and opposite reaction.

Newton argued that these laws apply not only to observable matter on earth but also to the motion of planets in their orbits. He showed that planets did not remain in their orbits because circular motion was "natural" or because crystalline spheres kept them in place. Rather, said Newton, planets keep to their orbits because every body in the universe exercises a force on every other body, a force that he called *universal gravitation.* Gravity is operative throughout the universe, whether on earth or in the heavens, and it is capable of mathematical expression. Newton built his theory on the work of other scientific giants, notably Kepler and Galileo; yet no one before him had possessed the breadth of vision, mathematical skill, and dedication to rigorous observation to combine this knowledge into one grand synthesis.

With Newton's discovery of universal gravitation, the Scientific Revolution reached its culmination. The universe could now be described as matter in motion; it was governed by invisible forces that operated everywhere, both on earth and in the heavens, and these forces could be expressed mathematically. The medieval picture of the universe as closed, earthbound, and earth-centered was replaced by a universe seen to be infinite and governed by universal laws. The earth was now regarded as simply another planet.

But what was God's role in this new universe? Newton and his circle labored to create a mechanical world picture that retained a central place for a providential deity who operates constantly in the universe; at one time he believed that gravity was simply the will of God operating on the universe. As Newton said in the *Optiks,* the physical order "can be the effect of nothing else than the wisdom and skill of a powerful ever-living agent." Newton, a scientific genius, was also a deeply religious thinker who was committed to the maintenance of Protestantism in England.

Biology, Medicine, and Chemistry

The spectacular advances made in physics and astronomy in the sixteenth and seventeenth centuries were not matched in the biological sciences. Indeed, the day-to-day practice of medicine throughout western Europe changed little in the period from 1600 to 1700, for much of medical practice relied frequently on astrology. Doctors clung to the teachings of the ancient practitioners Galen and Hippocrates.

In general, Galenic medicine paid little attention to the discovery of specific cures for particular diseases. As a follower of Aristotle, Galen emphasized the elements that make up the body—he called their manifestations *humors.* A person with an excess of blood was sanguine; a person with too much bile was choleric. Health consisted of a restoration of balances among these various elements, so Galenic doctors often prescribed purges of one sort or another. The most famous of these was bloodletting, but sweating was also a favorite remedy. These methods were often as dangerous as the diseases they sought to cure, but they were taught religiously in the medical schools of Europe.

In 1543, the same year that Copernicus published his heliocentric theory, Andreas Vesalius (1514–1564), a Belgian surgeon, published *The Structure of the Human Body*. Opposing Galenic practice, Vesalius argued that observation and anatomical dissection were the keys to knowing how the human body works. By the late seventeenth century, doctors had learned a great deal about the body's structure and chemistry.

In *The Motion of the Heart and Blood in Animals* (1628), William Harvey (1578–1657), a British physician, showed that blood circulates in the body because of the pumping action of the heart muscle, breaking with Galen's view that the liver was the source of the blood in the veins and the heart was the source of arterial blood. In describing the heart as a mechanical pump, Harvey demonstrated the same tendency to mechanize nature that marked the revolution in astronomy and physics. Drawing conclusions after carefully observing and experimenting with living animals, Harvey employed the inductive method championed by Sir Francis Bacon.

Robert Boyle (1627–1691) was an English scientist who adopted the atomic explanation that matter is made up of small, hard, indestructible particles that behave with regularity and explain changes in gases, fluids, and solids. Boyle pioneered in the experimental method with such exciting and accurate results that by the time of his death, no serious scientist could attempt chemical experiments without following his guidelines. Thus the science of chemistry acquired its characteristic experimentalism; it was also based on an atomic theory of matter. But not until late in the eighteenth century was this new discipline applied to medical research.

Prophets and Proponents of the New Science

The accomplishments of the Scientific Revolution extend beyond the creation of a new model of the universe and new knowledge of the human body. They also include the formulation of a new method of inquiring into nature and the recognition that science can serve humanity. Two thinkers instrumental in articulating these implications of scientific advances were Sir Francis Bacon and René Descartes.

Bacon

Sir Francis Bacon (1561–1626), an English statesman and philosopher, vigorously supported the advancement of science and the scientific method. Although he had no laboratory and made no discoveries, he is deservedly regarded as a prophet of modern science because of his advocacy of the scientific method. Bacon recognized that medieval scholasticism was not suited for an emerging age of science, and he attributed science's limited progress over the ages to the interference of scholastic theologians who bent theories of nature to the requirements of Scripture. The scholastics, said Bacon, engaged in arid verbalism; they constructed elaborate systems that had little to do with the empirical world and did not increase understanding of nature. Bacon also attacked practitioners of astrology, magic, and alchemy for their errors, secretiveness, and enigmatic writings; he advocated instead cooperative, methodical, and publicly criticizable scientific research.

The method that Bacon championed as the best way to truth and new knowledge was the inductive approach: careful observation of nature, systematic accumulation of data, and experimentation. Because he gave supreme value to the direct observation of nature, Bacon is one of the founders of the empirical tradition in modern philosophy. The Baconian vision of progress in science leading to an improvement of the human condition inspired much scientific activity in the seventeenth century, particularly in England.

Descartes

The scientific method encompasses two approaches to knowledge, which usually complement each other: the empirical (inductive) and the rational (deductive). In the inductive approach, which is employed in descriptive sciences, such as biology, anatomy, and geology, general principles are derived from the analysis of data collected through observation and experiment. The essential features of the inductive method were championed by Bacon. In the deductive approach, which is employed in mathematics and theoretical physics, truths are derived in successive steps from first principles, or indubitable axioms. In the seventeenth century, the deductive method was formulated by René Descartes (1596–1650), a French mathematician and philosopher.

In his *Discourse on Method*, Descartes expressed his disenchantment with the learning of his day and "resolved to seek no other knowledge than that which I might find within myself, or perhaps in the great book of nature." Rejecting as "absolutely false anything of which I could have the least doubt," Descartes, who longed for certainty, searched for an incontrovertible truth that could serve as the first principle of knowledge, the basis of an all-encompassing philosophic system.

Descartes found there was one thing of which he was certain, one truth that was unshakable: that it was he who was doing the doubting and thinking. In his dictum "I think, therefore I am," he had his starting point of knowledge. Descartes is viewed as the founder of modern philosophy because he called for the individual to question and, if necessary, to overthrow all traditional beliefs, and he proclaimed the mind's inviolable autonomy and importance—its ability and right to comprehend truth.

Descartes held that it is the method of mathematics that produces certain knowledge. By applying mathematical reasoning to philosphic problems, we can achieve the same certainty and clarity evidenced in geometry. The mathe-

René Descartes by Frans Hals
(c. 1580–1666). Descartes is both the father of modern philosophy and the prophet of modern science. He placed his faith above all in the human intellect and its ability to achieve scientific knowledge, and made significant practical contributions in algebra. (*Royal Museum of Fine Arts, Copenhagen*)

matical or deductive approach he favored consists of finding a self-evident principle, such as a geometric axiom, and then deducing other truths from it through logical reasoning. Descartes was convinced that through *a priori* reasoning from general mathematical principles, one could deduce a complete and comprehensive system of nature. His deductive method, with its mathematical emphasis, perfectly complements Bacon's inductive approach, which stresses observation and experimentation. The scientific achievements of modern times have arisen from the skillful synchronization of induction and deduction.

Like Bacon, Descartes held that science served "the general good of mankind." It produced useful knowledge that enables us "to enjoy without any trouble the fruits of the earth and all its comforts . . . especially . . . the preservation of health." Bacon's and Descartes's confidence in science as a boon for humanity was bequeathed to the Age of Enlightenment.

The Meaning of the Scientific Revolution

The Scientific Revolution was decisive in shaping the modern mentality; it shattered the medieval view of the universe and replaced it with a wholly different world-view. Gone was the belief that a motionless earth lay at the center of a universe that was finite and enclosed by a ring of stars. Gone too was the belief that the universe was divided into higher and lower worlds and that different laws of motion operated in the heavens and on earth. The universe was now viewed as a giant machine functioning according to universal laws that could be expressed mathematically; nature could be mastered.

The methodology that produced this new view of nature—the new science—played a crucial historical role in reorienting Western thought away from medieval theology and metaphysics and toward the study of physical and human problems. In the later Middle Ages, most men of learning were Aristotelians and theologians. But by the mid-eighteenth century, knowledge of Newtonian science and the dissemination of useful learning had become the goal of the educated classes. All knowledge, it was believed, could emulate scientific knowledge; it could be based on observation, experimentation, and rational deduction; it could be systematic, verifiable, progressive, and useful. At every turn the advocates of this new approach to learning hailed the scientists of the sixteenth and seventeenth centuries as proof that no institution or dogma had a monopoly on truth—the scientific approach would yield knowledge that might, if properly applied for the good of all people, produce a new and better age. Such an outlook gave thinkers new confidence in the power of the human mind to master nature and led them to examine European institutions and traditions with an inquiring, critical, and skeptical spirit. Thus inspired, the reformers of the eighteenth century would seek to create an age of enlightenment.

The Scientific Revolution ultimately weakened traditional Christianity. Applied to religious doctrines, Descartes' reliance on methodical doubt and clarity of thought and Bacon's insistence on careful observation eventually led thinkers to question miracles, prophecies, and other Christian beliefs. Theology came to be regarded as a separate and somewhat irrelevant area of intellectual inquiry that was not fit for the interests of practical, well-informed people. Not only Christian doctrines but also various widespread and popular beliefs in magic, witchcraft, and astrology came under attack.

Gradually the science of Newton became the science of western Europe: nature mechanized, analyzed, regulated, and mathematicized. As a result of the Scientific Revolution, Western thinkers came to believe more strongly than ever that nature could be mastered. Mechanical science, applied to canals, engines, pumps, and levers, became the science of industry. Thus the Scientific Revolution, operating on both intellectual and commercial levels, laid the groundwork for two major developments of the modern West—the Industrial Revolution and the Age of Enlightenment.

The Age of Enlightenment

The German philosopher Immanuel Kant (1724–1804) defined the Enlightenment as the bringing of "light into the dark corners of the mind," the dispelling of ignorance and superstition. Kant went to the heart of one aspect of the Enlightenment, that is, its insistence that each individual should reason independently, without recourse to the authority of the schools, churches, and universities.

Philosophes—the thinkers who aspired to examine and order human institutions—were found most commonly in the major European cities; Paris became the center of the Enlightenment during the 1770s. In essays, monthly journals, works of fiction, and even mildly pornographic and anonymous tales, they attacked many of the abuses of eighteenth-century society—religious fanaticism and intolerance, the idleness and corruption of the aristocracy, the use of torture, terrible prison conditions, slavery, and violations of natural rights. In essence, the philosophes condemned all vestiges of medieval culture. Inevitably, modern liberal thought, initiated by the Enlightenment, emerged as hostile to scholastic learning, priests, and eventually, in some quarters, to Christianity itself. The philosophes expressed confidence in science and reason, espoused humanitarianism, and struggled for religious liberty and freedom of thought and person. Combining these values with a secular orientation and a belief in future progress, the philosophes helped shape, if not define, the modern outlook.

The Science of Religion
Christianity Under Attack

No single thread had united Western culture more powerfully than Christianity. Until the eighteenth century, educated people, especially rulers and servants of the state, had to give allegiance to one or another of the Christian churches, however un-Christian their actions. The Enlightenment, however, produced the first widely read and systematic assault on Christianity launched from within the ranks of the educated. The philosophes argued that many Christian dogmas defied logic—for example, the conversion of the substance of bread and wine into the body and blood of Christ during the Eucharist— and they ridiculed theologians for arguing over obscure issues that seemed irrelevant to the human condition and a hindrance to clear thinking. "Theology amuses me," wrote Voltaire. "That's where we find the madness of the human spirit in all its plenitude." In the same spirit, the philosophes denounced the churches for inciting the fanaticism and intolerance that led to the horrors of the Crusades, the Inquisition, and the wars of the Reformation. They viewed Christianity's preoccupation with salvation and its belief in the depravity of human nature, a consequence of Adam and Eve's defiance of God, as barriers to social improvement and earthly happiness.

The leaders of the Enlightenment sought to repudiate traditional Christianity and to put in its place a rational system of ethics and philosophy based on scientific truths. Although some philosophes were atheists, most were *deists* who tried to make religion compatible with a scientific understanding of nature. Deists believed only those Christian doctrines that could meet the test of reason. For example, they considered it reasonable to believe in God, for only with a creator, they said, could such a superbly organized universe have come into being. But after God set the universe in motion, according to the deists, he took no further part in its operations. Thus, although deists retained a belief in God the Creator, they rejected clerical authority, revelation, original sin, and miracles. They held that biblical accounts of the resurrection and of Jesus walking on water or waking the dead could not be reconciled with natural law. Deists viewed Jesus as a great moral teacher, not as the son of God, and they regarded ethics, not faith, as the essence of religion; rational people, they said, served God best by treating their fellow human beings justly.

David Hume (1711–1776), a Scottish skeptic, attacked both revealed religion and the deists' natural religion. He maintained that all religious ideas, including Christian teachings and even the idea of God, stemmed ultimately from human fears and superstitions. Hume rejected the deist argument that this seemingly orderly universe required a designing mind to create it. The universe, said Hume, might very well be eternal, and the seeming universal order simply a natural condition that requires no explanation. Hume's attack made it impossible to establish a necessary link between a mechanical universe and a creator. As a consequence of Hume's critique, Christian belief rested more than ever before on faith, not reason.

Voltaire, the Philosophe

As a poet and writer struggling for recognition in Paris, the young François Marie Arouet, known to the world as Voltaire (1694–1778), encountered some of the new ideas that were being discussed in private gatherings (called *salons*) in Paris. Care had to be taken in the French capital by those educated people who wanted to read books and discuss ideas hostile to the church or to the Sorbonne, the clerically controlled university. The French printing presses were among the most tightly controlled and censored in Europe. Individuals had been imprisoned for writing, publishing, or owning books hostile to Catholic doctrine. Although Voltaire learned something of the new enlightened culture in Paris, it was in 1726, when he journeyed to London, that Voltaire the poet became Voltaire the philosophe.

In England, Voltaire became acquainted with the ideas of John Locke (1632–1704) and Isaac Newton. From Newton, Voltaire learned the mathematical laws that govern the universe; he witnessed the power of human reason to establish general rules that seemed to explain the behavior of physical objects. From Locke, Voltaire learned that people should believe only those ideas received from the senses. Locke's theory of learning, his *epistemology*, impressed many of the proponents of the Enlightenment. Again, the implications for religion were most serious: if people believe only those things that they experience, they will be unable to accept mysteries and doctrines simply because they are taught by churches and the clergy. Voltaire experienced considerable freedom of thought in England and saw a religious toleration that

Mme. Geoffrin's Salon.   The High Enlightenment in the 1750s had Paris as its capital. The new thinking concentrated on social inequalities, especially those that stifled talented human beings. The salons of exclusive Parisian society, such as that of Mme. Geoffrin, became the forum for the next generation of philosophers after Voltaire and Diderot. (*Giraudon/Art Resource*)

stood in stark contrast to the absolutism of the French kings and the power of the French clergy. He also witnessed a freer mixing of bourgeois and aristocratic social groups than was permitted in France at this time.

Throughout his life, Voltaire was a fierce supporter of the Enlightenment and a bitter critic of churches and the Inquisition. Although his books were banned in France, he probably did more there than any other philosophe to popularize the Enlightenment and to mock the authority of the clergy. In *Letters Concerning the English Nation* (1733), Voltaire praised English society and offered constitutional monarchy, new science, and religious toleration as models to be followed by all of Europe.

Voltaire was a practical reformer who campaigned for the rule of law, a freer press, religious toleration, humane treatment of criminals, and a more effective system of government administration. His writings constituted a radical attack on aspects of eighteenth-century French society. Yet, like so many philosophes, Voltaire feared the power of the people, especially if goaded by the clergy. He supported rule by reform-minded kings—enlightened despots.

Political Thought

The Enlightenment built on the secular and rational tradition in political thought developed by Machiavelli during the Renaissance and Thomas Hobbes during the English Revolution of the seventeenth century. Three major European thinkers and a host of minor ones wrote treatises on politics that remain relevant to this day: John Locke, *Two Treatises of Government* (1690); Baron de la Brède et de Montesquieu, *The Spirit of the Laws* (1748); and Jean Jacques Rousseau, *The Social Contract* (1762). All repudiated the divine right of kings and were concerned with checking the power of monarchy; each offered different formulas for achieving that goal.

Hobbes

A prerequisite for all Enlightenment political theorists was the work of Thomas Hobbes (1588–1679). All accepted Hobbes's belief that self-interest is a valid reason for engaging in political activity and his refusal to bring God into his system to justify the power of kings. Hobbes said that power did not rest on divine right but arose out of a contract made among men (women are not included in his system) who agreed to elevate the state, and hence the monarch, to a position of power over them. That contract, once made, could not be broken. As a consequence, the power of the government, whether embodied in a king or a parliament, was absolute.

Hobbes published his major work, *Leviathan,* in 1651, soon after England had been torn by civil war; thus, he was obsessed with the issue of political stability. He feared that, left to their own devices, men would kill one another; the "war of all against all"[2] would prevail without the firm hand of a sovereign to stop it. Hobbes's vision of human nature was dark and forbidding. In the state of nature, the original men had lived lives that could only have been "nasty, brutish, and short." Their only recourse was to set up a power over themselves that would restrain them. For Hobbes the state was, as he put it, a "mortal god," the only guarantee of peace and stability. He was the first political thinker to realize the extraordinary power that had come into existence with the creation of strong centralized governments.

Most Enlightenment theorists, however, beginning with John Locke, denied that governments possessed absolute power over their subjects, and to that extent they repudiated Hobbes. Many European thinkers of the eighteenth century, including Rousseau, also rejected Hobbes's gloomy view that human nature is greedy and warlike. Yet Hobbes was essential to the Enlightenment. He was a secular political theorist, and he sounded the death knell for the theory of the divine right of kings. Enlightenment political theorists started where he left off.

Locke

Probably the most widely read political philosopher during the first half of the eighteenth century was John Locke. His *Two Treatises of Government* was seen as a justification for the Revolution of 1688–89 and the notion of government by consent of the people. (Although they were published in 1690, Locke wrote the treatises before the English Revolution; that fact, however, was not known during the Enlightenment.)

Locke's theory, in its broad outlines, stated that the right to govern derived from the consent of the governed and was a form of contract. When people gave their consent to a government, they expected it to govern justly, to protect their property, and to ensure certain liberties for the propertied. If a government attempted to rule absolutely and arbitrarily—if it violated the natural rights of the individual—it reneged on its contract and forfeited the loyalty of its subjects. Such a government could legitimately be overthrown. Locke believed that a constitutional government that limited the power of rulers was the best defense of property and individual rights.

Late in the eighteenth century, Locke's ideas were used to justify liberal revolutions in both Europe and America. Indeed, the importance of Locke's political philosophy was not simply his recourse to contract theory as a justification of constitutional government; it was also his assertion that the community could take up arms against its sovereign in the name of the natural rights of liberty and property. Locke's ideas about the foundation of government had greater impact on the Continent and in America during the eighteenth century than they did in England.

Montesquieu

Baron de la Brède et de Montesquieu (1689–1755) was a French aristocrat who, like Voltaire, visited England late in the 1720s and knew the writings of Locke. Montesquieu had little sympathy for revolutions, but he did approve of constitutional monarchy. His primary concern was to check the unbridled authority of the French kings. In opposition to the Old Regime (French society before the Revolution of 1789), Montesquieu proposed a balanced system of government, with an executive branch offset by a legislature whose members were drawn from the landed and educated elements in society. Montesquieu genuinely believed that the aristocracy possessed a natural and sacred obligation to rule and that their honor called them to serve the community.

In stressing the rule of law and the importance of nonmonarchical authority, Montesquieu became a source for legitimating the authority of representative institutions. Hardly an advocate of democracy, he was nonetheless seen as a powerful critic of royal absolutism. His writings, particularly *The Spirit of the Laws*, established Montesquieu both as a major philosophe who possessed republican tendencies and as a critic of absolute monarchy and the Old Regime in France.

Rousseau

Not until the 1760s did democracy find its champion, in Jean Jacques Rousseau (1712–1778). Rousseau based his politics on contract theory—the people choose their government, and in so doing effectively give birth to civil society. But Rousseau further demanded that the contract be constantly renewed and that government be made immediately and directly responsible to the will of the people. *The Social Contract* opened with this stirring cry for reform: "Man is born free; and everywhere he is in chains," and went on to ask how that restriction could be changed. Freedom is in the very nature of man: "to renounce liberty is to renounce being a man, to surrender the rights of humanity and even its duties."

In *The Social Contract,* Rousseau tried to resolve the conflict between individual freedom and the demands of the state. His solution was a small state, modeled after the ancient Greek city-state, where people participated actively and directly in politics and were willing to sacrifice self-interest to the community's needs. To the ancient Greek, said Rousseau, the state was a moral association that made him a better person, and good citizenship was the highest form of excellence. The state, said Rousseau, should be based on the *general will*—that which is best for the community, which expresses its common interests. Rousseau wanted laws of the state to coincide with the general will; he felt that people have the wisdom to arrive at laws that serve the common good, but to do so they have to set aside selfish interests for the good of the community. For Rousseau, freedom consisted of obeying laws prescribed by citizens inspired by the general will. Citizens themselves must constitute the law-making body; law making cannot be entrusted to a single person or a small group.

For Rousseau, those who disobey laws—who act according to their private will rather than in accordance with the general will as expressed in law—degrade themselves and undermine the community. Therefore, government has the right to force citizens to be obedient—to compel them to exercise their individual wills in the proper way. Because of this view, several contemporary thinkers see Rousseau not only as a spokesman of modern democracy but also as a forerunner of modern dictatorships.

No philosopher of the Enlightenment was more dangerous to the Old Regime than Rousseau. His ideas were perceived as truly revolutionary, a direct challenge to the power of kings, churches, and aristocrats. During the French Revolution, his name would be invoked to justify democracy.

Social Thought

Psychology and Education

Just as Locke's *Two Treatises of Government* was instrumental in shaping the political thought of the Enlightenment, his *Essay Concerning Human Understanding* (1689) provided the theoretical foundations for an unprecedented interest in education. Locke's view that at birth the mind is blank, a clean slate, or *tabula rasa,* held two important implications. First, if human beings were not born with innate ideas, then they were not, as Christianity taught, inherently sinful. Second, a person's environment was the decisive force in shaping that person's character and intelligence. Nine of every ten men, wrote Locke, "are good or evil, useful or not, [because of] their education." Such a theory was eagerly received by the reform-minded philosophes, who preferred attributing wickedness to faulty institutions, improper rearing, and poor education—which could be remedied—rather than to a defective human nature.

Locke's doctrine that knowledge comes primarily through experience found its most extreme expression in the writings of Rousseau on education. In *Émile* (1762), Rousseau argued that individuals learn from nature, from people, or from things. Indeed, Rousseau wanted the early years of a child's education to be centered on developing the senses, not spent chained to a schoolroom desk. Later, attention would be paid to intellectual pursuits, then finally to morality. Rousseau grasped a fundamental principle of modern psychology, that the child is not a small adult, and childhood is not merely preparation for adulthood but a particular stage, with its own distinguishing characteristics, in human development. Children, said Rousseau astutely, should be permitted to behave like children.

Humanitarianism

Crime and Punishment   No society founded on the principles of the Enlightenment could condone the torture of prisoners and the inhumanity of a corrupt legal system. On that view, all the philosophes were clear, and they had plenty of evidence from their own societies on which to base their condemnation of torture and the inhumanity of the criminal justice system. Prisoners were often starved or exposed to disease, or both. In many Continental countries, where torture was still legal, prisoners could be subjected to brutal interrogation or to random punishment.

Fittingly, the most powerful critique of the European system of punishment came from Italy, where the Inquisition and its torture chambers had reigned for centuries with little opposition. In *On Crimes and Punishments* (1764), Cesare Beccaria (1738–1794), an Italian economist and criminologist inspired in part by Montesquieu, condemned torture as inhuman. He called it "a criterion fit for a cannibal," and an irrational way of determining guilt or innocence, for there are "innumerable examples of innocent persons who have confessed themselves criminals because of the agonies of torture." Influenced by Beccaria's work, reform-minded jurists, legislators, and ministers called for the elimination of torture from codes of criminal justice, and several European lands abolished torture in the eighteenth century.

Slavery   On both sides of the Atlantic during the eighteenth century, criticism of slavery was growing. At first it came from religious thinkers like the Quakers, who held that the light of God's truth works in every man and woman. Many philosophes in both America and Europe were familiar with Quaker

Slaves Processing Sugar in a Colonial Plantation.   This diagram shows slaves running machinery to grind sugar cane into pulp. In the colonies of European countries in the New World and other lands, subjected peoples were used to perform hard labor in the plantations and mines. The immorality of slavery was raised initially by religious thinkers, especially the Quakers, and then taken up by Diderot in his *Encyclopedia*. (*Courtesy of the University of Minnesota Libraries*)

attacks on slavery. The Enlightenment must be credited with bringing the problem of slavery into the forefront of public discussion in Europe and the American colonies. Throughout the eighteenth century, the emphasis placed by the Enlightenment on moral sensibility produced a literature that used shock to emphasize over and over again, and with genuine revulsion, the inhumanity of slavery.

By the second half of the century, strongly worded attacks on slavery were issued by a new generation of philosophes. With Rousseau in the vanguard, they condemned slavery as a violation of the natural rights of man. In a volume issued in 1755, the great *Encyclopedia* of the Enlightenment, edited by Denis Diderot, condemned slavery in no uncertain terms: "There is not a single one of these hapless souls . . . who does not have the right to be declared free . . . since neither his ruler nor his father nor anyone else had the right to dispose of his freedom."

Women

Not entirely unlike slaves, women had few property rights within marriage, and their physical abuse by husbands was widely regarded as beyond the purview of the law. Women's education was slighted, and social theorists had for centuries regarded them as inferiors. By the 1750s in Paris, however, rich women had become the organizers of fashionable salons where writers and enlightened reformers gathered for free and open conversation. Diderot attended such a salon, but Baron d'Holbach, who led the most famous gathering of the 1770s, specifically excluded women because he believed that they lowered the tone and seriousness of the discussion.

Mary Wollstonecraft (1759–1797), an English writer familiar with Enlightenment ideas, extended the principles of the Enlightenment to the position and status of women. In *Vindication of the Rights of Woman* (1792), she argued that "from the tyranny of man the greater part of female follies proceed." Calling for the extension of the principle of liberty to women and urging that equal public education be made available for both men and women, Wollstonecraft's *Vindication* became a text on which nineteenth-century reformers could and did build.

Economic Thought

The Enlightenment's emphasis on property as the foundation for individual rights and its search for uniform laws inspired by Newton's scientific achievement led to the development of the science of economics. Appropriately, that intellectual achievement occurred in the most advanced capitalistic nation in Europe, Great Britain. Not only were the British in the vanguard of capitalist expansion; by the third quarter of the eighteenth century, that expansion had brought on the start of the Industrial Revolution. Britain's new factories and markets for the manufacture and distribution of goods provided a natural laboratory where theorists schooled in the Enlightenment's insistence on observation and experimentation could observe the ebb and flow of capitalist production and distribution. In contrast to the harsh criticisms it leveled against existing institutions and old elites, the Enlightenment on the whole approved of the independent businessman—the entrepreneur.

And there was no one more approving than Adam Smith (1732–1790), whose *Wealth of Nations* (1776) became a kind of bible for those who regarded capitalist activity as uniformly worthwhile, never to be inhibited by government regulation. A professor in Glasgow, Scotland, Smith actually went out and observed factories at work; he was one of the first theorists to see the importance of the division of labor in making possible the manufacture of more and cheaper consumer goods.

By the middle of the eighteenth century, enlightened theorists all over

Europe, especially in England, Scotland, and France, had decided that self-interest was the foundation of all human actions and that at every turn government should assist people in expressing their interests and thus in finding true happiness. Of course, in the area of economic life, government had for centuries regulated most aspects of the market. The classic economic theory behind such regulation was mercantilism. Mercantilists believed that a constant shortage of riches—bullion, goods, whatever—existed, and that governments must direct economic activity in their states so as to compete successfully with other nations for a share of the world's scarce resources. It required enormous faith in the inherent usefulness of self-interest to assert that government should cease regulating economic activity, that the market should be allowed to be free. This doctrine of *laissez faire*—to leave the market to its own devices—was the centerpiece of Adam Smith's massive economic study on the origins of the wealth of nations.

Smith was not distressed by the apparent randomness of market forces. Beneath this superficial chaos he saw order—the same order he saw in physical nature through his understanding of the new science. He used the metaphor of "the invisible hand" to explain the source of this order; by that he probably meant Newton's regulatory God, made very distant by Smith, who was a deist. That hand would invisibly reconcile self-interest to the common or public interest. With the image of the invisible hand, Smith expressed his faith in the rationality of commercial society and laid the first principle for the modern science of capitalist economics.

The High Enlightenment

More than any other political system in western Europe, the Old Regime in France was directly threatened by the doctrines and reforming impulse of the Enlightenment. The Roman Catholic church was deeply entrenched in every aspect of life—landownership, control over universities and presses, and access to both the court and, through the pulpit, the people. For decades the church had brought its influence to bear against the philosophes, yet by 1750 the Enlightenment had penetrated learned circles and academies in Paris and the provinces. Censorship had produced the opposite of the desired effect: the more irreligious and atheistic the book or manuscript was, the more attractive and sought-after it became.

The most important work of the French Enlightenment was the multivolume *Encyclopedia* edited by Denis Diderot (1713–1784), who had spent six months in jail for his writings. Published in 1751 and in succeeding years and editions, the *Encyclopedia* initiated a new stage in the history of Enlightenment publishing. The new era thus ushered in, called the High Enlightenment, was characterized by a violent attack on the church's privileges and the very foundations of Christian belief. From the 1750s to the 1780s, Paris became the capital of the Enlightenment. The philosophes were no longer a persecuted minority. Instead, they became cultural heroes. The *Encyclopedia* had to be read by anyone claiming to be educated.

In his preface to the *Encyclopedia,* Diderot's collaborator, Jean d'Alembert (c. 1717–1783), wrote a powerful summation of the Enlightenment's highest ideals. He extolled Newton's science. The progress of geometry and mechanics in combination, d'Alembert wrote, "may be considered the most incontestable monument of the success to which the human mind can rise by its efforts." In turn, he urged that revealed religion should be reduced to a few precepts to be practiced; religion should, he implied, be made scientific and rational. The *Encyclopedia* itself was self-consciously modeled on Bacon's admonition that the scientist should first of all be a collector of facts; in addition, it gave dozens of examples of useful new mechanical devices.

D'Alembert's preface also praised the psychology of Locke: all that is known, is known through the senses. He added that all learning should be catalogued and made easily and readily available, that the printing press should serve the needs of enlightenment, and that literary societies should be set up that would encourage men of talent. D'Alembert added that "they should banish all inequalities that might exclude or discourage men who are endowed with talents that will enlighten others."[3]

The High Enlightenment's systematic, sustained, and occasionally violent attacks on the abuses of French society link it with the French Revolution. Although the philosophes themselves were political moderates who aimed at a gradual evolutionary transformation of society, their criticism of the existing order had revolutionary implications.

War, Revolution, and Politics

Warfare and Revolution

The dreams of the philosophes, articulated in almost every area of human experience, seemed unable to forestall troublesome developments in power politics, war, and diplomacy. The eighteenth century was dominated by two areas of extreme conflict: Anglo-French rivalry over control of territory in the New World and intense rivalry between Austria and Prussia over control of central Europe.

In 1740 Prussia, ruled by the aggressive Frederick the Great, launched a successful war against Austria and was rewarded with Silesia, which augmented the Prussian population by 50 percent. Maria Theresa, the Austrian queen, never forgave Frederick, and in 1756 formed an alliance with France against Prussia. The ensuing Seven Years' War (1756–1763), which involved every major European power, did not significantly change Europe, but it did reveal Prussia's growing might.

At the same time, the French and English fought over their claims in the New World. England's victory in the conflict (known in American history as the French and Indian War) deprived France of virtually all of its North

American possessions and set in motion a train of events that culminated in the American Revolution. The war drained the British treasury, and now Britain had the additional expense of paying for troops to guard the new North American territories that it had gained in the war. As strapped British taxpayers could not shoulder the whole burden, the members of Parliament thought it quite reasonable that American colonists help pay the bill; they reasoned that Britain had protected the colonists from the French and was still protecting them in their conflicts with Indians. New colonial taxes and import duties imposed by Parliament produced vigorous protests from the Americans.

The quarrel turned to bloodshed in April and June 1775, and on July 4, 1776, delegates from the various colonies adopted the Declaration of Independence, written mainly by Thomas Jefferson. Applying Locke's theory of natural rights, this document declared that government derives its power from the consent of the governed, that it is the duty of a government to protect the rights of its citizens, and that people have the right to "alter or abolish" a government that deprives them of their "unalienable rights."

Why were the American colonists so ready to revolt? For one thing, they had brought with them a highly idealized understanding of English liberties; long before 1776, they had extended representative institutions to include small property owners who probably could not have voted in England. The colonists had come to expect representative government, trial by jury, and protection from unlawful imprisonment. Each of the thirteen colonies had an elected assembly that acted like a miniature parliament; in these assemblies, Americans gained political experience and quickly learned to be self-governing.

Familiarity with the thought of the Enlightenment and the republican writers of the English Revolution also contributed to the Americans' awareness of liberty. The ideas of the philosophes traversed the Atlantic and influenced educated Americans, particularly Thomas Jefferson and Benjamin Franklin. Like the philosophes, American thinkers expressed a growing confidence in reason, valued freedom of religion and of thought, and championed the principle of natural rights.

Another source of hostility toward established authority among the American colonists was their religious traditions, particularly that of the Puritans, who believed that the Bible was infallible and its teachings a higher law than the law of the state. Like their counterparts in England, American Puritans challenged political and religious authorities who, in their view, contravened God's law. Thus, Puritans acquired two habits that were crucial to the development of political liberty—dissent and resistance. When transferred to the realm of politics, these Puritan tendencies led Americans to resist authority that they considered unjust.

American victory came in 1783 as a result of several factors. George Washington proved a superior leader, able to organize and retain the loyalty of his troops. France, seeking to avenge its defeat in the Seven Years' War, helped the

Map 10.1   Europe, 1789 ▶

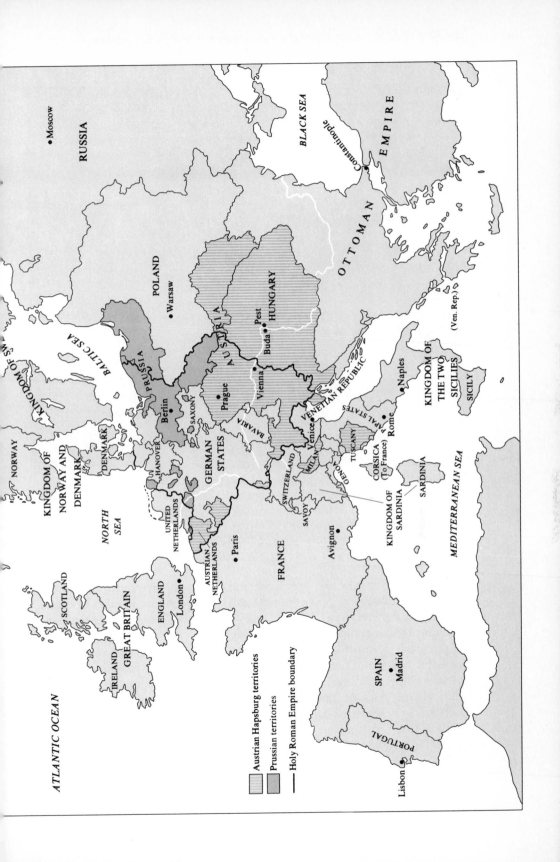

ATLANTIC OCEAN

IRELAND

SCOTLAND

GREAT BRITAIN

ENGLAND

London

NORTH SEA

NORWAY

KINGDOM OF NORWAY AND DENMARK

DENMARK

BALTIC SEA

KINGDOM OF SWE...

Moscow

RUSSIA

POLAND

Warsaw

PRUSSIA

Berlin

SAXONY

Prague

AUSTRIA

Vienna

Buda
Pest

HUNGARY

HANOVER

GERMAN STATES

BAVARIA

UNITED NETHERLANDS

AUSTRIAN NETHERLANDS

Paris

FRANCE

SWITZERLAND

SAVOY

AVignon

GENOA

VENETIAN REPUBLIC

Venice

Milan

TUSCANY

PAPAL STATES

Rome

CORSICA (To France)

KINGDOM OF SARDINIA

SARDINIA

Naples

KINGDOM OF THE TWO SICILIES

SICILY

(Ven. Rep.)

BLACK SEA

Constantinople

OTTOMAN EMPIRE

MEDITERRANEAN SEA

SPAIN

Madrid

PORTUGAL

Lisbon

Austrian Hapsburg territories

Prussian territories

Holy Roman Empire boundary

The Signing of the Declaration of Independence, July 4, 1776 (detail) by John Trumbull. The success of the American Revolution was hailed as a victory of liberty over tyranny. Jefferson and Franklin were intimately familiar with the thinking of the Enlightenment and stressed a confidence in reason, freedom of religion and thought, and the existence of natural rights. (*Copyright Yale University Art Gallery*)

Americans with money and provisions and then in 1778 entered the conflict. Britain had difficulty shipping supplies across three thousand miles of ocean, was fighting the French in the West Indies and elsewhere at the same time, and ultimately lacked commitment to the struggle.

Reformers in other lands quickly interpreted the American victory as a successful struggle of liberty against tyranny. During the Revolution the various states drew up constitutions based on the principle of popular sovereignty and included bills of rights that protected individual liberty. They also managed, somewhat reluctantly, to forge a nation. Rejecting both monarchy and hereditary aristocracy, the Constitution of the United States created a republic in which power derived from the people. A system of separation of powers and checks and balances set safeguards against the abuse of power, and the Bill of Rights provided for protection of individual rights. To be sure, the ideals of liberty and equality were not extended to all people—slaves knew nothing of the freedom that white Americans cherished, and women were denied the vote and equal opportunity. But to reform-minded Europeans, it seemed that Americans were fulfilling the promise of the Enlightenment; they were creating a freer and better society.

Enlightened Despotism

The philosophes used the term *enlightened despotism* to refer to an ideal shared by many of them: the strong monarch who would implement rational reforms and remove obstacles to freedom. When historians use the term *enlightened despotism,* they generally are describing the reigns of specific European monarchs and their ministers—Frederick the Great in Prussia; Catherine the Great in Russia; Charles III of Spain; Maria Theresa and, to a greater extent, her son Joseph II in Austria; and Louis XV of France. These eighteenth-century monarchs instituted specific reforms in education, trade, and commerce, and against the clergy.

Behind the reforms of enlightened despots lay the realization that the struggle for power in Europe called for efficient government administration and ample funds. Enlightened despots appointed capable officials to oversee the administration of their kingdoms, eliminate costly corruption, and collect taxes properly. Rulers strengthened the economy by encouraging the expansion of commerce through reduced taxes on goods and through agricultural reforms. In Central and Eastern Europe some rulers moved toward abolishing serfdom or at least improving conditions for serfs. (In Western Europe, serfdom had virtually died out.) Provisions were made to care for widows, orphans, and invalids. Censorship was eased, greater religious freedom was granted to minorities, criminal codes were made less harsh, and there were some attempts at prison reform. By these measures enlightened despots hoped to inspire greater popular support for the nation, an important factor in the European power struggle.

However, if the Enlightenment meant the endorsement of reason over force and of peace and cosmopolitan unity over ruthless competition, then the foreign policies of these enlightened monarchs can only be regarded as despotic. The evidence for this view lies in a long series of aggressions. There were no major philosophes who did not grow disillusioned with "enlightened" monarchs.

The Enlightenment and the Modern World

Enlightenment thought was the culmination of a trend instituted by Renaissance artists and humanists who attacked medieval otherworldliness and gave value to individual achievement and the worldly life. It was a direct outgrowth of the Scientific Revolution, which provided a new method of inquiry and verification and demonstrated the power and self-sufficiency of the human intellect. If nature were autonomous—that is, if it operated according to natu-

Chronology 10.1 ❧ The Scientific Revolution and the Enlightenment

1543	Publication of Copernicus' *On the Revolutions of the Heavenly Spheres* marks the beginning of modern astronomy
1605	Publication of Bacon's *Advancement of Learning*
1610	Publication of Galileo's *The Starry Messenger,* which asserts the uniformity of nature
1632	Galileo's teachings are condemned by the church and he is placed under house arrest
1687	Publication of Newton's *Principia Mathematica*
1690	Publication of Locke's *Two Treatises of Government*
1733	Publication of Voltaire's *Letters Concerning the English Nation*
1751–1765	Publication of Diderot's *Encyclopedia*
1776	The Declaration of Independence
1789	The French Revolution

ral laws that did not require divine intervention—then the human intellect could also be autonomous. Through its own powers, it could uncover those general principles that operate in the social world as well as in nature.

The philosophes sought to analyze nature, government, religion, law, economics, and education through reason alone, without any reference to Christian teachings, and they rejected completely the claims of clerics to a special wisdom. The philosophes broke decisively with the medieval view that the individual is naturally depraved, that heaven is the true end of life, and that human values and norms derive from a higher reality and are made known through revelation. Instead, they upheld the potential goodness of the individual, regarded the good life on earth as the true end of life, and insisted that individuals could improve themselves and their society solely by the light of reason.

In addition, the political philosophies of Locke, Montesquieu, and Rousseau were based on an entirely new and modern concept of the relationship between the state and the individual: states should exist not simply to accumulate power unto themselves but also to enhance human happiness. From that perspective, monarchy and even oligarchy not based on merit began to seem increasingly less useful. And if happiness is a goal, then it must be assumed that some sort of progress is possible in history.

The French leaders of the late Enlightenment, in fact, possessed a wholehearted belief in the infinite possibility of human progress. If human knowledge is ever-increasing and dependent only on the ability to sense and experience the world, then surely, they believed, the human condition can constantly improve. Western thought has never entirely relinquished this brave dream.

The philosophes wanted a freer, more humane, and more rational society, but they feared the people and their potential for revolutionary action. As an alternative to revolution, most philosophes offered science as the universal improver of the human condition. Faith in reform without the necessity of revolution proved to be a doctrine for the elite of the salons. In that sense the French Revolution can be said to have repudiated the essential moderation of philosophes such as Voltaire, d'Alembert, and Kant. Yet the Enlightenment established a vision of humanity so independent of Christianity and so focused on the needs and abuses of present society that no established institution, once grown corrupt and ineffectual, could long withstand its penetrating critique. To that extent the writings of the philosophes point toward the democratic revolutions of the late eighteenth century. The writers of the Enlightenment also point toward ideals that remain strong in most democratic Western societies: religious toleration, a disdain for prejudice and superstition, a fear of unchecked political authority, and, of course, a belief in the power of the human mind to rectify defective institutions and social injustice.

Notes

1. Excerpted in Stillman Drake, ed., *Discoveries and Opinions of Galileo* (New York: Doubleday, 1957), p. 28.
2. Thomas Hobbes, *Leviathan*, ed. by C. B. Macpherson (Harmondsworth, England: Penguin, 1977), p. 189.
3. Jean Le Rond d'Alembert, *Preliminary Discourse to the Encyclopedia of Diderot*, trans. by Richard N. Schwab (New York: Bobbs-Merrill, 1963), pp. 101–102.

Suggested Reading

Anchor, Robert, *The Enlightenment Tradition* (1967). Good survey for the student.

Anderson, M. S., *Europe in the Eighteenth Century, 1713–1783* (1961). A good general survey of the century with excellent chapters on cultural and intellectual life.

Becker, Carl, *The Heavenly City of the Eighteenth-Century Philosophers* (1932). Still a provocative assessment of the Enlightenment's relation to Christianity.

Bernal, J. D., *Science in History* (1969). A learned classic that discusses the meaning of science in history.

Briggs, Robin, *The Scientific Revolution of the Seventeenth Century* (1969). A clearly written survey with documents.

Brumfitt, J. H., *The French Enlightenment* (1972). A useful survey.

Butterfield, Herbert, *The Origins of Modern Science* (1957). An analysis of the emergence of modern science.

Cassirer, Ernst, *The Philosophy of the Enlightenment* (1951). A classic and basic account of Enlightenment philosophy; difficult reading.

Cohen, I. B., *The Birth of a New Physics* (1960). Authoritative, but difficult for the novice.

Drake, Stillman, ed., *Discoveries and*

Opinions of Galileo (1957). A good place to start to learn Galileo's most important ideas.

Gay, Peter, *The Enlightenment, An Interpretation* (1967). A good survey.

Jacob, Margaret C., *The Cultural Meaning of the Scientific Revolution* (1988). Offers a general interpretation of the social context of the Scientific Revolution.

Kearney, Hugh, *Science and Social Change, 1500–1700* (1971). Includes a discussion of the social setting of the Scientific Revolution.

Woloch, Isser, *Eighteenth-Century Europe: Tradition and Progress, 1715–1789* (1982). An interesting general survey.

Review Questions

1. What was the difference between the scientific understanding of the universe and the medieval understanding of it?
2. Describe the major achievements of Copernicus, Kepler, Galileo, and Newton.
3. What role did the Scientific Revolution play in shaping the modern mentality?
4. What is meant by the Age of Enlightenment? Where did the Enlightenment begin, and what contributed to its spread?
5. How did Christianity come under attack by deists and skeptics?
6. In what ways does Voltaire exemplify the philosophes?
7. What were the essential characteristics of the political thought of each of the following: Hobbes, Locke, Montesquieu, and Rousseau? Make relevant comparisons and contrasts.
8. Describe Locke's theory of learning. What was its significance for the Enlightenment?
9. In what ways was the American Revolution based on Enlightenment principles?
10. The Enlightenment was a pivotal period in the shaping of the modern mentality. Discuss this statement.

The Great Exhibition of 1851, Painted by Dickinson.   The exhibition was held at the Crystal Palace in London; it drew millions to view the products and processes of machine and craft industries. (*By permission of the Houghton Library, Harvard University*)

IV

The Modern West: From the French Revolution to the Industrial Age

1789–1914

Chapter ⦿ 11

The Era of the French Revolution: The Affirmation of Liberty and Equality

The outbreak of the French Revolution in 1789 stirred the imagination of Europeans. Both participants and observers sensed that they were living in a pivotal age. On the ruins of the old order founded on privilege and despotism, a new era was forming that promised to realize the ideals of the Enlightenment. These ideals included the emancipation of the human personality from superstition and tradition, the triumph of liberty over tyranny, the refashioning of institutions in accordance with reason and justice, and the tearing down of barriers to equality. It seemed that the natural rights of the individual, hitherto a distant ideal, would now reign on earth, ending centuries of oppression and misery. Never before had people shown such confidence in the power of human intelligence to shape the conditions of existence. Never before had the future seemed so full of hope. ⦿

The Old Regime

The causes of the French Revolution reach back into the aristocratic structure of society in the Old Regime. Eighteenth-century French society was divided into three orders, or Estates: the clergy constituted the First Estate, the nobility the Second Estate, and everyone else (about 96 percent of the population) the Third Estate. The clergy and nobility, totaling about 400,000 out of a population of 26 million, enjoyed special privileges. The semifeudal social structure of the Old Regime, based on inequalities sanctioned by law, produced the tensions that precipitated the Revolution.

The First Estate

The powers and privileges of the French Catholic church made it a state within a state. As it had done for centuries, the church registered births, marriages, and deaths; collected tithes (a tax on products from the soil); censored books considered dangerous to religion and morals; operated schools; and distributed relief to the poor. Although its land brought in an immense revenue, the church paid no taxes. Instead it made a "free gift" to the state—the church determined the amount—which was always smaller than direct taxes would have been.

The clergy reflected the social divisions in France. The upper clergy shared the attitudes and way of life of the nobility from which they sprang. The parish priests, commoners by birth, resented the haughtiness and luxurious living of the upper clergy. In 1789, when the Revolution began, many priests sympathized with the reform-minded people of the Third Estate.

The Second Estate

Like the clergy, the nobility was a privileged order. Nobles held the highest positions in the church, army, and government. They were exempt from most taxes (or used their influence to evade paying taxes), collected manorial dues from peasants, and owned between one-quarter and one-third of the land. In addition to the income that they drew from their estates, nobles were becoming increasingly involved in such nonaristocratic enterprises as banking and finance. Nobles were the leading patrons of the arts. Many key philosophes— Montesquieu, Condorcet, d'Holbach—were nobles. Most nobles, however, were suspicious of and intolerant of the liberal ideas advanced by the philosophes.

All nobles were not equal; there were gradations of dignity among the 200,000 to 250,000 members of the nobility. Enjoying the most prestige were *nobles of the race*—families who could trace their aristocratic status back to time immemorial. The highest of the ancient nobles were engaged in the social whirl at Versailles and Paris, receiving pensions and sinecures from the king but performing few useful services for the state. Most nobles of the race, unable to afford the gilded life at court, remained on their provincial estates, the poorest of them barely distinguishable from prosperous peasants.

Alongside this ancient nobility, a new nobility had arisen, created by the monarchy. To obtain money, reward favorites, and weaken the old nobility, French kings had sold titles of nobility to members of the bourgeoisie and had conferred noble status on certain government offices bought by wealthy members of the bourgeoisie. Particularly significant were the *nobles of the robe*, whose ranks included many former bourgeois who had purchased judicial offices in the parlements, the high law courts. In the late eighteenth century the nobles of the robe vigorously championed the cause of aristocratic privilege.

In the eighteenth century, nobles sought to regain the power that they had lost under Louis XIV. This resurgence was led by the new nobility, the nobles of the robe, who used the parlements to oppose royal policy that threatened aristocratic and provincial privileges. This "feudal reaction" triggered the Revolution.

However, all nobles did not think alike. A minority, influenced by the liberal ideals of the philosophes, sought to reform France; they wanted to end royal despotism and establish a constitutional government. To this extent, the liberal nobility had a great deal in common with the bourgeoisie. These liberal nobles saw the king's difficulties in 1788 as an opportunity to regenerate the nation under enlightened leadership. But the majority of nobles, hostile to liberal ideals, resisted enlightened reforms. In doing so, they contributed to the destruction of the aristocracy in 1789.

The Third Estate

The Third Estate was composed of the bourgeoisie, peasants, and urban laborers. Although the bourgeoisie provided the leadership for the Revolution, its success depended on the support given by the rest of the Third Estate.

The Bourgeoisie   The bourgeoisie consisted of merchant-manufacturers, wholesale merchants, bankers, master craftsmen, doctors, lawyers, intellectuals, and government officials below the top ranks. Although the bourgeois had wealth, they lacked social prestige. A merchant, despite his worldly success, felt that his occupation denied him the dignity enjoyed by the nobility. Traditionally, some bourgeoisie had risen socially either by purchasing a judicial or political office that carried with it a title of nobility, or by gaining admission to the upper clergy and the officer ranks of the army. As long as these avenues of upward social mobility remained open, the bourgeoisie did not challenge the existing social structure, including the special privileges of the nobility.

But in the last part of the eighteenth century it became increasingly difficult for the bourgeois to gain the most honored offices in the land. Finding the road to social dignity and advancement blocked, the bourgeois came to resent a social system that valued birth more than talent. Increasingly, members of the bourgeoisie, imbued with the rational outlook of the Enlightenment, sought to abolish the privileges of birth and to open careers to talent.

By 1789 the bourgeois had many grievances. They wanted all positions in church, army, and state open to men of talent, regardless of birth. They sought a parliament; a constitution that would limit the king's power and guarantee freedom of thought, a fair trial, and religious toleration; and administrative reforms that would eliminate waste, inefficiency, and interference with business. When they challenged the Old Regime, the bourgeois felt that they were fulfilling the ideals of the philosophes and serving all humanity.

The Peasantry   The condition of the more than 21 million French peasants was a paradox. On the one hand, they were better off than peasants in Austria, Prussia, Poland, and Russia, where serfdom still predominated. In France, serfdom had largely disappeared; many peasants owned their own land, and some were even prosperous. On the other hand, most French peasants lived in poverty, which worsened in the closing years of the Old Regime.

The typical peasant holding was barely large enough to eke out a living. The rising birthrate (between 1715 and 1789 the population may have increased from 18 million to 26 million) led to the continual subdivision of farms among heirs. Moreover, many peasants did not own their own land but rented it from a nobleman or a prosperous neighbor. Others worked as sharecroppers, turning over to their creditors a considerable share of the harvest.

An unjust and corrupt system of taxation weighed heavily on the peasantry. Louis XIV had maintained his grandeur and financed his wars by milking ever more taxes from the peasants, a practice that continued throughout the eighteenth century. An army of tax collectors victimized the peasantry. In addition to royal taxes, peasants paid the tithe to the church and manorial dues to lords.

Although serfdom had ended in most parts of France, lords continued to demand obligations from peasants as they had done in the Middle Ages. In addition to performing labor services on the lord's estate, peasants still had to grind their grain in the lord's mill, bake their bread in his oven, press their grapes in his winepress, and give him part of their produce in payment. In addition, the lord exercised exclusive hunting rights on lands tilled by peasants. The last was a particularly onerous right, for the lord's hunting parties damaged crops. Lords were determined to hold on to these privileges not only because of the income they brought, but because they were symbols of authority and social esteem.

Urban Laborers   The urban laboring class in this preindustrial age consisted of journeymen working for master craftsmen, factory workers in small-scale industries, and wage earners such as day laborers, gardeners, handymen, and deliverymen, who were paid by those they served. The poverty of the urban poor, like that of the peasant wage earners, had worsened in the late eighteenth century. From 1785 to 1789 the cost of living increased by 62 percent, while wages rose only 22 percent. For virtually the entire decade of the Revolution, urban workers struggled to keep body and soul together in the face of food shortages and rising prices, particularly that of their staple food, bread. Material want drove the urban poor to acts of violence that affected the course of the Revolution.

Inefficient Administration and Financial Disorder

The administration of France was complex, confusing, and ineffective. The practice of buying state offices from the king, introduced as a means of raising money, resulted in many incompetent officeholders. Tariffs on goods shipped from one province to another and differing systems of weights and measures hampered trade. No single law code applied to all the provinces; instead, there were overlapping and conflicting law systems based on old Roman law or customary feudal law, which made the administration of justice slow, arbitrary, and unjust. To admirers of the philosophes, the administrative system was an insult to reason. The Revolution would sweep the system away.

Financial disorders also contributed to the weakness of the Old Regime. In the last years of the Old Regime the government could not raise sufficient funds to cover expenses. By 1787, it still had not paid off the enormous debt incurred during the wars of Louis XIV, let alone the costs of succeeding wars during the eighteenth century, particularly France's aid to the colonists in the American Revolution. The king's gifts and pensions to court nobles and the extravagant court life further drained the treasury.

Finances were in a shambles not because France was impoverished, but because of an inefficient and unjust tax system. The financial crisis, although serious, was solvable if the clergy, nobility, and bourgeoisie would pay their fair share of taxes. With France on the brink of bankruptcy, the king's ministers proposed that the nobility and church surrender some of their tax exemptions, but the privileged orders resisted. The resistance of the nobility forced the government, in July 1788, to call for a meeting of the Estates General—a medieval representative assembly that had last met in 1614—to deal with the financial crisis. Certain that they would dominate the Estates General, the nobles intended to weaken the power of the throne and to regain power that they had lost under Louis XIV. Once in control of the government, they would introduce financial reforms. But the revolt of the nobility against the crown had unexpected consequences; it opened the way for revolutions by the Third Estate that destroyed the Old Regime and with it the aristocracy and its privileges.

The Moderate Stage, 1789–1791

Formation of the National Assembly

As the Estates General prepared to meet, reform-minded Frenchmen held great hopes for the regeneration of France and the advancement of liberty. There was general agreement that a constitutional government in which laws (including the levying of taxes) were promulgated by an assembly that met regularly was preferable to absolute monarchy. At this stage, with a significant number of nobles sympathetic to reform, there was no insuperable gulf between the bourgeoisie and the nobility. But it soon became clear that the hopes of reformers clashed with the intentions of many aristocrats. What had started as a struggle between the crown and the aristocracy was turning into something far more significant—a conflict between the two privileged orders on one side and the Third Estate on the other. One pamphleteer, Abbé Sieyès (1748–1836), expressed the hatred the bourgeoisie held for the aristocracy. "The privileged

Approval of the Tennis Court Oath (detail). On June 17, 1789, the Third Estate declared itself the National Assembly. On June 20, they met on a nearby tennis court when they found their customary meeting hall locked. They vowed not to disband until a constitution had been drawn up for the entire nation. In this painting by Jacques Louis David, aristocrat, clergyman, and commoner embrace before a cheering National Assembly. (*Versailles/Cliché des Musées Nationaux*)

order has said to the Third Estate: 'Whatever be your services, whatever be your talents, you shall go thus far and no farther. It is not fitting that you be honored.' " The higher positions in the land, said Sieyès, should be the "reward for talents," not the prerogative of birth. Without the Third Estate, "nothing can progress"; without the nobility, "everything would proceed infinitely better."[1]

The Estates General convened at Versailles on May 5, 1789, but was stalemated by the question of procedure. Seeking to control the assembly, the nobility insisted that the three Estates follow the traditional practice of meeting separately and voting as individual bodies. Since the two privileged orders were likely to stand together, the Third Estate would always be outvoted, two to one. But the delegates from the Third Estate, unwilling to allow the nobility and the higher clergy to dominate the Estates General, proposed instead that the three Estates meet as one body and vote by head. There were some 610 delegates from the Third Estate; the nobility and clergy together had an equivalent number. Since the Third Estate could rely on the support of sympathetic parish priests and liberal nobles, it would be assured a majority if all orders met together.

On June 17, the Third Estate made a revolutionary move. It declared itself the National Assembly. On June 20, locked out of their customary meeting hall (apparently by accident), the Third Estate delegates moved to a nearby tennis court and took a solemn oath not to disband until a constitution had been drawn up for France. Louis XVI commanded the National Assembly to separate into orders, but the Third Estate held firm. The steadfastness of the delegates and the menacing actions of Parisians who supported the National Assembly forced Louis XVI to yield. On June 27 he ordered the nobility (some had already done so) and the clergy (a majority had already done so) to join with the Third Estate in the National Assembly.

But the victory of the bourgeoisie was not yet secure, for most nobles had not resigned themselves to a bourgeois-dominated National Assembly. It appeared that Louis XVI, influenced by court aristocrats, had resolved to use force against the National Assembly and to stop the incipient revolution. At this point, uprisings by the common people of Paris and peasants in the countryside saved the National Assembly and ensured the victory of the forces of reform.

Storming of the Bastille

In July 1789, the level of tension in Paris was high for three reasons. First, the calling of the Estates General had aroused hopes for reform. Second, the price of bread was soaring: in August 1788, a Parisian laborer had spent 50 percent of his income on bread; by July 1789 he was spending 80 percent. A third element in the tension was the fear of an aristocratic plot to crush the National Assembly. Fearful that royal troops would bombard and pillage the city, Parisians searched for weapons.

On July 14, eight hundred to nine hundred Parisians gathered in front of the Bastille, a fortress used as a prison and a despised symbol of royal despotism. They gathered primarily to obtain gunpowder and to remove the cannon that threatened a heavily populated working-class district. As the tension mounted, the Parisians stormed and captured the Bastille. The fall of the Bastille had far-reaching consequences: a symbol of the Old Regime had fallen; some court nobles hostile to the Revolution decided to flee the country; the frightened king told the National Assembly that he would withdraw the troops ringing Paris. The revolutionary act of the Parisians had indirectly saved the National Assembly and with it the bourgeois revolution.

The Great Fear

Revolution in the countryside also served the interests of the reformers. Inflamed by economic misery and stirred by the uprisings of the Parisians, peasants began to burn manor houses and to destroy the registers on which were inscribed their obligations to the lords. The flames of the peasants' insurrection were fanned by rumors that aristocrats were organizing bands of brigands to attack the peasants. The mythical army of brigands never materialized, but the Great Fear, as this episode is called, led more peasants to take up arms.

Women's March to Versailles.   A bread shortage and high prices sparked the protest march of thousands of women to Versailles in October 1789. The king was compelled to return to Paris, a sign of his diminishing power, and many aristocrats hostile to the Revolution fled the country. (*Bibliothèque Nationale, Paris*)

Suspicious of an aristocratic plot to thwart efforts at reform and releasing centuries of stored-up hatred for the nobles, the peasants attacked the lords' chateaux with great fury.

The peasant upheavals in late July and early August, like the insurrection in Paris, worked to the advantage of the reformers. It provided the National Assembly with an opportunity to strike at noble privileges by putting into law what the peasants had accomplished with the torch—the destruction of feudal remnants. On the night of August 4, 1789, aristocrats seeking to restore calm in the countryside surrendered their special privileges—exclusive hunting rights, tax exemptions, monopoly of highest offices, manorial courts, and the right to demand labor services from peasants.

In the decrees of August 5 and 11, the National Assembly implemented the resolutions of August 4. The assembly also declared that the planned constitution should be prefaced by a declaration of rights. On August 26, it adopted the Declaration of the Rights of Man and the Citizen. The August Decrees and the Declaration of Rights marked the death of the Old Regime.

October Days

Louis XVI, cool to these reforms, postponed his approval of the August Decrees and the Declaration of Rights. It would require a second uprising by the Parisians to force the king to agree to the reforms and to nail down the victory of the reformers. On October 5, 1789, Parisian women and men marched twelve miles to Versailles to protest the lack of bread to the National Assembly and the king. A few hours later, 20,000 Paris Guards, a citizen militia sympathetic to the Revolution, also set out for Versailles in support of the protesters. The king had no choice but to promise bread and to return with the demonstrators to Paris. Aware that he had no control over the Parisians and fearful of further violence, Louis XVI approved the August Decrees and the Declaration of the Rights of Man and the Citizen. Nobles who had urged the king to use force against the assembly and had tried to block reforms fled the country in large numbers.

Reforms of the National Assembly

With resistance enfeebled, the National Assembly continued the work of reform begun in the summer of 1789. Its reforms, which follow, destroyed the Old Regime.

1. *Abolition of special privileges.* By ending the special privileges of the nobility and the clergy in the August Decrees, the National Assembly pronounced the equality that the bourgeoisie had demanded. The aristocratic structure of the Old Regime, a remnant of the Middle Ages that had hindered the progressive bourgeoisie, had been eliminated.

2. *Statement of human rights.* The Declaration of the Rights of Man and the Citizen expressed the liberal and universal goals of the philosophes. In proclaiming the inalienable right to liberty of person and thought and to equal treatment under the law, the Declaration affirmed the dignity of human personality; it asserted that government belonged not to any ruler but to the people as a whole, and that its aim was the preservation of the natural rights of the individual. Because the Declaration stood in sharp contrast to the principles espoused by an intolerant clergy, a privileged aristocracy, and a despotic monarch, it has been called the death warrant of the Old Regime.

3. *Subordination of church to state.* The National Assembly also struck at the privileges of the Roman Catholic church. The August Decrees declared the end of tithes. To obtain badly needed funds, the Assembly in November 1789 confiscated church lands and put them up for sale. In 1790 the Assembly passed the Civil Constitution of the Clergy, which altered the boundaries of the dioceses, reducing the number of bishops and priests, and transformed the clergy into government officials elected by the people and paid by the state.

Almost all bishops and many priests opposed the Civil Constitution, which divided the French and gave opponents of the Revolution an emotional issue around which to rally supporters.

4. *Constitution for France.* In September 1791 the National Assembly issued a constitution limiting the power of the king and guaranteeing all French citizens equal treatment under the law. Citizens paying less than a specified amount in taxes could not vote. Probably about 30 percent of the males over

age twenty-five were excluded by this stipulation, and only the more well-to-do citizens qualified to sit in the Legislative Assembly, a unicameral parliament created to succeed the National Assembly. Despite this restriction, suffrage requirements under the Constitution of 1791 were far more generous than in Britain.

5. *Administrative and judicial reforms.* The National Assembly replaced the patchwork of provincial units with eighty-three new administrative units, or departments, approximately equal in size.

Judicial reforms complemented the administrative changes. A standardized system of courts replaced the innumerable jurisdictions of the Old Regime, and the sale of judicial offices was ended. In the penal code completed by the National Assembly, torture and barbarous punishments were abolished.

6. *Aid for business.* The National Assembly abolished all tolls and duties on goods transported within the country, established a uniform system of weights and measures, eliminated the guilds (medieval survivals that blocked business expansion), and forbade workingmen to form unions or to strike.

By ending absolutism, striking at the privileges of the nobility, and preventing the mass of people from gaining control over the government, the National Assembly consolidated the rule of the bourgeoisie. With one arm, it broke the power of aristocracy and throne; with the other, it held back the common people. Although the reforms benefited the bourgeoisie, it would be a mistake to view them merely as a selfish expression of bourgeois interests. The Declaration of the Rights of Man and the Citizen was addressed to all; it proclaimed liberty and equality as the right of all and called for citizens to treat each other with respect.

The Radical Stage, 1792–1794

The Sans-Culottes

Pleased with their accomplishments—equality before the law, careers open to talent, a written constitution, parliamentary government—the men of 1789 wished the Revolution to go no further. But revolutionary times are unpredictable. Soon the Revolution moved in a direction neither anticipated nor desired by the reformers. A counterrevolution was led by irreconcilable nobles and alienated churchmen; supported by socially unprogressive and strongly Catholic peasants, it threatened the Revolution, forcing the revolutionary leadership to resort to extreme measures.

Also propelling the Revolution in the direction of radicalism was the discontent of the *sans-culottes*—small shopkeepers, artisans, and wage earners. Although they had played a significant role in the Revolution, particularly in the storming of the Bastille and the October Days, they had gained little. The sans-culottes, says French historian Albert Soboul, "began to realize that a privilege of wealth was taking the place of a privilege of birth. They foresaw that the bourgeoisie would succeed the fallen aristocracy as the ruling class."[2] Inflamed by poverty and their hatred of the rich, the sans-culottes insisted that it was the government's duty to guarantee them the "right of existence," a policy that ran counter to the economic individualism of the bourgeoisie. They demanded that the government increase wages, set price controls on food supplies, end food shortages, and pass laws to prevent extremes of wealth and poverty. Whereas the men of 1789 sought equality of rights, liberties, and opportunities, the sans-culottes expanded the principle of equality to include narrowing the gap between rich and poor. To reduce economic inequality, the sans-culottes called for higher taxes for the wealthy and the redistribution of land. Politically, they favored a democratic republic in which the common man had a voice.

In 1789 the bourgeoisie had demanded equality with the aristocrats—the right to hold the most honored position in the nation and an end to the special privileges of the nobility. By the end of 1792 the sans-culottes were demanding equality with the bourgeois—political reforms that would give the poor a voice in the government and social reforms that would improve their lot.

Despite the pressures exerted by reactionary nobles and clergy on the one hand and discontented sans-culottes on the other, the Revolution might not have taken a radical turn had France remained at peace. The war that broke out with Austria and Prussia in April 1792 exacerbated internal dissensions, worsened economic conditions, and threatened to undo the reforms of the Revolution. It was under these circumstances that the Revolution moved from its moderate stage into a radical one that historians refer to as the Second French Revolution.

Foreign Invasion

In June 1791, Louis XVI and the royal family, traveling in disguise, fled Paris for the northeast of France to join with *émigrés* (nobles who had left revolutionary France and were organizing a counterrevolutionary army) and to rally foreign support against the Revolution. Discovered at Varennes by a village postmaster, they were brought back to Paris as virtual prisoners. The flight of the king turned many French people against the monarchy, strengthening the position of radicals who wanted to do away with kingship altogether and establish a republic. But it was foreign invasion that led ultimately to the destruction of the monarchy.

On April 20, 1792, fearful that Austria intended to overthrow the Revolution and eager to spread revolutionary ideals, France declared war on Austria. Commanded by the Duke of Brunswick, a combined Austrian and Prussian army crossed into France. Into an atmosphere already charged with tension, the Duke of Brunswick issued a manifesto declaring that if the royal family were harmed he would exact a terrible vengeance on the Parisians. On August 10, 1792, enraged Parisians and militia from other cities attacked the king's palace, killing several hundred Swiss guards.

In early September, as foreign troops advanced deeper into France, rumors spread that jailed priests and aristocrats were planning to break out of their cells to support the Duke of Brunswick. The Parisians panicked. Driven by fear, patriotism, and murderous impulses, they raided the prisons and massacred 1,100 to 1,200 prisoners. Most of the victims were not political prisoners but ordinary criminals.

On September 21–22, the National Convention (the new lawmaking body) abolished the monarchy and established a republic. In December 1792, Louis XVI was placed on trial, and in January 1793 he was executed for conspiring against the liberty of the French people. The uprising of August 10, the September Massacres, the creation of a republic, and the execution of Louis XVI all confirmed that the Revolution was falling into radicalism.

Meanwhile the war continued. Short of supplies, hampered by bad weather, and possessing insufficient manpower, the Duke of Brunswick never did reach Paris. Outmaneuvered at Valmy on September 20, 1792, the foreign forces retreated to the frontier, and the armies of the republic took the offensive. By the beginning of 1793, French forces had overrun Belgium (then a part of the Austrian Empire), the German Rhineland, and the Sardinian provinces of Nice and Savoy. To the peoples of Europe the National Convention had solemnly announced that it was waging a popular crusade against privilege and tyranny, against aristocrats and princes.

Frightened by these revolutionary social ideas, by the execution of Louis XVI, and, most important, by French expansion that threatened the balance of power, the rulers of Europe, urged on by Britain, formed an anti-French alliance by the spring of 1793. The allies' forces pressed toward the French borders. The republic was endangered.

Counterrevolutionary insurrections further undermined the fledgling republic. Led by local nobles, peasants of the Vendée waged a guerrilla war for religion, royalism, and their traditional way of life. In other quarters, federalists revolted in the provinces, objecting to the power wielded by the centralized government in Paris. The republic was unable to exercise control over much of the country.

The Jacobins

As the republic tottered under the weight of foreign invasion, internal insurrection, and economic crisis, the revolutionary leadership grew still more radical. In June 1793, the Jacobins replaced the Girondins as the dominant group in the National Convention. Whereas the Girondins favored a government in which the departments would exercise control over their own affairs, the Jacobins wanted a strong central government with Paris as the center of power. Both Girondins and Jacobins came from the bourgeoisie, but the Girondins opposed government interference with business, whereas the Jacobins would support temporary government controls to deal with the needs of war and economic crisis. This last point was crucial; it won the Jacobins the support of the sans-culottes. On June 2, 1793, some 80,000 armed sans-culottes surrounded the Convention and demanded the arrest of Girondin delegates—an act that enabled the Jacobins to gain control of the government.

The problems confronting the Jacobins were staggering. They had to cope with civil war, particularly in the Vendée, economic distress, blockaded ports, and foreign invasion. They lived with the terrible dread that if they failed, the Revolution for liberty and equality would perish. Only strong leadership could save the republic.

The Jacobins continued the work of reform. A new constitution in 1793 expressed Jacobin enthusiasm for political democracy. It contained a new Declaration of Rights that affirmed and amplified the principles of 1789. By giving all adult males the right to vote, it overcame sans-culotte objections to the constitution of 1791. However, because of the threat of invasion and the revolts, implementation of the constitution of 1793 was postponed, and it never was put into effect. By abolishing both slavery in the French colonies and imprisonment for debt and by making plans for free public education, the Jacobins revealed their humanitarianism and their debt to the philosophes. To halt inflation and gain the support of the poor—both necessary for the war effort—the Jacobins decreed the *law of the maximum,* which fixed prices on bread and other essential goods and raised wages.

The Nation in Arms

To fight the war against foreign invaders, the Jacobins, in an act that anticipated modern conscription, drafted unmarried men between eighteen and twenty-five years of age. They mobilized all the resources of the nation, infused the army with a love for *la patrie* (the nation), and in a remarkable demonstration of administrative skill, equipped an army of more than 800,000 men. In creating the nation in arms, the Jacobins heralded the emergence of modern warfare. The citizen-soldiers of the republic, commanded by officers who had proved their skill on the battlefield and inspired by the ideals of liberty, equality, and fraternity, won decisive victories. In May and June of 1794, the French routed the allied forces on the vital northern frontier, and by the end of July, France had become the triumphant master of Belgium.

In demanding complete devotion to the nation, the Jacobin phase of the Revolution also heralded the rise of modern nationalism. In the schools, in newspapers, speeches, and poems, on the stage, and at rallies and meetings of patriotic societies, the French people were told of the glory won by republican soldiers on the battlefield and were reminded of their duties to *la patrie.* "The citizen is born, lives, and dies for the fatherland." These words were written in public places for all citizens to read and ponder. The soldiers of the Revolution fought not for money or for a king, but for the nation. Could this heightened sense of nationality, which concentrated on the special interests of the French people, be reconciled with the Declaration of the Rights of Man, whose principles were addressed to all humanity? The revolutionaries themselves did not understand the implications of the new force that they had unleashed.

The Republic of Virtue and the Reign of Terror

At the same time that the Jacobins were forging a revolutionary army to deal with external enemies, they were also waging war against internal opposition. The pivotal personality in this struggle was Maximilien Robespierre (1758–1794), who had a fervent faith in the rightness of his beliefs and a total commitment to republican democracy.

Robespierre wanted to create a better society founded on reason, good citizenship, and patriotism. In his Republic of Virtue, there would be no kings or nobles; men would be free, equal, and educated; reason would be glorified and superstition ridiculed; there would be no extremes of wealth or poverty; man's natural goodness would prevail over vice and greed; laws would preserve, not violate, inalienable rights. He pursued his ideal society with religious zeal. Knowing that the Republic of Virtue could not be established while France was threatened by foreign and civil war, Robespierre urged harsh treatment for enemies of the republic, who "must be prosecuted by all not as ordinary enemies, but as rebels, brigands, and assassins."

The Jacobin leadership, with Robespierre playing a key role, attacked those they considered enemies of the republic: Girondins who challenged Jacobin authority, federalists who opposed a strong central government emanating from Paris, counterrevolutionary priests and nobles and their peasant supporters, and profiteers who hoarded food. The Jacobins even sought to discipline the ardor of the sans-culottes who had given them power. Fearful that sans-culotte spontaneity would undermine central authority and promote anarchy, Robespierrists brought about the dissolution of sans-culotte societies. They also executed sans-culotte leaders known as *enragés,* who threatened insurrection against Jacobin rule and pushed for more social reforms than the Jacobins would allow. The enragés wanted to set limits on income and on the size of farms and businesses—policies considered far too extreme by the supporters of Robespierre.

To preserve republican liberty, the Jacobins made terror a deliberate government policy. Perhaps as many as 40,000 people perished during the Reign of Terror. Robespierre and his fellow Jacobins did not resort to the guillotine because they were bloodthirsty or power-mad. Instead, they sought to establish a temporary dictatorship in a desperate attempt to save the republic and the Revolution. Deeply devoted to republican democracy, the Jacobins viewed themselves as bearers of a higher faith. Like all visionaries, Robespierre was convinced that he knew the right way, that the new society he envisaged would benefit all humanity, and that those who impeded its implementation were not just opponents but sinners who had to be liquidated for the good of humanity.

The Jacobins did save the republic. Their regime expelled foreign armies, crushed the federalist uprisings, contained the counterrevolutionaries in the Vendée, and prevented anarchy. Without the discipline, order, and unity imposed on France by the Robespierrists, it is likely that the republic would have collapsed under the twin blows of foreign invasion and domestic anarchy.

Nonetheless, the Reign of Terror poses fundamental questions about the

M.M.J.ROBERSPIERRE

Robespierre, an Engraving by Fiésinger After a Drawing by Pierre-Narcisse Guérin.   To create a Republic of Virtue where men would be free and equal, Maximilien Robespierre considered terror necessary. Robespierre lost favor with his own party and was himself guillotined. (*Bibliothèque Nationale, Paris*)

meaning of the French Revolution and the validity of the Enlightenment conception of man. To what extent was the Terror a reversal of the ideals of the Revolution as formulated in the Declaration of the Rights of Man? To what extent did the feverish passions and fascination for violence demonstrated in the mass executions in the provinces and in the public spectacles in Paris indicate a darker side of human nature, beyond control of reason? Did Robespierre's religion of humanity revive the fanaticism and cruelty of the wars of religion that had so disgusted the philosophes? Did the Robespierrists, who considered themselves the staunchest defenders of the Revolution's ideals, soil and subvert these ideals by their zeal? By mobilizing the might of the nation, by creating the mystique of *la patrie,* by imposing temporary dictatorial rule in defense of liberty and equality, and by legalizing and justifying terror committed in the people's name, were the Jacobins unwittingly unleashing new forces that in later years would be harnessed by totalitarian regimes consciously resolved to stamp out the liberal heritage of the Revolution?

The Fall of Robespierre

Opponents of Robespierre in the convention, feeling the chill of the guillotine blade on their own necks, ordered the arrest of Robespierre and some of his

Chronology 11.1 ⊕ The French Revolution

July 1788	Calling of the Estates General
June 17, 1789	The Third Estate declares itself the National Assembly
July 14, 1789	The storming of the Bastille
Late July 1789	The Great Fear
August 4, 1789	Nobles surrender their special privileges
April 20, 1792	The Legislative Assembly declares war on Austria
September 21–22, 1792	Abolition of the monarchy
June 1793	Jacobins replace the Girondins as the dominant group in the National Convention
July 27, 1794	Robespierre is guillotined

supporters. On July 27, 1794, the ninth of Thermidor according to the new republican calendar, Robespierre was guillotined. After the fall of Robespierre, the machinery of the Jacobin republic was dismantled.

Leadership passed to the property-owning bourgeois who had endorsed the constitutional ideas of 1789–1791, the moderate stage of the Revolution. The new leadership, known as *Thermidoreans* until the end of 1795, wanted no more of the Jacobins or of Robespierre's society. They had considered Robespierre a threat to their political power because he would have allowed the common people a considerable voice in the government, and a threat to their property because he would have introduced some state regulation of the economy to aid the poor.

The Thermidorean reaction was a counterrevolution. The new government purged the army of officers who were suspected of Jacobin leanings, abolished the law of the maximum, and declared void the Constitution of 1793. A new constitution, approved in 1795, re-established property requirements for voting. The counterrevolution also produced a counterterror, as royalists and Catholics massacred Jacobins in the provinces.

At the end of 1795, the new republican government, called the *Directory,* was burdened by war, a sagging economy, and internal unrest. The Directory crushed insurrections by Parisian sans-culottes maddened by hunger and hatred of the rich (1795, 1796) and by royalists seeking to restore the monarchy (1797). As military and domestic pressures worsened, power began to pass into the hands of generals. One of them, Napoleon Bonaparte, seized control of the government in November 1799, pushing the Revolution into yet another stage.

Napoleon and France: Return to Autocratic Rule

Napoleon was born on August 15, 1769, on the island of Corsica, the son of a petty noble. After finishing military school in France, he became an artillery officer; the wars of the French Revolution afforded him an opportunity to advance his career, and in 1796 he was given command of the French Army of Italy. In Italy, against the Austrians, Napoleon demonstrated a dazzling talent for military planning and leadership that earned him an instant reputation. Having tasted glory, he could never do without it; having experienced only success, nothing seemed impossible. He sensed that he was headed for greatness.

In 1799, Napoleon was leading a French army in Egypt when he decided to return to France and make his bid for power. He joined a conspiracy that overthrew the Directory and set up an executive of three consuls. As first consul, Napoleon monopolized power. In 1802 he was made first consul for life, with the right to name his successor. And on December 2, 1804, in a magnificent ceremony at the Cathedral of Notre Dame in Paris, Napoleon crowned himself emperor of the French. General, first consul, and then emperor—it was a breathless climb to the heights of power. And Napoleon, who once said he loved "power as a musician loves his violin," was determined never to lose it.

An Enlightened Despot

Napoleon did not identify with the republicanism and democracy of the Jacobins, but rather he belonged to the tradition of eighteenth-century enlightened despotism. Like the reforming despots, Napoleon admired administrative uniformity and efficiency, hated feudalism, religious persecution, and civil inequality, and favored government regulation of trade and industry. He saw in enlightened despotism a means of ensuring political stability and strengthening the state. Napoleon did preserve several gains of the Revolution: equality under the law, careers open to men with talent, promotion of secular education, weakening of clerical power. But he suppressed political liberty.

Napoleon succeeded in giving France a strong central government and administrative uniformity. An army of officials, subject to the emperor's will, reached into every village, linking together the entire nation. This centralized state suited Napoleon's desire for orderly government and rational administration, enabled him to concentrate power in his own hands, and provided him with the taxes and soldiers needed to fight his wars. To suppress irreconcilable opponents, primarily die-hard royalists and republicans, Napoleon used the instruments of the police state—secret agents, arbitrary arrest, summary trials, executions.

Napoleon also shaped public opinion to prevent hostile criticism of his rule

Map 11.1   Napoleon's Europe, 1810   ▶

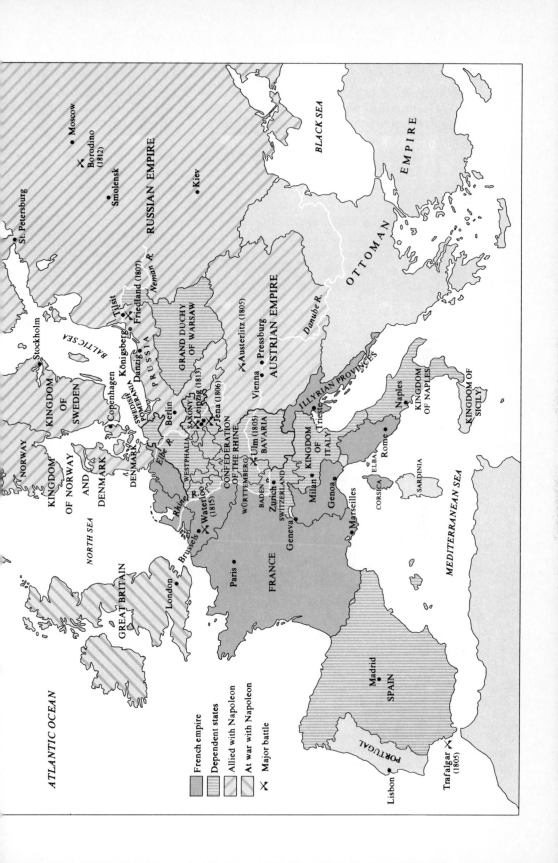

ATLANTIC OCEAN

RUSSIAN EMPIRE

• Moscow

✕ Borodino (1812)

• Smolensk

• Kiev

• St. Petersburg

BLACK SEA

OTTOMAN EMPIRE

Neman R.

✕ Friedland (1807)

Tilsit

• Königsberg

Danzig

BALTIC SEA

Stockholm

KINGDOM OF SWEDEN

GRAND DUCHY OF WARSAW

✕ Austerlitz (1805)

• Pressburg

AUSTRIAN EMPIRE

Danube R.

PRUSSIA

NORWAY

KINGDOM OF NORWAY AND DENMARK

Copenhagen

DENMARK

SWEDISH POMERANIA

• Berlin

SAXONY

✕ Leipzig (1813)

✕ Jena (1806)

• Vienna

Elbe R.

WESTPHALIA

CONFEDERATION OF THE RHINE

✕ Ulm (1805)

BAVARIA

ILLYRIAN PROVINCES

• Trieste

KINGDOM OF NAPLES

• Naples

KINGDOM OF SICILY

NORTH SEA

✕ Waterloo (1815)

Rhine R.

Brussels

WÜRTTEMBERG

BADEN

Zürich

SWITZERLAND

KINGDOM OF ITALY

• Milan

Genoa

ELBA

Rome •

SARDINIA

MEDITERRANEAN SEA

GREAT BRITAIN

• London

Paris •

FRANCE

Geneva

Marseilles

CORSICA

Lisbon

PORTUGAL

Madrid •

SPAIN

✕ Trafalgar (1805)

French empire

Dependent states

Allied with Napoleon

At war with Napoleon

✕ Major battle

and to promote popular support for his policies and person. In these actions, he was a precursor of twentieth-century dictators. Liberty of the press came to an end. Printers swore an oath of obedience to the emperor, and newspapers were converted into government mouthpieces.

Napoleon attempted to close the breach between the state and the Catholic church that had emerged during the Revolution. Such a reconciliation would gain the approval of the mass of the French people, who remained devoted to their faith, and would reassure those peasants and bourgeois who had bought confiscated church lands. For these reasons, Napoleon negotiated an agreement with the pope. The Concordat of 1801 recognized Catholicism as the religion of the great majority of the French, rather than as the official state religion (the proposal that the pope desired). Napoleon had achieved his aim. The Concordat made his regime acceptable to Catholics and to owners of former church lands.

Legal, Educational, and Financial Policies

Under the Old Regime, France was plagued with numerous and conflicting law codes. Reflecting local interests and feudal traditions, these codes obstructed national unity and administrative efficiency. Efforts by the revolutionaries to draw up a unified code of laws bogged down. Recognizing the value of such a code in promoting effective administration throughout France, Napoleon pressed for the completion of the project. The Code Napoléon incorporated many principles of the Revolution: equality before the law, the right to choose one's profession, freedom of conscience, protection of property rights, the abolition of serfdom, and the secular character of the state.

The code also had its less liberal side, denying equal treatment to workers in their dealings with employers, to women in their relations with their husbands, to children in their relations with their fathers. In making wives inferior to their husbands in matters of property, adultery, and divorce, the code reflected both Napoleon's personal attitude and the general view of the times toward women and family stability.

Napoleon's educational policy was in many ways an elaboration of the school reforms initiated during the Revolution. Like the revolutionaries, Napoleon favored a system of public education with a secular curriculum and a minimum of church involvement. For Napoleon, education served a dual purpose: it would provide him with capable officials to administer his laws and trained officers to lead his armies, and it would indoctrinate the young in obedience and loyalty. He established the University of France, a giant board of education that placed education under state control. To this day the French school system, unlike that in the United States, is strictly centralized, with curriculum and standards set for the entire state.

Napoleon's financial and economic policies were designed to strengthen France and enhance his popularity. To stimulate the economy and to retain the favor of the bourgeois who supported his seizure of power. Napoleon aided industry through tariffs and loans and fostered commerce (while also speeding

Napoleon at Arcole by Antoine-Jean Gros. Gros idealized Napoleon in this ultra-Romantic portrait. Here he is a conqueror of nations and a political visionary. In his reminiscences written at St. Helena, the exiled emperor depicted himself as a defeated unifier of Europe who had sought peace and a restoration of order. (*Louvre/Cliché des Musées Nationaux*)

up troop movements) by building or repairing roads, bridges, and canals. To protect the currency from inflation, he established the Bank of France, which was controlled by the nation's leading financiers. By keeping careers open to talent, he endorsed one of the key demands of the bourgeoisie during the Revolution. Fearing a revolution based on lack of bread, he provided food at low prices and stimulated employment for the laboring poor. He endeared himself to the peasants by not restoring feudal privileges and by allowing them to keep the land they had obtained during the Revolution.

Napoleon and Europe: Diffusion of Revolutionary Institutions

Napoleon, the Corsican adventurer, realized Louis XIV's dream of French mastery of Europe. Between 1805 and 1807, he inflicted decisive defeats on Austria, Prussia, and Russia, to become the virtual ruler of Europe. In these campaigns, as in his earlier successes in Italy, Napoleon demonstrated his greatness as a military commander.

By 1810, Napoleon dominated the Continent, except for the Balkan Peninsula. The *Grand Empire* comprised lands annexed to France, vassal states, and cowed allies. The French Republic had already annexed Belgium and the German Left Bank of the Rhine. Napoleon incorporated several other areas into France: German coastal regions as far as the western Baltic and large areas of Italy, including Rome, Geneva and its environs, Trieste, and the Dalmatian Coast. Vassal states in the Grand Empire included five kingdoms ruled by Napoleon's relatives, two of them in Italy, the Kingdom of Holland, the Kingdom of Westphalia, and Spain.

Besides the five satellite kingdoms there were several other vassal states within the Grand Empire. Napoleon formed the Confederation of the Rhine in 1806. Its members, a loose association of sixteen (later eighteen) German states, were subservient to the emperor, as were the nineteen cantons of the Swiss confederation. The Grand Duchy of Warsaw, formed in 1807 from Prussia's Polish lands, was placed under the rule of the German King of Saxony, one of Napoleon's vassals. Finally, the Grand Empire included states compelled to be French allies—Austria, Prussia, and Russia, as well as Sweden and Denmark.

With varying degrees of determination and success, Napoleon extended the reforms of the Revolution to other lands. His officials instituted the Code Napoléon, organized an effective civil service, opened careers to talent, and equalized the tax burden. They abolished serfdom, manorial payments, and the courts of the nobility. They did away with clerical courts, promoted freedom of religion, permitted civil marriage, pressed for civil rights for Jews, and fought clerical interference with secular authority. They abolished guilds, introduced a uniform system of weights and measures, did away with internal tolls, and built roads, bridges, and canals. They promoted secular education and improved public health. Napoleon had launched a Europe-wide social revolution that attacked the privileges of the aristocracy and the clergy—who regarded him as that "crowned Jacobin"—and worked to the advantage of the bourgeoisie. This diffusion of revolutionary institutions weakened the Old Regime irreparably in much of Europe and speeded up the modernization of nineteenth-century Europe.

Pleased by the overhaul of feudal practices and the reduction of clerical power, many Europeans, particularly the progressive bourgeoisie, welcomed Napoleon as a liberator. But there was another side to Napoleon's rule. Napoleon, the tyrant of Europe, turned conquered lands into satellite kingdoms and exploited them for the benefit of France—a policy that gained him the enmity of many Europeans.

The Fall of Napoleon

In addition to the hostility of subject nationals, Napoleon had to cope with the determined opposition of Great Britain. Its subsidies and encouragement kept resistance to the emperor alive. But perhaps Napoleon's greatest obstacle was his own boundless ambition, which warped his judgment; from its short-lived peak, the emperor's career slid downhill from defeat to dethronement to deportation.

Failure to Subdue England

Britain was Napoleon's most resolute opponent. It could not be otherwise, for any power that dominated the Continent could organize sufficient naval might to threaten British commerce, challenge its sea power, and invade the island kingdom. Britain would not make peace with any state that sought European hegemony, and Napoleon's ambition would settle for nothing less.

Unable to invade Britain while British warships commanded the English Channel, Napoleon decided to bring what he called "the nation of shopkeepers" to its knees by damaging the British economy. His plan, called the *Continental System,* was to bar all countries under France's control from buying British goods. However, by smuggling goods onto the Continent and increasing trade with the New World, Britain, although hurt, escaped economic ruin. Moreover, the Continental System punished European lands dependent on British imports; the bourgeoisie, generally supportive of Napoleon's social and administrative reforms, turned against him because of the economic distress it caused. Furthermore, Napoleon's efforts to enforce the system enmeshed him in two catastrophic blunders: the occupation of Spain and the invasion of Russia.

The Spanish Ulcer

An ally of France since 1796, Spain proved a disappointment to Napoleon. It failed to prevent the Portuguese from trading with Britain and contributed little military or financial aid to France's war effort. Napoleon decided to incorporate Spain into his empire; in 1808 he deposed the Spanish ruler, and designated his brother Joseph as king of Spain.

Napoleon believed the Spanish would rally round the gentle Joseph and welcome his liberal reforms. This confidence was a fatal illusion. Spanish nobles and clergy feared French liberalism; the overwhelmingly peasant population, illiterate and credulous, intensely proud, fanatically religious, and easily aroused by the clergy, viewed Napoleon as the devil's agent. Loyal to the Spanish monarchy and faithful to the church, the Spanish fought a "War to the Knife" against the invaders.

Seeking to keep the struggle against Napoleon alive, Britain came to the aid of the Spanish insurgents. The intervention of British troops commanded by Sir Arthur Wellesley, the future Duke of Wellington, led to the ultimate defeat of Joseph in 1813. The "Spanish ulcer" drained Napoleon's treasury, tied down hundreds of thousands of French troops, enabled Britain to gain a foothold on the Continent from which to invade southern France, and inspired patriots in other lands to resist the French emperor.

The German War of Liberation

Anti-French feeling also broke out in the German states. Hatred of the French invaders evoked a feeling of national outrage among some Germans, who up to this time had thought only in terms of their own particular state and prince. Some German intellectuals, using the emotional language of nationalism,

And There Is No Remedy—Etching by Francisco Goya (1746–1828). Napoleon could not understand the resistance of Spain to his grand plan. Spaniards rejected Napoleon's gentle brother as their new monarch. Their revolt was a "war to the knife." Executions and repression followed. Napoleon would state, "That miserable Spanish affair killed me." (*Philadelphia Museum of Art: SmithKline Beckman Corporation Fund*)

called for a war of liberation against Napoleon and, in some instances, for the creation of a unified Germany.

In addition to arousing a desire for national independence and unity, the disastrous defeat of the Prussians at Jena (1806) and French domination of Germany stimulated a movement for reform among members of the Prussian high bureaucracy and officer corps. If Prussia were to survive in a world altered by the French Revolution, it would have to learn the principal lessons of the Revolution—that aroused citizens fighting for a cause make better soldiers than mercenaries and oppressed serfs, and that officers selected for daring and intelligence command better than nobles possessing only a gilded birthright. The reformers believed that the elimination of social abuses would overcome defeatism and apathy and encourage Prussians to serve the state willingly and to fight bravely for national honor. A revitalized Prussia could then deal with the French.

Among the important reforms introduced in Prussia between 1807 and

1813 were the abolition of serfdom, the granting to towns of a large measure of self-administration, the awarding of army commissions on the basis of merit instead of birth, the elimination of cruel punishment in the ranks, and the establishment of national conscription. In 1813 the reform party forced King Frederick William III to declare war on France. The military reforms did improve the quality of the Prussian army. In the War of Liberation (1813), Prussian soldiers demonstrated far more enthusiasm and patriotism than they had at Jena in 1806, and the French were driven from Germany. The German War of Liberation came on the heels of Napoleon's disastrous Russian campaign.

Disaster in Russia

Deteriorating relations between Russia and France led Napoleon to his fatal decision to attack the Eastern giant. His creation of the Grand Duchy of Warsaw irritated the tsar, who feared a revival of Polish power and resented French influence on Russia's border. Another source of friction between the tsar and Napoleon was Russia's illicit trade with Britain, in violation of the Continental System. No doubt Napoleon's inexhaustible craving for power also compelled him to strike at Russia.

In June 1812, the Grand Army, 614,000 strong, crossed the Neman River into Russia. Fighting only rear-guard battles and retreating according to plan, the tsar's forces lured the invaders into the vastness of Russia far from their lines of supply. On September 14, the Grand Army, its numbers greatly reduced by disease, hunger, exhaustion, desertion, and battle, entered Moscow, which the Russians had virtually evacuated. Taking up headquarters in Moscow, Napoleon waited for Alexander I to admit defeat and come to terms. But the tsar remained intransigent.

Napoleon was in a dilemma: to penetrate deeper into Russia was certain death; to stay in Moscow with winter approaching meant possible starvation. Faced with these alternatives, Napoleon decided to retreat westward. On October 19, 1812, 95,000 troops and thousands of wagons loaded with loot left Moscow for the long trek back. In early November came the first snow and frost. Army stragglers were slaughtered by Russian Cossacks and peasant partisans. In the middle of December, with the Russians in pursuit, the remnants of the Grand Army staggered across the Neman River into east Prussia.

Final Defeat

After the destruction of the Grand Army, the empire crumbled. Although Napoleon raised a new army, he could not replace the equipment, cavalry horses, and experienced soldiers squandered in Russia. Now he had to rely on schoolboys and overage veterans. Most of Europe joined in a final coalition against France. In October 1813, allied forces from Austria, Prussia, Russia, and Sweden defeated Napoleon at Leipzig; in November, Anglo-Spanish forces crossed the Pyrenees into France. Finally, in the spring of 1814, the allies captured Paris. Napoleon abdicated and was exiled to the tiny island of Elba off the coast of Italy. The Bourbon dynasty was restored to the throne of France in the person of Louis XVIII, younger brother of the executed Louis XVI and the acknowledged leader of the émigrés.

Only forty-four years of age, Napoleon did not believe that it was his destiny to die on Elba. On March 1, 1815, he landed on the French coast with a thousand soldiers, and three weeks later he entered Paris to a hero's welcome. Raising a new army, Napoleon moved against the allied forces in Belgium. There the Prussians, led by Field Marshal Gebhard von Blucher, and the British, led by the Duke of Wellington, defeated Napoleon at Waterloo in June 1815. Napoleon's desperate gamble to regain power—the famous "hundred days"—had failed. This time the allies sent Napoleon to St. Helena, a lonely island in the South Atlantic a thousand miles off the coast of southern Africa. On this gloomy and rugged rock, Napoleon Bonaparte, emperor of France and would-be conqueror of Europe, spent the last six years of his life.

The Meaning of the French Revolution

The French Revolution was a decisive period in the shaping of the modern West. It implemented the thought of the philosophes, destroyed the hierarchic and corporate society of the Old Regime, promoted the interests of the bourgeoisie, and speeded the growth of the modern state.

The French Revolution weakened the aristocracy. With their feudal rights and privileges eliminated, the nobles became simply ordinary citizens. Throughout the nineteenth century, France would be governed by both the aristocracy and the bourgeoisie; property, not noble birth, determined the composition of the new ruling elite.

The principle of careers open to talent gave the bourgeoisie access to the highest positions in the state. Possessing wealth, talent, ambition, and now opportunity, the bourgeoisie would play an ever more important role in French political life. Throughout the Continent, the reforms of the French Revolution served as a model for progressive bourgeois, who sooner or later would challenge the Old Regime in their own lands.

The French Revolution transformed the dynastic state of the Old Regime into the modern state: national, liberal, secular, and rational. When the Declaration of the Rights of Man and of the Citizen stated that "the source of all sovereignty resides essentially in the nation," the concept of the state took on a new meaning. The state was no longer merely a territory or a federation of provinces; it was not the private possession of the king claiming to be God's lieutenant on earth. In the new conception, the state belonged to the people as a whole, and the individual, formerly a subject, was now a citizen with both rights and duties and was governed by laws that drew no distinction on the basis of birth.

The liberal thought of the Enlightenment found practical expression in the reforms of the Revolution. Absolutism and divine right of monarchy, repudiated in theory by the philosophes, were invalidated by constitutions that set limits to the powers of government and by elected parliaments that represented the governed. By providing for equality before the law and the protection of human rights—habeas corpus, trial by jury, freedom of religion, speech, and the press—the Revolution struck at the abuses of the Old Regime. These gains seemed at times more theoretical than actual, because of violations and interruptions; nevertheless, these liberal ideals reverberated throughout the Continent. During the nineteenth century the pace of reform would quicken.

By disavowing any divine justification for the monarch's power and by depriving the church of its special position, the Revolution accelerated the secularization of European political life. Sweeping aside the administrative chaos of the Old Regime, the Revolution attempted to impose rational norms on the state. The sale of public offices that produced ineffective and corrupt administrators was eliminated, and the highest positions in the land were opened to men of talent, regardless of birth. The Revolution abolished the peasantry's manorial obligations that hampered agriculture and swept away barriers to economic expansion. It based taxes on income and streamlined their collection. The destruction of feudal remnants, internal tolls, and the guilds speeded up the expansion of a competitive market economy. In the nineteenth century, reformers in the rest of Europe would follow the lead set by France.

By spreading revolutionary ideals and institutions, Napoleon made it impossible for the traditional rulers to restore the Old Regime intact after the emperor's downfall. The destruction of feudal remnants, the secularization of society, the transformation of the dynastic state into the modern national state, and the prominence of the bourgeoisie were assured.

The French Revolution also unleashed two potentially destructive forces identified with the modern state: total war and nationalism. These contradicted the rational and universal aims of the reformers as stated in the Declaration of the Rights of Man. Whereas eighteenth-century wars were fought by professional soldiers for limited aims, the French Revolution brought conscription and the mobilization of all the state's resources for armed conflict. The world wars of the twentieth century are the terrible fulfillment of this new development in warfare. The French Revolution also gave birth to modern nationalism. During the Revolution, loyalty was directed to the entire nation, not to a village or province or to the person of the king. The whole of France became the fatherland. Under the Jacobins, the French became converts to a secular faith preaching total reverence for the nation.

The Revolution attempted to reconstruct society on the basis of Enlightenment thought. The Declaration of the Rights of Man and of the Citizen, whose spirit permeated the reforms of the Revolution, upheld the dignity of the individual, demanded respect for the individual, attributed to each person natural rights, and barred the state from denying these rights. It insisted that society and state have no higher duty than to promote the freedom and auton-

Chronology 11.2 ✿ Napoleon's Career

1796	Napoleon gets command of French Army of Italy
November 10, 1799	He helps overthrow the Directory's rule, establishing a strong executive in France
December 2, 1804	He crowns himself emperor of the French
October 21, 1805	The battle of Trafalgar—French and Spanish fleets are defeated by the British
October 1806	He defeats the Prussians at Jena, and French forces occupy Berlin
1808–1813	The Peninsular War—Spaniards, aided by the British, fight against French occupation
October–December 1812	The Grand Army retreats from Russia
October 1813	Allied forces defeat Napoleon at Leipzig
1814	Paris is captured and Napoleon is exiled to Elba
March 20, 1815	Escaping, he enters Paris and begins 100 days' rule
June 1815	Defeated at Waterloo, he is exiled to St. Helena

omy of the individual. The tragedy of the Western experience is that this humanist vision, brilliantly expressed by the Enlightenment and given recognition in the reforms of the French Revolution, would be undermined in later generations. And, ironically, by spawning total war, nationalism, terror as government policy, and a revolutionary mentality that sought to change the world through violence, the French Revolution itself contributed to the shattering of this vision.

Notes

1. Excerpted in John Hall Stewart, ed., *A Documentary Survey of the French Revolution* (New York: Macmillan, 1951), pp. 43–44.

2. Albert Soboul, *The Parisian Sans-Culottes and the French Revolution, 1793–1794,* trans. by Gwynne Lewis (London: Oxford University Press, 1964), pp. 28–29.

Suggested Reading

Chandler, David, *The Campaigns of Napoleon* (1966). An exhaustive analysis of Napoleon's art of war.

Connelley, Owen, *Napoleon's Satellite Kingdoms* (1965). Focuses on the kingdoms in Naples, Italy, Holland, Spain, and Westphalia, which were created by Napoleon and ruled by his relatives.

Cronin, Vincent, *Napoleon Bonaparte* (1972). A highly acclaimed biography.

Doyle, William, *Origins of the French Revolution* (1980). In recent decades, several historians have challenged the traditional view that the French Revolution was an attempt by the bourgeoisie to overthrow the remnants of aristocratic power and privilege, that it was a victory of a capitalist bourgeois order over feudalism. This book summarizes the new scholarship and argues that the nobility and bourgeoisie had much in common prior to the Revolution.

Gershoy, Leo, *The Era of the French Revolution* (1957). A brief survey with useful documents.

Gottschalk, Louis, and Donald Lach, *Toward the French Revolution* (1973). A survey of the eighteenth-century background to the French Revolution.

Herold, J. Christopher, ed., *The Mind of Napoleon* (1955). A valuable selection from the written and spoken words of Napoleon.

———, *The Horizon Book of the Age of Napoleon* (1965). Napoleon and his time.

Higgins, E. L., ed. *The French Revolution* (1938). Excerpts from contemporaries.

Holtman, Robert B., *The Napoleonic Revolution* (1967). Napoleon as revolutionary innovator who influenced every aspect of European life; particularly good on Napoleon the propagandist.

Lefebvre, Georges, *The French Revolution*, 2 vols. (1962, 1964). A detailed analysis by a master historian.

———, *The Coming of the French Revolution* (1967). A brilliant analysis of the social structure of the Old Regime and the opening phase of the Revolution.

Markham, Felix, *Napoleon* (1963). A first-rate short biography.

———, *Napoleon and the Awakening of Europe* (1965). Napoleon's influence on other lands.

Palmer, R. R., *The Age of the Democratic Revolution*, 2 vols. (1959, 1964). The French Revolution as part of a revolutionary movement that spread on both sides of the Atlantic.

———, *Twelve Who Ruled* (1965). An admirable treatment of the Terror.

Rudé, George, *The Crowd in the French Revolution* (1959). An analysis of the composition of the crowds that stormed the Bastille, marched to Versailles, and attacked the king's palace.

———, *Robespierre: Portrait of a Revolutionary Democrat* (1976). A biography of the revolutionary leader.

Stewart, J. H., *A Documentary Survey of the French Revolution* (1951). A valuable collection of documents.

Review Questions

1. Analyze the causes of the French Revolution.
2. Identify and explain the significance of the following: formation of the National Assembly, storming of the Bastille, the Great Fear, and the October Days.
3. Analyze the nature and significance of the reforms of the National Assembly.
4. What were the grievances of the sans-culottes?
5. What were the accomplishments of the Jacobins?
6. Describe Robespierre's basic philosophy.
7. Napoleon both preserved and destroyed the ideals of the French Revolution. Discuss this statement.
8. Account for Napoleon's downfall. What were Napoleon's greatest achievements? What were his greatest failures?
9. Why was the era of the French Revolution a decisive period in the shaping of the West?

Chapter · 12

Ferment of Ideas:
Romanticism, Conservatism,
Liberalism, Nationalism

After the defeat of Napoleon, the traditional rulers of Europe, some of them just restored to power, were determined to protect themselves and society from future revolutions. As defenders of the status quo, they attacked the reformist spirit of the philosophes that had produced the Revolution. In *conservatism,* which championed tradition over reason, hierarchy over equality, and the community over the individual, they found a philosophy to justify their assault on the Enlightenment and the French Revolution.

But the forces unleashed by the French Revolution had penetrated European consciousness too deeply to be eradicated. One force for revolution was *liberalism,* which aimed to secure the liberty and equality proclaimed by the French Revolution. Another was *nationalism,* which called for the liberation of subject peoples and the unification of broken nations.

The postrevolutionary period also saw a new cultural orientation. *Romanticism,* with its plea for the liberation of human emotions and the free expression of personality, challenged the Enlightenment stress on rationalism. Although primarily a literary and artistic movement, Romanticism also permeated philosophy and political thought, particularly conservatism. ❧

Lord Byron (1788–1824). One of the leading romantic poets, Byron created the "Byronic hero," a lonely and mysterious figure. His own short life exalted the emotions and the senses. He went to Greece in 1824 to aid the revolutionaries and died there from poor health. (*Historical Pictures Service, Chicago*)

Romanticism: A New Cultural Orientation

The Romantic Movement, which began in the closing decades of the eighteenth century, dominated European cultural life in the first half of the nineteenth century. Most of Europe's leading cultural figures came under the influence of the Romantic Movement. Among the exponents of romanticism were the poets Shelley, Wordsworth, Keats, and Byron in England; the novelist Victor Hugo and the Catholic philosopher Chateaubriand in France; the writers A. W. and Friedrich Schlegel and the philosophers Schiller and Schelling in Germany. Caspar David Friedrich in Germany and John Constable in England expressed the romantic mood in art, and Beethoven, Schubert, Chopin, and Wagner expressed it in music.

Exalting Imagination and Feelings

Perhaps the central message of the romantics was that the imagination of the individual should determine the form and content of an artistic creation. This outlook ran counter to the rationalism of the Enlightenment, which itself had been a reaction against the otherworldly Christian orientation of the Middle Ages. The philosophes had attacked faith because it thwarted and distorted reason; romantic poets, philosophers, and artists now denounced the rationalism of the philosophes because it crushed the emotions and impeded creativity. The philosophes, said the romantics, had turned flesh-and-blood human beings into soulless thinking machines, and vibrant nature into lifeless wheels, cogs, and pulleys. For human beings to be restored to their true nature, to become whole again, they must be emancipated from the tyranny of excessive intellectualizing; the feelings must be nourished and expressed. Taking up one of Rousseau's ideas, romantics yearned to rediscover a pristine freedom and creativity in the human soul that had been squashed by habits, values, rules, and standards imposed by civilization.

The philosophes had concentrated on people in general—those elements of human nature shared by all people. Romantics, on the other hand, emphasized human diversity and uniqueness—those traits that set one human being apart from others. They urged each to discover and express his or her true self; to play his or her own music; to write his or her own poetry; to paint his or her own personal vision of nature; to live, suffer, and love in his or her own way.

Whereas the philosophes had regarded the feelings as an obstacle to clear thinking, to the romantics they were the human essence. People could not live by reason alone, said the romantics. They agreed with Rousseau, who wrote: "For us, to exist is to feel and our sensibility is incontestably prior to our reason."[1] For the romantics, reason was cold and dreary, its understanding of people and life meager and inadequate. Reason could not comprehend or express the complexities of human nature nor the richness of human experience. By always dissecting and analyzing, by imposing deadening structure and form, and by demanding adherence to strict rules, reason crushed inspiration and creativity and barred true understanding. "The Reasoning Power in Man," said William Blake, the British poet, artist, and mystic, is "an incrustation over my immortal Spirit."[2]

For the romantics, the avenue to truth was not the intellect but spontaneous human emotions. By cultivating instincts and imagination, individuals could experience reality and realize their authentic selves. The romantics wanted people to feel and to experience—to "bathe in the waters of life," said Blake. For this reason, the romantics insisted that imaginative poets had a greater insight into life than analytical philosophers did. "I am certain of nothing but of the holiness of the Heart's affections and the truth of Imagination," wrote John Keats. "O for a Life of Sensations rather than of Thoughts."[3]

The Enlightenment mind had been clear, critical, and controlled. It had adhered to standards of aesthetics, thought to be universal, that had dominated European cultural life since the Renaissance. Romantic poets, artists, and musicians broke with these traditional styles and austere rules and created new cultural forms and techniques. "We do not want either Greek or Roman Models," said Blake, but should be "just and true to our own Imaginations."[4] For the romantics, one did not learn how to write poetry or paint pictures by following textbook rules; one could not comprehend the poet's or artist's intent by judging works according to fixed standards. The romantics also explored the inner life of the mind, which Freud would later call *the unconscious*. It was this layer of the mind—mysterious, primitive, more elemental and more powerful than reason, the wellspring of creativity—that the romantics yearned to revitalize and release.

Nature, God, History

The philosophes had viewed nature as a lifeless machine—a giant clock, all of whose parts worked together in perfect precision and harmony. Nature's laws, operating with mathematical certainty, were uncovered by the methodology of science. To the romantics, nature was alive and suffused with God's presence. Nature stimulated the creative energies of the imagination; it taught human beings a higher form of knowledge, as William Wordsworth wrote:

> *One impulse from a vernal wood*
> *May teach you more of man,*
> *Of moral evil and of good,*
> *Than all the sages can.*[5]

The philosophes had seen God as a great watchmaker—a detached observer of a self-operating mechanical universe—and they tried to reduce religion to a series of scientific propositions. Many romantics viewed God as an inspiring spiritual force, and condemned the philosophes for weakening Christianity by submitting its dogmas to the test of reason. For the romantics, religion was not science and syllogism but a passionate and authentic expression of human nature.

The philosophes had viewed the Middle Ages as an era of darkness, superstition, and fanaticism and regarded surviving medieval institutions and traditions as barriers to progress. The romantics, on the other hand, revered the Middle Ages. To the romantic imagination, the Middle Ages abounded with Christian mysteries, heroic deeds, and social harmony.

Romantics and philosophes held differing conceptions of history. For the philosophes, history served a didactic purpose by providing examples of human folly. Such knowledge assisted people in preparing for a better future, and for that reason alone history should be studied. To the romantics, a historical period, like an individual, was a unique entity with its own soul. They wanted the historian to portray and analyze the variety of nations, traditions, and institutions that constituted the historical experience. The command of the romantics to study the specific details of history and culture and to comprehend them within the context of their times is the foundation of modern historical scholarship.

Searching for universal principles, the philosophes had dismissed folk traditions as peasant superstitions and impediments to progress. The romantics, on the other hand, rebelling against the standardization of culture, saw native languages, songs, and legends as the unique creations of a people and the deepest expression of national feeling. The romantics regarded the legends, myths, and folk traditions of a people as the wellspring of poetry and art, the spiritual source of a people's cultural vitality, creativity, and identity. Hence they examined these earliest cultural expressions with awe and reverence. In this way, romanticism was instrumental in the shaping of modern nationalism.

The Impact of the Romantic Movement

The romantic revolt against the Enlightenment had an important and enduring impact on European history. By focusing on the creative capacities inherent in the emotions—intuition, instinct, passion, will, empathy—the romantics shed light on a side of human nature that the philosophes had often overlooked or undervalued. By encouraging personal freedom and diversity in art, music, and literature, they greatly enriched European cultural life. Future artists, writers, and musicians would proceed along the path opened by the romantics. Modern art, for example, owes much to the Romantic Movement's emphasis on the legitimacy of human feeling and its exploration of the hidden world of dreams and fantasies. By recognizing the distinctive qualities of historical periods, peoples, and cultures, the romantics helped to create the modern historical outlook. By valuing the nation's past, romanticism contributed to modern nationalism and conservatism.

But there was a potentially dangerous side to the Romantic Movement. By waging their attack on reason with excessive zeal, the romantics undermined the rational foundations of the West. The romantic idealization of the past and glorification of ancient folkways, native soil, and native language introduced a highly charged, nonrational component into political life. In the decades to come, romanticism, particularly in Germany, fused with political nationalism and "created a general climate of inexact thinking, an intellectual . . . dream world and an emotional approach to problems of political action to which sober reasoning should have been applied."[6]

The philosophes would have regarded the romantics' veneration of a people's history and traditions, their search for a nation's soul in an archaic culture, as barbarous—a regression to superstition, the triumph of myth over philosophy. Indeed, when transferred to the realm of politics, the romantics' idealization of the past did reawaken a mythic way of thinking about the world, which rested more on feeling than on reason. In the process, people became committed to ideas that were fraught with danger.

Conservatism: The Value of Tradition

To the traditional rulers of Europe—kings, aristocrats, clergy—the French Revolution was a great evil that had inflicted a near-fatal wound on civilization. Disgusted and frightened by the revolutionary violence, terror, and warfare, the traditional rulers sought to refute the philosophes' world-view that had spawned the Revolution. To them, natural rights, equality, the goodness of man, and perpetual progress were perverse doctrines that had produced the Jacobin "assassins." In conservatism they found a political philosophy to counter the Enlightenment ideology.

Edmund Burke's *Reflections on the French Revolution* (1790) was instrumental in shaping conservative thought. Burke (1729–1797), a British philosopher and statesman, wanted to warn his countrymen of the dangers inherent in the ideology of the revolutionaries. Although writing in 1790, he astutely predicted that the Revolution would lead to terror and military dictatorship. To Burke, fanatics armed with pernicious principles—abstract ideas divorced from historical experience—had dragged France through the mire of revolution. Burke developed a coherent political philosophy that served as a counterweight to the ideology of the Enlightenment and the Revolution.

Hostility to the French Revolution

The philosophes and French reformers, entranced by the great discoveries in science, had believed that the human mind could also transform social institutions and ancient traditions according to rational models. Progress through reason became their faith. Dedicated to creating a new future, the revolutionaries abruptly dispensed with old habits, traditional authority, and familiar ways of thought.

To conservatives, who like the romantics venerated the past, this was supreme arrogance and wickedness. They regarded the revolutionaries as presumptuous men who recklessly severed society's links with ancient institutions and traditions and condemned venerable religious and moral beliefs as ignorance. By attacking time-honored ways, the revolutionaries had deprived French society of moral leadership and had opened the door to anarchy and terror.

The philosophes and French reformers had expressed unlimited confidence in the power of human reason to understand and to change society. While appreciating human rational capacities, conservatives also recognized the limitations of reason. They saw the Revolution as a natural outgrowth of an arrogant Enlightenment philosophy that overvalued reason and sought to reshape society in accordance with abstract principles.

For conservatives, human beings were not by nature good. Human wickedness was not due to a faulty environment, as the philosophes had proclaimed, but was at the core of human nature, as Christianity taught. Evil was held in check not by reason but by tried and tested institutions, traditions, and beliefs. Without these habits inherited from ancestors, said conservatives, the social order was threatened by sinful human nature.

Because monarchy, aristocracy, and the church had endured for centuries, argued the conservatives, they had worth. By despising and uprooting these ancient institutions, revolutionaries had hardened the people's hearts, perverted their morals, and caused them to commit terrible outrages upon each other and society. For conservatives, revolutionaries had divorced people and society from their historical settings and reduced them to abstractions; they had drawn up constitutions based on the unacceptable principle that government derives its power from the consent of the governed.

For conservatives, God and history were the only legitimate sources of political authority; states were not made, but were an expression of the nation's moral, religious, and historical experience. No legitimate or sound constitution could be drawn up by a group assembled for that purpose. Scraps of paper with legal terminology and philosophic visions could not produce an effective government; instead, a sound political system evolved gradually and inexplicably in response to circumstances.

The Quest for Social Stability

The liberal philosophy of the Enlightenment and the French Revolution started with the individual. The philosophes and the revolutionaries envisioned a society in which the individual was free and autonomous. Conservatives believed that society was not a mechanical arrangement of disconnected individuals, but a living organism held together by centuries-old bonds. Individualism would imperil social stability, destroy obedience to law, and fragment society into self-seeking isolated atoms. Conservatives held that the community was more important than the individual. Whereas the philosophes had attacked Christianity for promoting superstition and fanaticism, conservatives saw religion as the basis of civil society. Catholic conservatives in particular held that God had constituted the church and monarchy to check sinful human nature.

Conservatives viewed equality as another pernicious abstraction that contradicted all historical experience. For conservatives, society was naturally hierarchical, and they believed that some men, by virtue of their intelligence, education, wealth, and birth, were best qualified to rule and instruct the less able. They said that by denying the existence of a natural elite and uprooting a long-established ruling elite that had learned its art through experience, the revolutionaries had deprived society of effective leaders, brought internal disorder, and prepared the way for a military dictatorship.

Conservatism pointed to a limitation of the Enlightenment. It showed that human beings and social relationships are far more complex than the philosophes had imagined. People do not always accept the rigorous logic of the philosopher and are not eager to break with ancient ways, however illogical they appear. They often find familiar customs and ancestral religions more satisfying guides to life than the blueprints of philosophers. The granite might of tradition remains an obstacle to all the visions of reformers.

Liberalism: The Value of the Individual

The decades after 1815 saw a spectacular rise of the bourgeoisie. Talented and ambitious bankers, merchants, manufacturers, professionals, and officeholders wanted to break the stranglehold that the landed nobility, the traditional elite, held on political power and social prestige; they also wanted to eliminate restrictions on the free pursuit of profits.

The political philosophy of the bourgeoisie was most commonly liberalism.

Nicolò Paganini (1782–1840) by Jean Auguste Dominique Ingres (1780–1867).   The structure and order of classical music gave way to sweeping melodies and rich harmonies. Paganini, the composer-performer, stunned audiences with his virtuosity. Paganini's name became synonymous with the violin, as Franz Liszt's was with the piano. (*Louvre/Cliché des Musées Nationaux*)

While conservatives sought to strengthen the foundations of traditional society, which has been severely shaken in the period of the French Revolution and Napoleon, liberals wanted to alter the status quo and to carry out the promise of the Enlightenment and the French Revolution. Conservatives extolled the community, but liberals gave central concern to individual freedom. Conservatives tried to preserve a social hierarchy based on inherited aristocracy, but liberals insisted that a person's value was measured not by birth but by achievement. Conservatives held that the state rests on tradition, but liberals sought the rational state, in which political institutions and procedures were based on intelligible principles. Conservatives wanted individuals, inherently evil, to obey their betters. Liberals, in contrast, had confidence in the goodness of human nature and the capacity of individuals to control their own lives.

The Sources of Liberalism

In the long view of Western civilization, liberalism is an extension and development of the democratic practices and rational outlook that originated in ancient Greece. Also flowing into the liberal tradition is Judeo-Christian respect for the individual. But the immediate historical roots of nineteenth-century liberalism extended back to seventeenth-century England. At that time, the struggle for religious toleration by English Protestant dissenters established the principle of freedom of conscience, which is easily transferred into freedom of opinion and expression in all matters. The Glorious Revolution of 1688 set limits on the power of the English monarchy. In that same century John Locke's natural-rights philosophy declared that the individual was by nature entitled to freedom, and it justified revolutions against rulers who deprived citizens of their lives, liberty, or property.

The French philosophes were instrumental in the shaping of liberalism. From Montesquieu, liberals derived the theory of the separation of powers and of checks and balances—principles intended to guard against autocratic government. The philosophes had supported religious toleration and freedom of thought, expressed confidence in the capacity of the human mind to reform society, maintained that human beings are essentially good, and believed in the future progress of humanity—all fundamental principles of liberalism.

The American and French revolutions were crucial phases in the history of liberalism. The Declaration of Independence gave expression to Locke's theory of natural rights; the Constitution of the United States incorporated Montesquieu's principles and demonstrated that people could create an effective government; the Bill of Rights protected the person and rights of the individual. In destroying the special privileges of the aristocracy and opening careers to talent, the French National Assembly of 1789 had implemented the liberal ideal of equality under the law. They also drew up the Declaration of the Rights of Man and the Citizen, which affirmed the dignity and rights of the individual, and a constitution that limited the king's power. Both the American and French revolutions explicitly called for the protection of property rights, another basic premise of liberalism.

Individual Liberty

The liberals' primary concern was the enhancement of individual liberty. They agreed with German philosopher Immanuel Kant that every person exists as an end in himself or herself and not as an object to be used arbitrarily by others. If uncoerced by government and churches and properly educated, a person could develop into a good, productive, and self-directed human being.

Liberals rejected a legacy of the Middle Ages, the classification of the individual as a commoner or aristocrat on the basis of birth. They held that a man was not born into a certain station in life but made his way through his own efforts. Taking their cue from the French Revolution, liberals called for an end to all privileges of the aristocracy.

In the tradition of the philosophes, liberals stressed the pre-eminence of reason as the basis of political life. Unfettered by ignorance and tyranny, the mind could eradicate evils that had burdened people for centuries and begin an age of free institutions and responsible citizens. For this reason, liberals supported the advancement of education.

Liberals attacked the state and other authorities that prevented the individual from exercising the right of free choice, that interfered with the right of free expression, and that prevented the individual from self-determination and self-development. They agreed with John Stuart Mill, the British philosopher, who declared that "over his own body and mind, the individual is sovereign. ... that the only purpose for which power can be rightfully exercised over any member of a civilized community, against his will, is to prevent harm to others."[7]

To guard against the absolute and arbitrary authority of kings, liberals demanded written constitutions that granted freedom of speech, the press, and religion; freedom from arbitrary arrest; and the protection of property rights. To prevent the abuse of political authority, liberals called for a freely elected parliament and the distribution of power among the various branches of government. Liberals held that a government that derived its authority from the consent of the governed, as given in free elections, was least likely to violate individual freedom. A corollary of this principle was that the best government is one that governs least—that is, one that interferes as little as possible with the economic activities of its citizens and does not involve itself in their private lives or their beliefs.

Adopting the laissez-faire theory of Adam Smith, liberals maintained that a free economy, in which private enterprise would be unimpeded by government regulations, was as important as political freedom to the well-being of the individual and the community. When people acted from self-interest, the liberals said, they worked harder and achieved more; self-interest and natural competitive impulses spurred economic activity and ensured the production of more and better goods at the lowest possible price, thereby benefiting the entire nation. For this reason, the government must neither block free competition nor deprive individuals of their property, which was their incentive to work hard and efficiently. Believing that individuals were responsible for their own misfortunes, liberals were often unmoved by the misery of the poor and considered social reforms to alleviate poverty as unwarranted and dangerous meddling with the natural laws of supply and demand.

Liberalism and Democracy

Many bourgeois liberals viewed with horror the democratic creed that all people should share in political power. To them, the participation of commoners in politics meant a vulgar form of despotism and the end to individual liberty. The masses—uneducated, unpropertied, inexperienced, and impatient—had neither the ability nor the temperament to maintain liberty and protect property.

Because bourgeois liberals feared that democracy could crush personal freedom as ruthlessly as any absolute monarch could, they called for property requirements for voting and officeholding. They wanted political power to be concentrated in the hands of a safe and reliable—that is, a propertied and educated—middle class. Such a government would prevent revolution from below, a prospect that caused anxiety among bourgeois liberals.

Early nineteenth-century liberals engaged in revolutions, to be sure, but their aims were always limited. Once they had destroyed absolute monarchy and gained a constitution and a parliament or a change of government, they quickly tried to terminate the revolution. When the fever of revolution spread to the masses, liberals either withdrew or turned counterrevolutionary, for they feared the stirrings of the multitude.

Although liberalism was the political philosophy of a middle class generally hostile to democracy, the essential ideals of democracy flowed logically from liberalism. Eventually, democracy became a later stage in the evolution of liberalism, because the masses, their political power enhanced by the Industrial Revolution, would press for greater social, political, and economic equality. Thus, by the early twentieth century, many European states had introduced universal suffrage, abandoned property requirements for officeholding, and improved conditions for workers.

But the fears of nineteenth-century liberals were not without foundation. In the twentieth century, the participation of common people in politics has indeed threatened freedom. Impatient with parliamentary procedures, the masses, particularly when troubled by economic problems, have in some instances given their support to demagogues who promised swift and decisive action. The granting of political participation to the masses has not always made people more free. The confidence of democrats has been shaken in the twentieth century by the seeming willingness of the masses to trade freedom for authority, order, economic security, and national power. Liberalism is based on the assumption that human beings can and do respond to rational argument, that reason will prevail over base human feelings. The history of our century shows that this may be an overly optimistic assessment of human nature.

Nationalism: The Sacredness of the Nation

Nationalism is a conscious bond shared by a group of people who possess a common culture and history marked by shared glories and sufferings and who feel strongly attached to a particular land. Nationalism is accompanied by a conviction that one's highest loyalty and devotion should be given to the nation. Nationalists exhibit great pride in their people's history and traditions and often feel that their nation has been specially chosen by God or history. Like a religion, nationalism provides the individual with a sense of community and with a cause worthy of self-sacrifice.

Thus, in an age when Christianity was in retreat, nationalism became the dominant spiritual force in nineteenth-century European life. Nationalism provided new beliefs, martyrs, and "holy" days that stimulated reverence; it offered membership in a community, which satisfied the overwhelming psychological need of human beings for fellowship and identity. And nationalism gave a mission—the advancement of the nation—to which people could dedicate themselves.

The Emergence of Modern Nationalism

The essential components of nationalism emerged at the time of the French Revolution. The Revolution asserted the principle that sovereignty derived from the nation, from the people as a whole—the state was not the private possession of the ruler but the embodiment of the people's will. The nation-state was above king, church, estate, guild, or province; it superseded all other loyalties. The French people must view themselves not as subjects of the king, not as Bretons or Normans, not as nobles or bourgeois, but as citizens of a united fatherland, *la patrie*. These two ideas—that the people possess unlimited sovereignty and that they are united in a nation—were crucial in fashioning a nationalist outlook.

As the Revolution moved from the moderate to the radical stage, French nationalism gained in intensity. In 1793–94, when the republic was threatened by foreign invasion, the Jacobins created a national army, demanded ever greater allegiance to and sacrifice for the nation, and called for the expansion of France's borders to the Alps and the Rhine. With unprecedented success, the Jacobins used every means—press, schoolroom, rostrum—to instill a love of country.

The Romantic Movement also awakened nationalist feelings. By examining the language, literature, and folkways of their people, romantic thinkers instilled a sense of national pride in their compatriots. Johann Gottfried Herder (1744–1803) conceived the idea of the *Volksgeist*—the soul of the people. For Herder, each people was unique and creative; each expressed its genius in language, literature, monuments, and folk traditions. Herder did not make the theoretical jump from a spiritual or cultural nationalism to political nationalism; he did not call for the formation of states based on nationality. But his emphasis on the unique culture of a people stimulated a national consciousness among Germans and the various Slavic peoples who lived under foreign rule. Fascination with the *Volksgeist* prompted intellectuals to investigate the past of their own people, to rediscover their ancient traditions, and to extol their historic language and culture. From this cultural nationalism it was only a short step to a political nationalism that called for national liberation, unification, and statehood.

The romantics were the earliest apostles of German nationalism. They restored to consciousness memories of the German past, and they emphasized the peculiar qualities of the German folk and the special destiny of the German nation. The romantics glorified medieval Germany and valued hereditary monarchy and aristocracy as vital links to the nation's past. They saw the existence of each individual as inextricably bound up with folk and fatherland, and they found the self-realization for which they yearned in the unification of their own egos with the national soul. To these romantics, the national community was a vital force that gave the individual both an identity and a purpose in life. And the nation stood above the individual; the national spirit bound isolated souls into a community of brethren.

Eugène Delacroix (1799–1863): Liberty Leading the People, 1830.   Early nineteenth-century reformers found their rallying call in liberty, a legacy of the French Revolution. In this painting, Delacroix, the leader of French romantic artists, glorifies liberty. (*Louvre/Cliché des Musées Nationaux*)

Nationalism and Liberalism

In the early nineteenth century, liberals were the principal leaders and supporters of nationalist movements. They viewed the struggle for national rights—the freedom of a people from foreign rule—as an extension of the struggle for the rights of the individual. There could be no liberty, said nationalists, if people were not free to rule themselves in their own land.

Liberals called for the unification of Germany and Italy, the rebirth of Poland, the liberation of Greece from Turkish rule, and the granting of autonomy to the Hungarians of the Austrian Empire. Liberal nationalists envisioned a Europe of independent states based on nationality and popular sovereignty. Free of foreign domination and tyrant princes, these newly risen states would protect the rights of the individual and strive to create a brotherhood of nationalities in Europe.

In the first half of the nineteenth century, few intellectuals recognized the dangers inherent in nationalism or understood the fundamental conflict between liberalism and nationalism. For the liberal, the idea of universal natural rights transcended all national boundaries. Inheriting the cosmopolitanism of the Enlightenment, liberalism emphasized what all people had in common, called for all individuals to be treated equally under the law, and preached toleration. Nationalists, manifesting the particularist attitude of the in-group and the tribe, regarded the nation as the essential fact of existence. Consequently, they often willingly subverted individual liberty for the sake of national grandeur. Whereas the liberal sought to protect the rights of all within the state, the nationalist often ignored or trampled on the rights of individuals and national minorities. Whereas liberalism grew out of the rational tradition of the West, nationalism derived from the emotions. Because it fulfilled an elemental yearning for community and kinship, nationalism exerted a powerful hold over human hearts often driving people to political extremism. Liberalism demanded objectivity in analyzing tradition, society, and history, but nationalism evoked a mythic and romantic past that often distorted history.

In the last part of the nineteenth century, the irrational and mythic quality of nationalism would intensify. By stressing the unique qualities and history of a particular people, nationalism would promote hatred between nationalities. By kindling deep love for the past, including a longing for ancient borders, glories, and power, nationalism would lead to wars of expansion. By arousing the emotions to a fever pitch, nationalism would shatter rational thinking, drag the mind into a world of fantasy and myth, and introduce extremism into politics. Love of nation would become an overriding passion threatening to extinguish the liberal ideals of reason, freedom, and equality.

Notes

1. Quoted in H. G. Schenk, *The Mind of the European Romantics* (Garden City, N.Y.: Doubleday, 1969), p. 4.
2. William Blake, *Milton*, 40.34–35.
3. Letter of John Keats, November 22, 1817, in Hyder E. Rollins, ed., *The Letters of John Keats* (Cambridge, Mass.: Harvard University Press, 1958), 1: 184–185.
4. Blake, *Milton*, Preface.
5. From "The Tables Turned," in An-
drew J. George, ed., *The Complete Poetical Works of Wordsworth* (Boston: Houghton Mifflin, 1904, rev. ed., 1982), p. 83.
6. Horst von Maltitz, *The Evolution of Hitler's Germany* (New York: McGraw-Hill, 1973), p. 127.
7. John Stuart Mill, *On Liberty*, ed. by Currin V. Shields (Indianapolis: Bobbs-Merrill, 1956), ch. 1.

Suggested Reading

Arblaster, Anthony, *The Rise and Decline of Western Liberalism* (1984). A critical analysis of liberalism, its evolution and characteristics.

Bullock, Alan, and Maurice Shock, eds., *The Liberal Tradition* (1956). Selections from the works of British liberals, preceded by an essay on the liberal tradition.

de Ruggiero, Guido, *The History of European Liberalism* (1927). A classic study.

Epstein, Klaus, *The Genesis of German Conservatism* (1966). An analysis of German conservative thought as a response to the Enlightenment and the French Revolution.

Harris, R. W., *Romanticism and the So-*

cial Order, 1780–1830 (1969). Involvement of English romantics in social and political questions.

Hayes, Carlton J. H., *Historical Evolution of Modern Nationalism* (1931). A pioneering work in the study of nationalism.

Honour, Hugh, *Romanticism* (1979). A study of the influence of Romanticism on the visual arts.

Kohn, Hans, *The Idea of Nationalism* (1961). A comprehensive study of nationalism from the ancient world through the eighteenth century by a leading student of the subject.

——, *Prelude to Nation-States* (1967). The emergence of nationalism in France and Germany.

Schapiro, J. S., *Liberalism: Its Meaning and History* (1958). A useful survey with readings.

Schenk, H. G., *The Mind of the European Romantics* (1966). A comprehensive analysis of the Romantic Movement.

Shafer, B. C., *Faces of Nationalism* (1972). The evolution of modern nationalism in Europe and the non-European world; contains a good bibliography.

Smith, A. D., *Theories of Nationalism* (1972). The relationship between nationalism and modernization.

Weiss, John, *Conservatism in Europe, 1770–1945* (1977). Conservatism as a reaction to social modernization.

Review Questions

1. The Romantic Movement was a reaction against the dominant ideas of the Enlightenment. Discuss this statement.
2. What was the significance of the Romantic Movement?
3. What were the attitudes of the conservatives toward the philosophes and the French Revolution?
4. What were the sources of liberalism?
5. The central concern of liberals was the enhancement of individual liberty. Discuss this statement.
6. How did the French Revolution and romanticism contribute to the rise of modern nationalism?
7. What is the relationship between nationalism and liberalism?
8. Account for nationalism's great appeal.

Chapter ⚡ 13

Surge of Nationalism:
From Liberal to
Extreme Nationalism

A clash between the forces unleashed by the French Revolution and
the traditional outlook of the Old Regime took place during the years
1815 through 1848. The period opened with the Congress of Vienna,
which drew up a peace settlement after the defeat of Napoleon, and
closed with the revolutions that swept across most of Europe in 1848.
Much of the Old Regime outside of France had survived the stormy
decades of the French Revolution and Napoleon. Monarchs still held
the reins of political power. Aristocrats, particularly in central and
eastern Europe, retained their traditional hold over the army and administration, controlled the peasantry and local government, and enjoyed tax exemptions. Determined to enforce respect for traditional
authority and to smother liberal ideals, the conservative ruling elites
resorted to censorship, secret police, and armed force. Inspired by the
revolutionary principles of liberty, equality, and fraternity, liberals
and nationalists continued to engage in revolutionary activity. ⚱

The Congress of Vienna

Statesmen and Issues

After the defeat of Napoleon, a congress of European powers met at Vienna
(1814–1815) to draw up a peace settlement. The pivotal figure at the Congress
of Vienna was Prince Klemens von Metternich (1773–1859) of Austria. Belonging to the old order of courts and kings, Metternich believed that domestic

order and international stability depended on rule by monarchy and respect for aristocracy. The misguided liberal belief that society could be reshaped according to the ideals of liberty and equality, said Metternich, had led to twenty-five years of revolution, terror, and war. To restore stability and peace, the old Europe must suppress liberal ideas and quash the first signs of revolution.

Metternich also feared the new spirit of nationalism. As a multinational empire, Austria was particularly vulnerable to nationalist unrest. If its ethnic groups—Poles, Czechs, Magyars, Italians, South Slavs, Rumanians—became infected with the nationalist virus, they would shatter the Hapsburg Empire. Moreover, Metternich felt that by arousing the masses and setting people against people, nationalism could undermine the foundations of the European civilization that he cherished.

Metternich sought to return to power the ruling families deposed by more than two decades of revolutionary warfare, and to restore the balance of power so that no one country could be in a position to dominate the European continent as Napoleon had. Metternich was determined to end the chaos of the Napoleonic period and restore stability to Europe. There must be no more Napoleons who obliterate states, topple kings, and dream of European hegemony.

Other nations at the Congress of Vienna included Britain, Russia, France, and Prussia. Representing Britain was Robert Stewart, Viscount Castlereagh (1769–1822), the British foreign secretary, who was realistic and empirically minded. Although an implacable enemy of Napoleon, Castlereagh demonstrated mature statesmanship by not seeking to punish France severely. Tsar Alexander I (1777–1825) attended the Congress himself. Showing signs of mental instability and steeped in Christian mysticism, the Russian tsar wanted to create a European community based on Christian teachings. Alexander regarded himself as the savior of Europe, an attitude that caused other diplomats to regard him with distrust. Representing France was Prince Charles Maurice de Talleyrand-Périgord (1754–1838). A devoted patriot, Talleyrand sought to remove from France the stigma of the Revolution and Napoleon. The aging Prince Karl von Hardenberg (1750–1822) represented Prussia. Like Metternich, Castlereagh, and Talleyrand, the Prussian statesman believed that the various European states, in addition to pursuing their own national interests, should concern themselves with the well-being of the European community as a whole.

Two interrelated issues threatened to disrupt the conference and enmesh the Great Powers in another war. One was Prussia's intention to annex the German kingdom of Saxony; the other was Russia's demand for Polish territories. The tsar wanted to combine the Polish holdings of Russia, Austria, and Prussia into a new Polish kingdom under Russian control. Both Britain and Austria regarded such an extension of Russia's power into central Europe as a threat to the balance of power.

Prince Talleyrand of France suggested that Britain, Austria, and France conclude an alliance to oppose Prussia and Russia. This clever move by Talleyrand restored France to the family of nations. Now France was no longer the

Congress of Vienna, 1815, by Jean Baptiste Isabey (1767–1855). The delegates to the Congress of Vienna (Metternich is standing before a chair at the left) in 1815 sought to re-establish many features of the Europe that existed before the French Revolution and Napoleon. The delegates can be called shortsighted; nevertheless, the balance of power that they formulated preserved international peace. (*The New York Public Library*)

hated enemy, but a necessary counterweight to Russia and Prussia. Threatened with war, Russia and Prussia moderated their demands and the crisis ended.

The Settlement

After months of discussion, quarrels, and threats, the delegates to the Congress of Vienna finished their work. Resisting Prussia's demands for a punitive peace, the allies did not punish France severely. They feared that a humiliated France would only prepare for a war of revenge. Moreover, Metternich continued to need France to balance the power of both Prussia and Russia. France had to pay a large indemnity over a five-year period and submit to allied occupation until the obligation was met.

Although it lost most of its conquests, France emerged with somewhat more land than it possessed before the Revolution. To guard against a resurgent France, both Prussia and Holland received territories on the French border. Holland obtained the southern Netherlands (Belgium); Prussia gained the Rhineland and part of Saxony, but not as much as the Prussians had desired.

Nevertheless, Prussia emerged from the settlement significantly larger and stronger. Russia obtained Finland and a considerable part of the Polish territories, but not as much as the tsar had anticipated; the Congress prevented further Russian expansion into central Europe. The northern Italian province of Lombardy was restored to Austria, which also received adjacent Venetia. England obtained strategic naval bases: Helgoland in the North Sea, Malta and the Ionian Islands in the Mediterranean, the Cape Colony in South Africa, and Ceylon in the Indian Ocean. Germany was organized into a confederation of thirty-eight (later thirty-nine) states. Norway was given to Sweden. The legitimate rulers, who had been displaced by the Revolution and the wars of Napoleon, were restored to their thrones in France, Spain, Portugal, the Kingdom of the Two Sicilies, the Papal States, and many German states.

The conservative delegates at the Congress of Vienna have often been criticized for ignoring the liberal and nationalist aspirations of the different peoples and turning the clock back to the Old Regime. Critics have castigated the Congress for dealing only with the rights of thrones and not the rights of peoples. But after the experience of two world wars in the twentieth century, some historians today are impressed with the peacemakers' success in restoring a balance of power that effectively stabilized international relations. No one country was strong enough to dominate the Continent; no Great Power was so unhappy that it resorted to war to undo the settlement. Not until the unification of Germany in 1870–1871 was the balance of power upset; not until World War I in 1914 did Europe have another general war of the magnitude of the Napoleonic wars.

Revolutions, 1820–1829

Russia, Austria, Prussia, and Great Britain agreed to act together to preserve the territorial settlement of the Congress of Vienna and the balance of power. After paying its indemnity, France was admitted into this Quadruple Alliance, also known as the *Concert of Europe*. Metternich intended to use the Concert of Europe to maintain harmony between nations and internal stability within nations. Toward this end, conservatives in their respective countries censored books and newspapers and imprisoned liberal and nationalist activists.

But repression could not contain the liberal and nationalist ideals unleashed by the French Revolution. The first revolution after the restorations of legitimate rulers occurred in Spain in 1820. Fearing that the Spanish uprising, with its quasi-liberal overtones, would inspire revolutions in other lands, the Concert of Europe empowered France to intervene. In 1823, 100,000 French troops crushed the revolution.

Revolutionary activity in Italy also frightened the Concert of Europe. In

Map 13.1 Europe's Age of Revolutions ▶

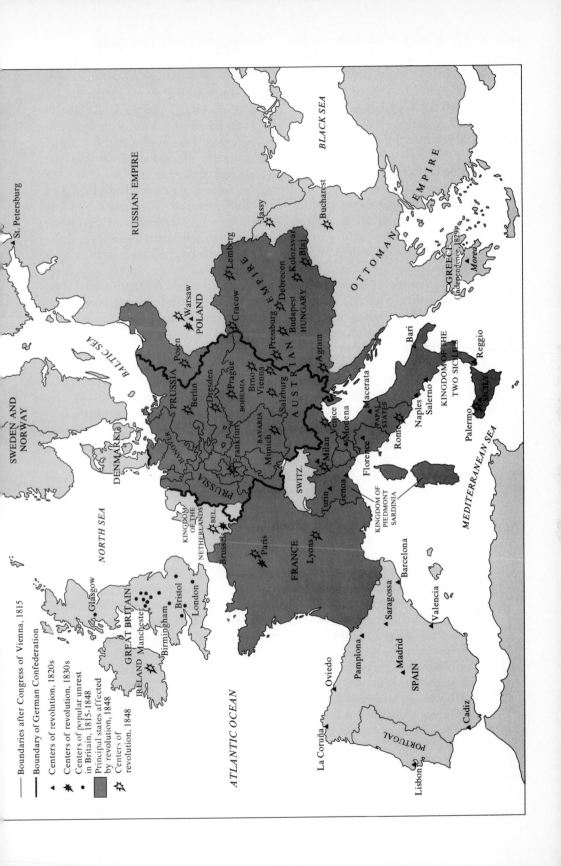

Boundaries after Congress of Vienna, 1815

Boundary of German Confederation

▲ Centers of revolution, 1820s

✳ Centers of revolution, 1830s

• Centers of popular unrest in Britain, 1815–1848

Principal states affected by revolution, 1848

✳ Centers of revolution, 1848

St. Petersburg

SWEDEN AND NORWAY

BALTIC SEA

NORTH SEA

DENMARK

RUSSIAN EMPIRE

Warsaw
POLAND

Posen

Cracow

Lemberg

Blaj
Kolozsvar
Debrecen
Budapest
HUNGARY
Pressburg
Agram

AUSTRIAN EMPIRE

Bucharest

Jassy

BLACK SEA

OTTOMAN EMPIRE

GREAT BRITAIN

Glasgow

IRELAND

Manchester
Birmingham
Bristol
London

PRUSSIA

Berlin
Dresden
Prague
BOHEMIA
Brno
Vienna
Salzburg

HANOVER

Frankfurt
BAVARIA
Munich

KINGDOM OF THE NETHERLANDS

BEL.

Brussels

Paris

Lyons

FRANCE

SWITZ.

Turin

Genoa

KINGDOM OF PIEDMONT SARDINIA

Milan
Modena
Venice

Florence

PAPAL STATES

Macerata

Rome

Naples
Salerno

KINGDOM OF THE TWO SICILIES

Bari

Reggio

SICILY

Palermo

MEDITERRANEAN SEA

GREECE
(independence, 1829)

Morea

ATLANTIC OCEAN

La Coruña

Oviedo

Pamplona

Saragossa

Madrid
SPAIN

Barcelona

Valencia

Cadiz

PORTUGAL

Lisbon

1815, Italy consisted of several separate states. In the south, a Bourbon king ruled the Kingdom of the Two Sicilies; the pope governed the Papal States in central Italy; Hapsburg Austria ruled Lombardy and Venetia in the north; Hapsburg princes subservient to Austria ruled the duchies of Tuscany, Parma, and Modena. Piedmont in the northwest and the island of Sardinia were governed by an Italian dynasty, the House of Savoy.

Besides all these political divisions, Italy was divided economically and culturally. Throughout the peninsula, attachment to the local region was stronger than devotion to national unity. Economic ties between north and south were weak; inhabitants of the northern Italian cities felt little closeness to Sicilian peasants. Except for the middle class, most Italians clung to the values of the Old Regime.

An expanding intellectual elite, through novels, poetry, and works of history, awakened interest in Italy's glorious past. They insisted that a people who had built the Roman Empire and had produced the Renaissance must not remain weak and divided, their land occupied by Austrians. These sentiments appealed particularly to university students and the middle class. But the rural masses, illiterate and preoccupied with the hardships of daily life, had little concern for this struggle for national revival.

Secret societies kept alive the hopes for liberty and independence from foreign rule in the period after 1815. The most important of these societies was the Carbonari, which had clubs in every state in Italy. In 1820 the Carbonari, its members drawn largely from the middle class and the army, enjoyed a few months of triumph in the Kingdom of the Two Sicilies. Supported by the army and militia, they forced King Ferdinand I to grant a constitution and a parliamentary government. But Metternich feared that the germ of revolution would spread to other countries. Supported by Prussia and Russia, Austria suppressed the constitutional government in Naples and another revolution that broke out in Piedmont. In both cases, Austria firmly fixed an absolute ruler on the throne.

A revolution also failed in Russia. During the Napoleonic wars and the occupation of France, Russian officers were introduced to French ideas. Contrasting French liberal ideas and ways with Russian autocracy, some officers resolved to change conditions in Russia. Like their Western counterparts, they organized secret societies and disseminated liberal ideas within Russia. When Alexander I died, these liberal officers struck. Their uprising in December 1825 was easily smashed by the new tsar, Nicholas I, and the leaders were severely punished.

The revolutions in Spain, Italy, and Russia were suppressed, but the Concert of Europe also suffered setbacks. Stimulated by the ideals of the French Revolution, the Greeks revolted against their Turkish rulers in 1821. Although the Turkish sultan was the legitimate ruler, Russia, France, and Britain aided the Greek revolutionaries, for they were Christians, while the Turks were Muslims; moreover, pro-Greek sentiments were very strong among educated western Europeans who had studied the literature and history of ancient Greece. To them the Greeks were struggling to regain the freedom of their ancient forebears. Not only the pressure of public opinion but fear of Russian motives led Britain to join in intervention. If Russia carried out its intention of aiding the Greeks on its own, no doubt the Russian bear would never release Greece from its hug. Britain could not permit this extension of Russian power in the eastern Mediterranean. Despite Metternich's objections, Britain, France, and Russia took joint action against the Turks, and in 1829, Greece gained its independence.

Revolutions, 1830–1832

After Napoleon's defeat, a Bourbon king, Louis XVIII (1814–1824), ascended the throne of France. Recognizing that the French people would not accept a return to the old order, Louis pursued a moderate course. Although his pseudoconstitution, the Charter, declared that the king's power rested on divine right, it also stipulated that citizens possessed fundamental rights— freedom of thought and religion and equal treatment under the law—and it set up a two-house parliament. But peasants, urban workers, and most bourgeois could not meet the property requirements for voting. Louis XVIII was resisted by diehard aristocrats, called *ultras,* who wanted to erase the past twenty-five years of French history and restore the power and privileges of church and aristocracy. Their leader was the king's younger brother, the Comte d'Artois, who after Louis' death in 1824 ascended the throne as Charles X (1824– 1830).

The new government aroused the hostility of the bourgeoisie by indemnifying the émigrés for the property they had lost during the Revolution, by censoring the press, and by giving the church greater control over education. In the election of 1830, the liberal opposition to Charles X won a decisive victory. Charles responded with the July Ordinances, which dissolved the newly elected chamber; the Ordinances also deprived rich bourgeois of the vote and severely curtailed the press.

The bourgeois, students, and workers rebelled. They hoped to establish a republic, but the wealthy bourgeois who took control of their revolution feared republican radicalism. They offered the throne to the Duc d'Orléans; Charles X abdicated and went into exile in Britain. The new king, Louis Philippe (1830–1848), never forgot that he owed his throne to the rich bourgeois. And the Parisian workers who had fought for a republic and economic reforms to alleviate poverty felt betrayed by the outcome, as did the still-disenfranchised petty bourgeois.

The Revolution of 1830 in France set off shock waves in Belgium, Poland, and Italy. The Congress of Vienna had assigned Catholic Belgium to Protestant Holland; from the outset the Belgians had protested. Stirred by the events in Paris, Belgian patriots proclaimed their independence from Holland and established a liberal government. Inspired by the uprisings in France and Belgium, Polish students, intellectuals, and army officers took up arms against their

Honoré Daumier (1808–1879): The Uprising.   Daumier, caricaturist and painter, sided with his French compatriots against oppressive French regimes. He was imprisoned by Louis Philippe for a brief time in the 1830s because of his pictorial attacks against the government. Best known for his satirical lithographs of the society of his day, Daumier was also an early Impressionist painter. (*The Phillips Collection, Washington, D.C.*)

Russian overlords. The revolutionaries wanted to restore Polish independence, a dream that poets, musicians, and intellectuals had kept alive. Polish courage, however, was no match for Russian might, and Warsaw fell in 1831. The tsar took savage revenge on the revolutionaries. In 1831–32, the Austrians suppressed another insurrection by the Carbonari in the Papal States. During these uprisings the peasants gave the Carbonari little support; indeed, they seemed to side with the traditional rulers.

The Revolutions of 1848: France

Eighteen-forty-eight is often called *the year of revolution,* for throughout Europe, uprisings for political liberty and nationhood took place. The economic crisis of the previous two years aggravated discontent with the existing regimes, but "it was the absence of liberty," concludes historian Jacques Droz, "which . . . was most deeply resented by the peoples of Europe and led them to take up arms."

The February Revolution

An uprising in Paris set in motion the revolutionary tidal wave that was to engulf much of Europe in 1848. The Revolution of 1830 had broken the back of the ultras in France. There would be no going back to the Old Regime. But King Louis Philippe and his ministers, moderates by temperament and philosophy, had no intention of going forward to democracy.

The government of Louis Philippe was run by a small elite consisting of bourgeois bankers, merchants, and lawyers, and aristocrats who had abandoned the hope of restoring the Old Regime. This ruling elite championed the revolutionary ideas of equal treatment under the law and of careers open to talent, but feared democracy and blocked efforts to broaden the franchise (Only about 3 percent of adult French males were qualified to vote.) Radical republicans, or democrats, in opposition, wanted to abolish monarchy and grant all men the vote. The situation reached a climax in February 1848, when bourgeoisie, students, and workers took to the streets to demand reforms; this led to a violent confrontation with soldiers. Unable to pacify the enraged Parisians, Louis Philippe abdicated, and France became a republic.

The June Days: Revolution of the Oppressed

The new bourgeois leaders were committed to political democracy, but only a few favored the social reforms demanded by the laboring poor. A meager harvest in 1846 and an international financial crisis in 1847, which drastically curtailed French factory production, aggravated the misery of the working class. Workers who could find jobs labored twelve and fourteen hours a day under brutalizing conditions. In some districts, one out of three children died before the age of five, and everywhere in France, beggars, paupers, prostitutes, and criminals were evidence of the struggle to survive. Prevented by law from striking, unable to meet the financial requirements for voting, and afflicted with unemployment, the urban workers wanted relief.

The middle-class leaders of the new republic had little comprehension of or sympathy for the plight of these people. By occupation and wealth, the middle class considered itself to be apart from the working class. To the bourgeoisie, the workers were dangerous creatures, "the wild ones," "the vile mob." But the inhabitants of the urban slums could no longer be ignored. They felt, as Alexis de Tocqueville stated, "that all that is above them is incapable and unworthy of governing them; that the distribution of goods prevalent until now . . . is unjust; that property rests on a foundation which is not an equitable one."[1]

The new leaders gave all adult males the vote and abolished censorship; however, their attempts to ease the distress of the urban poor were insincere and halfhearted. The government limited the workday to ten hours, legalized labor unions, and established national workshops that provided food, medical benefits, and employment on public works projects. But to the workers, this was a feeble effort to deal with their monumental distress. To the property-owning peasantry and bourgeoisie, the national workshops were a hateful concession to socialist radicalism and a waste of government funds. When the government closed the workshops, working-class hostility and despair turned to open rebellion. Again barricades went up in the streets of Paris.

The June Revolution in Paris was a revolt against poverty and a cry for the redistribution of property. The workers stood alone. To the rest of the nation, they were barbarians attacking civilized society. Aristocrats, bourgeois, and peasants feared that no one's property would be safe if the revolution succeeded. From hundreds of miles away, Frenchmen flocked to Paris to crush what they considered to be the madness within their midst. After three days of vicious street fighting and atrocities on both sides, the army extinguished the revolt. Some 1,460 lives had been lost, including four generals. The June Days left deep scars on French society. For many years, workers would never forget that the rest of France had united against them; the rest of France would remain terrified of working-class radicalism.

In December 1848, the French people in overwhelming numbers elected Louis Napoleon, nephew of the great emperor, as president of the Second Republic. They were attracted by the magic of Louis Napoleon's name, and they expected him to prevent future working-class disorders. The election, in which all adult males could vote, demonstrated that most Frenchmen were socially conservative; they were unsympathetic to working-class poverty and deeply suspicious of socialist programs.

The Revolutions of 1848: Germany, Austria, and Italy

Like an epidemic, the fever of revolution that broke out in Paris in February raced across the Continent. Liberals, excluded from participation in political life, fought for parliaments and constitutions; many liberals were also nationalists who wanted unity or independence for their nations.

The German States: Liberalism Discredited

After the Congress of Vienna, Germany consisted of a loose confederation of thirty-nine independent states, of which Austria and Prussia were the most powerful. Jealous of the states' independence and determined to preserve their own absolute authority, the ruling princes detested liberal and nationalist ideals.

The German nationalism that had emerged during the French occupation gained in intensity during the restoration (the post-Napoleonic period), as intellectuals, inspired in part by the ideas of the romantics, insisted that Germans, who shared a common language and culture, should also be united politically. During the restoration, the struggle for German unity and liberal reforms continued to be waged primarily by students, professors, writers, lawyers, and other educated people. The great mass of people, knowing only loyalty to their local prince, remained unmoved by appeals for national unity.

The successful revolt against Louis Philippe, hostility against absolute princes, and the general economic crisis combined to produce uprisings in the capital cities of the German states in March 1848. Throughout Germany, liberals clamored for constitutions, parliamentary government, freedom of thought, and an end to police intimidation. Some called for the creation of a unified Germany governed by a national parliament and headed by a constitutional monarch. The poor of town and countryside, their plight worsened by the great depression of the 1840s, joined the struggle.

Terrified that these disturbances would lead to anarchy, the princes made concessions to the liberals whom they previously had censored, jailed, and exiled. During March and April 1848, the traditional rulers in Prussia and other German states replaced reactionary ministers with liberals, eased censorship, established jury systems, framed constitutions, formed parliaments, and ended peasant obligations to lords.

Liberals took advantage of their successes to form a national assembly charged with the task of creating a unified and liberal Germany. Representatives from all the German states attended the assembly, which met at Frankfurt. After many long debates, the Frankfurt Assembly approved a federation of German states. The German union would have a parliament and would be headed by the Prussian king. Austria, with its many non-German nationalities, would be excluded from the federal union. The deputies selected Frederick William as emperor of the new Germany, but the Prussian king refused; he would never wear a crown given to him by common people during a period of revolutionary agitation. While the delegates debated, the ruling princes recovered from the first shock of revolution and ordered their armies to crush the revolutionaries. One by one the liberal governments fell.

German liberalism had failed to unite Germany or to create a constitutional government dominated by the middle class. Liberalism, never securely rooted in Germany, was discredited. In the following decades, many Germans, identifying liberalism with failure, abandoned liberal values and turned to authoritarian Prussia for leadership in the struggle for unification. The fact that authoritarians hostile to the spirit of parliamentary government eventually united Germany had deep implications for future German and European history.

Austria: Hapsburg Dominance

The Hapsburg (Austrian) Empire, the product of dynastic marriage and inheritance, had no common nationality or language; it was held together only by the reigning Hapsburg dynasty, its army, and its bureaucracy. The ethnic composition of the empire was enormously complex. The Germans dominated; concentrated principally in Austria, they constituted about 25 percent of the empire's population. The Magyars predominated in the Hungarian lands of the empire. The great bulk of the population consisted of Slavs— Czechs, Poles, Slovaks, Slovenes, Croats, Serbs, Ruthenians. In addition, there were Italians in northern Italy and Rumanians in Transylvania. The Hapsburg dynasty, aided by the army and the German-dominated civil service, prevented the multinational empire from collapsing into anarchy.

Metternich, it is often said, suffered from a "dissolution complex": he understood that the new forces of nationalism and liberalism could break up the Austrian Empire. Liberal ideas could lead Hapsburg subjects to challenge the authority of the emperor, and nationalist feelings could cause the different peoples of the empire to rebel against German domination and Hapsburg rule. To keep these ideas from infecting Austrian subjects, Metternich's police imposed strict censorship, spied on professors, and expelled from the universities students caught reading forbidden books. Despite Metternich's political police, the universities still remained hotbeds of liberalism.

In 1848, revolutions spread throughout the Austrian Empire, starting in Vienna. Aroused by the abdication of Louis Philippe, Viennese liberals denounced Hapsburg absolutism and demanded a constitution, relaxation of censorship, and restrictions on the police. Intimidated by the revolutionaries, the government allowed freedom of the press, accepted Metternich's resignation, and promised a constitution. The Constitutional Assembly was convened and in August voted the abolition of serfdom. At the same time that the Viennese insurgents were tasting the heady wine of reform, revolts in other parts of the empire—Bohemia, Hungary, and northern Italy—added to the distress of the monarchy.

But the revolutionaries' victory was only temporary, and the defeat of the old order only illusory; the Hapsburg government soon began to recover its balance. The first government victory came with the crushing of the Czechs in Bohemia. In 1848, Czech nationalists wanted the Austrian Empire reconstructed along federal lines that would give the Czechs equal standing with Germans. General Windischgrätz bombarded Prague, the capital of Bohemia, into submission and re-established Hapsburg authority.

In October 1848, the Hapsburg authorities ordered the army to bombard Vienna. Against the regular army, the courageous but disorganized and divided students and workers had little hope. In March 1849, the Hapsburg rulers replaced the liberal constitution drafted by the popularly elected Constitutional Assembly with a more conservative one drawn up by its own ministers.

The most serious threat to the Hapsburg realm came from the Magyars in Hungary. Some 12 million people lived in Hungary, 5 million of whom were Magyars. The other nationalities consisted of South Slavs (Croats and Serbs) and Rumanians. Louis Kossuth (1802–1894), a member of the lower nobility, called for both social reform and a deepening of national consciousness in Hungary. Led by Kossuth, the Magyars demanded local autonomy. Hungary would remain within the Hapsburg Empire, but would have its own constitution and national army and would control its own finances. The Hungarian leadership introduced liberal reforms—suffrage for all males who could speak Magyar and owned some property, freedom of religion, freedom of the press, the termination of serfdom, and the end of the privileges of nobles and church. Within a few weeks, the Hungarian parliament changed Hungary from a feudal to a modern liberal state.

But the Hungarian leaders' nationalist dreams towered above their liberal ideals. The Magyars intended to incorporate lands inhabited by Serbs, Slovaks, and Rumanians into their kingdom and transform these people, whom they regarded as inferiors, into Hungarians. In the spring of 1849, the Hungarians renounced their allegiance to the Hapsburgs and proclaimed Hungary an independent state, with Kossuth as president.

The Hapsburg rulers took advantage of such ethnic animosities inside and outside Hungary. They encouraged Rumanians and South Slavs to resist the new Hungarian government. When Hapsburg forces moved against the Magyars, they were joined by an army of South Slavs whose nationalist aspirations had been flouted by the Hungarians. The recently ascended Hapsburg emperor, Francis Joseph, also appealed to Tsar Nicholas I for help. The tsar complied, fearing that a successful revolt by the Hungarians might lead the Poles to rise up against their Russian overlords. The Hungarians fought with extraordinary courage but were overcome by superior might.

Italy: *Continued Fragmentation*

Italian nationalists, eager to end the humiliation of Hapsburg occupation and domination and to unite the disparate states into a unified and liberal nation, rose in rebellion in 1848. Revolution broke out in Sicily six weeks before the February Revolution in Paris. Bowing to the revolutionaries' demands, King Ferdinand II of Naples granted a liberal constitution. The Grand Duke of Tuscany, King Charles Albert of Piedmont-Sardinia, and Pope Pius IX, ruler of the Papal States, also felt compelled to introduce liberal reforms.

Then the revolution spread to the Hapsburg lands in the north. After "Five Glorious Days" (March 18–22) of street fighting, the citizens of Milan forced the Austrians to withdraw. The people had liberated their city. On March 22, the citizens of Venice declared their city free of Austria and set up a republic. King Charles Albert, who hoped to acquire Lombardy and Venetia, declared war on Austria. Intimidated by the insurrections, the ruling princes of the Italian states and Hapsburg Austria had lost the first round.

But soon everywhere in Italy the forces of reaction recovered and reasserted their authority. The Austrians defeated the Sardinians and reoccupied Milan, and Ferdinand II crushed the revolutionaries in the south. Revolutionary disorders in Rome had forced Pope Pius IX to flee in November 1848; in February 1849 the revolutionaries proclaimed Rome "a pure democracy with the glorious title of the Roman Republic." Heeding the pope's call for assistance, Louis Napoleon attacked Rome, destroyed the infant republic, and allowed Pope Pius to return. The last city to fall to the reactionaries was Venice, which the

Austrians subjected to a merciless bombardment. Italy was still a fragmented nation.

The Revolutions of 1848: An Assessment

The revolutions of 1848 began with much promise, but they all ended in defeat. The revolutionaries' initial success was due less to their strength than to the governments' hesitancy to use their superior force. The reactionary leaders of Europe overcame their paralysis, however, and moved decisively to smash the revolutions. The courage of the revolutionaries was no match for regular armies. Thousands were killed and imprisoned; many fled to America.

Class divisions weakened the revolutionaries. The union between middle-class liberals and workers, which brought success in the opening stages of the revolutions, was only temporary. Bourgeois liberals favoring political reforms—constitution, parliament, and protection of basic rights—grew fearful of the laboring poor, who demanded social reforms—jobs and bread. To the bourgeois, the workers were an uneducated mob driven by dark instincts. When the working class engaged in revolutionary action, a terrified middle class deserted the cause of revolution or joined the old elites in subduing the workers.

Intractable nationalist animosities helped to destroy all the revolutionary movements against absolutism in central Europe. In many cases the different nationalities hated each other more than they hated the reactionary rulers. Hungarian revolutionaries dismissed the nationalist yearnings of the South Slavs and Rumanians living in Hungary, who in turn helped the Hapsburg dynasty to extinguish the nascent Hungarian state. The Germans of Bohemia resisted Czech demands for self-government and the equality of the Czech language with German. When German liberals at the Frankfurt Assembly debated the boundary lines of a united Germany, the problem of Prussia's Polish territories emerged. In 1848, Polish patriots wanted to re-create the Polish nation, but German delegates at the convention by an overwhelming majority opposed returning the Polish lands seized by Prussia in the late eighteenth century.

Before 1848, democratic idealists envisioned the birth of a new Europe of free people and liberated nations. The revolutions in central Europe showed that nationalism and liberalism were not natural allies, that nationalists were often indifferent to the rights of other peoples. Disheartened by these nationalist antagonisms, John Stuart Mill, the English liberal statesman and philosopher, lamented that "the sentiment of nationality so far outweighs the love of liberty that the people are willing to abet their rulers in crushing the liberty and independence of any people not of their race or language."[2]

The liberal and nationalist aims of the revolutionaries were not realized, but liberal gains were not insignificant. All French men obtained the right to vote; the labor services of peasants were abolished in Austria and the German states; parliaments, dominated to be sure by princes and aristocrats, were established in Prussia and other German states. In the decades to come, liberal reforms would become more widespread. These reforms would be introduced peacefully, for the failure of the Revolutions of 1848 convinced many people, including liberals, that popular uprisings were ineffective ways of changing society. The Age of Revolution initiated by the French Revolution of 1789 had ended.

The Unification of Italy

In 1848, liberals had failed to drive the Austrians out of Italy and to unite the Italian nation. By 1870, however, Italian unification had been achieved. The success of Italian unification was due to the efforts of three men—Mazzini, Cavour, and Garibaldi.

Giuseppe Mazzini (1805–1872) dedicated his life to the creation of a united and republican Italy—a goal he pursued with extraordinary moral intensity and determination. Mazzini was both a romantic and a liberal. As a liberal, he fought for republican and constitutional government and held that national unity would enhance individual liberty. As a romantic, he believed that an awakened Italy would lead to the regeneration of humanity. Just as Rome had provided law and unity in the ancient world, and the Roman pope had led Latin Christendom during the Middle Ages, Mazzini believed that a third Rome, a newly united Italy, would usher in a new age of free nations, personal liberty, and equality.

Mazzini had great charisma, determination, courage, and eloquence; he was also a prolific writer. His idealism attracted the intelligentsia and youth and kept alive the spirit of national unity. He infused the *Risorgimento,* the movement for Italian unity, with spiritual intensity. After his release from prison for participating in the insurrection of 1831, Mazzini went into exile and founded a new organization—Young Italy. Consisting of dedicated revolutionaries, many of them students, Young Italy was intended to serve as the instrument for the awakening of Italy and the transformation of Europe into a brotherhood of free peoples. Mazzini believed that a successful revolution must come from below—from the people, moved by a profound love for their nation. They must overthrow the Hapsburg princes and create a democratic republic.

Cavour and Victory over Austria

The failure of the Revolution of 1848 contained an obvious lesson: Mazzini's approach—an armed uprising by aroused masses—did not work. The reasons for failure were that the masses were not deeply committed to the nationalist cause, and that the revolutionaries were no match for the Austrian army. Italian nationalists now hoped that the Kingdom of Piedmont-Sardinia, ruled by an Italian dynasty, would expel the Austrians and lead the drive for unity. Count Camillo Benso di Cavour (1810–1861), the chief minister of Piedmont-Sardinia, became the architect of Italian unity.

Cavour, unlike Mazzini, was neither a dreamer nor a speechmaker but a tough-minded practitioner of *Realpolitik,* "the politics of reality." Focusing on the world as it actually was, he dismissed ideals as illusions. A cautious and practical politician, Cavour realized that mass uprisings could not succeed against Austrian might. Moreover, mistrusting the common people, he did not approve of Mazzini's goal of a democratic republic. Cavour had no precise blueprint for unifying Italy. His immediate aim was to increase the territory of Piedmont by driving the Austrians from northern Italy and incorporating Lombardy and Venetia into Piedmont-Sardinia.

To improve Piedmont's image in foreign affairs, Cavour launched a reform program to strengthen the economy. He reorganized the currency, taxes, and the national debt; in addition, he had railways and steamships built, fostered improved agricultural methods, and encouraged new businesses. Within a few years, Piedmont had become a progressive modern state.

In 1855, Piedmont joined England and France in the Crimean War against Russia. Cavour had no quarrel with Russia, but sought the friendship of Britain and France and a chance to be heard in world affairs. At the peace conference, Cavour was granted an opportunity to denounce Austria for occupying Italian lands. He soon found a supporter in Napoleon III (1852–1870), the French emperor, who hoped that a unified northern Italy would become an ally and client of France.

In 1858, Cavour and Napoleon III reached an agreement. If Austria attacked Piedmont, France would aid the Italian state. Piedmont would annex Lombardy and Venetia and parts of the Papal States. For its assistance, France would obtain Nice and Savoy from Piedmont. With this agreement in his pocket, Cavour cleverly maneuvered Austria into declaring war, for it had to appear that Austria was the aggressor.

Supported by French forces and taking advantage of poor Austrian planning, Piedmont conquered Lombardy and occupied Milan. But Napoleon III quickly had second thoughts. If Piedmont took any of the pope's territory, French Catholics would blame their own leader. Even more serious was the fear that Prussia, suspicious of French arms, would aid Austria. For these reasons Napoleon III, without consulting Cavour, signed an armistice with Austria. Piedmont would acquire Lombardy, but no more. An outraged Cavour demanded that his state continue the war until all northern Italy was liberated, but King Victor Emmanuel of Piedmont accepted the Austrian peace terms. The Piedmont-Sardinian victory, however, proved greater than Cavour had anticipated. During the conflict, patriots in Parma, Modena, Tuscany, and Romagna (one of the Papal States) had seized power. These new revolutionary governments voted to join with Piedmont.

Garibaldi and Victory in the South

Piedmont's success spurred revolutionary activity in the Kingdom of the Two Sicilies. In the spring of 1860, some one thousand red-shirted adventurers and patriots led by Giuseppe Garibaldi (1807–1882) landed in Sicily, determined

Victor Emmanuel and Garibaldi at the Bridge of Teano, 1860. The unification of Italy was the work of the romantic liberal Giuseppe Mazzini, the practical politician Count Cavour, and the seasoned revolutionary Giuseppe Garibaldi. Selflessly, Garibaldi turned over his conquests in the south to Victor Emmanuel in 1861. (*Scala/Art Resource*)

to liberate the land from its Bourbon ruler. After the liberation of Sicily in 1860, Garibaldi invaded the mainland. He occupied Naples without a fight and prepared to advance on Rome. Cavour feared that an assault on Rome by Garibaldi would lead to French intervention. Napoleon III had pledged to defend the pope's lands, and a French garrison had been stationed in Rome since 1849.

Moreover, Cavour considered Garibaldi too impulsive and rash, too attracted to republican ideals, too popular, to lead the struggle for unification. Garibaldi held exceptional views for his day. He supported the liberation of all subject nationalities, female emancipation, the right of workers to organize, racial equality, and the abolition of capital punishment. But the cause of Italian national unity was his true religion.

Cavour persuaded Napoleon III to approve an invasion of the Papal States by Piedmont to head off Garibaldi. A papal force offered only token opposition, and the Papal States of Umbria and the Marches soon voted for union with Piedmont, as did Naples and Sicily. Refusing to trade on his prestige with the masses to fulfill personal ambition, Garibaldi turned over his conquests to the Sardinian king, Victor Emmanuel, who was declared king of Italy in 1861.

Italian Unification Completed

Two regions still remained outside the control of the new Italy: the city of Rome, ruled by the pope and protected by French troops; and Venetia, occupied by Austria. Cavour died in 1861, but the march toward unification continued. During the conflict between Prussia and Austria in 1866, Italy sided with the victorious Prussians and was rewarded with Venetia. During the Franco-Prussian War of 1870, France withdrew its garrisons from Rome; much to the anger of the pope, Italian troops marched in, and Rome was declared the capital of Italy.

The Unification of Germany

In 1848, German liberals and nationalists, believing in the strength of their ideals, had naively underestimated the power of the conservative old order. After the failed revolution, some disenchanted revolutionaries retained only a halfhearted commitment to liberalism or embraced conservatism; others fled the country, weakening the liberal leadership. All liberals came to doubt the effectiveness of revolution as a way to transform Germany into a unified state; all gained a new respect for the realities of power. Abandoning idealism for realism, liberals now thought that German unity would be achieved through Prussian arms, not liberal ideals.

Prussia, Agent of Unification

During the late seventeenth and eighteenth centuries, Prussian kings had fashioned a rigorously trained and disciplined army. The state bureaucracy, often staffed by ex-soldiers, perpetuated the military mentality. As the chief organizations in the state, the army and the bureaucracy drilled into the Prussian people a respect for discipline and authority.

The Prussian throne was supported by the Junkers; these powerful aristocrats, who owned vast estates farmed by serfs, were exempt from most taxes, and dominated local government in their territories. The Junkers' commanding position made them officers in the royal army, diplomats, and leading officials in the state bureaucracy. The Junkers knew that a weakening of the king's power would lead to the loss of their own aristocratic prerogatives.

In late-eighteenth-century France, a powerful and politically conscious middle class had challenged aristocratic privileges. The Prussian monarchy and the Junkers had faced no such challenge, for the Prussian middle class at that time

Map 13.2   Unification of Germany, 1866–1871

was small and without influence. The idea of the rights of the individual did not deeply penetrate Prussian consciousness nor undermine the Prussian tradition of obedience to military and state authority. Liberalism did not take firm root in Germany.

In 1834, under Prussian leadership, the German states, with the notable exception of Austria, established the *Zollverein*, a customs union that abolished tariffs between the states. The customs union stimulated economic activity and promoted a desire for greater unity. The Zollverein led many Germans to view Prussia, not Austria, as the leader of the unification movement.

Bismarck and the Road to Unity

Austria was the principal barrier to the extension of Prussian power in Germany. This was one reason why Frederick William I (1861–1888) called for a drastic reorganization of the Prussian army. But the liberals in the lower chamber of the Prussian parliament blocked passage of the army reforms, for they feared that the reforms would greatly increase the power of the monarchy and the military establishment. Unable to secure passage, William withdrew the reform bill and asked the lower chamber for additional funds to cover government expenses. When parliament granted these funds, he used the money to institute the army reforms. Learning from its mistake, the lower chamber would not approve the new budget in 1862 without an itemized breakdown. If the liberals won this conflict between the liberal majority in the lower chamber and the crown, they would, in effect, establish parliamentary control over the king and the army.

At this critical hour, King William asked Otto von Bismarck (1815–1898) to lead the battle against parliament. Descended on his father's side from an old aristocratic family, Bismarck was a staunch supporter of the Prussian monarchy and the Junker class and a devout patriot. He yearned to increase the territory and prestige of his beloved Prussia and to protect the authority of the Prussian king who, Bismarck believed, ruled by the grace of God. Like Cavour, Bismarck was a shrewd and calculating practitioner of realpolitik.

Liberals were outraged by his domineering and authoritarian manner and his determination to preserve monarchical power and the aristocratic order. Set on continuing the reorganization of the army and not bowing to parliamentary pressure, Bismarck ordered the collection of taxes without parliament's approval—an action that would have been unthinkable in Britain or the United States. He dismissed the lower chamber, imposed strict censorship on the press, arrested outspoken liberals, and fired liberals from the civil service. The liberals protested against these arbitrary and unconstitutional moves. What led to a resolution of the conflict was Bismarck's extraordinary success in foreign affairs.

Wars with Denmark and Austria   To Bismarck, a war between Austria and Prussia seemed inevitable, for only by removing Austria from German affairs could Prussia extend its dominion over the other German states. Bismarck's first move, however, was not against Austria but against Denmark in 1864 over the disputed duchies of Schleswig and Holstein. Austria joined as Prussia's ally, because it hoped to prevent Prussia's annexing the territories. After Denmark's defeat, Austria and Prussia quarrelled over the ultimate disposition of the territory. Bismarck used the dispute to goad Austria into war. The Austrians, on their side, held that Prussia must be defeated for Austria to retain its influence over German affairs.

In 1866, with astonishing speed, Prussia assembled its forces and overran Austrian territory. At the battle of Sadowa (or Königgrätz), Prussia decisively defeated the main Austrian forces and the Seven Weeks' War ended. Prussia took no territory from Austria, but the latter agreed to Prussia's annexation of Schleswig and Holstein and a number of small German states. And Prussia organized a Confederation of North German States from which Austria was excluded. In effect, Austria was removed from German affairs, and Prussia became the dominant power in Germany.

The Triumph of Nationalism and Conservatism over Liberalism   The Prussian victory had a profound impact on political life within Prussia. Bismarck was the man of the hour, the great hero who had extended Prussia's power. Most liberals forgave Bismarck for his authoritarian handling of parliament. The liberal press that had previously denounced Bismarck for running roughshod over the constitution embraced him as a hero. Prussians were urged to concentrate on the glorious tasks ahead and to put aside the constitutional struggle, which in contrast appeared petty and insignificant.

Bismarck recognized the great appeal of nationalism and used it to expand Prussia's power over other German states and to strengthen Prussia's voice in European affairs. By heralding his state as the champion of unification, Bismarck gained the support of nationalists throughout Germany. In the past, the nationalist cause had been the property of liberals, but Bismarck appropriated it to promote Prussian expansion and conservative rule.

Prussia's victory over Austria, therefore, was a triumph for conservatism and nationalism and a defeat for liberalism. The liberal struggle for constitutional government in Prussia collapsed. The Prussian monarch retained the right to override parliamentary opposition and act on his own initiative. In 1848, Prussian might had suppressed a liberal revolution; in 1866, liberals beguiled by Bismarck's military triumphs gave up the struggle for responsible parliamentary government. They had traded political freedom for Prussian military glory and power.

The capitulation of Prussian liberals demonstrated the essential weakness of the German liberal tradition. German liberals displayed a diminishing commitment to the principles of parliamentary government, and a growing fascination with force, military triumph, and territorial expansion. Enthralled by Bismarck's achievement, many liberals abandoned liberalism and threw their support behind the authoritarian Prussian state. And Germans of all classes acquired an adoration for Prussian militarism and for the power-state, with its Machiavellian guideline that all means are justified if they result in the expansion of German power. In 1848, German liberals had called for "Unity and Freedom." What Bismarck gave them was unity and authoritarianism.

War with France   Prussia emerged from the war with Austria as the leading power in the North German Confederation; the Prussian king controlled the armies and foreign affairs of the states within the confederation. To complete the unification of Germany, Bismarck would have to draw the South German states into the new German confederation. But the South German states, Catholic and hostile to Prussian authoritarianism, feared being absorbed by Prussia.

Bismarck hoped that a war between Prussia and France would ignite the

Otto von Bismarck and William II, 1888.   Between 1862 and 1871, Bismarck worked tirelessly to unite Germany under the Prussian monarchy. Bismarck's wars against Denmark, Austria, and France led to the unification of Germany and earned him the admiration of the German people. (*Bildarchiv Preussischer Kulturbesitz*)

nationalist feelings of the South Germans, causing them to overlook the differences that separated them from Prussia. If war with France would serve Bismarck's purpose, it was also not unthinkable to Napoleon III, the emperor of France. The creation of a powerful North German Confederation had frightened the French, and the prospect that the South German states might one day add their strength to the new Germany was terrifying. Both France and Prussia had parties who advocated war.

A cause for war arose over the succession to the vacated Spanish throne. King William of Prussia discussed the issue with the French ambassador and sent Bismarck a telegram informing him of what had ensued. With the support of high military leaders, Bismarck edited the telegram. The revised version gave the impression that the Prussian king and the French ambassador had insulted each other. Bismarck wanted to inflame French feeling against Prussia and arouse German opinion against France. He succeeded. In both Paris and Berlin, crowds of people, gripped by war fever, demanded satisfaction. When

France declared a general mobilization, Prussia followed suit; Bismarck had his war.

The South German states, as Bismarck had anticipated, came to the aid of Prussia. Quickly and decisively routing the French forces and capturing Napoleon III, the Prussians went on to besiege Paris. Faced with starvation, Paris surrendered in January 1871. France was compelled to pay a large indemnity and to cede to Germany the border provinces of Alsace and Lorraine—a loss that French patriots could never accept.

The Franco-Prussian War completed the unification of Germany. On January 18, 1871, at Versailles, the German princes granted the title of German Kaiser (emperor) to William I. A powerful nation had arisen in central Europe. Its people were educated, disciplined, and efficient; its industries and commerce were rapidly expanding; its army was the finest in Europe. Vigorous, confident, and intensely nationalistic, the new German Empire would be eager to play a greater role in world affairs. No nation in Europe was a match for the new Germany. Metternich's fears had been realized—a Germany dominated by Prussia had upset the balance of power. The unification of Germany created fears, tensions, and rivalries that would culminate in world war.

Nationality Problems in the Hapsburg Empire

In Italy and Germany, nationalism had led to the creation of unified states; in Austria, nationalism eventually caused the destruction of the centuries-old Hapsburg dynasty. A mosaic of different nationalities, each with its own history and traditions, the Austrian Empire could not survive in an age of intense nationalism. The Austrian Empire had to weld together and reconcile antagonistic nationalities when nationalistic consciousness was high. The empire's collapse in the final stages of World War I marked the end of years of antagonism between its different peoples.

In the first half of the nineteenth century, the Germans, constituting less than one-quarter of the population, were the dominant national group in the empire. But Magyars, Poles, Czechs, Slovaks, Croats, Rumanians, Ruthenians, and Italians were experiencing national self-awareness. Poets and writers who had been educated in Latin, French, and German began to write in their mother tongues and extol their splendor. By searching their past for glorious ancestors and glorious deeds, writers kindled pride in their native history and folklore and aroused anger against past and present injustices.

In 1848–49 the Hapsburg monarchy had extinguished the Magyar bid for independence, the Czech revolution in Prague, and the uprisings in the Italian provinces of Lombardy and Venetia. Gravely frightened by these revolutions, the Austrian power structure resolved to resist pressures for political rights by strengthening autocracy and tightening the central bureaucracy. German and Germanized officials took over administrative and judicial duties formerly handled on a local level. An expanded secret police stifled liberal and nationalist expressions. The various nationalities, of course, resented these efforts at centralization and repression.

The defeats by France and Piedmont in 1859 and by Prussia in 1866 cost Austria its two Italian provinces. The defeat by Prussia also forced the Hapsburg monarchy to make concessions to the Magyars, the strongest of the non-German nationalities; without a loyal Hungary, the Hapsburg monarchy could suffer other humiliations. The Settlement of 1867 split the Hapsburg territories into Austria and Hungary. The two countries retained a common ruler, Francis Joseph (1848–1916), who was emperor of Austria and king of Hungary. Hungary gained complete control over its internal affairs—the administration of justice and education. Foreign and military affairs and common financial concerns were conducted by a ministry consisting of delegates from both lands.

With the Settlement of 1867, Magyars and Germans became the dominant nationalities in the empire. The other nationalities felt that the German-Magyar political, economic, and cultural domination blocked their own national aspirations. Nationality struggles in the half-century following the Settlement of 1867 consumed the energies of the Austrians and Hungarians. In both lands, however, the leaders failed to solve the minority problems, a failure that ultimately led to the dissolution of the empire during the last weeks of World War I.

The Rise of Racial Nationalism

In the first half of the nineteenth century, nationalism and liberalism went hand in hand. Liberals sought both the rights of the individual and national independence and unification. Liberal nationalists believed that a unified state free of foreign subjugation was in harmony with the principle of natural rights, and they insisted that love of country led to love of humanity. As nationalism grew more extreme, however, its profound difference from liberalism became more apparent. The extreme nationalism of the late nineteenth and early twentieth centuries was the seedbed of totalitarian nationalism. It contributed to World War I and to the rise of fascism after the war.

Concerned exclusively with the greatness of the nation, extreme nationalists rejected the liberal emphasis on political liberty. They regarded liberty as an obstacle to national power and maintained that authoritarian leadership was needed to meet national emergencies. The needs of the nation, they said, transcended the rights of the individual. Extreme nationalists also rejected the liberal ideal of equality. Placing the nation above everything, nationalists became increasingly intolerant of minorities within the nation's borders and hateful of other peoples. In the name of national power and unity, they persecuted minorities at home and stirred up hatred against other nations. In the pursuit of national power, nationalists increasingly embraced militaristic, imperialistic, and racist doctrines. At the founding of the Nationalist Association in Italy in 1910, one leader declared: "Just as socialism teaches the proletariat the value of class struggle, so we must teach Italy the value of international struggle. But international struggle is war? Well, then, let there be war! And nationalism will arouse the will for a victorious war, . . . the only way to national redemption."[3]

Interpreting politics with the logic of emotions, extreme nationalists insisted that they had a sacred mission to regain lands once held in the Middle Ages, to unite with their kinfolk in other lands, or to rule over peoples considered inferior. Loyalty to the nation-state was elevated above all other allegiances. The ethnic state became an object of religious reverence; the spiritual energies that formerly had been dedicated to Christianity were now channeled into the worship of the nation-state.

By the beginning of the twentieth century, conservatives had become the staunchest advocates of nationalism, and the nationalism preached by conservative extremists was stripped of Mazzinian ideals of liberty, equality, and the fellowship of nations. Landholding aristocrats, generals, and clergy, often joined by big industrialists, saw nationalism as a convenient instrument for gaining a mass following in their struggle against democracy and socialism. Championing popular nationalist myths and dreams, a newly radicalized right hoped to harness the instinctual energies of the masses, particularly the peasants and the lower middle class—shopkeepers, civil servants, white-collar workers—to conservative causes. Peasants viewed liberalism and socialism as threats to traditional values, while the lower bourgeoisie feared the proletariat. These people were receptive to the rhetoric of ultranationalists who denounced democracy and socialism as threats to national unity and Jews as aliens who endangered the nation.

Volkish Thought

Extreme nationalism was a general European phenomenon, but it was especially dangerous in Germany. Bismarck's triumphs lured Germans into a dreamworld. Many started to yearn for the extension of German power throughout the world. The past, they said, belonged to France and Britain; the future, to Germany.

The most ominous expression of German nationalism (and a clear example of mythical thinking) was *Volkish* thought. (*Volk* means "folk" or "people.") German Volkish thinkers sought to bind together the German people through a deep love of their language, traditions, and fatherland. These thinkers felt that Germans were animated by a higher spirit than that found in other peoples. To Volkish thinkers, the Enlightenment and parliamentary democracy were foreign ideas that corrupted the pure German spirit. With fanatical devotion, Volkish thinkers embraced all things German—the medieval past, the German landscape, the simple peasant, the village—and denounced the liberal-humanist tradition of the West as alien to the German soul.

Volkish thought attracted Germans frightened by all the complexities of the modern age—industrialization, urbanization, materialism, class conflicts, alienation. Seeing their beloved Germany transformed by these forces of modernity, Volkish thinkers yearned to restore the sense of community that they attributed to the preindustrial age. Only by identifying with their sacred soil and sacred traditions could modern Germans escape from the evils of industrial society. Only then could the different classes band together in an organic unity.

The Volkish movement had little support from the working class, which was concerned chiefly with improving its standard of living. It appealed mainly to farmers and villagers who regarded the industrial city as a threat to native values and a catalyst for foreign ideas; to artisans and small shopkeepers threatened by big business; and to scholars, writers, teachers, and students, who saw in Volkish nationalism a cause worthy of their idealism. The schools were leading agents for the dissemination of Volkish ideas.

Volkish thinkers glorified the ancient Germanic tribes that overran the Roman Empire; they contrasted their courageous and vigorous German ancestors with the effete and degenerate Romans. A few tried to harmonize ancient Germanic religious traditions with Christianity. Such attitudes led Germans to see themselves as a heroic people fundamentally different from and better than the English and French. It also led them to regard German culture as unique— innately superior to and in opposition to the humanist outlook of the Enlightenment. Volkish thinkers, like their romantic predecessors, held that the German people and culture had a special destiny and a unique mission. They pitted the German soul against the Western intellect, feeling and spirit against a drab rationalism. To be sure, the Western humanist tradition still had its supporters in Germany, but the counterideology of Volkish thought was becoming increasingly widespread.

Volkish thinkers were especially attracted to racist doctrines. Racist thinkers held that race was the key to history, and that not only physical features but moral, esthetic, and intellectual qualities distinguished one race from another. In their view, a race demonstrated its vigor and achieved greatness when it preserved its purity; intermarriage between races was contamination that would result in genetic, cultural, and military decline. Like their Nazi successors, Volkish thinkers claimed that the German race was purer than and therefore superior to all other races. Its superiority was revealed in such physical characteristics as blond hair, blue eyes, and fair skin—all signs of inner qualities lacking in other races.

German racial nationalists insisted that as a superior race, Germans had a national right to dominate other peoples, particularly the "racially inferior" Slavs of the East: "The racial-biological ideology tells us that there are races that lead and races that follow. Political history is nothing but the history of struggles among the leading races. Conquests, above all, are always the work of the leading races. Such men can conquer, may conquer, and shall conquer."[4]

Anti-Semitism

German racial nationalists singled out Jews as the most wicked of races and a deadly enemy of the German people. Anti-Semitism, which was widespread in late-nineteenth-century Europe, provides a striking example of the perennial appeal, power, and danger of mythical thinking. Anti-Semitic organizations and political parties sought to deprive Jews of their civil rights, and anti-Semitic publications proliferated.

Edouard Drumont, a French journalist, held that the Jews, racially inferior and believers in a primitive religion, had gained control of France. Like medieval Christian anti-Semites, Drumont accused Jews of deicide and of using Christian blood for ritual purposes. Drumont's newspaper (founded with Jesuit funds) blamed all the ills of France on the Jews, called for their expulsion from the country, and predicted that they would be massacred.

In Rumania and Austria, Jews faced barriers in education and government. Rumania barred most Jews from holding office and from voting, imposed various economic restrictions on them, and restricted their admission into secondary schools and universities. The Rumanian government even financed an international congress of anti-Semites that met in Bucharest in 1886. In German-speaking Austria, Karl Lueger, a leader of the Christian Socialist party founded by conservative German nationalists, exploited anti-Semitism to win elections in overwhelmingly Catholic Vienna. Georg von Schönerer, founder of the German National party in Austria, wanted to eliminate Jews from all areas of public life.

Russia placed a quota on the number of Jewish students admitted to secondary schools and higher educational institutions, confined Jews to certain regions of the country, and, "to purify the sacred historic capital," expelled some 20,000 Jews from Moscow. Some government officials encouraged and even organized *pogroms* (mob violence) against Jews. Between 1903 and 1906, pogroms broke out in 690 towns and villages, most of them in the Ukraine, traditionally a hotbed of anti-Semitism. (Ukrainian folk songs and legends glorified centuries-old massacres of Jews.) The attackers looted, burned, raped, and murdered, generally with impunity. In Russia and several other lands, Jews were put on trial for slaughtering Christian children as part of a Passover ritual—a deranged accusation that survived from the Middle Ages.

Anti-Semitism had a long and bloodstained history in Europe, stemming both from an irrational fear and hatred of outsiders with noticeably different ways and from the commonly accepted myth that the Jews as a people were collectively and eternally cursed for rejecting Christ. Christians saw Jews as the murderers of Christ—an image that promoted terrible anger and hatred. Periodically mobs humiliated, tortured, and massacred Jews, and rulers expelled them from their kingdoms. Often barred from owning land and excluded from the craft guilds, medieval Jews concentrated in trade and moneylending—occupations that frequently earned them greater hostility. By the sixteenth century, Jews in a number of lands were forced by law to live in separate quarters of the town called *ghettos*. Medieval Christian anti-Semitism, which depicted the Jew as vile and Judaism as repulsive, fertilized the soil for modern anti-Semitism.

In the nineteenth century, under the aegis of the liberal ideals of the Enlightenment and the French Revolution, Jews gained legal equality in most Euro-

Anti-Semitism: Bodies of Jewish Fugitives, Shot While Crossing the Dniester Between the Ukraine and Rumania.   In Russia, some government officials at times encouraged and supported anti-Semitic outrages. (*Brown Brothers*)

pean lands. They could leave the ghetto and participate in many activities that had been closed to them. Traditionally an urban people, the Jews, who were concentrated in the leading cities of Europe, took advantage of this new freedom and opportunity. Motivated by the fierce desire of outsiders to prove their worth and aided by deeply embedded traditions that valued education and family life, many Jews achieved striking success as entrepreneurs, bankers, lawyers, journalists, doctors, scientists, scholars, and performers. For example, in 1880, Jews, who constituted about 10 percent of the Viennese population, accounted for 38.6 percent of the medical students and 23.3 percent of the law students in Vienna. Viennese cultural life before World War I was to a large extent shaped by Jewish writers, artists, musicians, critics, and patrons. All but one of the major banking houses were Jewish. But most European Jews— peasants, peddlers, and laborers—were quite poor. Perhaps 5,000 to 6,000 Jews of Galicia in Austria-Hungary died of starvation annually, and many Russian Jews fled to the United States to escape from desperate poverty.

Those Jews who were members of the commercial and professional classes, like other bourgeois, gravitated toward liberalism. Moreover, as victims of persecution, they naturally favored societies that were committed to the liberal ideals of legal equality, toleration, the rule of law, and equality of opportunity. As strong supporters of parliamentary government and the entire system of values associated with the Enlightenment, the Jews became targets for conservatives and Volkish thinkers who repudiated the humanist and cosmopolitan outlook of liberalism and professed a militant nationalism.

Anti-Semites blamed the Jews for all the social and economic ills caused by the rapid growth of industries and cities and for all the new ideas that were undermining the old order. Their anxieties and fears concentrated on the Jews, to whom they attributed everything they considered evil in the modern age, all that threatened the German Volk. The thought processes of Volkish anti-Semites demonstrate the mind's monumental capacity for irrational thinking.

In the Middle Ages, Jews had been persecuted and humiliated primarily for religious reasons. In the nineteenth century, national-racial considerations supplemented a traditional, biased Christian perception of Jews and Judaism. However, whereas Christian anti-Semites believed that through conversion, Jews could escape the curse of their religion, racial anti-Semites, who used the language of Social Darwinism, said that Jews were indelibly stained and eternally condemned by their genes (see Chapters 15 and 16). Their evil and worthlessness derived from inherited racial characteristics, which could not be altered by conversion.

The Jewish population of Germany was quite small: in 1900 it was only about 497,000, or 0.95 percent, of the total population of 50,626,000. Jews were proud of their many contributions to German economic and intellectual life (by the 1930s, 30 percent of the Nobel Prize winners in Germany were Jews); they considered themselves patriotic Germans and regarded Germany as an altogether desirable place to live—a place of refuge in comparison to Russia, where Jews lived in terrible poverty and suffered violent attacks.

German anti-Semitic organizations and political parties failed to get the state to pass anti-Semitic laws, and by the early 1900s these groups had declined in political power and importance. But the mischief had been done. In the minds of many Germans even in respectable circles, the image of the Jew as an evil and dangerous creature had been firmly planted. It was perpetuated by schools, youth groups, the Pan-German Association, and an array of racist pamphlets and books. Late-nineteenth-century racial anti-Semites had constructed an ideological foundation on which Hitler would later build his movement. In words that foreshadowed Hitler, Paul de Lagarde said of the Jews: "One does not have dealings with pests and parasites; one does not rear them and cherish them; one destroys them as speedily and thoroughly as possible."[5]

It is, of course, absurd to believe that a nation of 50 million was threatened by a half-million citizens of Jewish birth, or that the 11 million Jews of the world (by 1900) had organized to rule the planet. The Jewish birthrate in Germany was low, the rate of intermarriage high, and the desire for complete assimilation into German life great. Within a few generations the Jewish community in Germany might well have disappeared. Moreover, despite the paranoia of the anti-Semite, the German Jews and the Jews in the rest of Europe were quite powerless. There were scarcely any Jews in the ruling circles of governments, armies, civil services, or heavy industries. As events were to

Chronology 13.1 ✒ The Surge of Nationalism	
1821	Austria crushes revolts in Italy
1823	French troops crush revolt in Spain
1825	Uprising in Russia crushed by Nicholas I
1829	Greece gains its independence from Turkey
1830	The July Ordinances in France are followed by a revolution that forces Charles X to abdicate; Belgians declare their independence from Holland, establishing the liberal government
1831	The Polish revolution fails
1831–32	Austrian forces crush a revolution in Italy
1848	The year of revolution
1862	Bismarck becomes chancellor of Prussia
1864	Austria and Prussia defeat Denmark in a war over Schleswig-Holstein
1866	Seven Weeks' War between Austria and Prussia; Prussia emerges as the dominant power in Germany
1870–71	Franco-Prussian War; German unification completed
January 18, 1871	William I becomes German kaiser

prove, the Jews, who had no army or state and who dwelt among people many of whom despised them, were the weakest of peoples. But the race mystics, convinced that they were waging a war of self-defense against a satanic foe, were impervious to rational argument. Anti-Semites, said Theodor Mommsen, the great nineteenth-century German historian, would not listen to "logical and ethical arguments. . . . They listen only to their own envy and hatred, to the meanest instincts. Nothing else counts for them. They are deaf to reason, right, morals. One cannot influence them. . . . [Anti-Semitism] is a horrible epidemic, like cholera—one can neither explain nor cure it."[6]

Thus racial nationalists attacked and undermined the Enlightenment tradition. They denied equality, scorned toleration and cosmopolitanism, and made myth and superstition vital forces in political life. That many people believed these racial theories was an ominous sign for Western civilization. It showed how tenuous the rational tradition of the Enlightenment is, how receptive the mind is to dangerous myths, and how easily human behavior can degenerate into inhumanity.

Notes

1. *The Recollections of Alexis de Tocqueville,* trans. by Alexander Teixeira de Mattos (Cleveland: Meridian Books, 1969), pp. 11–12.
2. Quoted in Hans Kohn, *Nationalism: Its Meaning and History* (Princeton, N.J.: D. Van Nostrand, 1965), pp. 51–52.
3. Quoted in Edward R. Tannenbaum, *1900: The Generation Before the Great War* (Garden City, N.Y.: Doubleday, 1976), p. 337.

4. Quoted in Horst von Maltitz, *The Evolution of Hitler's Germany* (New York: McGraw-Hill, 1973), p. 33.
5. Quoted in Helmut Krausnick, et al., *Anatomy of the SS State,* trans. by Richard Barry, et al. (London: William Collins' Sons, 1968), p. 9.
6. Quoted in Peter G. J. Pulzer, *The Rise of Political Anti-Semitism in Germany and Austria* (New York: Wiley, 1964), p. 299.

Suggested Reading

Beales, Derek, *The Risorgimento and the Unification of Italy* (1971). A comprehensive overview followed by documents.

Droz, Jacques, *Europe Between Revolutions* (1967). A fine survey of the period 1815–1848.

Fasel, George, *Europe in Upheaval: The Revolutions of 1848* (1970). A good introduction.

Fejtö, François, ed., *The Opening of an Era: 1848* (1973). Contributions by nineteen eminent European historians.

Hibbert, Christopher, *Garibaldi and His Enemies* (1965). A vivid portrait of the Italian hero.

Holburn, Hajo, *A History of Modern Germany, 1840–1945* (1969). A standard reference work.

Katz, Jacob, *From Prejudice to Destruction* (1980). A survey of modern anti-Semitism; holds that modern anti-Semitism is an outgrowth of traditional Christian anti-Semitism.

Kohn, Hans, *Nationalism: Its Meaning and History* (1955). A concise history of modern nationalism by a leading student of the subject.

Langer, W. L., *Political and Social Upheaval, 1832–1852* (1969). Another volume in *The Rise of Modern Europe* series by its editor. Rich in data and interpretation; contains a valuable bibliographical essay.

Mosse, George L., *The Crisis of German Ideology* (1964). Explores the dark side of German nationalism; an excellent study of Volkish thought.

Pauley, B. F., *The Habsburg Legacy, 1867–1939* (1972). A good brief work on a complex subject.

Pulzer, Peter G. J., *The Rise of Political Anti-Semitism in Germany and Austria* (1964). Relationship of anti-Semitism to changing socioeconomic conditions; impact of anti-Semitism on politics.

Robertson, Priscilla, *Revolutions of 1848* (1960). Vividly portrays the events and the personalities involved.

Rodes, John E., *The Quest for Unity: Modern Germany, 1848–1970* (1971). A good survey of German history.

Stearns, Peter N., *1848: The Revolutionary Tide in Europe* (1974). Strong on social factors.

Talmon, J. L., *Romanticism and Revolt* (1967). The forces shaping European history from 1815 to 1848.

Review Questions

1. How did the Congress of Vienna violate the principle of nationalism? What was the principal accomplishment of the Congress?

2. Between 1820 and 1832, where were revolutions suppressed, and how? Where were revolutions successful, and why?
3. What were the complaints of the urban poor to the new French government after the February Revolution in 1848? What was the significance of the June Days in French history?
4. Why did the Revolutions of 1848 fail in the German states, the Austrian Empire, and Italy?
5. What were the liberal gains of the Revolutions of 1848? Why were liberals and nationalists disappointed with the results of the Revolutions of 1848?
6. Mazzini was the soul, Cavour the brains, and Garibaldi the sword in the struggle for the unification of Italy. Discuss their participation in and contributions to the struggle.
7. Prussia's victory over Austria was a triumph for conservatism and a defeat for liberalism. Discuss this statement.
8. What was the significance of the Franco-Prussian War for European history?
9. In the Hapsburg Empire, nationalism was a force for disunity. Discuss this statement.
10. Why is racial nationalism a repudiation of the Enlightenment tradition and a regression to mythical thinking?
11. Anti-Semites attributed to Jews everything that they found repellent in the modern world. Discuss this statement.

Chapter ✥ 14

The Industrial Revolution:
The Transformation of Society

In the last part of the eighteenth century, as a revolution for liberty and equality swept across France and sent shock waves across Europe, a different kind of revolution, a revolution in industry, was transforming life in Great Britain. In the nineteenth century the Industrial Revolution spread to the United States and to the European continent. Today, it encompasses virtually the entire world; everywhere the drive to substitute machines for human labor continues at a rapid pace.

After 1760, dramatic changes occurred in Britain in the way goods were produced and labor organized. New forms of power, particularly steam, replaced animal strength and human muscle. Better ways of obtaining and using raw materials were discovered, and a new form of organizing production and workers—the factory—came into common use. In the nineteenth century, technology moved from triumph to triumph with a momentum unprecedented in human history. The resulting explosion in economic production and productivity transformed society with breathtaking speed. ✥

The Rise of the Industrial Age
The Roots of Industrialization

The process of industrialization began in western Europe for a number of reasons. Western Europe was wealthier than much of the world, and its wealth was spread across more classes of people. Contributing to the accumulation of capital was the rapid expansion of trade, both overseas and on the Continent, during the sixteenth and seventeenth centuries (the Commercial Revolution).

This expansion resulted from an aggressive search for new markets and tapped the wealth of a much larger area of the world than the Mediterranean lands accessible to earlier generations. Thus the resources, both human and material, of the New World and of Africa fueled Europe's accumulation of wealth.

Engaged in fierce military and commercial rivalries, early modern states, with varying degrees of success, actively promoted industries to manufacture weaponry, uniforms, and ships, and encouraged commerce for tax revenues. The ensuing growth in commerce nurtured a greatly expanded economy in which many levels of society participated—great estate owners, merchant princes, innovative entrepreneurs, sugar plantation colonials, slave traders, sailors, and peasants.

The rise in population and agricultural productivity also helped spur industrialization. The enormous European population growth of the eighteenth century provided industry with both consumers and labor. The population expanded rapidly, partly because the number of deaths from war, famine, and disease declined. More efficient agriculture and better food distribution reduced malnutrition, which meant better health, more births, and fewer deaths. Developments in agriculture contributed greatly to the coming of the industrial age in Europe. Over the centuries, the decline of serfdom and manorial obligations and the increasing efficiency of agriculture freed people for new forms of labor. By the eighteenth century, traditional patterns of farming were breaking up in western Europe. Agriculture became more and more a capitalist enterprise; production was undertaken for the market, not for family or village consumption.

Land formerly used in common by villagers for grazing animals was claimed for private use. Usually the great landowners took advantage of their power or of the law and laid claim to these common lands. This process of *enclosure,* or fencing off formerly communal land for private use, took place over much of Europe. Once the peasants were gone, landlords could bring these lands under cultivation and produce a surplus for the marketplace. Consequently, land use grew more efficient. Through convertible husbandry, which cycled land from grain production through soil-restoring crops of legumes and then pasturage, farmers could keep all their fields in production rather than leave some fallow, as had been the practice for centuries.

Finally, two European cultural traditions played crucial roles in the rise of industrialism. One was individualism, which during the era of the Commercial Revolution produced hard-driving, ambitious merchants and bankers. This spirit of individualism, combined with the wide latitude states gave to private economic activity, fostered the development of dynamic capitalist entrepreneurs. A second cultural tradition promoting industrialization was the high value westerners gave to the rational understanding and control of nature. Both individualism and the tradition of reason, concludes historian David S. Landes, "gave Europe a tremendous advantage in the invention and adoption of new technology. The will to mastery, the rational approach to problems that we call scientific method, the competition for wealth and power—to-

Map 14.1   Industrial Growth in England, Mid-1800s

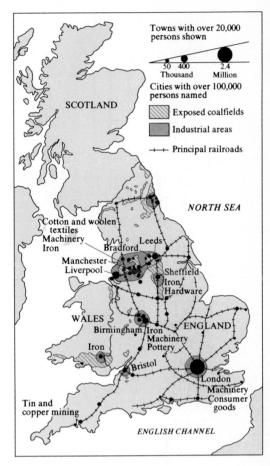

gether these broke down the resistance of inherited ways and made change a positive good."[1]

Britain First

Britain possessed several advantages that enabled it to take the lead. Large and easily developed supplies of coal and iron had given the British a long tradition of metallurgy and mining. In the early stages of industrialization, Britain's river transportation system was supplemented by canals and toll roads (turnpikes) that private entrepreneurs financed and built for profit. In addition, Britain had a labor pool of farmers who could no longer earn a living for themselves and their families on the land.

Britain had capital available for investment in new industries. These funds came from wealthy landowners and merchants who had grown rich through commerce, including the slave trade. Interest rates on loans fell in the eigh-

Woman at Hargreaves's Spinning Jenny. The textile trade was one of the first to be mechanized. In the cottage industries, farmers and their families were weavers and spinners—sometimes even inventors. (*Mary Evans Picture Library*)

teenth century, which served as a stimulus for investment. Britain's expanding middle class provided a home market for emerging industries; so too did its overseas colonies, which also provided raw materials, particularly cotton that was needed for the developing textile industry. A vigorous spirit of enterprise and the opportunity for men of ability to rise from common origins to riches and fame also help to explain the growth of industrialization.

Changes in Technology

The Cotton Industry   Long the home of an important wool trade, Britain in the eighteenth century jumped ahead in the production of cotton, the industry that first showed the possibility of unprecedented growth rates. British cotton production expanded tenfold between 1760 and 1785, and another tenfold between 1785 and 1825. A series of inventions revolutionized the industry and drastically altered the social conditions of the work.

In 1733, long before expansion started, a simple invention—John Kay's flying shuttle—made it possible for weavers to double their output. The flying shuttle enabled weavers to produce faster than spinners could spin until James

Hargreaves's spinning jenny, perfected by 1768, allowed an operator to work several spindles at once—powered only by human energy. Within five years, Richard Arkwright's water frame spinning machine could be powered by water or animals, and Samuel Crompton's spinning mule (1779) powered many spindles, first by human power, later by animal and water energy. These changes improved spinning productivity so much that bottlenecks in weaving developed until Edmund Cartwright developed a power loom in 1787.* To the end of the century there was a race to speed up the spinning part of the process and then the weaving part by applying water power to looms or new, larger devices to the jenny.

Arkwright's water frame made it more efficient to bring many workers together, rather than sending work out to individuals in their own homes. This development was the beginning of the factory system, which within a generation would revolutionize the conditions of labor. Because water power drove these early machines, mills were located near rivers and streams. Towns thus grew up where machinery could be powered by water; the factory system concentrated laborers and their families near the factories.

The Steam Engine   James Watt, a Scottish engineer, developed the steam engine in the 1760s. Because steam engines ran on coal or wood, not water power, they allowed greater flexibility in locating textile mills. Factories were no longer restricted to the power supplied by a river or a stream or to the space available beside flowing water; they could be built anywhere. With steam, the whole pattern of work changed, because weaker, younger, and less skilled workers could be taught the few simple tasks necessary to mind the machine. The shift from male to female and child labor was a major social change.

The Iron Industry   Although steam power made it possible to hire weaker people to operate machinery, it required machines made of stronger metal to withstand the forces generated by a stronger power source. By the 1780s, trial and error had perfected the production of wrought iron, which became the most widely used metal until steel began to be cheaply produced in the 1860s.

The iron industry made great demands on the coal mines to fuel its furnaces. Because steam engines enabled miners to pump water from the mines more efficiently and at a much deeper level, rich veins in existing mines became accessible for the first time. The greater productivity in coal allowed the continued improvement of iron smelting. Then, in 1856, Henry Bessemer developed a process for converting pig iron into steel by removing the impurities in the iron. In the 1860s, William Siemens and Pierre and Émile Martin (broth-

---

*Technological developments in America helped meet the growing demand for raw cotton. Eli Whitney's cotton gin (1793) removed the seeds from raw cotton quickly and cheaply, leading farmers and plantation owners to devote more land to cotton. Within a generation, more laborers were required for the fields and fewer to process the cotton. The increased demand for slave labor brought far-reaching repercussions.

ers) developed the open-hearth process, which could handle much greater amounts of metal than Bessemer's converter. Steel became so cheap to produce that it quickly replaced iron in industry because of its greater tensile strength and durability.

Transportation   The steam engine, iron, and steel brought a new era in transport. As machines speeded up factory production, methods of transportation also improved. In 1830 the first railway line was built in England, connecting Manchester and Liverpool; this triggered an age of railway building throughout much of the world. Shipping changed radically with the use of vessels without sails, which had greater tonnage capacity.

Society Transformed

The changes in agricultural production, business organization, and technology had revolutionary consequences for society, economics, and politics. People were drawn from the countryside into cities, and traditional ways of life changed. Much of the old life persisted, however, particularly during the first half of the nineteenth century. Landed property was still the principal form of wealth, and large landowners continued to exercise political power. From England to Russia, families of landed wealth (often the old noble families) continued to constitute the social elite. European society remained overwhelmingly rural; as late as the middle of the century, only England was half urban. Still, contemporaries were so overwhelmed by industrialization that they saw it as a sudden and complete break with the past—the shattering of traditional moral and social patterns.

Cities grew in number, size, and population as a result of industrialization. For example, between 1801 and 1851 the population of Birmingham grew from 73,000 to 250,000, and that of Liverpool from 77,000 to 400,000. Industrial cities expanded rapidly, without planning or much regulation by local or national government. So much growth with so little planning or control led to cities with little sanitation, no lighting, wretched housing, poor transportation, and little security.

Rich and poor alike suffered in this environment of disease, crime, and ugliness, although the poor obviously bore the brunt of these evils. They lived in houses that were several stories high and jammed together as near the factories as possible, separated from one another by a courtyard. Sometimes a whole family huddled together in one room or even shared a room with another family. Open sewers, polluted rivers, factory smoke, and filthy streets allowed disease to spread. In Britain, about twenty-six out of every one hundred children died before the age of five. Almost universally, those who wrote about industrial cities—England's Manchester, Leeds, and Liverpool, and France's Lyons—described the stench, the filth, the inhumane crowding, the poverty, and the immorality.

Map 14.2   Industrial Growth on the Continent, Mid-1800s

Changes in Social Structure

The Industrial Revolution destroyed forever the old division of society into clergy, nobility, and commoners. The development of industry and commerce caused a corresponding development of a bourgeoisie, a middle class comprised of people of common birth who engaged in trade and other capitalist ventures. The wealthiest bourgeois were bankers, factory and mine owners, and merchants, but the middle class also included shopkeepers, managers, lawyers, and doctors. The virtues of work, thrift, ambition, and caution characterized the middle class as a whole, as did the perversion of these virtues into materialism, selfishness, callousness, harsh individualism, and smugness.

From the eighteenth century on, as industry and commerce developed, the middle class grew in size, first in England and then throughout western Europe.

Throughout the eighteenth and nineteenth centuries, the middle class struggled against the entrenched aristocracy to end political, economic, and social discrimination. By the end of the nineteenth century, bourgeois politicians held the highest offices in much of western Europe and shared authority with aristocrats, whose birth no longer guaranteed them the only political and social power in the nation. As industrial wealth became more important, the middle class became more influential. It was common throughout Europe for wealthy bourgeois to spend fortunes buying great estates and emulating aristocratic manners and pleasures. The middle class also valued respectability. In this and many other ways, its members copied the aristocracy for most of the century.

Industrialization may have reduced some barriers between the landed elites and the middle class, but it sharpened the distinctions between the middle class and the laboring class. Like the middle class, the proletariat encompassed different economic levels: rural laborers, miners, and city workers. Many gradations existed among city workers, from artisans to factory workers to servants. Factory workers were the newest and most rapidly growing social group; at midcentury, however, they did not constitute the majority of laboring people in any major city. For example, as late as 1890 they comprised only one-sixth of London's population.

The artisans were the largest group of workers in the cities for the first half of the nineteenth century, and in some places for much longer than that. They worked in construction, in printing, in small tailoring or dress-making establishments, in food preparation and processing, and in crafts producing such luxury items as furniture, jewelry, lace, and velvet. Artisans were distinct from factory workers; their technical skills were difficult to learn, and traditionally their crafts were acquired in guilds, which still functioned as both social and economic organizations. Artisans were usually educated (they could read and write), lived in one city or village for generations, and maintained stable families, often securing places for their children in their craft. As the Industrial Revolution progressed, however, they found it difficult to compete with cheap factory-produced goods, and their livelihoods were threatened.

Servants were especially numerous in capital cities. In the first half of the nineteenth century in cities like Paris and London where the number of factories was not great, there were more servants than factory workers. Servants usually had some education. If they married and had a family, they taught their children to read and write and sometimes to observe the manners and values of the household in which the parent had worked. Many historians believe that these servants passed on to their children their own deference to authority and their aspirations to bourgeois status, which may have limited social discontent and radical political activity.

Working-Class Life

Life was not easy for those whose labor contributed to the industrializing process. Usually factory workers were recent arrivals from agricultural areas, where they had been driven off the land. They frequently moved to the city without their families, leaving them behind until they could afford to support them in town. These people entered rapidly growing industries where long hours—sometimes fifteen a day—were not unusual; farming had meant long hours, too, as had the various forms of labor for piecework rates in the home, but the pace of the machine, the dull routine, and dangerous conditions in factories and mines made work even more oppressive. Miners, for example, labored under the hazards of cave-ins, explosions, and deadly gas fumes. Deep under the earth's surface, life was dark, cold, wet, and tenuous. Their bodies stunted and twisted, their lungs wrecked, miners labored their lives away in "the pits."

Sometimes, compared to their lives in the country, the workers' standard of living rose, particularly if they were part of a whole family that found work; the pay for a family might be better than they could have earned for agricultural labor. But working conditions were terrible, as were living conditions. The factories were dirty, hot, unventilated, and frequently dangerous. Workers toiled long hours, were fined for mistakes and even for accidents, were fired at the will of the employer and foreman, and suffered from job insecurity. They often lived in overcrowded and dirty housing. If they were unmarried or had left their family in the country, they often lived in a barracks with other members of their sex. If they lost their jobs, they also lost their shelter.

In the villages they had left, they had been poor but were socially connected to family, church, and even to local landlords. But in the cities, factory workers labored in plants with twenty to a hundred workers and had little contact with their employers; instead, they were pushed by foremen to work hard and efficiently, to keep up with the machines. Workers had little time on the job to socialize with others; they were fined for talking to one another, for lateness, and for many petty infringements. They often became competitors in order to keep their jobs. Lacking organization, a sense of comradeship, education, and experience of city life, factory workers found little comfort when times were bad.

Many workers developed a life around the pub, the café, or some similar gathering place, where there were drinks and games and the gossip and news of the day. On Sundays, their one day off, workers drank and danced; absenteeism was so great on Monday that the day was called "holy Monday." Gin drinking was denounced on all sides; workers and reformers alike urged temperance. Many workers played sports, and some social organizations grew up around their sporting games. In these and other ways, workers developed a culture of their own—a culture that was misunderstood and often deplored by middle-class reformers.

Many contemporaries felt that the poor—those who were so unfortunate that they needed the assistance of others—were growing in numbers, that their condition was deplorable, and that it had actually deteriorated in the midst of increased wealth. If machines could produce so much wealth and so many products, social observers wondered why poor people were so numerous. Parliamentary reports and investigations of civic-minded citizens documented the suffering for all to read.

Historians still debate about how bad workers' conditions were in the early stages of industrialization. Most workers experienced periods of acute distress, but historians generally conclude that the standard of living slowly improved during the eighteenth and nineteenth centuries. Although historians take an optimistic view about the long-range effects of industrialization, nonetheless the rapidity of change worked great hardships on the workers of all countries, who endured cruel conditions in factories and slums.

The Rise of Reform in Britain

Although it was the freest state in Europe in the early decades of the nineteenth century, Britain was far from democratic. A constitutional monarchy, with many limits on the powers of king and state, Britain was nonetheless dominated by aristocrats. Landed aristocrats controlled both the House of Lords and the House of Commons—the House of Lords because they constituted its membership and the House of Commons because they patronized or sponsored men favorable to their interests. The vast majority of people, middle class as well as working class, could not vote. Many towns continued to be governed by corrupt groups. New industrial towns were not allowed to elect representatives to Parliament; often lacking a town organization, they could not even govern themselves effectively.

The social separation of noble and commoner was not as rigid in Britain as on the Continent. Younger sons of aristocrats did not inherit titles and were therefore obliged to make careers in law, business, the military, and the church. The upper and middle classes mingled much more freely than on the Continent, and the wealthiest merchants tended to buy lands, titles, and husbands for their daughters. Nonetheless, Parliament, the courts, local government, the established Anglican church, the monarch—all were a part of a social and political system dominated by aristocratic interests and values. This domination had changed little despite the vast changes in social and economic structure that had taken place in the process of industrialization during the second half of the eighteenth century.

Some members of Parliament urged timely reforms. In 1828 Parliament repealed a seventeenth-century act that in effect barred Catholics and Nonconformists (non-Anglican Protestants) from government positions and from universities. In 1833, slavery was abolished within the British empire. (The British slave trade had been abolished earlier.) The Municipal Corporations Act (1835) granted towns and cities greater authority over their affairs. This measure created town and city governments that could, if they wished, begin to solve some problems of urbanization and industrialization. These municipal corporations could institute reforms such as sanitation, which Parliament encouraged by passing the first Public Health Act, in 1848.

Increasingly, reform centered on extension of the suffrage and enfranchisement of the new industrial towns. Middle-class men, and even workers, hoped

Gustave Doré (1833–1883): Engraving of a London Slum.   A population explosion took place between 1700 and 1850, as well as a population shift that peopled the new industrial cities. Rapid industrialization and inadequate city planning gave rise to urban slums with their disease, crime, and squalor. (*The Granger Collection, New York*)

to gain the right to vote. Because of population shifts, some sparsely populated regions—called *rotten boroughs*—sent representatives to the House of Commons, while many densely populated factory towns had little or no representation; and in many cases a single important landowner controlled many seats in the Commons. Voting was public, which allowed for intimidation, and candidates frequently tried to influence voters with drinks, food, and even money.

Intense and bitter feelings built up during the campaign for the Reform Bill of 1832. The House of Commons passed the bill to extend the suffrage by some 200,000, almost double the number who were then entitled to vote. The House of Lords, however, refused to pass the bill. There were riots and strikes in many cities, and mass meetings, both of workers and of middle-class people, took place all over the country. King William IV (1830–1837) became convinced, along with many politicians, that the situation was potentially revolutionary. To defuse it, he threatened to increase the number of the bill's supporters in the House of Lords by creating new peers. This threat brought reluctant peers into line, and the bill was passed. The Reform Act of 1832 extended the suffrage to the middle class and made the House of Commons more representative. The rotten boroughs lost their seats, which were granted to towns. Suffrage did not extend to workers, however, because there were high property qualifications.

Workers did gain some relief when humanitarians pressured Parliament to pass the Factory Act (1833), which legislated that no child under thirteen could work more than nine hours a day and that no one aged thirteen to eighteen could work more than sixty-nine hours a week. The act also provided some inspectors to investigate infractions and to punish offenders. Parliament responded in the same year by banning children under ten from the mines. The Factory Act of 1847 stipulated that boys under eighteen and women could work no more than ten hours a day in the mines and factories. At first workers resented the prohibition of child labor because it would greatly reduce their family income if their children could not work, but they gradually came to approve of this law. The ten-hour day for adult male workers would not be enacted until 1874.

Outside the government, the Chartist movement, a very diverse and complicated affair, attracted very different kinds of people with widely varying visions of the future. Its adherents came from the ranks of both intellectual radicals and workers. They pressed for political, not economic, reforms. During the 1830s and 1840s, the Chartists agitated for democratic measures, such as universal manhood suffrage, the secret ballot, salaries and the abolition of property qualifications for members of Parliament, and annual meetings of Parliament. The Chartist platform remained the democratic reform program for the rest of the century, long after the death of Chartism itself at midcentury. All of the Chartists' demands, except for annual elections for members of Parliament, were eventually realized.

The last political effort by the Chartists was led by Feargus O'Connor, a charismatic Irishman, who organized a mass demonstration to present a huge petition of six demands to Parliament in 1848. The cabinet ignored the great charter, which had signatures of at least 2 million names. The movement died out just as most of Europe burst into revolution. The working-class leadership of Chartism turned away from political programs almost exclusively to economic activity, such as trade unions that could bring immediate benefits to workers.

At the beginning of the nineteenth century, elementary education in Britain was managed by private individuals and church organizations. Schools were financed by contributions, grants, and fees paid by students. The government neither financed nor promoted education. As a result, very few poor children attended school. Indeed, many government officials feared that educating the poor would incite unrest. If the lower classes read publications attacking Christianity and challenging authority, they would become insolent to their superiors. One member of Parliament declared that schooling would teach the poor "to despise their lot in life, instead of making them good servants in agriculture and other laborious employments to which their rank in society had destined them." However, many British, inheriting the Enlightenment's confidence in education, favored schooling for the poor. In 1833, Parliament began to allocate small sums for elementary education. These funds were inadequate; in 1869, only about half of all children of school age attended school. The Education Act of 1870 gave local governments the power to establish elementary schools. By 1891 these schools were free and attendance was required.

Many workers and radicals believed that the only hope for their class lay in unified action through trade unions. At first Parliament fought the unions, passing the Combination Acts (1799–1800), which made unions illegal. In 1825, Parliament allowed workers to unionize but forbade them to strike. Unions made some headway in protecting their members from unemployment and dangerous working conditions, but strikes (which remained officially illegal until 1875) were rarely successful and were often suppressed by force.

Unlike the continental states, England avoided revolution. British politicians thought it was because they had made timely reforms in the 1830s and 1840s, and that belief itself became a force in political life. Whenever times were hard, there were always political leaders who would say that the remedy was reform and that reform would prevent revolution. The political experience of the first half of the nineteenth century laid the foundation for British parliamentary practices, which came to be the model of liberal, progressive, and stable politics. Britain was the symbol for all those who argued for reform rather than revolution. In the rest of Europe in 1848, however, such arguments were meeting with little success.

Responses to Industrialization

Liberalism

Liberalism evolved as a political movement to protect the rights of the individual against oppressive governments. Fearful of state power and committed to laissez-faire economics, British liberals at first opposed government intervention to deal with the plight of the working class and other problems created by rapid industrialization and urbanization. They drew comfort from Thomas Malthus's *Essay on the Principles of Population* (1798), which supported laissez-faire economics. Malthus argued that the population always increases at a faster rate than the food supply, so government programs to aid the poor and provide higher wages would only encourage larger families and thus perpetuate poverty. Malthus seemed to supply "scientific" justification for opposing state action to help the poor. Poverty, argued Malthusians, was not the fault of factory owners; it was an iron law of nature, the result of population pressure on resources, and could not be eliminated by state policies.

Fellow economist David Ricardo (1772–1823) used Malthus's idea to form another theory that also made poverty seem inevitable and irremediable. Wages, he said, tended to remain at the minimum needed to maintain workers. An increase in wages encouraged laborers to increase their families. As the supply of workers increased, competition for jobs also increased, causing wages to decline. Ricardo's disciples made his law inflexible—an "Iron Law of Wages" offered dismal prospects.

Many workers felt the new science of economics offered little hope for them.

They argued that the liberals were only concerned with their class and national interests, that they were hard, callous, and apathetic toward the sufferings of the poor.

Early in the nineteenth century, liberals feared that state interference in the economy to redress social ills would threaten individual rights and the free market that they thought was essential to personal liberty. In time, the liberals modified their position, first supporting government action to provide education or opportunity for all and then accepting the principle of state aid to the poor. They came to believe that justice required some protection against the economy's ravages for those who were powerless. They thought reform was possible without losing the advantages of capitalism and without sacrificing personal liberty.

Early Socialism

A new group called socialists went further than the liberals, demanding the creation of a new society based on the spirit of cooperation rather than on competition. Reflecting the spirit of the Enlightenment and the French Revolution, socialists were convinced that people could create a better world according to the principles of reason. They espoused a new social and economic system in which production and distribution of goods would be planned for the general good of society. They denied that human beings reached the peak of their achievements as individuals, arguing that people achieved more happiness for themselves and for others as a community that worked together and experienced solidarity. Their thought influenced Karl Marx and Friedrich Engels, who in the second half of the nineteenth century became the most influential formulators and propagators of socialism.

Saint-Simon   Henri Comte de Saint-Simon (1760–1825) renounced his title during the French Revolution and enthusiastically preached the opportunity for a new society. Saint-Simon believed that he had a mission to set society right by providing an understanding of the new age being shaped by science and industry. He argued that just as Christianity had provided social unity and stability during the Middle Ages, scientific knowledge would bind the society of his time. The scientists, industrialists, bankers, artists, and writers would replace the clergy and the aristocracy as the social elite and harness technology for the betterment of humanity. Saint-Simon's disciples championed efforts to build great railway and canal systems, including the Suez and Panama canals. His vision of a scientifically organized society led by trained experts was a powerful force among intellectuals in the nineteenth century and is very much alive today among those who believe in a technocratic society.

Fourier   Another early French socialist was Charles Fourier (1772–1837), who believed, as the romantics did, that society conflicted with the natural needs of human beings and that this tension was responsible for human misery. Only the reorganization of society so that it would satisfy people's desire for pleasure and satisfaction would end that misery. Whereas Saint-Simon and his followers had elaborate plans to reorganize society on the grand scale of large industries and giant railway and canal systems. Fourier sought to create small communities to allow men and women to enjoy life's simple pleasures. These communities of about 1,600 people, called *phalansteries,* would be organized according to the unchanging needs of human nature. Everyone would work at tasks that interested them and would produce things that brought themselves and others pleasure. Like Adam Smith, Fourier understood that specialization bred boredom and alienation from work and life. Unlike Smith, he did not believe that vastly increased productivity compensated for the evils of specialization. In the phalansteries, money and goods would not be equally distributed; those with special skills and responsibilities would be rewarded accordingly. This system of rewards accorded with nature because people have a natural desire to be rewarded.

Fourier thought that marriage distorted the natures of both men and women, because monogamy restricted their sexual needs and narrowed their lives' scope to the family alone. Instead, people should think of themselves as part of the family of all humanity. Because married women had to devote all their strength and time to household and children, they had no time or energy left to enjoy life's pleasures. Fourier did not call for the abolition of the family, but he did hope that it would disappear of its own accord as society adjusted to his theories. Men and women would find new ways of fulfilling themselves sexually, and the community would be organized so that it could care for the children. Fourier's ideas found some reception in the United States, where in the 1840s at least twenty-nine communities were founded on Fourierist principles. None, however, lasted more than five or six years.

Owen   In 1799, Robert Owen (1771–1858) became part owner and manager of the New Lanark cotton mills in Scotland. Distressed by widespread mistreatment of workers, Owen resolved to improve the lives of his employees and to prove that it was possible to do so without destroying profits. He raised wages, upgraded working conditions, refused to hire children under ten, and provided workers with neat homes, food, and clothing, all at reasonable prices. He set up schools for children and for adults. In every way, he demonstrated his belief that healthier, happier workers produced more than the less fortunate ones. Like Saint-Simon, Owen believed industry and technology could and would enrich humankind, if organized according to the proper principles. Visitors came from all over Europe to see Owen's factories.

Just like many philosophes, Owen also held that the environment was the principal shaper of character—that the ignorance, alcoholism, and crime of the poor derived from bad living conditions. Public education and factory reform, said Owen, would make better citizens of the poor. Owen came to believe that the entire social and economic order must be replaced by a new system based on harmonious group living rather than on competition. He established a model community at New Harmony, Indiana, but it was short-lived.

Karl Marx (left) and Friedrich Engels (right) with Marx's Three Daughters, 1860s.   Marx saw history solely in terms of economic and social interrelationships, a struggle between laborers and the owners of the means of production. He called for the proletariat to overthrow capitalism and to establish a classless society. (*Culver Pictures*)

Marxism

Karl Marx (1818–1883) was born of German-Jewish parents (both descendants of prominent rabbis). To save his job as a lawyer, Marx's father converted to Protestantism. Enrolled at a university to study law, Marx switched to philosophy. In 1842, he was editing a newspaper that was soon suppressed by the Prussian authorities for its outspoken ideas. Leaving his native Rhineland, Marx went to Paris, where he met another German, Friedrich Engels (1820–1895), who was the son of a prosperous textile manufacturer. Marx and Engels entered into a lifelong collaboration and became members of socialist groups. In February 1848 they published the *Communist Manifesto,* which called for a working-class revolution to overthrow the capitalist system. Forced to leave France in 1849 because of his political views, Marx moved to London, where he spent the rest of his life. There he spent years writing *Capital,* a study and critique of the modern capitalistic economic system, which he predicted would be destroyed by a socialist revolution.

A Science of History   As did other thinkers influenced by the Enlightenment, Marx believed that human history, like the operations of nature, was governed by scientific law. Marx was a strict materialist; rejecting all religious and metaphysical interpretations of both nature and history, he sought to fashion an empirical science of society. He viewed religion as a human creation—a product of people's imagination and feelings, a consolation for the oppressed—and the happiness it brought as an illusion. Real happiness would come, said Marx, not by transcending the natural world but by improving it. Rather than deluding oneself by seeking refuge from life's misfortunes in an imaginary world, one must confront the ills of society and reform them. This last point is crucial. "The philosophers have only *interpreted* the world in different ways; the point is to *change* it."[2]

The world could be rationally understood and changed, said Marx. People were free to make their own history, but to do so effectively, they must comprehend the inner meaning of history—the laws governing human affairs in the past and operating in the present. To Marx, history was not an assortment of unrelated and disconnected events; rather, like the growth of a plant, it proceeded according to its own inner laws. Marx claimed to have uncovered these laws. He said that economic and technological factors—the way in which goods are produced and wealth is distributed—were the moving forces in history. They accounted for historical change and were the basis of all culture—politics, law, religion, morals, and philosophy. "The history of humanity," concluded Marx, "must therefore always be studied and treated in relation to the history of industry and exchange."[3]

Marx said that material technology—the methods of cultivating land and the tools for manufacturing goods—determined society's social and political arrangements and its intellectual outlooks. For example, the hand mill, the loose yoke, and the wooden plow had given rise to feudal lords, whereas power-driven machines had spawned the industrial capitalists.

Class Conflict   Throughout history, said Marx, there has been a class struggle between those who own the means of production and those whose labor has been exploited to provide wealth for this upper class. This opposing tension between classes has pushed history forward into higher stages. In the ancient world, when wealth was based on land, the struggle was between master and slave, patrician and plebeian; during the Middle Ages, when land was still the predominant mode of production, the struggle was between lord and serf. In the modern industrial world, two sharply opposed classes were confronting each other—the capitalists owning the factories, mines, banks, and transportation systems, and the exploited wage earners (the proletariat).

The class with economic power also controlled the state, said Marx and Engels. That class used political power to protect and increase its property and to hold down the laboring class. "Thus the ancient State was above all the slaveowners' state for holding down the slaves," said Engels, "as a feudal State was the organ of the nobles for holding down the . . . serfs, and the modern representative State is the instrument of the exploitation of wage-labor by capital."[4]

Marx and Engels said too that the class that controlled material production also controlled mental production; that is, the ideas held by the ruling class became the dominant ideas of society. These ideas, presented as laws of nature or moral and religious standards, were regarded as the truth by oppressor and oppressed alike. In reality, however, these ideas merely reflected the special economic interests of the ruling class. Thus, said Marx, bourgeois ideologists would insist that natural rights and laissez-faire economics were laws of nature having universal validity. But these "laws" were born of the needs of the bourgeoisie in its struggle to wrest power from an obsolete feudal regime and to protect its property from the state. Similarly, nineteenth-century slaveholders convinced themselves that slavery was morally right—that it had God's approval and was good for the slave. Slaveowners and capitalist employers alike may have defended their labor systems by citing universal principles that they thought were true, but in reality their systems rested on a simple economic consideration: slave labor was good for the pocketbook of the slaveowner, and wage labor was good in the same way for the capitalist.

The Destruction of Capitalism   Under capitalism, said Marx, the worker knew only poverty. He worked long hours for low wages, suffered from periodic unemployment, and lived in squalid, overcrowded dwellings. Most monstrous of all, he was forced to send his young children into the factories.

Capitalism also produced another kind of poverty, said Marx—poverty of the human spirit. Under capitalism, the factory worker was reduced to a laboring beast, performing tedious and repetitive tasks in a dark, dreary, dirty cave, an altogether inhuman environment that deprived people of their human sensibilities. Unlike the artisans in their own shops, factory workers found no pleasure and took no pride in their work; they did not have the satisfaction of creating a finished product that expressed their skills. Work, said Marx, should be a source of fulfillment for people. It should enable people to affirm their personalities and develop their potential. By treating people not as human beings but as cogs in the production process, capitalism alienated people from their work, themselves, and one another.

Marx believed that capitalist control of the economy and the government would not endure forever. The capitalist system would perish just as the feudal society of the Middle Ages and the slave society of the ancient world had perished. From the ruins of a dead capitalist society a new economic-social system, socialism, would emerge. Marx predicted how capitalism would be destroyed. Periodic unemployment would increase the misery of the workers and intensify their hatred of capitalists. Small businessmen and shopkeepers, unable to compete with the great capitalists, would sink into the ranks of the working class, greatly expanding its numbers. Society would become polarized into a small group of immensely wealthy capitalists and a vast proletariat, poor, embittered, and desperate. This monopoly of capital by the few would become a brake on the productive process. Growing increasingly conscious of their misery, the workers—aroused, educated, and organized by communist intellectuals—would revolt. "Revolution is necessary," said Marx, "not only because the *ruling* class cannot be overthrown in any other way, but also because only in a revolution can *the class which overthrows it* rid itself of the accumulated rubbish of the past and become capable of reconstructing society."[5] The working-class revolutionaries would smash the government that helped the capitalists maintain their dominance. Then they would confiscate the property of the capitalists, abolish private property, place the means of production in the workers' hands, and organize a new society. The *Communist Manifesto* ends with a ringing call for revolution: "The Communists . . . openly declare that their ends can be attained only by the forcible overthrow of all existing social conditions. Let the ruling classes tremble at a Communist revolution. The proletarians have nothing to lose but their chains. They have a world to win. Workingmen of all countries, unite!"[6]

Marx did not say a great deal about the new society that would be ushered in by the socialist revolution. With the destruction of capitalism, the distinction between capitalist and worker would cease and with it the class conflict. No longer would society be divided into haves and have-nots, oppressor and oppressed. Since this classless society would contain no exploiters, there would be no need for a state, which was merely an instrument for maintaining and protecting the power of the exploiting class. Thus, the state would eventually wither away. The production and distribution of goods would be carried out through community planning and communal sharing, replacing the capitalist system of competition. People would work at varied tasks, rather than being confined to one form of employment, just as Fourier had advocated. No longer factory slaves, people would be free to fulfill their human potential, to improve their relationships on a basis of equality with others, and to work together for the common good.

The Influence of Marx   Marxism had immense appeal for both the downtrodden and intellectuals. It promised to end the injustices of industrial society; it claimed the certainty of science; it assured adherents that the triumph of their cause was guaranteed by history. In many ways, Marxism was a secular religion—the proletariat become a chosen class endowed with a mission to achieve worldly salvation for humanity.

Marx's influence grew during the second wave of industrialization in the closing decades of the nineteenth century, when class bitterness between the proletariat and the bourgeoisie seemed to worsen. Many workers thought that liberals and conservatives had no sympathy for their plight and that the only way to improve their lot was through socialist parties.

Marx's emphasis on economic forces has immeasurably broadened the perception of historians, who now explore the economic factors in historical developments. This approach has greatly expanded our understanding of Rome's decline, the outbreak of the French Revolution and the American Civil War, and other crucial developments. Marx's theory of class conflict has provided social scientists with a useful tool for analyzing social process. His theory of alienation has been adapted by sociologists and psychologists. Of particular value to social scientists is Marx's insight that the ideas people hold to be true and the values they consider valid often veil economic interests. On the political level, both the socialist parties of western Europe, which pressed for reform through parliamentary methods, and the communist regimes in Russia and China, which came to power through revolution, claimed to be heirs of Marx.

Critics of Marx   Critics point out serious weaknesses in Marxism. The rigid Marxist who tries to squeeze all historical events into an economic framework is at a disadvantage. Economic forces alone will not explain the triumph of Christianity in the Roman Empire, the fall of Rome, the Crusades, the French Revolution, modern imperialism, World War I, or the rise of Hitler. Economic explanations fall particularly flat in trying to account for the emergence of modern nationalism, whose appeal, resting on deeply ingrained emotional needs, crosses class lines. The great struggles of the twentieth century have not been between classes but between nations.

Many of Marx's predictions or expectations have not materialized. Workers in Western lands did not become the oppressed and impoverished working class that Marx described in the mid-nineteenth century. Western workers, because of increased productivity and the efforts of labor unions and reform-minded governments, improved their lives considerably, so that they now enjoy the highest standard of living in history. The tremendous growth of a middle class of professionals, civil service employees, and small-business persons belies Marx's prediction that capitalist society would be polarized into a small group of very rich capitalists and a great mass of destitute workers. Marx believed that socialist revolutions would break out in the advanced industrialized lands. But the socialist revolutions of the twentieth century have occurred in underdeveloped, predominantly agricultural states. The state in communist lands, far from withering away, has grown more centralized, powerful, and oppressive. In no country where communist revolutionaries have seized power have people achieved the liberty that Marx desired. All these failed predictions and expectations seem to contradict Marx's claim that his theories rested on an unassailable scientific foundation.

Industrialism in Perspective

Like the French Revolution, the Industrial Revolution was instrumental in the modernization of Europe; eventually it transformed every facet of society. In preindustrial society—Europe in the mid-eighteenth century—agriculture was the dominant economic activity and peasants were the most numerous class. Peasant life centered around the family and the village, which country folk rarely left. The new rational and critical spirit associated with the Enlightenment hardly penetrated rural Europe; there, religious faith, clerical authority, and ancient superstition remained firmly entrenched. The richest and most powerful class was the aristocracy, whose wealth stemmed from land; nobles dominated the countryside and enjoyed privileges protected by custom and law. Eighteenth-century aristocrats, like their medieval forebears, viewed society as a hierarchy in which a person's position in life was determined by his or her inherited status. By championing the ideals of liberty and equality, the French Revolution undermined the traditional power structure—king, aristocracy, and clergy; by advocating the rational and secular outlook of the Enligh-

Chronology 14.1 ◊ The Industrial Revolution

1764–1767	The spinning jenny is invented by the Hargreaves
1769	Watt invents the modern steam engine
1785	Cartwright develops the power loom
1825	Workers are allowed to unionize but not to strike
1830	The first railway line is built in England
1832	The Reform Bill of 1832 expands British voting rights
1848	Publication of *The Communist Manifesto*

tenment, the French reformers dismantled further the religious and political pillars of traditional society.

Europe in the eighteenth century was predominantly rural. By 1800, 20 percent of the population of Britain, France, and Holland lived in cities; in Russia the figure was only 5 percent. Artisan manufacturing in small shops and trade for local markets were the foundations of the urban economy, although some cities did produce luxury goods for wider markets. Textile manufacturing was conducted through the putting-out system, in which wool was turned into cloth in private dwellings, usually the homes of peasants.

The Industrial Revolution accelerated the pace of modernization. In time, agricultural villages and handicraft manufacturing were eclipsed in importance by cities and factories. In the society fashioned by industrialization and urbanization, aristocratic power and values declined; at the same time, the bourgeoisie increased in number, wealth, importance, and power. A person was judged increasingly by talent rather than by birth, and opportunities for upward social mobility grew. The Industrial Revolution was a great force for democratization; during the nineteenth century, first the middle class and then the working class gained the vote. The Industrial Revolution also hastened the secularization of European life. In the cities, former villagers, separated from traditional communal ties, drifted away from their ancestral religion. In a world being reshaped by technology, industry, and science, Christian mysteries lost their force, and for many, salvation became a distant concern. Modernization did not proceed everywhere at the same pace and with the same thoroughness. Generally, premodern social and institutional forms remained deeply entrenched in eastern and southern Europe, and persisted well into the twentieth century.

Although the Industrial Revolution created many problems, some of which still endure, it was a great triumph. Ultimately it made possible the highest standard of living in human history and created new opportunities for social advancement, political participation, and educational and cultural development. It also widened the gap between the West and the rest of the world in terms of science and technology, enabling western states to extend their power by 1900 over virtually the entire globe, completing a trend that had begun with the Age of Exploration.

Notes

1. David S. Landes, *The Unbound Prometheus* (Cambridge, Mass.: Harvard University Press, 1969), p. 33.
2. Karl Marx, *Theses on Feuerbach,* excerpted in T. B. Bottomore and Maximilien Rubel, eds., *Karl Marx: Selected Writings in Sociology and Social Philosophy* (London: Watts, 1956), p. 69.
3. Karl Marx, *The German Ideology* (New York: International Publishers, 1939), p. 18.
4. Friedrich Engels, *The Origin of the Family, Private Property and the State,* in Emile Burns, *A Handbook of Marxism* (New York: Random House, 1935), p. 330.
5. Karl Marx, *The German Ideology,* p. 69.
6. Karl Marx, *The Communist Manifesto,* trans. by Samuel Moore (Chicago: Henry Regnery, 1954), pp. 81–82.

Suggested Reading

Deane, Phyllis, *The First Industrial Revolution, 1750–1850* (1965). An excellent introduction.

Floud, Roderick, and Donald McCloskey, *The Economic History of Britain Since 1900,* 2 vols. (1981). This work incorporates the latest scholarship on British industrialization.

Himmelfarb, Gertrude, *The Idea of Poverty: England in the Early Industrial Age* (1983). A brilliant history of English social thought focused on the condition of the poor.

Hobsbawm, Eric, *The Age of Revolution: 1789–1848* (1964). A survey of this tumultuous period, stressing the connections between economic, social, and political revolution.

Landes, David S., *The Unbound Prometheus: Technological Change and Industrial Development in Western Europe from 1750 to the Present* (1969). A classic treatment of a complex subject.

Langer, William L., *Political and Social Upheaval: 1832–1852* (1969). An excellent source with good references and bibliography.

Thompson, E. P., *Making of the English Working Class* (1966). A very readable, dramatic, enormously influential, and controversial book.

Webb, R. K., *Modern England from the Eighteenth Century* (1967 and 1980). A text that is balanced, well-written, well-informed, and up-to-date on historical controversies.

Review Questions

1. What were the causes of the Industrial Revolution? Why did it begin in Britain?
2. How did the Industrial Revolution transform the social structure?
3. What problems did the Industrial Revolution create for the working class?
4. How did Parliament respond to demands for reform from 1815 to 1848?
5. Why are Saint-Simon, Fourier, and Owen regarded as early socialists?
6. What did Marx have in common with the philosophes of the Enlightenment?
7. Why did Marx think that capitalism was doomed? How, according to Marx, would its destruction happen?

Chapter ⚘ 15

Europe in the Industrial Age: Modernization and Imperialism

In the last part of the nineteenth century, the accelerated pace of industrialization transformed European and American societies. Simultaneously, Western nations built governmental machinery for including and controlling great numbers of citizens. This strengthening and centralizing process—*state-building* in modern terminology—became the major activity of Western governments. State-building meant not only strengthening central authority but also absorbing previously excluded classes into the community, primarily through the power of nationalism, which governments fostered. A state's power grew enormously as its government affected the lives of ordinary citizens through military conscription, public education, and broad taxation.

Industrialization facilitated trends toward centralization with the concentration of factory workers in cities and the loosening of traditional rural ties. Industrialization greatly affected international relations as well. The amount of coal and iron production, the mileage and tonnage of railways and navies, the mechanization of industry, and the skill of the populace became important components of national power. Industrialization also led European nations and the United States to extend their power over Asian, African, and Latin American lands. ⚘

The Advance of Industry

Historians call the second half of the nineteenth century the Second Industrial Revolution because of the great increase in the speed and scale of economic and social transformation. This changed world was characterized by techno-logical advances, by new forms of business and labor organization, by the rise of the middle class to political and social power corresponding to its economic power, by the decline of traditional groups or classes, and by dramatic changes in the role of women and children in the family.

At midcentury, farming was still the main occupation of people everywhere, including Britain, where industrialization was most advanced. Even in Britain there were more domestic servants than factory workers and twice as many agricultural laborers as textile and clothing workers. Large factories were few, and handicrafts still flourished. Sailing ships still outnumbered steamships, and horses carried more freight than trains.

After midcentury, however, much changed radically during two important spurts. First, between 1850 and 1870 in Europe and America, the shift from hand to machine production accelerated, leading to the concentration of fac-tory workers in industrial cities and to the growth of unions. The standard of living for most workers rose. New machines and processes, legislation, and trade-union bargaining relieved the worst conditions of early industrialization; also, the first regulations of urban development and sanitation began to im-prove living conditions. In the more advanced industrial areas the social or-ganization of the workplace changed; the introduction of heavy equipment resulted in men replacing women and children in the factories, and the some-what higher wages for skilled male laborers meant that women in their families no longer were compelled by dire necessity to work in factories. Women forced out of factories (they would return during World War I) were not freed for a life of leisure, however; they worked as domestics, pieceworkers, seamstresses, laundresses, and similar workers. Children became students as the state and the economy demanded that they acquire at least a minimal education.

From the 1890s to World War I, there was a marked change in the scale of development: giant firms run by boards of directors, including financiers, operated far-flung enterprises of enormous, mechanized factories manned by unskilled, low-paid, often seasonal workers. These industrial giants were able to control the output, price, and distribution of commodities; they dominated smaller firms, financed and controlled research and development, and ex-panded far beyond their national frontiers. The "captains of industry," the owners or managers of these large firms, possessed such extraordinary eco-nomic power that they often commanded political power as well. The emer-gence and concentration of heavy industry in large firms, capitalized by specialist banks, characterized the post-1890 period all over Europe. Such rapid growth caught the imagination of businessmen as well as socialist critics.

Revolutionary technological changes furthered the growth of industry. At midcentury, all Europe caught the railroad mania that had seized Britain in the 1840s. This epic expansion of railroads was paralleled in shipping. In 1850, 5 percent of the world's tonnage of ships were steam-powered; by 1893, the figure had advanced to half of all tonnage. At the turn of the century, two German engineers, Gottfried Daimler and Carl Benz, joined to perfect the internal combustion engine. Then the American Henry Ford used mass-

Isambard Kingdom Brunel, 1857.
Brunel, an engineer, was photographed in front of the chains of a
checking drum belonging to the
steamship the *Great Eastern*. In the
1840s, the railroads had transformed the face of Europe. Countries were unified, and economies
expanded. The steamship came to
the fore during the last decades of
the nineteenth century. The world
now had easy access to goods of
European and U.S. industry, transported by steamship speed and
efficiency. (*Victoria and Albert
Museum*)

production assembly-line techniques to produce his Model T for "the ordinary
man," and the automobile age was born. The invention of the diesel engine by
another German in 1897 meant cheaper, more efficient fuel could be used.
Diesel engines soon replaced steam engines on giant cargo ships, warships, and
luxury liners. Developments in communications, too, revolutionized people's
lives with the advent of telegraph, telephone, and later radio.

Economic development was extremely uneven, though. Central, southern,
and eastern Europe remained backward areas in many respects and stayed so
until World War I and after. In these overwhelmingly agricultural societies,
manufacturing consisted for the most part of consumer-oriented, small-scale
operations in textiles and food processing, in which craftsmen maintained their
place.

The Acceleration of Urbanization

More rapid industrialization increased the numbers of northwestern Europeans and Americans who lived in cities, which became more numerous,

larger, and more densely populated. London, although not an industrial city, had become a megalopolis of 5 million people by 1880 and was home to 7 million by 1914. Paris increased from 2 to 3 million between midcentury and World War I. Berlin, a city of only half a million in 1866, reached 2 million by World War I. There were only three German cities of more than 100,000 on the eve of unification, but by 1903 there were fifteen.

In the cities, the middle class rose to political, economic, and social prominence, often expressing its newfound importance and prosperity by civic activity. As machinery replaced handcraftsmen, the artisan working class experienced a sharp decline. Factory workers, their ranks swelled by peasants and artisans, emerged as an important social group in cities. Cut off from the regions of their birth, factory-working peasants and artisans shed their old loyalties; in the cities, some found a place for themselves in their neighborhoods, some in union and party activities, and some not at all. Industrialization also created a new "white collar" group of clerks who tried to differentiate themselves from factory workers.

The Rise of Socialist Parties

Over the years from 1850 to 1914, workers' lives improved because of trade-union organization, government intervention in the economy, and the general increase in productivity brought on by industrialization. Still, members of the working class faced problems and inequities that drew them to socialist parties, which strove for government control of industry and worker control of government and workplace. Most workers, and their families, lived in overcrowded, bleak tenements, without central heating or running water. They worked long hours, as much as 55 hours a week in trades where governments restricted the length of the work week, and as much as 70 to 75 hours in unregulated trades. Their jobs were exhausting and monotonous. They suffered from malnutrition; the English men and boys who appeared for medical exams to serve in the Boer War were found to be so physically unfit that their condition prompted reforms to improve the health and education of the laboring class. The working class as a whole suffered from diseases, particularly tuberculosis, and from lack of medical care. Women often died in childbirth owing to inadequate treatment, and men, particularly miners and dockworkers, commonly experienced job accidents that maimed and killed. Socialists believed that these conditions were due to the capitalist profit system, which exploited and impoverished workers and enriched the owners.

Socialist parties grew phenomenally in Germany and rapidly in much of the rest of Europe. Even Russia, which was scarcely industrial, had a Marxist socialist party. The growth of socialism reflected the workers' growing consciousness that they had special needs that other political parties did not fulfill. Socialists, however, were divided about tactics. "Orthodox" Marxists believed that socialist-led revolution was the necessary first step for change; among the orthodox Marxists were Wilhelm Liebknecht and August Bebel of Germany and Jules Guesde of France. Others, "revisionist" Marxists, influenced by the

German theoretician Edward Bernstein, urged socialists to use the political and economic systems to build a socialist society without revolution.

Great Britain: Reform and Unrest

Reform

The process of reform, begun with the Reform Bill of 1832 and the Factory Acts, continued in the era of the Second Industrial Revolution. The Reform Bill of 1867, skillfully maneuvered through Parliament by Benjamin Disraeli (1804–1881), gave the vote to the working class, doubling the electorate. Some of Disraeli's fellow Conservative party members feared that extending the vote to the largely uneducated masses would ruin the nation, but Disraeli maintained that this democratic advance would strengthen the bonds between the people and the state. Moreover, he believed that the Conservatives' social program and imperialist foreign policy would win the newly enfranchised poor to the party.

The work of electoral reform was continued by the Liberal party under the leadership of William Gladstone (1809–1898), who served four terms as prime minister. The Ballot Act (1872) provided for the secret ballot, which enabled working-class voters to avoid intimidation by their employers. Next the Reform Bill of 1884 enfranchised rural laborers; now virtually all adult males had the right to vote.

Unlike their continental brothers, British workers on the whole had never been attracted to socialism, particularly not to Marxism. In the 1880s, however, widespread poverty and new trends in industry—particularly monopolies, cartels, and foreign competition—led some labor leaders to urge greater militancy. These conditions fostered the creation of the Labour party. This party might never have grown without the Taff Vale decision (1901), which awarded damages to an employer picketed by a union. If workers could be fined for picketing or other actions restraining trade, their unions could be broken and they would lose the economic gains of half a century. Galvanized by the Taff Vale decision and eager to win reforms for the working class, labor took to politics; in the elections of 1906 the new Labour party gained twenty-nine members, an important faction since Conservatives and Liberals were almost equal in number.

Between 1906 and 1911, the Liberals, led by David Lloyd George (1863–1945) and the then-Liberal Winston Churchill (1874–1965), introduced a series of important social measures. Aided by the Labour party, they enacted a program of old-age pensions, labor exchanges to help the unemployed find work, unemployment and health insurance (a program deeply influenced by Bismarckian social legislation), and minimum wages for certain industries. Parliament also repealed the Taff Vale decision. In the process, however, a constitutional crisis developed between the Liberals, who had Labour support, and the Conservatives, who dominated the House of Lords. The crisis ended with the Parliament Act of 1911, which decreed that the House of Lords could only delay, not prevent, the passage of a bill that the House of Commons had approved.

Feminist Agitation

On the issue of women's suffrage, British democracy was lagging. Influenced by the ideals of the American and French revolutions, women had begun to protest their unequal status. In 1837 the English novelist and economist Harriet Martineau commented: "One of the fundamental principles announced in the Declaration of Independence is that governments derive their just power from the consent of the governed. How can the political condition of women be reconciled with this?" In 1867, John Stuart Mill, philosopher and member of Parliament, proposed that the vote be extended to women. Parliament rejected the proposal, but 74 members voted in favor (194 opposed it). The following year, Lydia Becker became the first English woman to speak in public for women's suffrage. Many people, both men and women, viewed female suffrage as too radical a break with tradition. Some asserted that women were represented by their husbands or male relatives, so the vote was unnecessary; others protested that women lacked the ability to participate responsibly in political life. Queen Victoria, who supported other reforms, called women's suffrage "that mad, wicked folly."

Many Liberals and some Labourites favored women's suffrage, but women were advised by the leader of the Liberals "to keep on pestering . . . but exercise the virtue of patience." For those women who felt the advice patronized them and whose patience was running out, a family of feminists advocated a more militant course of action. Emmeline Pankhurst and her daughters Sylvia and Christabel urged demonstrations, invasions of the House of Commons, destruction of property, and hunger strikes. They did not urge these dramatic actions all at once, but when their petitions and demands were ignored, they moved to more and more shocking actions. Suffragettes began a campaign of breaking windows, starting fires in mailboxes, and chaining themselves to the gates at Parliament. As a gesture of protest, in 1913 one militant threw herself to her death under King Edward VII's horse at the races.

When feminists were arrested for violating the law, they staged hunger strikes. Ugly situations resulted, with the police force-feeding the demonstrators and subjecting them to ridicule and rough treatment. Often the police would release half-starved feminists and, when they had recovered their health, would reimprison them. Ridiculed, humiliated, and punished—but above all legally ignored—the feminists refused to accept the passive role that a male-dominated society had assigned them. When women played a major part on the home front in World War I, many of the elite changed their minds, and in 1918, British women over the age of thirty gained the vote. In 1928, Parliament lowered the voting age for women to twenty-one, the same qualifying age for male voters.

The Irish Question

Feminist agitation was one explosive issue confronting prewar Britain. Another was the Irish question. While moderate Irish nationalists called for *home rule* (self-government within the British Empire), something favored by many members of Parliament, Irish Catholic extremists, such as the Irish Republican Brotherhood and the Gaelic League, pressed for full independence. Fearing Catholic domination, the Protestant Irish (Ulstermen) in the northern counties of Ulster strongly opposed independence for Ireland. The Ulster Volunteers recruited a large private army and openly trained it for revolution in the event that home rule was enacted. Gangs smuggled guns, soldiers fired on demonstrators, violence bred violence, and civil war seemed close. In 1916, the Easter Rebellion, an Irish insurrection led by Sir Roger Casement, was suppressed and its leaders executed. At that moment Lloyd George negotiated a settlement that was carried out after the war: Ireland was divided, the overwhelmingly Catholic south gaining independence and a republican government, and the six predominantly Protestant counties of Ulster remaining part of the United Kingdom.

At the beginning of the twentieth century, labor, Irish, and female militancy marred Britain's image of a stable, liberal, constitutional regime. Nevertheless, British parliamentary government survived every crisis and proved itself able to carry the nation successfully through a grueling world war.

France: A Troubled Nation

In 1852, Louis Napoleon (1808–1873), who had been elected president of the Second French Republic in 1848, took the title emperor in the tradition of his illustrious uncle. Napoleon III ruled in an authoritarian manner, permitting no opposition, censoring the press, and allowing the legislature little power. But in the 1860s, in a drastic shift, he introduced liberal reforms, pardoning political prisoners, removing press censorship, allowing workers the right to form unions, and approving a new constitution with safeguards for individual liberty. His reforms have perplexed historians. Was Napoleon III a sincere believer in liberal ideals who waited until his power was firmly established before implementing these ideals, or did he introduce reforms only because he feared unrest?

Defeat in the Franco-Prussian War brought down the empire of Napoleon III. Bitter frustration with defeat and hatred of the Prussian invaders led the people of Paris to rise against the armistice signed by the provisional government—the politicians who had replaced Napoleon. The Paris Commune (1871) began as a patriotic refusal to accept defeat and as a rejection of Napoleon's rule, but it became a rejection of the provisional government as well. Ultimately, the Communards (as those who resisted the Prussians and the provisional government were called) also challenged property owners.

The Communards included followers of the anarchist Joseph Proudhon and groups of republican and socialist veterans of the Revolution of 1848, gathered from prisons, from hiding, and from exile. For two months in the spring of 1871, these revolutionaries ruled Paris. Then Adolphe Thiers, head of the provisional government that still governed the rest of France, ordered a siege of Paris. The fighting was bitter and desperate, with many acts of terrorism and violence. Both sides in this civil war set fires that destroyed large parts of the city they loved. The Communards were defeated and treated as traitors: 20,000 of them were executed without trial, and those who were tried received harsh sentences (death, life imprisonment, and deportation to prison colonies). Governing classes across Europe viewed the Paris Commune as a sign that the people should be ruled with an iron fist.

At first it seemed that a monarchy would succeed the empire of Napoleon III. But disunity among the monarchists enabled France to become a republic by default. Unlike Britain with its two-party system, the Third French Republic had many political parties, which contributed to instability. No one party had sufficient strength within parliament to provide strong leadership. Prime ministers resigned in rapid succession; cabinets rose and fell frequently, giving the impression of a state without direction. Political life seemed to be one of wheeling and dealing, but in the process, legislation was enacted that made elementary education free and compulsory and legalized trade unions. The Third Republic survived, but not without major crises, the principal one being the Dreyfus affair.

In 1894, Captain Alfred Dreyfus, an Alsatian-Jewish artillery officer, was wrongly accused of having sold secrets to the Germans. After a court martial, he was condemned to life imprisonment on Devil's Island. Anti-Semitic elements joined with the republic's opponents—monarchists, army leaders, clerics, and nationalists—to denounce and block every attempt to clear Dreyfus of the charges against him. In the beginning, few people defended Dreyfus; the vast majority felt that the honor of France and the army was at stake. Then individuals, mainly radical republicans, came to his defense, including the writers Anatole France and Émile Zola and the future republican leader Georges Clemenceau, along with university students. They protested and demonstrated, insisting on a retrial and a revision of the verdict. After many humiliations, Dreyfus was finally cleared in 1906.

The result of the victory of the radical republicans, however, was a fierce campaign to root out those opposing the republic. The radicals attacked the church, expelled religious orders, confiscated their property, and waged a vigorous campaign to replace the influence of the parish priest with that of the district schoolmaster. Complete separation of church and state was ordered. France became a secular state, and taxes no longer supported the parishes and schools.

Despite progress in the middle of the nineteenth century, French economic development lagged. France had fewer and smaller industries than Britain or Germany, and more French people lived in rural areas or in small communities. In the 1880s, both trade unionism and political parties with a socialist program began to make headway and to press for social reform through the democratic parliamentary institutions of the republic. France was very slow, however, to enact social measures such as pensions and regulations governing working conditions, wages, and hours. Such measures, which might have improved the lives of ordinary people, were regarded by the ruling elite as socialism and as socialist tokens to buy off workers.

France was a troubled country, and the Third Republic was not a popular regime. The church, the army, socialism, and even memories of the monarchy and the empire inspired deeper passions than the republic, which survived only because the dissension among its enemies allowed it to. France approached World War I as a deeply divided country. Yet when World War I broke out, the French people rallied to defend the nation.

Germany: The Power-State

Prussia's victory over France in the Franco-Prussian War of 1870–71 completed the struggle for German unification. The new government, the German Reich (empire), was headed by the king of Prussia. Though the Reichstag (lower house) was elected by universal suffrage, real power lay in the hands of the emperor and Bismarck, the "Iron Chancellor," who was responsible only to the emperor. The German kaiser (emperor), unlike the British monarch, had considerable control over lawmaking and foreign affairs and commanded the army and navy. The emperor alone could remove the chancellor or the cabinet members from office. The sole control over Bismarck was the Reichstag's refusal to pass the budget, an extreme measure that politicians were usually unwilling to take. German liberals did not vigorously struggle for basic political and civil liberties; they tolerated evasions of principle and practices that British politicians would never have allowed. While Britain, France, the United States, and other Western states were becoming more democratic, Germany remained a semiautocratic state. The failure of democratic attitudes and procedures to take root in Germany was to have dangerous consequences for the future.

Bismarck's political practices weakened liberal and democratic elements, and he regarded parties as incapable of making policy for the country. In Bismarck's mind, the Catholics and the socialists were internationalists who did not place the interests of Germany first. He began to persecute Catholics, who comprised about 40 percent of the population. The *Kulturkampf*, struggle for culture, was a series of laws passed in 1873 that tried to subject the church to the state. The laws discriminated against the Jesuits and required state supervision of the church and training of priests in state schools. Catholics were required to be married by the state. Churchmen who refused to accept these laws were imprisoned or exiled. The German liberals did not defend the civil liberties of the Catholics against these laws. Persecution only strengthened the German Catholics' loyalty, however, and the Catholic Center party gained

German Industry: Krupp Works at Essen, Manufacturing Guns.   The beginning of Kaiser William II's reign coincided with the explosion of German industrial and corporate capitalism. Calls for expansionist colonial policies were complemented by heavy industry that was willing and able to support German imperialism. (*Culver Pictures*)

support. Prussian conservatives, though Protestant in religion, resented Bismarck's anticlerical policy, which could hurt Lutherans as well as Catholics. With the succession of Leo XIII to the papacy in 1878, Bismarck quietly opened negotiations for peace with the church.

When two attempts on William I's life occurred in 1878, Bismarck demanded that the socialists be suppressed. In reality, the socialists, few in number, were not a threat—their immediate practical program was a demand for civil liberties and democracy in Germany. Only the narrowest of conservative views would have seen the socialists as a danger, but many in Germany, particularly the Prussian Junker class, held such a narrow view. The liberals once again did not oppose Bismarck's special legislation outlawing subversive organizations and authorizing the police to ban meetings and newspapers. The Social Democratic party, like the Catholic Center party before, survived the persecution; it grew stronger and better disciplined as the liberals grew weaker, discredited by their unwillingness to act.

Bismarck's policy was not merely repressive. He tried to win the workers by paternalistic social legislation. Like many conservatives, he was disturbed by the effects of industrialization, which had developed at rapid pace in the 1850s and 1860s. Germany was the first state to enact a program of social legislation for the proletariat, which included insurance against sickness, disability, accidents, and old age. The employer, the state, and the worker each contributed small amounts to an insurance fund. Many people called the legislation *state socialism.*

Despite Bismarck's attempts to woo the workers away from socialism, the German working class continued to support the Social Democratic party in elections. On the eve of World War I, union membership was roughly 3 million, and the Social Democratic party was the largest single party in Germany. The socialists talked revolution, but the unions, the largest and most powerful in Europe, and many party members, favored policies of gradual reform. Great numbers of German workers were patriotic, even imperialistic, and thought their government deserved their loyalty.

By 1900, Germany had equalled and in some areas surpassed Britain in economic growth. Aided by the skill of its scientists and inventors, Germany became a leader in the chemical and electrical industries. It possessed the most extensive sector of large-scale and concentrated industrial and corporate capitalism. Within a short period of time Germany had become a powerful industrialized state, ready and eager to play an important role in world affairs. Its growing industrial and military might, combined with an aggressive nationalism, alarmed other states. This combination of German vitality, aggressiveness, and the fears of its rivals helped lead to World War I.

Italy: Unfulfilled Expectations

Italian nationalists expected greatness from the unification of their country, so long conquered, plundered, divided, and ruled by absolute princes. But the newly unified Italy faced serious problems. An overwhelmingly Roman Catholic country, it was split by religious controversy. Liberals and republicans wanted a secular state, with civil marriage and public education, which was anathema to the church. Another divisive factor was Italy's long tradition of separate and rival states. Many Italians doubted that the central government would deal justly with every region. Furthermore, few Italians could participate in the constitutional monarchy. Of the 27 million citizens, only about 2 million could vote—even after the reforms of 1881 that tripled the electorate. Liberals could point out that almost every literate male could vote, but this achievement was small consolation to those who had fought for unification but now were denied voting privileges because they did not pass a literacy test.

Among Italian workers, cynicism about the government was so deep that many turned to radical movements that advocated the rejection of authority and the tactics of terrorism, assassination, and general strikes. Disgust with parliamentary government led the workers to believe that direct action would gain more than elections and parties. Other alienated Italians included peasants in some rural areas, particularly in the south. They were so isolated from the national political and economic life that traditional patterns of loyalty to the local landowner, now also a political leader, persisted. Catholic, loyal to their landlord, and bitterly unhappy with their economic situation, they saw few signs of the new state other than taxation and conscription.

The ruling elite brushed aside Italy's difficult social and economic problems and concentrated instead on issues more easily expressed to an inexperienced political nation: nationalism, foreign policy, and military glory. The politicians trumpeted Italy's ambitions for Great Power status to justify military expenditures beyond the means of such a poor state. They furnished the rationale for Italy's scramble for African and Mediterranean territories by promising that their expansionist foreign policy would provide the solution to all Italy's social ills: the profits from exploiting others would pay for badly needed social reforms, and the raw materials gained would fuel industrialization. None of these promises came true, which deepened the cynicism of a disillusioned people. As a foreign and as a domestic policy, this pursuit of glory was too costly for the fragile nation.

Before World War I, Italy was deeply divided politically. A wave of strikes and rural discontent gave sufficient warning to political leaders that they declared neutrality, deciding, unlike Russia, not to risk the shaky regime by entering the war. But the appeals of expansionism were too great for them to maintain this policy.

The Emergence of the New Imperialism

Causes

The Second Industrial Revolution coincided with an age of imperialism as European states extended their hegemony over much of the globe. What accounted for the struggle of Europeans to claim and control the entire world? Some historians suggest that the *new* imperialism (to differentiate it from the *colonialism* of settlement and trade of the sixteenth to eighteenth centuries) was a direct result of industrialization. With intensified economic activity and competition, Europeans struggled for raw materials, markets for their commodities, and places to invest their capital. In the late nineteenth century, many politicians and industrialists believed that the only way their nations could ensure their economic necessities was the acquisition of overseas territories.

Captains of industry defended the new empires to their sometimes reluctant governments and countrymen, predicting dire consequences if their nation failed to get its share of the world markets. However, their expectations often did not materialize. Historians point to the fact that most areas claimed by Europeans and Americans did not possess profitable sources of raw materials nor wealth enough to be good markets. For Europeans and Americans the primary trading and investment areas were Europe and America rather than Asia or Africa. Some individual businesses made colonial profits, but most colonies proved unprofitable for the Western taxpayer.

The economic motivations of imperialism are inseparable from the intensely nationalistic one—the desire to win glory for the nation. Newly unified, Germany and Italy demanded colonies as recognition of their Great Power status. German and Italian nationalists were convinced that Britain's status depended on colonies and naval power, and they wanted their nations to "have a place in the sun." Having lost ingloriously to Prussia in 1870, France also turned overseas, hoping to recoup some prestige and to add to its manpower and wealth for future European struggles. The nationalistic competition between the Europeans led them, for a time, to extend their power struggles to Africa and Asia.

The most extreme ideological expression of nationalism was Social Darwinism (see Chapter 16), with its image of national vitality and competition between fit and unfit. Social Darwinists vigorously advocated empire. They argued that the strong nations—by definition, those that were successful at expanding industry and empire—would survive and that others would not. To these elitists, all white men were better fit than non-whites to prevail in the struggle for dominance, but among Europeans, some nations were deemed more fit than others for the competition. Social Darwinists were not embarrassed by the fact that their arguments were blatantly racist. In the popular mind, the concepts of evolution justified the exploitation of "lesser breeds without the law" by superior races. This language of race and conflict, of superior and inferior people, was widely expressed in the Western states.

Not all advocates of empire were Social Darwinists, however. Some did not think of themselves as racists. In fact, they believed that the extension of empire, law, order, and industrial civilization would raise "backward peoples" up the ladder of evolution and civilization. Many Westerners believed it was their duty as Christians to set an example and to educate others. Missionaries were the first to meet and learn about many peoples and the first to develop writing for those without a written language. Christian missionaries were ardently opposed to slavery, and throughout the century they had gone to unexplored African regions to preach against slavery, which was still carried on by Arab and African traders. But to end slavery, many of them believed that Europeans must furnish law, order, and stability.

Some of the passion for imperialism was sparked by interest in exotic places. At the turn of the nineteenth century, the expeditions by Mungo Park, a Scottish explorer, on the Niger River in West Africa stimulated the romantic imagination. The explorations of David Livingstone in the Congo Basin and of Richard Burton and John Speke (who raced with each other and with Livingstone to find the source of the Nile River) fascinated many Europeans.

A Christian Missionary in Togoland (Ghana).   Throughout the nineteenth century, Christian missionaries had gone to Asia, Africa, and Latin America to preach and to carry on the crusade against slavery. Many of these Christians devoted their lives to accomplishing their goals; at the same time, many carried with them the ethnocentric values and judgments of their compatriots who thought that non-Europeans were backward and uncivilized. (*Culver Pictures*)

Control and Resistance

Aided by superior technology and the machinery of the modern state, Europeans established varying degrees of political control over much of the rest of the world. Control could mean outright annexation and the governing of a territory as a colony. In this way Germany controlled Tanganyika (East Africa) after 1886, and Britain ruled much of India. Control could also mean status as a protectorate, in which the local ruler continued to rule but was directed, or "protected," by a Great Power. In this way the British controlled Egypt after 1882 and maintained authority over their dependent Indian princes, and France guarded Tunisia. There were also spheres of influence, in which, without military or political control, a European nation had special trading and legal privileges other Europeans did not have. At the turn of the century the Russians in the north and the British in the south, each recognizing the other's sphere of influence, divided Persia (Iran). In some non-Western lands, the governing authorities granted *extraterritoriality,* or the right of Europeans to trial by their own laws in foreign countries. Europeans often also lived a segregated and privileged life in quarters, clubs, and whole sections of foreign lands or cities in which no native was allowed to live.

Many non-Europeans resisted American and European economic penetration and political control in varied ways, and the very process of resistance shaped their history and their self-awareness. Such resistance became a statement of both national and individual identity. A few out of the many instances of such resistance include the Sudan Muslims' holy war led by the Mahdi Mohammed Ahmed against both Egyptian fellow Muslims, who were regarded as agents of the European nonbelievers, and the Europeans; the Boxer Rebellion in China; and the Sepoy Mutiny in India. Still others reacted to Western penetration with strongly nationalistic feelings and fought to strengthen the nationalism of their people, sometimes even going to Western universities, military schools, and factories to master the advanced technology. Mohandas Gandhi, Jawaharlal Nehru, Sun Yat-sen, Chiang Kai-shek, and Mustapha Kemal Atatürk are the most famous examples of nationalistic resistance to the West.

European Domination of Asia
India

In the last part of the eighteenth century, the British East India Company became a territorial power in India. It gained the upper hand by making alliances with warring princes, by carrying on trade and collecting taxes, and by commanding armies of *sepoys* (native soldiers). Parliament regulated the chartered monopoly enterprise, but in fact did not control it much until the Sepoy Mutiny of 1857–58. (The Indians call this massive act of resistance the Great Rebellion.) This major popular uprising joined Muslim and Hindu soldiers with some native princes who finally perceived that the British, rather than neighboring princes, were the true threat to their authority. The British, with the aid of faithful troops from the Punjab, repressed the uprising. The rebellion caused parliament to abolish the East India Company and to make India an integral part of the British Empire. The British ruled some states through dependent Indian princes, but about two-thirds of the subcontinent was ruled directly by about a thousand British officials in the civil service.

At first, the civil service was entirely British, its officials confident of the superiority of their people, law, and society. Later, an elite of Indians educated in English and trained in administration became part of it. Indian civil servants, along with soldiers who were recruited from peoples with military traditions, such as the Gurkhas and the Punjabis, carried out British laws, adding their interpretations, customs, and traditions. By 1900, a civil service of 4,000 Europeans and half a million Indians ruled over more than 300 million

Indians representing almost 200 language groups and several religions, races, and cultures. Under the impact of British imperialism the subcontinent gained some political unity, an English-educated elite, and a focus for discontent—the common resentment of the British.

The British built a modern railroad and communications system and developed agriculture and industry to meet the needs of the world market. The railroad, as a link to areas of food surplus, reduced the incidence and impact of local famines, which had plagued India's history. British rule also ended internal war and disorder. Population increased as fewer people died of starvation and lives were saved by Western medical practices. But many students of history believe that the Indian masses did not benefit from economic progress because they could not pay their debts in money as their landlords demanded, and the British flooded the Indian market with cheap, machine-produced English goods, which drove native artisans out of business or even deeper into debt.

The racism that excluded the Indian elite from British clubs, hotels, and social gatherings and from top government positions alienated the leaders that British rule had created. Many of the older elite of princes and landlords who may have profited from British connections resented the lack of respect for Indian traditions and culture. Educated Indians, demanding equality and self-government, created the Indian National Congress in the 1880s. The Congress party ultimately organized masses of Indians to work toward independence.

In 1919, partly in response to agitation and partly as a reward for loyal Indian service during the war, the British granted India a legislative assembly representing almost a million of the 247 million in the subcontinent. The British granted some powers to this assembly, but retained most of them. At the same time, agitation and unrest became very bitter. In 1919, at Amritsar in Punjab, a British officer commanded his Gurkha troops to fire into a peaceful demonstration until their ammunition was exhausted. Three hundred seventy-nine Indians died and twelve hundred were wounded; women and children were among the victims. The government punished the officer, but the Indian British community gave him a fortune, honoring him for what he had done. The massacre and the behavior of the Britons stung Indians to action, including former supporters of the British and advocates of self-government within the British Empire.

Out of this feverish period emerged a gentle but nonetheless determined revolutionary leader, Mohandas K. Gandhi (1869–1948). In South Africa he had led the resistance of Indians to the vicious system of racial discrimination there, and in the process developed a doctrine of civil disobedience and nonviolent resistance. He believed that the power of love and spiritual purity would ultimately overthrow British rule in India. His was a spiritually uplifting message—and a shrewd political tactic as well. Gandhi called on the Indian elite to give up the privileges allotted by the British—to resign their positions, to

Map 15.1   Asia in 1914 ▶

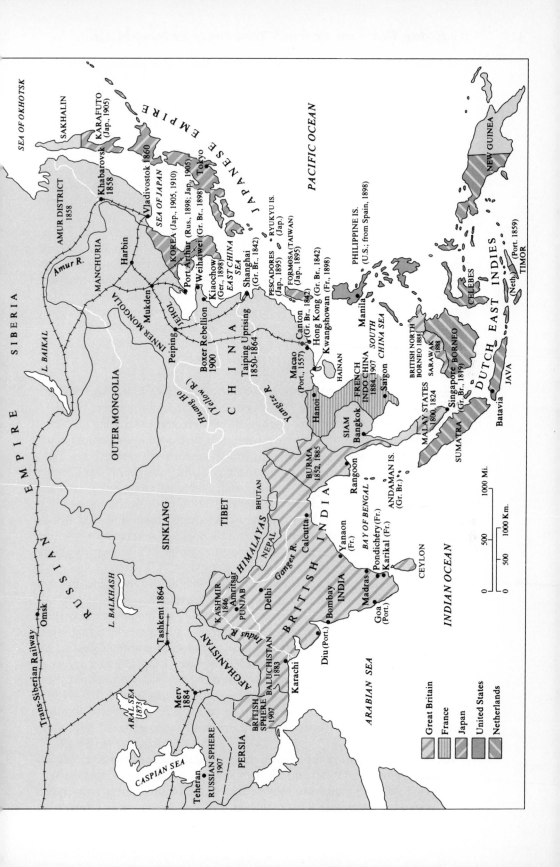

SEA OF OKHOTSK

SAKHALIN

KARAFUTO (Jap. 1905)

JAPANESE EMPIRE

PACIFIC OCEAN

Khabarovsk 1858

AMUR DISTRICT 1858

Amur R.

MANCHURIA

Harbin

Vladivostok 1860

Tokyo

SEA OF JAPAN

KOREA (Jap., 1905, 1910)

NEW GUINEA

SIBERIA

L. BAIKAL

Peiping

Mukden

JEHOL

INNER MONGOLIA

OUTER MONGOLIA

Port Arthur (Rus., 1898; Jap., 1905)

Weihaiwei (Gr. Br.) 1898

Kiaochow (Ger.) 1898

Shanghai (Gr. Br.) 1842

EAST CHINA SEA

RYUKYU IS. (Jap.)

FORMOSA (TAIWAN) (Jap., 1895)

PESCADORES (Jap., 1895)

PHILIPPINE IS. (U.S.: from Spain, 1898)

Boxer Rebellion 1900

CHINA

Taiping Uprising 1850–1864

Huang Ho (Yellow R.)

Yangtze R.

Macao (Port., 1557)

Canton (Gr. Br., 1842)

Hong Kong (Gr. Br., 1842)

Kwangshowan (Fr., 1898)

HAINAN

Manila

Hanoi

FRENCH INDOCHINA 1884, 1907

SOUTH CHINA SEA

Saigon

BRITISH NORTH BORNEO 1888

SARAWAK 1888

BORNEO

DUTCH EAST INDIES

CELEBES

TIMOR (Neth. (Port. 1859))

RUSSIAN EMPIRE

SINKIANG

TIBET

HIMALAYAS

BHUTAN

NEPAL

BURMA 1852, 1885

SIAM

Bangkok

Rangoon

ANDAMAN IS. (Gr. Br.)

MALAY STATES 1800, 1824

Singapore (Gr. Br.) 1819

SUMATRA

JAVA

Batavia

Trans-Siberian Railway

Omsk

L. BALKHASH

Tashkent 1864

KASHMIR 1846

Amritsar

PUNJAB

Delhi

Indus R.

AFGHANISTAN

BALUCHISTAN 1883

BRITISH SPHERE 1907

Karachi

Ganges R.

Calcutta

B R I T I S H   I N D I A

Yanaon (Fr.)

Pondichéry (Fr.)

Karikal (Fr.)

BAY OF BENGAL

CEYLON

Madras

INDIA

Bombay

Goa (Port.)

Diu (Port.)

ARABIAN SEA

INDIAN OCEAN

Merv 1884

ARAL SEA (1873)

PERSIA

Teheran

RUSSIAN SPHERE 1907

CASPIAN SEA

1000 Mi.

1000 Km.

500

500

0

0

Great Britain

France

Japan

United States

Netherlands

boycott British schools, and finally, to boycott all foreign goods. He dramatically rallied mass support with "the march to the sea," a mass refusal to pay taxes on salt. When imprisoned, Gandhi and his followers fasted for spiritual discipline, but their tactic also threatened the British with the possibility that the confined leaders would starve to death, setting off more civil disturbances. Gandhi also emphasized the boycott of foreign goods by spinning cottons and wearing simple native dress. To gain independence, Gandhi was even willing to sacrifice the higher standard of living that an industrial economy could bring to India.

After World War II had exhausted British resources and reduced British power, independence came: India was partitioned into Muslim Pakistan and predominantly Hindu India. Independence was achieved without a war between Britain and India, an accomplishment that many credit to the strength of Gandhi's moral leadership. But even his leadership could not prevent conflict between Hindu and Muslim, as bloody massacres at independence so clearly revealed.

China

Defeat by the British in the Opium War of 1839–1842 forced the Manchu Dynasty to open trade with the West. Before the war, any commerce had been limited, controlled by native monopolists who were granted trading privileges by the emperor. When the Chinese government destroyed Indian opium being traded by the East India Company, the British aggressively asserted their right to free trade and demanded compensation. In the subsequent war, Britain seized several trading cities along the coast, including Hong Kong, and the Chinese capitulated. In the Treaty of Nanking (1842), the British insisted that they determine the tariffs the Chinese might charge them and that British subjects in China have the right to be tried according to their own law (the right of extraterritoriality). Both provisions undermined the emperor's ability to control the foreigners in his country.

Defeat in the Opium War also forced change on the emperor. He drew on China's mandarins to revitalize the Manchu bureaucracy, by cleaning out much of the official corruption that weighed heavily on the poorest taxpayers and by strengthening China against the Westerners, sometimes by hiring Westerners to train Chinese armies. Nevertheless, widespread economic discontent, hatred of the Manchu (who were regarded by many Chinese as foreign conquerors, even though the conquest had taken place some two hundred years earlier), and religious mysticism inspired the Taiping Rebellion of 1850–1864. This uprising seriously threatened the dynasty, which was able to suppress the rebels with Western assistance. Britain and France extorted additional concessions.

For a time the Europeans seemed content with trading rights in coastal towns and preferential treatment for their subjects. But the Sino-Japanese War of 1894–95, which Japan won easily because of China's weakness, encouraged the Europeans to mutilate China. Britain, France, Russia, and Germany all

"The Real Trouble Will Come with the 'Wake' " by Joseph Keppler, 1900.   The Great Powers were unable to carve up China as they had Africa. The Europeans were able to wring such concessions as Hong Kong, trading, and special privileges from the weak empire. The American late-comers insisted that China be kept open for the trade of all—the Open Door policy. With the overthrow of the Manchu Dynasty in 1911, China became a republic, plagued by civil war and foreign aggression until the end of World War II. This lithograph from the August 1900 issue of *Puck* shows the Chinese dragon being fought over by the Great Powers. (*Library of Congress*)

scrambled for concessions, protectorates, and spheres of influence. China might have been carved up like Africa, but each Western nation, afraid of its rivals, resisted any partition that might possibly give another state an advantage. The United States, which insisted that it be given any trading concession that any other state received, proclaimed an "Open Door" policy stating that trade should be open to all, and that the Great Powers should respect the territorial integrity of China. The U.S. action may have restrained the Western powers from partitioning China, but it was also a way to ensure American interests in China.

Chinese traditionalists organized secret societies to expel foreigners and to punish Chinese who accepted Christianity or any other form of westernization. In 1900, encouraged by the Empress Tzu-hsi, the Society of Righteous and Harmonious Fists (called the Boxers by Europeans) attacked foreigners throughout the north of China. An international army of Europeans, Japanese, and Americans suppressed the rebellion, seized Chinese treasures, and forced China to pay an indemnity. They also made China accede to foreign troops stationed on its soil.

Chinese discontent with the dynasty deepened, as did unrest and nationalistic opposition to the foreigners. When the Japanese defeated the Russians in 1905, many Chinese argued that the only way to protect their country was to imitate the West, as the Japanese had done. Many signs of growing nationalism appeared. In 1911, nationalist revolutionaries, strongly present among soldiers, workers, and students, overthrew the Manchu and declared a republic. Sun Zhongshan (Sun Yat-sen, 1866–1925), who was in the United States when the revolution broke out, returned to China to become the first president of the republic and the head of the Nationalist party.

Espousing the Western ideas of democracy, nationalism, and social welfare (the three principles of the people, as Sun called them), the republic struggled to establish its authority over a China torn by civil war and ravaged by foreigners—Russia was claiming Mongolia and Britain was claiming Tibet. The northern warlords, who were regional leaders with private armies, resisted any attempt to strengthen the republic's army because it might diminish their power. In the south, the republic more or less maintained control. After Sun's death, the Guomindong (Kuomintang), under the authoritarian leadership of Jiang Jieshi (Chiang Kai-shek, 1887–1975), tried to westernize by using the military power of the state and introducing segments of a modern economic system. But faced with civil war, attacked from both the right and the communist left under Mao Zedong (Mao Tse-tung, 1893–1976), and by the Japanese after 1931, the Kuomintang made slow progress. A divided China continued to be at the mercy of outside interests until after World War II.

Japan

Japan, like China, was opened to the West against its will. The Japanese had expelled Europeans in the seventeenth century and kept isolated for the next two centuries. By the 1850s, as in India and China, social dissension within Japan and foreign pressure combined to force the country to admit outside trade. Americans in particular refused to accept Japanese prohibitions on commercial and religious contacts. Like China, Japan succumbed to superior technological power. In 1853, Commodore Matthew C. Perry sailed into Tokyo Bay, making a show of American strength and forcing the Japanese to sign a number of treaties that granted Westerners extraterritoriality and control over tariffs.

A flood of unrest was unleashed. A group of *samurai*, the warrior nobility, seized the government, determined to preserve Japan's independence. This takeover—the Meiji Restoration of 1867—returned power to the emperor, or Meiji, from the feudal aristocracy that had ruled in his name for almost seven hundred years. The new government enacted a series of reforms turning Japan into a powerful modern unitary state. Large landowners were persuaded to turn their estates over to the emperor in exchange for compensation and high-level positions in the government. All classes were made equal before the law. Universal military service was required, as in France and Germany, which diminished social privilege and helped to imbue Japanese of all classes with nationalism. The Japanese modeled their constitution on Bismarck's: there was a parliament, but the emperor held the most authority, which he delegated to his ministers to govern in his name without much control from the parliament.

The Meiji regime introduced modern industry and economic competition. Japanese visited factories all over the West and hired Westerners to teach industrial skills. The government, like central and eastern European governments, built defense industries, backed heavy industry and mining, and developed a modern communication system of railroads, roads, and telegraph. Industry in Japan adopted traditional Japanese values and emphasized cooperation more than competition; relations between employer and employee were paternalistic rather than individualistic and deferential rather than hostile. Within little more than a generation of the Meiji Restoration, Japan moved from economic backwardness to a place among the top ten industrial nations. To underdeveloped countries, Japan became a model of a nation that borrowed from the West yet preserved its traditional values and social structure.

By 1900, Japan had ended the humiliating treaties with the West and become an imperialist power in its own right. It had won Taiwan and Korea in its war with China (1894–95), although the Great Powers intervened, forcing the Japanese to return some of the spoils of victory while they themselves grabbed greater spheres of influence from the helpless Chinese. Their self-serving maneuvering infuriated the Japanese. Finally, in 1904, conflict over influence in Manchuria brought Japan and Russia to war, which Japan won. The victory of an Asian power over a Western power had a tremendous impact on Asian nationalists. If Japan could unite its people with nationalism and strong leadership, others should be able to do so. Japan's victory inspired anti-Western and nationalist movements throughout China, Indochina, India, and the Middle East.

How Japan would exercise its hard-won power was an open question in the post–World War I era. In the 1920s, the prosperous economy fortified the middle class and increased the importance of the working class, strengthening democratic institutions. But Japan's dependence on foreign trade meant the nation was hard hit by the Great Depression of 1929, when the major states subjected its trade to tariffs. The depression weakened the elements that contributed to peace, stability, and democracy in Japan and strengthened the militarist and fascist groups that were set on imperialism in Manchuria and China. To Asians in the 1930s, Japan seemed to champion Asian racial equality and to oppose Western imperialism. Many leaders of nationalist movements in Burma, India, Indochina, and Indonesia were attracted for a time by Japan's pose. World War II, however, brought Japanese occupation and exploitation, not freedom and equality for Asians.

The Scramble for Africa

The most rapid European expansion took place in Africa. Up to the 1870s, Great Power interest in Africa seemed marginal and likely to decline even further. As late as 1880, European nations ruled just a tenth of the continent. Only three decades later, by 1914, Europeans had claimed all of Africa except Liberia (a small territory of freed slaves from the United States) and Abyssinia (Ethiopia), which had successfully held off Italian invaders at Adowa in 1896.

The astounding activities of Leopold II, king of Belgium, spurred expansion. In 1876, as a private entrepreneur, he formed the International Association for the Exploration and Civilization of Central Africa. Leopold sent Henry Stanley (1841–1904) to the Congo River basin to establish trading posts, sign treaties with the chiefs, and claim the territory for the association. Stanley, an adventurer and a newspaper reporter who had fought on both sides of the American Civil War, had earlier led an expedition to central Africa in search of David Livingstone, the popular missionary-explorer who was believed to be in danger. For men like Stanley, Leopold's private development efforts promised profit and adventure. For the Africans, they promised brutal exploitation. The French responded to Leopold's actions by immediately establishing a protectorate on the north bank of the Congo. The scramble was on.

The Berlin Conference

Bismarck and Jules Ferry, the premier of France, called an international conference of the Great Powers in Berlin in 1884 to lay some ground rules for the development of Africa south of the Sahara. The Berlin Conference established the rule that a European country had to occupy territory effectively in order to claim it. This led to a mad race to the interior of Africa; it was a field day for explorers and soldiers. As Europeans rushed to claim territory, they ignored both natural and cultural frontiers. Even today the map of Africa reveals many straight (and thus artificial) boundary lines rather than the irregular lines of natural boundaries, such as rivers and mountains.

The conference declared that Leopold (as an individual, not as the king of Belgium) was the personal ruler of the Congo Free State. Before long, Leopold's Congo Association was trying to turn a profit with practices as vicious as those of the African slave traders. At the turn of the century, Edward D. Morel, an English humanitarian, produced evidence that slavery, mutilation, brutality, and murder were commonly practiced to force blacks to work for the rubber plantations in the Congo. In response to the outcry of public opinion, the Belgian parliament declared the territory a Belgian colony in 1908, putting an end to Leopold's private enterprise.

Map 15.2   Africa in 1914 ▶

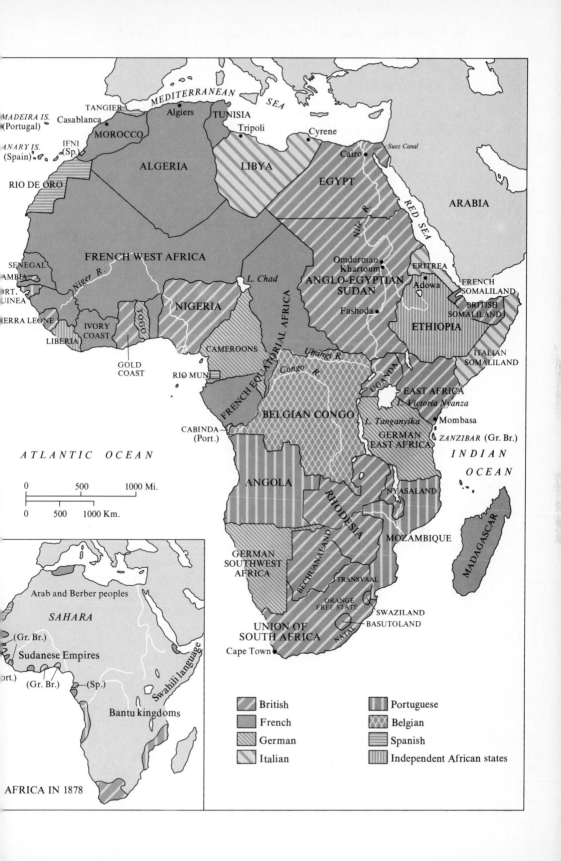

MADEIRA IS.
(Portugal)

TANGIER
Casablanca

MOROCCO

ANARY IS.
(Spain)

IFNI
(Sp.)

RIO DE ORO

MEDITERRANEAN

SEA

Algiers

TUNISIA

Tripoli

ALGERIA

LIBYA

Cyrene

Suez Canal

Cairo

EGYPT

ARABIA

RED SEA

Nile R.

SENEGAL
AMBIA

ORT.
UINEA

IERRA LEONE

LIBERIA

Niger R.

FRENCH WEST AFRICA

L. Chad

NIGERIA

IVORY
COAST

TOGO

GOLD
COAST

RIO MUNI

CAMEROONS

Omdurman
Khartoum

ERITREA

FRENCH
SOMALILAND

ANGLO-EGYPTIAN
SUDAN

Adowa

BRITISH
SOMALILAND

Fashoda

ETHIOPIA

ITALIAN
SOMALILAND

FRENCH EQUATORIAL AFRICA

Ubangi R.

Congo R.

BELGIAN CONGO

UGANDA

EAST AFRICA
L. Victoria Nyanza

CABINDA
(Port.)

L. Tanganyika

Mombasa

GERMAN
EAST AFRICA

ZANZIBAR (Gr. Br.)

ATLANTIC OCEAN

INDIAN

OCEAN

0   500   1000 Mi.

0   500   1000 Km.

ANGOLA

RHODESIA

NYASALAND

MOZAMBIQUE

MADAGASCAR

GERMAN
SOUTHWEST
AFRICA

BECHUANALAND

TRANSVAAL

Arab and Berber peoples

SAHARA

ORANGE
FREE STATE

SWAZILAND

BASUTOLAND

(Gr. Br.)

Sudanese Empires

ort.)

(Gr. Br.)

(Sp.)

Swahili language

UNION OF
SOUTH AFRICA

Cape Town

NATAL

Bantu kingdoms

British

Portuguese

French

Belgian

German

Spanish

Italian

Independent African states

AFRICA IN 1878

The British in Africa

For much of the nineteenth century, British interest in Africa was minimal. The opening of the Suez Canal in 1869, which Britain viewed as a vital highway to India, greatly increased the strategic value of Egypt, officially a part of the Ottoman Empire but effectively independent of the Ottoman sultan since the 1830s. When a nearly bankrupt Egypt could not pay its foreign debts and was threatened with internal rebellion, Britain intervened as "protector" in 1882. Prime Minister Gladstone, a "little Englander" (one who opposed empire), promised to withdraw British troops once the situation stabilized.

Not only did the British fail to withdraw from Egypt, they also moved further south into the Sudan, to quell a Muslim holy war against Egyptian authority and British influence. In 1885, the Sudanese, led by the Mahdi, who viewed himself as the successor to Muhammad, captured Khartoum and killed General Gordon, who had been sent to command the Egyptian forces. In 1898 the British, armed with machine guns, mowed down charging Muslims at Omdurman. The casualties were reported to be 11,000 Muslims and 28 Britons.

Immediately after the battle, British forces confronted the French at Fashoda in the Sudan. In the diplomatic crisis that followed, Britain and France were brought to the brink of war, and public passions were inflamed. Too divided by the Dreyfus affair at home to risk a showdown with Britain, however, the French cabinet ordered retreat.

The British also sought territory in South Africa. Cecil Rhodes (1853–1902), who had gone to South Africa for his health in 1870 and made a fortune in diamonds and gold, dreamed of expanding the British Empire. "The British," he declared, "are the finest race in the world and the more of the world we inhabit the better it is for the human race."[1] Rhodes was responsible for acquiring Rhodesia, a sizable and wealthy territory, for Britain. He also plotted to involve Britain in a war with the Boers, Dutch farmers and cattlemen who had settled in South Africa in the seventeenth century.

During the Napoleonic wars, the British had gained Cape Town, at the southern tip of Africa, a useful provisioning place for trading ships bound for India. Despising British rule and refusing to accept the British abolition of slavery in 1834, the Boers moved northward in a migration called the Great Trek (1835–1837), warring with African tribes along the way. They established two republics, the Transvaal and the Orange Free State, whose independence the British recognized in the 1850s. The republics' democratic practices did not extend to black Africans, who were denied political rights. In 1877, the British annexed Transvaal, but Boer resistance forced them in 1881 to recognize the Transvaal's independence again.

The discovery of rich deposits of gold and diamonds in the Boer lands reinforced Rhodes's dream to build a great British empire in Africa. In 1895, his close friend Leander Jameson led some 600 armed men into the Transvaal, hoping to create a pretext for a British invasion. Although the raid failed and both Jameson and Rhodes were disgraced, tensions between Britain and the Boer republics worsened, and in 1899 the Anglo-Boer War broke out.

Yoruba Carving of a European.
The African artist who carved this
figure has captured the spirit of the
old colonialism and the new imperialism with the symbols of the
European man with a gun and a
horse. Aztec, Chinese, Japanese, and
Indian artists also conveyed in their
works the sense of the intruder with
power. (*Neg. #327026, Courtesy
Department of Library Services,
American Museum of Natural
History*)

The Boers were formidable opponents—farmers by day and commandos by
night, armed with the latest French and German rifles. To deal with their
stubborn foe, the British herded or "concentrated" thousands of Boers, including women and children, into compounds where some 25,000 perished. After
three years, the nasty war ended in 1902. The British, hoping to live together in
peace with the Boers, drew up a conciliatory treaty. In 1910 the former Boer
republics were joined with the British territories into the Union of South Africa. Self-government within the British Empire for the British settlers and the
Boers did not help the majority black population, who had to cope with the
Boers' deeply entrenched racist attitudes.

Other European Countries in Africa

The cost of imperialism in Africa seemed high not only to the British but to
other imperialists as well. The Italians' defeat at Adowa (1896) by Ethiopians
belied Italian dreams of empire and national glory. (Bismarck scoffed that the
Italians had enormous appetites but very poor teeth.) Germans could take little
heart from their African acquisitions—Southwest Africa (Namibia), East Africa (Tanzania, but not Zanzibar, which was British), the Cameroons, and
Togo (part of Ghana today). The German colonies were the most efficiently

governed (critics said the most ruthlessly controlled), but they yielded few benefits other than pride of ownership, because they were costly to govern. And the Belgians had obviously gained no prestige from the horrors perpetrated in the Congo. Serious thinkers, contemplating the depths to which Europeans would sink in search of fortune and fame, began to suggest that barbarity characterized the Europeans more than the Africans. The Europeans seemed to be the moral barbarians, as novelist Joseph Conrad and others pointed out. Honor was fleeting and profits illusory, for the most part, in these new African empires.

The Legacy of Imperialism

World War I was a turning point in the history of imperialism, though neither mother countries nor colonies seemed aware of it at the time. The principle of self-determination, championed for European nationalities at the peace conference, was seized on by Asian and African intellectuals, who intensified their anti-imperialist efforts. After World War II, the exhausted colonial powers were reluctant to fight rebellious colonies. Moreover, after waging war to destroy Nazi imperialism and racism, European colonial powers had little moral justification to deny other peoples self-determination.

Today, almost a century after the rapid division of the world among the European and U.S. powers and decades after the decolonization of most of the world, the results of imperialism persist. Imperialism has left a legacy of deep animosity in countries of Asia, Africa, and Latin America. Although most nations have political independence, Western economic and cultural domination still exists and often influences the policies of autonomous governments. Much of the world is still poor and suffers from insufficient capital, unskilled leaders, and unstable governments. Many people in these poor areas believe that their countries' condition has resulted from a century of Western exploitation. They also believe that any political turmoil in their areas is due to the fact that the superpowers regard the areas as strategic to their interests or important in their ideological power struggle.

Imperialism has been a source of great bitterness to former colonial peoples not only because of its economic exploitation but also because of its encouragement of racism and callous disregard of other cultures. Thus, non-Western nationalism has often included anti-Western elements. Today, European nations and the United States must deal in the areas of economics and politics with nations acutely conscious of their nationhood and quick to condemn any policy that they perceive as imperialistic.

Imperialism accelerated the growth of a global market economy, completing a trend that began with the Commercial Revolution of the sixteenth and seventeenth centuries. At the beginning of the twentieth century, in many parts of Europe, even the working classes and the peasantry were able to buy goods

Chronology 15.1 ✿ Expansion of Western Power

1839–1842	The Opium War—defeat of the Chinese by the British, resulting in their annexing treaty ports in China and opening it to Western trade
1851	Louis Napoleon Bonaparte overthrows the Second Republic, becoming Emperor Napoleon III
1853	Commodore Perry, with U.S. naval forces, opens Japan to trade
1857–58	The Sepoy Mutiny—Britain replaces the East India Company and governs India through a viceroy
1867	Second Reform Bill doubles the English electorate
1869	The opening of the Suez Canal
1870	The Third French Republic is established
1870–71	The Franco-Prussian War; the Paris Commune; creation of the German Empire with William I as kaiser and Bismarck as chancellor
1876	Stanley sets up posts in the Congo for Leopold II of Belgium
1881	The French take control of Tunisia
1882	Britain occupies Egypt
1883–1885	The French fight the Chinese to claim Indochina
1884	The Berlin Conference on Africa; Reform Bill grants suffrage to most English men
1894–1906	The Dreyfus affair in France
1898	The Spanish-American War—the United States acquires the Philippines and Puerto Rico and occupies Cuba; the battle of Omdurman
1899–1902	The Boer War between the British and the Afrikaners
1900	The Boxers rebel against foreign presence in China
1904–1905	Russo-Japanese War—the Japanese defeat the Russians
1911	Parliament Act limits the power of the House of Lords
1919	Britain grants a legislative assembly in India; Gandhi's passive resistance movement broadens with the Amritsar Massacre

from faraway places that had previously been available only to the very wealthy. The underdeveloped areas of the world in turn found markets for their crops and were able to buy European commodities—at least, the wealthy could.

But being part of the world economy also created problems. Increasing crop production to satisfy European and American markets often meant turning land that had grown food for families over to export crops like coffee or indigo, thus reducing the food supply; it also often meant consolidation of small peasant holdings in the hands of richer peasants or landlords. Thus, market forces drove the poorer peasants off the land, into debt to the landlord or to the usurer, and into cities. For most of the nineteenth century, the peasants felt bonded to their traditional masters, but in the twentieth century they came to see themselves as enslaved by foreigners who controlled either the government or the world market. The passionate desire to escape this bondage has fueled revolutionary movements throughout the world.

Imperialism has also led to the spread of Western civilization around the globe. The influence of Western ideas, institutions, techniques, language, and culture is everywhere. English and to some extent French are international languages. African and Asian lands have adopted, often with limited success, democracy and parliamentary government from the West. Socialism, a Western ideology, has been transplanted in Third World countries. Industrialism and modern science, both achievements of the West, have become globalized. So too have Western agricultural techniques, business practices, medicine, legal procedures, school curricula, architecture, music, dress. That Turkish women are no longer required to wear the veil, that Chinese women no longer have their feet bound, that Indians have outlawed untouchability, that Arabs, Africans, and Indians no longer practice slavery—all occurred under the influence of Western ideas. (To be sure, cultural forms have not moved in only one direction; African and Asian ways have also influenced Western lands.) The impact of Western ways on the Third World is one of the most crucial developments of our time.

Notes

1. Joseph E. Flint, *Cecil Rhodes* (Boston: Little Brown, 1974), p. 248.

Suggested Reading

Brunschwig, Henri, *French Colonialism: 1871–1914. Myths and Realities* (trans. 1964). The best book on French imperialism.

Craig, Gordon, *Politics of the Prussian Army* (1955). A very valuable study with important implications for German and European history.

Ford, Colin, and Brian Harrison, *A Hundred Years Ago* (1983). An excellent social history of Britain with fine photographs.

Hobsbawm, Eric, *The Age of Capital* (1988). A Marxist interpretation of mid-nineteenth-century Europe.

Holborn, Hajo, *History of Modern Germany, 1840–1945, vol. 3 (1969). A definitive work.

Joll, James, *Europe Since 1870* (1973). A valuable general survey, particularly good on socialism in the individual nations.

Mack Smith, Denis, *Italy: A Modern History*, rev. ed. (1969). An excellent survey, with emphasis on the theme of the failure of Italy to develop viable liberal institutions or economic solutions.

Robinson, R. E., John Gallagher, and Alice Denny, *Africa and the Victo-rians: The Official Mind of Imperialism* (1961). An essential book for this fascinating subject; well-written and controversial.

Thornton, A. P., *The Imperial Idea and Its Enemies: A Study in British Power*, 2nd ed. (1985). An interesting study of the ideas and policies of British imperialism.

Webb, R. K., *Modern England from the Eighteenth Century to the Present* (1968). A well-informed, readable book that is balanced on controversial issues.

Review Questions

1. Why is the last part of the nineteenth century described as "the second Industrial Revolution"?
2. What was the difference between orthodox and revisionist Marxists?
3. Characterize the domestic histories of each of the following countries in the last part of the nineteenth century: Britain, France, Germany, and Italy.
4. Account for the rise of the new imperialism in the last part of the nineteenth century.
5. Why and how were Europeans able to dominate African and Asian lands?
6. What role did each of the following play in the history of imperialism: Cecil Rhodes, Sun Yat-sen, Matthew C. Perry, Henry Stanley, King Leopold II?
7. What is the legacy of imperialism for the contemporary world?

Chapter · 16

Changing Patterns of Thought and Culture: Reason, Antireason, and Modern Consciousness

The second half of the nineteenth century was characterized by great progress in science, a surge in industrialism, and a continuing secularization of life and thought. The principal intellectual currents of the century's middle decades reflected these trends. Realism, positivism, Darwinism, Marxism, and liberalism all reacted against romantic, religious, and metaphysical interpretations of nature and society and focused on the empirical world; adherents of these movements relied on careful observation and strove for scientific accuracy. This emphasis on objective reality helped to stimulate a growing criticism of social ills; for despite unprecedented material progress, reality was often sordid, somber, and depressing.

By the end of the nineteenth and beginning of the twentieth centuries, extraordinary creativity in thought and the arts produced a shift in European consciousness. Thinkers and scientists achieved revolutionary insights into human nature, the social world, and the physical universe; writers and artists opened up hitherto unimagined possibilities for artistic expression. The mechanical model of the universe that had dominated the Western outlook since Newton had to be altered; the Enlightenment view of human rationality and goodness was questioned; the belief in natural rights and objective standards governing morality was attacked; rules of aesthetics that had governed the arts since the Renaissance were dispensed with. However imaginative and fruitful these changes were for Western intellectual and cultural life, they also helped create the disoriented, fragmented, and troubled era that is the twentieth century. ✷

Realism and Naturalism

Realism, the dominant movement in art and literature in the mid-nineteenth century, opposed the romantic veneration of the inner life and romantic sentimentality. The romantics exalted passion and intuition, let their imaginations transport them to a presumed idyllic medieval past, and sought subjective solitude amid nature's wonders. Realists, in contrast, were preoccupied with the external world, with social conditions and contemporary manners, with the familiar details of everyday life. With clinical detachment and meticulous care, they analyzed how people looked, worked, and behaved.

Like scientists, realist writers and artists carefully investigated the empirical world. For example, Gustave Courbet (1819–1877), who exemplified realism in painting, sought to practice what he called a "living art," painting common people and commonplace scenes—laborers breaking stones, peasants tilling the soil or returning from a fair, a country burial, wrestlers, bathers, family groups. In a matter-of-fact style, without any attempt at glorification, realist artists also depicted floor scrapers, rag pickers, prostitutes, and beggars. Seeking to portray reality as it is, realist writers frequently dealt with social abuses and the sordid aspects of human behavior and social life. Harriet Beecher Stowe's *Uncle Tom's Cabin* (1852) graphically described the horrors of slavery. Ivan Turgenev's *Sketches* (1852) described rural conditions in Russia and expressed compassion for the brutally difficult life of serfs. In *War and Peace* (1863–1869), Leo Tolstoy vividly described the manners and outlook of the Russian nobility and the tragedies that attended Napoleon's invasion of Russia. In *Anna Karenina* (1873–1877), he treated the reality of class divisions and the complexities of marital relationships. Many regard Gustave Flaubert's *Madame Bovary* (1857) as the prototype of the realistic novel; it tells the story of a self-centered wife who shows her hatred for her devoted, hard-working, but dull husband by committing adultery. In *Bleak House* (1853), *Hard Times* (1854), and several other works, Charles Dickens portrayed the squalor of life, the hypocrisy of society, and the drudgery of labor in British industrial cities.

Literary realism evolved into naturalism when writers tried to demonstrate that there was a causal relationship between human character and the social environment—that certain conditions of life produced predictable character traits in human beings. This belief that human behavior was governed by a law of cause and effect reflected the immense prestige attached to science in the closing decades of the nineteenth century. Émile Zola, the leading naturalist novelist, probed the slums, brothels, mining villages, and cabarets of France, examining how people were conditioned by the squalor of their environment.

The Norwegian Henrik Ibsen, the leading naturalist playwright, examined with clinical precision the commercial and professional classes, their personal ambitions and family relationships. In the *Pillars of Society* (1877), Ibsen treated bourgeois social pretensions and hypocrisy; in *A Doll's House* (1879) a woman leaves her husband in search of a more fulfilling life—a theme that shocked a late-nineteenth-century bourgeois audience.

In aiming for a true-to-life portrayal of human behavior and the social environment, realism and naturalism coincided with an attitude of mind shaped by science, industrialism, and secularism. Both movements reasserted the importance of the external world. The same outlook also gave rise to positivism in philosophy.

Positivism

Positivists viewed science as the highest achievement of the mind and sought to apply a strict empirical approach to the study of society. They believed that the philosopher must proceed like a scientist, carefully assembling and classifying data and formulating general rules that demonstrate regularities in the social experience. Such knowledge based on concrete facts would provide the social planner with useful insights. Positivists rejected metaphysics, which in the tradition of Plato tried to discover ultimate principles through reason alone, rather than through observation of the empirical world. For the positivist, any effort to go beyond the realm of experience to a deeper reality would be a mistaken and fruitless endeavor.

Auguste Comte (1798–1857), the father of positivism, called for a purely scientific approach to history and society: only by a proper understanding of the laws governing human affairs could society, which was in a state of intellectual anarchy, be rationally reorganized. Comte called his system *positivism* because he believed that it rested on sure knowledge derived from observed facts and was therefore empirically verifiable. Like others of his generation, Comte believed that scientific laws underlay human affairs and that they were discoverable through the methods of the empirical scientist—that is, through recording and systematizing observable data. "I shall bring factual proof," he said, "that there are just as definite laws for the development of the human race as there are for the fall of a stone."[1]

One of the laws that Comte believed he had discovered was the "law of the three stages." Comte held that the human mind had progressed through three broad historical stages—the theological, the metaphysical, and the scientific. In the theological stage, the most primitive, the mind found a supernatural explanation for the origins and purpose of things, and society was ruled by priests. In the metaphysical stage, which included the Enlightenment, the mind tried to explain things through abstractions—"nature," "equality," "natural rights," "popular sovereignty"—that rested on hope and belief rather than on empirical investigation. The metaphysical stage was a transitional period between the infantile theological stage and the highest stage of society, the scientific or positive stage. In this culminating stage the mind breaks with all illusions inherited from the past, formulates laws based on careful observation of the empirical world, and reconstructs society in accordance with these laws. People remove all mystery from nature and base their social legislation on laws of society similar to the laws of nature discovered by Newton.

Although Comte attacked the philosophes for delving into abstractions instead of fashioning laws based on empirical knowledge, he was also influenced by the spirit of eighteenth-century philosophy. Like the philosophes he valued science, criticized supernatural religion, and believed in progress. In this way he accepted the Enlightenment's legacy, including the empirical and anti-theological spirit of Diderot's *Encyclopedia* and Montesquieu's quest for historical laws governing society. Because Comte advocated the scientific study of society, he is regarded as a principal founder of modern sociology.

Darwinism

In a century distinguished by scientific discoveries, perhaps the most important scientific advance was the theory of evolution formulated by Charles Darwin (1809–1882), an English naturalist. Darwin did for his discipline what Newton had done for physics; he made biology an objective science based on general principles. The Scientific Revolution of the seventeenth century had given people a new conception of space; Darwin radically altered our conception of time.

Natural Selection

During the eighteenth century, almost all people had adhered to the Biblical account of creation contained in Genesis: God had instantaneously created the universe and the various species of animal and plant life; and he had given every river and mountain and each species of animal and plant a finished and permanent form distinct from every other species. God had designed the bird's wings so that it could fly, the fish's eyes so that it could see under water, and the human legs so that people could walk. All this, it was believed, had occurred some six thousand years ago.

Gradually, this view was questioned. In 1830–1833, Sir Charles Lyell published his three-volume *Principles of Geology*, which showed that the planet had evolved slowly over many ages. In 1794, Erasmus Darwin, the grandfather of Charles Darwin, published *Zoonomia, or the Laws of Organic Life*, which offered evidence that the earth had existed for millions of years before the appearance of people and that animals experienced modifications that they passed on to their offspring.

In December 1831, Darwin sailed as a naturalist on the H.M.S. *Beagle*, which surveyed the shores of South America and some Pacific islands. During

Charles Darwin with His Eldest Son, William.   Darwin's theory of evolution was grounded in empirical observation and sound scientific reasoning. His theory also had a revolutionary impact on religion and social philosophy. (*Courtesy of Down House, Kent*).

the five-year expedition, Darwin collected and examined specimens of plant and animal life; he concluded that many animal species had perished, that new species had emerged, and that there were links between extinct and living species. In the *Origin of Species* (1859) and the *Descent of Man* (1871), Darwin used empirical evidence to show that the wide variety of animal species was due to a process of development over many millennia, and he supplied a convincing theory that explained how evolution operates.

Darwin adopted the Malthusian idea (see page 387) that the population reproduces faster than the food supply, causing a struggle for existence. Not all infant organisms grow to adulthood; not all adult organisms live to old age. The principle of *natural selection* determines which members of the species have a better chance for survival. The offspring of lions, giraffes, or insects are not exact duplications of their parents. A baby lion might have the potential for being slightly faster or stronger than its parents; a baby giraffe might grow up to have a longer neck than its parents; an insect might have a slightly different color. These small variations give the organism a crucial advantage in the struggle for food and against natural enemies. The organism favored by nature is more likely to reach maturity, to mate, and to pass on its superior qualities to its offspring, some of which will acquire the advantageous trait to an even greater degree than the parent. Over many generations the favorable characteristic becomes more pronounced and more widespread within the species. Over millennia, natural selection causes the death of old, less adapt-able species and the creation of new ones. Very few of the species that dwelt on earth ten million years ago still survive today, and many new ones, including human beings, have emerged. People themselves are products of natural selec-tion, evolving from earlier, lower, nonhuman forms of life.

Darwinism and Christianity

Like Newton's law of universal gravitation, Darwin's theory of evolution had revolutionary consequences in areas other than science. Evolution challenged traditional Christian belief. To some, it undermined the infallibility of Scrip-ture and the conviction that the Bible was indeed the Word of God. Darwin's theory touched off a great religious controversy between fundamentalists who defended a literal interpretation of Genesis and advocates of the new biology. In time, most religious thinkers tried to reconcile evolution with the Christian view that there was a Creation and that it had a purpose. These Christian thinkers held that God was the creator and the director of the evolutionary processes.

Darwinism ultimately helped end the practice of relying on the Bible as an authority in questions of science, completing a trend initiated earlier by Galileo. Darwinism contributed to the waning of religious belief and to a growing secular attitude, which dismissed or paid scant attention to the Christian view of a universe designed by God and a soul that rises to heaven. For many, the conclusion seemed inescapable: nature contained no divine design or purpose, and the human species itself was a chance product of impersonal forces. The core idea of Christianity—that people were children of God participating in a drama of salvation—rested more than ever on faith rather than reason. Some even talked openly about the death of God. The notion that people are sheer accidents of nature was shocking. Copernicus had deprived people of the comforting belief that the earth had been placed in the center of the universe just for them; Darwin deprived people of the privilege of being God's special creation, thereby contributing to the feeling of anxiety that characterizes the twentieth century.

Social Darwinism

Darwin's theories were extended by others beyond the realm in which he had worked. Social thinkers, who recklessly applied Darwin's conclusions to the social order, produced theories that had dangerous consequences for society. Social Darwinists—those who transferred Darwin's scientific theories to social and economic issues—used the terms "struggle for existence" and "survival of the fittest" to buttress economic individualism and political conservatism. Suc-cessful businessmen, they said, had demonstrated their fitness to succeed in the competitive world of business. Their success accorded with nature's laws and therefore was beneficial to society; those who lost out in the social-economic struggle had demonstrated their unfitness. Using Darwin's model of organisms evolving and changing slowly over tens of thousands of years, conservatives insisted that society too should experience change at an unhurried pace. Instant reforms conflicted with nature's laws and wisdom and resulted in a deterioration of the social body.

The application of Darwin's biological concepts to the social world, where they did not apply, also buttressed imperialism, racism, nationalism, and militarism. Social Darwinists insisted nations and races were engaged in a struggle for survival in which only the fittest survive and deserve to survive. Karl Pearson, a British professor of mathematics, wrote in *National Life from the Standpoint of Science* (1900): "History shows me only one way, and one way only in which a higher state of civilization has been produced, namely the struggle of race with race, and the survival of the physically and mentally fitter race."[2] "We are a conquering race," said U.S. Senator Albert J. Beveridge. "We must obey our blood and occupy new markets, and if necessary, new lands."[3] "War is a biological necessity of the first importance,"[4] exclaimed the Prussian General von Bernhardi in *Germany and the Next War* (1911).

Darwinian biology was used to promote the belief in Anglo-Saxon (British and American) and Teutonic (German) racial superiority. These peoples attributed the growth of the British Empire, the expansion of the United States to the Pacific, and the extension of German power to their racial qualities. The domination of other peoples—American Indians, Africans, Asians, Poles— was regarded as the natural right of the superior race.

The theory of evolution was a great achievement of the rational mind, but in the hands of the Social Darwinists it served to undermine the Enlightenment tradition. Whereas the philosophes emphasized human equality, Social Darwinists divided humanity into racial superiors and inferiors. Whereas the philosophes believed that states would increasingly submit to the rule of law to reduce violent conflicts, Social Darwinists regarded racial and national conflict as a biological necessity, a law of history, and a means to progress. In propagating a tooth-and-claw version of human and international relations, Social Darwinists dispensed with the humanitarian and cosmopolitan sentiments of the philosophes and distorted the image of progress. Their views promoted territorial aggrandizement and military buildup and led many to welcome World War I. The Social Darwinist notion of the struggle of races for survival became a core doctrine of the Nazi party after World War I and helped to provide the "scientific" and "ethical" justification for genocide.

Irrationalism

The modern mentality may be said to have passed through two broad phases— an early modernity and a late modernity. Formulated during the era of the Scientific Revolution and the Enlightenment, the outlook of early modernity stressed confidence in reason, science, human goodness, and humanity's capacity to improve society for human betterment. In the late nineteenth and early twentieth centuries, a new outlook took shape. It broke with standards of aesthetics that had been established during the Renaissance, altered the view of nature shaped during the Scientific Revolution, and rejected the Enlightenment attitude toward reason and progress. Shattering old beliefs, late modernity left Europeans without landmarks, without generally accepted cultural standards or agreed-upon conceptions of the human person and life's meaning.

Exemplifying this shift in European consciousness in the late nineteenth century were those thinkers who repudiated the Enlightenment conception of human rationality, stressing instead the irrational side of human behavior. For these thinkers it seemed that reason exercised a very limited influence over human conduct; impulses, drives, instincts—all forces below the surface—determined behavior much more than logical consciousness did. Like the romantics, proponents of the irrational placed more reliance on feeling and intuition than on reason. They belittled the intellect's attempt to comprehend nature and society, praised outbursts of the irrational, and in some instances exalted violence.

Nietzsche

The principal figure in the "dethronement of reason" and the glorification of the irrational was the German philosopher Friedrich Nietzsche (1844–1900). Nietzsche's writings are not systematic treatises but collections of aphorisms, often containing internal contradictions. For this reason his philosophy lends itself to misinterpretation and misapplication, as manifested by Nazi theorists who distorted Nietzsche to justify their theory of the German master race.

Nietzsche attacked the accepted views and convictions of his day as a hindrance to a fuller and richer existence for man. He denounced social reform, parliamentary government, and universal suffrage, ridiculed the vision of progress through science, condemned Christian morality, and mocked the liberal belief in man's essential goodness and rationality. He said that man must understand that life, which is replete with cruelty, injustice, uncertainty, and absurdity, is not governed by rational principles. There exist no absolute standards of good and evil whose truth can be demonstrated by reflective reason. There is only naked man living in a godless and absurd world.

Modern bourgeois society, said Nietzsche, was decadent and enfeebled—a victim of the excessive development of the rational faculties at the expense of will and instinct. Against the liberal-rationalist stress on the intellect, Nietzsche urged recognition of the dark mysterious world of instinctual desires—the true forces of life. Smother the will with excessive intellectualizing and you destroy that spontaneity that sparks cultural creativity and ignites a zest for living. The critical and theoretical outlook destroyed the creative instincts. For man's manifold potential to be realized, he must forego relying on the intellect and nurture again the instinctual roots of human existence.

Christianity, with all its prohibitions, restrictions, and demands to conform, also crushes the human impulse for life, said Nietzsche. Christian morality must be obliterated, for it is fit only for the weak, the slave. The triumph of

Christianity in the ancient world, said Nietzsche, was a revolution of the meek to inherit the earth from the strong. Christian otherworldliness undermined man's will to control the world; Christian teachings saddled man with guilt, preventing him from expressing his instinctual nature.

Although the philosophes had rejected Christian doctrines, they had largely retained Christian ethics. Nietzsche, however, did not attack Christianity because it was contrary to reason, as the philosophes had; he attacked Christianity because he said it gave man a sick soul. It was life-denying; it blocked the free and spontaneous exercise of human instincts and made humility and self-abnegation virtues and pride a vice; in short, Christianity extinguished the spark of life in man. This spark of life, this inner yearning which is man's true essence, must again burn.

"God is dead," proclaimed Nietzsche. God is man's own creation; there are no higher worlds. Christian morality is also dead. The death of God and Christian values can mean the liberation of man, insisted Nietzsche. Man can create new values and achieve self-mastery. He can overcome the deadening uniformity and mediocrity of modern civilization. He can undo democracy and socialism, which have made masters out of cattlelike masses, and the shop-keeper's spirit, which has made man soft and degenerate. European society is without heroic figures; all belong to a vast herd but there are no shepherds. Europe can only be saved by the emergence of a higher type of man, the *superman* or *overman,* who would not be held back by the egalitarian rubbish preached by democrats and socialists. "It is necessary for *higher* man to declare war upon the masses," said Nietzsche, to end "the dominion of *inferior* men." Europe requires "the annihilation of universal suffrage—this is to say, that system by means of which the lowest natures prescribe themselves as a law for higher natures."[5] Europe needs a new breed of rulers, a true aristocracy of masterful men.

The superman is a new kind of man who breaks with accepted morality and sets his own standards. He does not repress his instincts but asserts them. He destroys old values and asserts his prerogative as master. Free of Christian guilt, he proudly affirms his own being; dispensing with Christian "thou shalt not," he instinctively says "I will." He dares to be himself. Because he is not like other people, traditional definitions of good and evil have no meaning for him. He does not allow his individuality to be stifled. He makes his own values, those that flow from his very being. He knows that life is meaningless but lives it laughingly, instinctively, fully. The superman's joyful and heroic assertion of the will rescues life from nothingness. He grasps that "the most fundamental desire in man [is] his drive for power,"[6] that human beings crave and strive for power ceaselessly and uncompromisingly. This will to power governs everyday life and is the determining factor in international affairs. The enhancement of power brings supreme enjoyment: "the love of power is the demon of men. Let them have everything—health, food, a place to live, entertainment—they are and remain unhappy and low-spirited; for the demon waits and waits and will be satisfied. Take everything from them and satisfy this and they are almost happy—as happy as men and demons can be."[7] The masses, cowardly and envious, will condemn the superman as evil; this has always been their way.

The influence of Nietzsche's philosophy is still a matter of controversy and conjecture. Perhaps better than anyone else, Nietzsche recognized the ills of modern Western civilization and urged confronting them without hypocrisy or compromise. But he had no constructive proposals for dealing with the malaise of modern society. No social policy could be derived from his radical individualism, which taught that "there are higher and lower men and that a single individual can . . . justify the existence of a whole millennia."[8] And his vitriolic attack on European institutions and values, immensely appealing to central European intellectuals, helped to erode the rational foundations of Western civilization. Many young people, attracted to Nietzsche's philosophy, welcomed World War I because they thought that it would clear a path to a new heroic age. They could not be blamed for taking literally Nietzsche's words: "A society that definitely and instinctively gives up war and conquest is in decline."[9]

Nazi theorists tried to make Nietzsche a forerunner of their movement. They sought from him philosophic justification for their own will to power, their ruthlessness, their glorification of action, and their cult of the heroic. Recasting Nietzsche in their own image, the Nazis regarded themselves as embodiments of Nietzsche's superman, the new aristocracy, the master race that would change the world. Nietzsche himself, who detested German nationalism and militarism, rejected racism and anti-Semitism, and denounced state-worship, would have abhorred Hitler. But Nietzsche's extreme and violent denunciation of Western democratic values, his praise of power, and his elitism provided a breeding ground for violent, antirational, and antidemocratic movements.

Bergson

Another thinker who reflected the growing irrationalism of the age was Henri Bergson (1859–1941), a French philosopher of Jewish background. Originally attracted to positivism, Bergson turned away from the positivistic claim that science could explain everything and fulfill all human needs. Such an emphasis on the intellect, said Bergson, sacrifices spiritual impulses, imagination, and intuition and reduces the soul to a mere mechanism.

The methods of science cannot reveal ultimate reality, Bergson insisted. European civilization must recognize the limitations of scientific rationalism. The method of intuition, whereby the mind strives to immerse itself in the object, to become one with it, can reveal more about reality than the method of analysis employed by science. The intuitive experience is a direct avenue to truth that is closed to the calculations and measurements of science. Bergson's philosophy pointed away from science toward religious mysticism. Its popularity was another indication of the nonrational's strength and appeal, a sign that people were searching for new alternatives to the Enlightenment world-view.

Sorel

Nietzsche proclaimed that irrational forces constitute the essence of human nature; Bergson held that a nonrational intuition provided insights unattainable by scientific thinking. Georges Sorel (1847–1922), a French social theorist, recognized the political potential of the nonrational. Like Nietzsche, Sorel was disillusioned with contemporary bourgeois society, which he considered decadent, soft, and unheroic. Whereas Nietzsche called for the superman to rescue society from decadence and mediocrity, Sorel placed his hopes in the proletariat, whose position made them courageous, virile, and determined. Sorel wanted the proletariat to destroy the existing order. This overthrow, said Sorel, would be accomplished through a general strike—a universal work stoppage that would bring down the government and give power to the workers.

The general strike had all the appeal of a great myth, said Sorel. What is important is not that the general strike actually takes place, but that its image stirs all the anticapitalist resentments of the workers and inspires them to their revolutionary responsibilities. Sorel understood the extraordinary potency of myths for eliciting total commitment and inciting heroic action. Because they appeal to the imagination and feelings, myths are an effective way of moving the masses to revolt. By believing in the myth of the general strike, workers would soar above the moral decadence of bourgeois society and bear the immense sacrifices that their struggle calls for. Sorel believed that the only recourse for workers was direct action and violence, which he regarded as ennobling, heroic, and sublime—a means of restoring grandeur to a flabby world.

Sorel's pseudoreligious exaltation of violence and mass action, his condemnation of liberal democracy and rationalism, and his recognition of the power and political utility of fabricated myths would find concrete expression in the fascist movements after World War I. Sorel heralded the age of mass political movements determined to destroy democracy and myths manufactured by propaganda experts.

Freud: A New View of Human Nature

In many ways Sigmund Freud (1856–1939), an Austrian Jewish doctor who spent most of his adult life in Vienna, was a child of the Enlightenment. Like the philosophes, Freud identified civilization with reason and regarded science as the avenue to knowledge. But unlike the philosophes, Freud focused on the massive power and influence of nonrational drives. Whereas Nietzsche glorified the irrational and approached it with a poet's temperament, Freud recognized its potential danger, sought to comprehend it scientifically, and wanted to regulate it in the interests of civilization. Unlike Nietzsche, Freud did not belittle the rational, but always sought to salvage respect for reason.

Freud held that people are not fundamentally rational; human behavior is governed primarily by powerful inner forces that are hidden from consciousness. These instinctual strivings, rather than rational faculties, constitute the greater part of the mind. Freud's great achievement was to explore the world

Freud and His Daughter Anna in the Dolomites, 1912.   Sigmund Freud, the father of psychoanalysis, penetrated the world of the unconscious in a scientific way. He concluded that powerful drives govern human behavior more than reason does. His explorations of the unconscious produced an image of the human being that broke with the Enlightenment's view of the individual's essential rationality. (*Mary Evans Picture Library*)

of the unconscious with the tools and temperament of a scientist. He considered not just the external acts of a person but also the inner psychic reality that underlies human behavior.

Freud sought to comprehend neuroses—disorders in thinking, feeling, and behavior that interfere with everyday acts of personal and social life. Neuroses can take several forms, including hysteria, anxiety, depression, and so on. To understand neuroses, said Freud, one had to look beyond a patient's symptoms and discover those unconscious factors, generally sexual in nature, that are at the root of the person's distress. The key to the unconscious, he said, was the interpretation of dreams.

The *id,* the subconscious seat of the instincts, constantly demands gratification, said Freud. Unable to endure tension, it demands sexual release, the termination of pain, the cessation of hunger. When the id is denied an outlet for its instinctual energy, people become frustrated, angry, and unhappy. Gratifying the id is our highest pleasure. But the full gratification of instinctual demands is detrimental to civilized life.

Freud postulated a terrible conflict between the relentless strivings of our instinctual nature and the requirements of civilization. Civilization, for Freud, requires the renunciation of instinctual gratification and the mastery of animal instincts, a thesis he developed in *Civilization and Its Discontents* (1930). While Freud's thoughts in this work were no doubt influenced by the great tragedy of World War I, the main theme could be traced back to his earlier writings. Human beings derive their highest pleasure from sexual fulfillment, said Freud, but unrestrained sexuality drains off psychic energy needed for creative artistic and intellectual life. Hence society, through the family, the priest, the teacher, and the police, imposes rules and restrictions on our animal nature. But this is immensely painful. People are caught in a tragic bind. Society's demand for the denial of full instinctual gratification causes terrible frustration; equally distressing, the violation of society's rules under the pressure of instinctual needs evokes terrible feelings of guilt. Either way people suffer; civilized life simply entails too much pain for people. It seems that the price we pay for civilization is neurosis. Most people cannot endure the amount of instinctual renunciation that civilization requires. There are times when our elemental human nature rebels against all the restrictions and "thou shalt nots" demanded by society, against all the misery and torment imposed by civilization.

"Civilization imposes great sacrifices not only on man's sexuality but also on his aggressivity,"[10] said Freud. People are not good by nature, as the philosophes had taught; on the contrary, they are "creatures among whose instinctual endowments is to be reckoned a powerful share of aggressiveness." Their first inclination is not to love their neighbor but to "satisfy their aggressiveness on him, to exploit his capacity for work without compensation, to use him sexually without his consent, to seize his possessions, to humiliate him, to cause him pain, to torture and to kill him." Man is wolf to man, concluded Freud. "Who has the courage to dispute it in the face of all the evidence in his own life and in history?" Civilization "has to use its utmost efforts in order to set limits to man's aggressive instincts," but "in spite of every effort these endeavors of civilization have not so far achieved very much." People find it difficult to do without "the satisfaction of this inclination to aggression." When circumstances are favorable, this primitive aggressiveness breaks loose and "reveals man as a savage beast to whom consideration towards his own kind is something alien." For Freud, "the inclination to aggression is an original self-subsisting disposition in man . . . that . . . constitutes the greatest impediment to civilization."[11] Aggressive impulses drive people apart, threatening society with disintegration. For Freud an unalterable core of human nature is ineluctably in opposition to civilized life. To this extent everyone is potentially an enemy of civilization.

Freud's awareness of the irrational and his general pessimism regarding people's ability to regulate it in the interests of civilization did not lead him to break faith with the Enlightenment tradition, for Freud did not celebrate the irrational. He was too aware of its self-destructive nature for that. Civilization is indeed a burden, but people must bear it, for the alternative is far worse. In the tradition of the philosophes Freud sought truth based on a scientific analysis of human nature and believed that reason was the best road to social improvement. Like the philosophes he was critical of religion, regarding it as a pious illusion—a fairy tale in conflict with reason. Freud wanted people to throw away what he believed was the crutch of religion—to break away from childlike dependency and stand alone. Also like the philosophes, Freud was a humanitarian who sought to relieve human misery by making people aware of their true nature, particularly their sexuality. He wanted society to soften its overly restrictive sexual standards because they were injurious to mental health.

Although Freud undoubtedly was a child of the Enlightenment, in crucial ways he differed from the philosophes. Regarding the Christian doctrine of original sin as myth, the philosophes had believed that people's nature was essentially good. If people took reason as their guide, evil could be eliminated. Freud, however, asserted, in secular and scientific terms, a pessimistic view of human nature. Freud saw evil as rooted in human nature rather than as a product of a faulty environment. Education and better living conditions will not eliminate evil, as the philosophes expected, nor will abolition of private property, as Marx had declared. The philosophes venerated reason; it had enabled Newton to unravel nature's mysteries and would permit people to achieve virtue and reform society. Freud, who wanted reason to prevail, understood that its soft voice had to compete with the thunderous roars of the id. Freud broke with the optimism of the philosophes. His awareness of the immense pressures that civilization places on our fragile egos led him to be generally pessimistic about the future. Unlike Marx, Freud had no vision of utopia.

The Modernist Movement
Breaking with Conventional Modes of Aesthetics

At the same time that Freud was breaking with the Enlightenment view of human nature, artists and writers were rebelling against traditional forms of artistic and literary expression that had governed European cultural life since the Renaissance. Their experimentations produced a great cultural revolution called *modernism*, which still profoundly influences the arts. In some ways, modernism was a continuation of the romantic movement that had dominated European culture in the early nineteenth century. Both movements subjected to searching criticism cultural styles that had been formulated during the Renaissance and had roots in ancient Greece.

But even more than romanticism, modernism aspired to an intense introspection—a heightened awareness of self—and saw the intellect as a barrier to the free expression of elemental human emotions. More than their romantic predecessors, modernist artists and writers abandoned conventional literary and artistic models and experimented with new modes of expression. The consequence of their bold venture, says literary critic and historian Irving

Howe, was nothing less than the "breakup of the traditional unity and continuity of Western culture."[12]

Like Freud, modernist artists and writers went beyond surface appearances in search of a more profound reality hidden in the human psyche. Writers like Thomas Mann, Marcel Proust, James Joyce, August Strindberg, D. H. Lawrence, and Franz Kafka explored the inner life of the individual and the psychopathology of human relations; they dealt with the predicament of men and women who rejected the values and customs of their day, and they depicted the anguish of people burdened by guilt, torn by internal conflicts, and driven by an inner self-destructiveness; they showed the overwhelming might of the irrational and the seductive power of the primitive and broke the silence about sex that had prevailed in Victorian literature.

From the Renaissance through the Enlightenment and into the nineteenth century, Western aesthetic standards had been shaped by the conviction that the universe embodied an inherent mathematical order. A corollary of this conception of the outer world as orderly and intelligible was the view that art should imitate reality, should mirror nature. Since the Renaissance, artists had deliberately made use of laws of perspective and proportion; musicians had used harmonic chords that brought rhythm and melody into a unified whole; writers had produced works according to a definite pattern that included a beginning, middle, and end.

Modernist culture, however, acknowledged no objective reality of space, motion, and time that means the same to all observers. Rather, reality can be grasped in many ways; a multiplicity of frames of reference apply to nature and human experience. Reality is what the viewer perceives it to be through the prism of the imagination. "There is no outer reality," said the modernist German poet Gottfried Benn, "there is only human consciousness, constantly building, modifying, rebuilding new worlds out of its own creativity."[13] Modernism is concerned less with the object itself than with how the artist experiences it, with the sensations that an object evokes in the artist's very being, with the meaning the artist's imagination imposes on reality. Sociologist Daniel Bell expresses this point in reference to painting:

> *Modernism . . . denies the primacy of an outside reality, as given. It seeks either to rearrange that reality, or to retreat to the self's interior, to private experience as the source of its concerns and aesthetic preoccupations. . . . There is an emphasis on the self as the touchstone of understanding and on the activity of the knower rather than the character of the object as the source of knowledge. . . . Thus one discerns the intentions of modern painting . . . to break up ordered space.*[14]

Dispensing with conventional forms of aesthetics that stressed structure and coherence, modernism propelled the arts into uncharted seas. Recoiling from a middle-class, industrial civilization that valued rationalism, organization, clarity, stability, and definite norms and values, modernist writers and artists were fascinated by the bizarre, the mysterious, the unpredictable, the primitive, the irrational, the formless. Writers, for example, experimented with new techniques to convey the intense struggle between the conscious and the unconscious, to connote the aberrations and complexities of human personality and the irrationality of human behavior. In particular they devised a new way—the stream of consciousness—to exhibit the mind's every level, both conscious reflection and unconscious strivings, and to capture how thought is punctuated by spontaneous outbursts, disconnected assertions, random memories, hidden desires, and persistent fantasies. Musicians like Igor Stravinsky and Arnold Schoenberg experimented with dissonance and primitive rhythms. When Stravinsky's ballet *The Rite of Spring* was performed in Paris in 1913, the theater audience rioted to protest the composition's break with tonality, its use of primitive jazz-like rhythms, and its theme of ritual sacrifice.

Modern Art

The modernist movement, which began near the end of the nineteenth century, was in full bloom before World War I and would continue to flower in the postwar world. Probably the clearest expression of the modernist viewpoint is found in art. In the late nineteenth century, artists began to turn away from the standards that had characterized art since the Renaissance. No longer committed to depicting how an object appears to the eye, they searched for new forms of expression.

Modern painting begins with impressionism, a movement centered in Paris that covered the years 1860 through 1886. Such impressionists as Edouard Manet, Claude Monet, Camille Pissaro, Edgar Degas, and Pierre Renoir tried to give their own immediate and personal impression of an object or an event as it appeared to the eye at a fleeting instant. In the late 1880s and 1890s postimpressionists further revolutionized the artist's sense of space and color in order to make art a vivid emotional and personal experience. French artist Paul Cézanne (1839–1906), seeking to portray his own visual perception of an object rather than a photographic copy of it, deliberately distorted perspective. He subordinated the appearance of the individual object to the requirements of the total design. The postimpressionists produced a revolution not only of space but also of color; thus Vincent van Gogh (1853–1890), a Dutchman who settled in France, used color as a language in and of itself, as a means of expressing the artist's feelings.

After the postimpressionists, art moved still further away from reproducing an exact likeness of a physical object or human being. Increasingly artists sought to penetrate the deepest recesses of the unconscious, which they saw as the wellspring of creativity and the fissured dwelling place of a higher truth. Paul Klee (1879–1940), a prominent Swiss painter, described modern art as follows: "Each [artist] should follow where the pulse of his own heart leads. . . . Our pounding heart drives us down, deep down to the source of all. What springs from this source, whether it may be called dream, idea or phantasy— must be taken seriously. . . ."[15]

Other styles included that of a group of avant-garde artists in France called the *fauves* (the wild beasts), who used color with great freedom to express

Vincent van Gogh (1853–1890): The Starry Night, 1889.   The intensity of van Gogh's feelings about the painting's subject matter are conveyed by the blazing yellow of the stars and the midnight blue of the landscape, as well as the whirling contours that translate the stars' energy. Oil on canvas, 29 × 36¼". (*Collection, The Museum of Modern Art, New York. Acquired through the Lillie P. Bliss Bequest.*)

intense feelings and heightened energy. Between 1909 and 1914, a new style called *cubism* was developed by Pablo Picasso (1881–1973) and Georges Braque (1882–1963). Exploring the interplay between the flat world of the canvas and the three-dimensional world of visual perception, they sought to paint a reality deeper than what the eye sees at first glance. One art historian describes cubism as follows: "The cubist is not interested in usual representational standards. It is as if he were walking around the object he is analyzing, as one is free to walk around a piece of sculpture for successive views. But he must represent all these views at once."[16]

Throughout the period from 1890 to 1914, artists were de-emphasizing subject matter and stressing the expressive power of such formal qualities as line, color, and space. It is not surprising that some artists, such as Piet Mondrian (1872–1944), a Dutch painter, and Wassily Kandinsky (1866–1944), a Russian residing in Germany, finally created abstract art, a nonobjective art totally devoid of reference to the visible world. In breaking with the Renaissance view of the world as inherently orderly and rational, modern artists opened up new possibilities for artistic expression. They all exemplified the growing appeal and force of the nonrational in European life.

Social Thought: Confronting the Irrational and the Complexities of Modern Society

The end of the nineteenth and the beginning of the twentieth centuries mark the great age of sociological thought. The leading sociological thinkers of the period all regarded science as the only valid model for arriving at knowledge, and all claimed that their thought rested on a scientific foundation. They struggled with some of the crucial problems of modern society. How can society achieve coherence and stability when religion no longer unites people? What are the implications of the nonrational for political life? How can people preserve their individuality in a society that is becoming increasingly regimented?

Durkheim

Émile Durkheim (1858–1917), a French scholar of Jewish background, and heir to Comte's positivism, was an important founder of modern sociology. Like Comte, he brought the scientific method to the study of society. Durkheim tried to show that the essential elements of modern times—secularism, rationalism, and individualism—threatened society with disintegration. In traditional society a person's place and function were determined by birth. Modern people, however, devoted to the principle of individualism, will not accept such restraints.

The weakening of the traditional ties that bind the individual to society constitutes, for Durkheim, the crisis of modern society. Without collective values and common beliefs, society is threatened with disintegration and the individual with disorientation. Modern people, said Durkheim, suffer from *anomie*—a condition of anxiety caused by the collapse of values. They do not feel integrated into a collective community and find no purpose in life. In *Suicide* (1897), Durkheim maintained that the pathology of modern society is demonstrated by its high rate of suicide. Modern people are driven to suicide by intense competition and the disappointment and frustration resulting from unfulfilled expectations and lack of commitment to moral principles. People must limit their aspirations and exercise discipline over their desires and passions. They must stop wanting more. Religion once spurred people to do these things, but it no longer can, said Durkheim.

Durkheim approved of modernity, but he noted that modern ways have not brought happiness or satisfaction to the individual. Modern scientific and industrial society requires a new set of binding principles—a secular-rational system of morality to replace Christian dogma—that will tie together the various classes into a cohesive social order and help to overcome those feelings of restlessness and dissatisfaction that torment people.

Durkheim focused on a crucial dilemma of modern life. On the one hand, modern urban civilization has provided the individual with unparalleled opportunities for self-development and material improvement. On the other hand, the breakdown of traditional communal bonds stemming from the spread of rationalism and individualism has produced a sense of isolation and alienation. Twentieth-century totalitarian movements sought to integrate these uprooted and alienated souls into new collectivities: a proletarian state based on workers' solidarity or a racial state based on ethnic "purity" and nationalism.

Pareto

Like Comte, Vilfredo Pareto (1848–1923), an Italian economist and sociologist, aimed to construct a system of sociology on the model of the physical sciences. His studies led him to conclude that social behavior does not rest primarily on reason but on nonrational instincts and sentiments. These deeply rooted and essentially changeless feelings are the fundamental elements in human behavior. Although society may change, human nature remains essentially the same. Whoever aims to lead and to influence people must appeal not to logic but to elemental feelings. Most human behavior is nonrational; nonlogical considerations also determine the beliefs that people hold. Like Marx and Freud, Pareto believed that we cannot accept a person's word at face value; in human instincts and sentiments we find the real cause of human behavior. People do not act according to carefully thought-out theories; they act first from nonlogical motivations and then construct a rationalization to justify their behavior. Much of Pareto's work was devoted to studying the nonrational elements of human conduct and the various beliefs invented to give the appearance of rationality to behavior that derives from feeling and instinct.

Pareto divided society into two strata—an elite and the masses. In the tradition of Machiavelli, Pareto held that a successful ruling elite must, with cunning, and if necessary violence, exploit the feelings and impulses of the masses to its own advantage. Democratic states, he said, delude themselves in thinking that the masses are really influenced by rational argument. Pareto predicted that new political leaders would emerge who would master the people through propaganda and force, appealing always to sentiment rather than reason. To this extent, Pareto was an intellectual forerunner of facism, which preached an authoritarian elitism. Mussolini praised Pareto and proudly claimed him as a source of inspiration. Pareto himself welcomed the advent of fascism, because it seemed to confirm his conviction that democracy was ready to collapse.

Weber

Probably the most prominent social thinker of the age and a leading shaper of modern sociology was Max Weber (1864–1920). To Weber, a German academic, Western civilization, unlike the other civilizations of the globe, had virtually eliminated myth, mystery, and magic from its conception of nature and society. This process of rationalization—the "disenchantment of the world," as Weber called it—was most conspicuous in Western science, but it was also evident in politics and economics. Weber considered Western science an attempt to understand and master nature through reason, and Western capitalism an attempt to organize work and production in a rational manner. The Western state has a rational written constitution, rationally formulated law, and a bureaucracy of trained government officials that administers the affairs of state according to rational rules and regulations.

Weber understood the terrible paradox of reason. Reason accounts for brilliant achievements in science and economic life, but it also despiritualizes life by ruthlessly eliminating centuries-old traditions, denouncing deeply felt religious beliefs as superstition, and regarding human feelings and passions as impediments to clear thinking. The process of disenchantment has given people knowledge, but it has also made people soulless and life meaningless. This is the dilemma of modern individuals, said Weber. Science cannot give people a purpose for living, and it cannot fulfill a human being's spiritual needs. The prospect existed that people would refuse to endure this violation of their spiritual needs and would reverse the process of disenchantment by seeking redemption in the irrational. Weber himself, however, was committed to the ideals of the Enlightenment and to perpetuating the rational scientific tradition.

Like Freud, Weber believed that to safeguard reason, it was necessary to comprehend human irrationality. One expression of the irrational that Weber analyzed in considerable depth was the charismatic leader who attracts people by force of personality. Charismatic leaders may be religious prophets, war heroes, demagogues, or others who possess this extraordinary personality that attracts and dominates others. People yearn for charismatic leadership, particularly during times of crisis. The leader claims a mission—a sacred duty—to lead the people during the crisis; the leader's authority rests on the people's belief in the mission and their faith in the leader's extraordinary abilities. A common allegiance to the charismatic leader unites the community. Weber's analysis of this phenomenon throws light on the popularity of twentieth-century dictators and demagogues.

Modern Physics

Until the closing years of the nineteenth century, the view of the universe held by the Western mind rested largely on the classical physics of Newton and included the following principles: (1) Time, space, and matter were objective realities that existed independently of the observer. (2) The universe was a giant machine whose parts obeyed strict laws of cause and effect. (3) The atom, indivisible and solid, was the basic unit of matter. (4) Heated bodies emitted radiation in continuous waves. (5) Through further investigation it would be possible to gain complete knowledge of the physical universe.

Between the 1890s and the 1920s this view of the universe was shattered by a second Scientific Revolution. The discovery of x rays by William Konrad Roentgen in 1895, of radioactivity by Henri Bequerel in 1896, and of the electron by J. J. Thomson in 1897 led science to abandon the conception of the atom as a solid and indivisible particle. Rather than resembling a billiard ball, the atom consisted of a nucleus of tightly packed protons separated from orbiting electrons by empty space.

In 1900 Max Planck (1858–1947), a German physicist, proposed the quantum theory, which holds that a heated body radiates energy not in a continuous unbroken stream, as had been believed, but in intermittent spurts or jumps called quanta. Planck's theory of discontinuity in energy radiation challenged a cardinal principle of classical physics, that action in nature was strictly continuous. In 1913, Niels Bohr, a Danish scientist, applied Planck's theory of energy quanta to the interior of the atom and discovered that the Newtonian laws of motion could not fully explain what happened to electrons orbiting an atomic nucleus. As physicists explored the behavior of the atom further, it became apparent that its nature was fundamentally elusive and unpredictable.

Newtonian physics says that given certain conditions, we can predict what will follow. For example, if an airplane is flying north at 400 miles per hour, we can predict its exact position two hours from now, assuming that the plane does not alter its course or speed. Quantum mechanics teaches that in the subatomic realm, we cannot predict with certainty what will take place; we can only say that given certain conditions, it is *probable* that a certain event will follow. This principle of uncertainty was developed in 1927 by German scientist Werner Heisenberg, who showed that it is impossible to determine at one and the same time both an electron's precise speed and its position. In the small-scale world of the electron, we enter a universe of uncertainty, probability, and statistical relationships. No improvement in measurement techniques will dispel this element of chance and provide us with complete knowledge of the universe.

The theory of relativity, developed by Albert Einstein (1879–1955), a German-Swiss physicist of Jewish lineage, was instrumental in the shaping of modern physics; it altered classical conceptions of space and time. Newtonian physics had viewed space as a distinct physical reality, a stationary and motionless medium through which light traveled and matter moved. Time was viewed as a fixed and rigid framework that was the same for all observers and existed independently of human experience. For Einstein, however, neither space nor time had an independent existence; neither could be divorced from human experience. Once asked to explain briefly the essentials of relativity, Einstein replied: "It was formerly believed that if all material things disappeared out of the universe, time and space would be left. According to the relativity theory, however, time and space disappear together with the things."[17]

Contrary to all previous thinking, relativity theory holds that time differs for

Albert Einstein.   Einstein was a principal architect of modern physics. Forced to flee Nazi Germany before World War II, he became a United States citizen. He was appointed to the Institute for Advanced Study at Princeton, N.J. (*Culver Pictures*)

two observers traveling at different speeds. Imagine twin brothers involved in space exploration, one as an astronaut, the other as a rocket designer who never leaves earth. The astronaut takes off in the most advanced spaceship yet constructed, one that achieves a speed close to the maximum attainable in our universe—the speed of light. After traveling several trillion miles, the spaceship turns around and returns to earth. According to the experience of the ship's occupant, the whole trip took about two years. But when the astronaut lands on earth, he finds totally changed conditions. For one thing, his brother has long since died, for according to earth's calendars some two hundred years have elapsed since the rocket ship set out on its journey. Such an occurrence seemed to defy all common-sense experience, yet experiments supported Einstein's claims.

Einstein's work encompassed motion, matter, and energy as well. Motion, too, is relative: the only way we can describe the motion of one body is to compare it with another moving body. This means that there is no motionless, absolute, fixed frame of reference anywhere in the universe. In his famous equation, $E = mc^2$, Einstein showed that matter and energy are not separate categories but two different expressions of the same physical entity. The source of energy is matter; and the source of matter is energy. Tiny quantities of matter could be transformed into staggering amounts of energy. The atomic age was dawning.

The discoveries of modern physics transformed the world of classical physics. Whereas nature had been regarded as something outside of the individual—an objective reality that existed independently of ourselves—modern physics teaches that our position in space and time determines what we mean by reality, and our very presence affects reality itself. When we observe a particle with our measuring instruments, we are interfering with it, knocking it off its course; we are participating in reality. Nor is nature fully knowable, as the classical physics of Newton had presumed; uncertainty, probability, and even mystery are inherent in the universe.

We have not yet felt the full impact of modern physics, but there is no doubt that it has been part of a revolution in human perceptions. Jacob Bronowski, a student of science and culture, concludes:

> *One aim of the physical sciences has been to give an exact picture of the material world. One achievement of physics in the twentieth century has been to prove that that aim is unattainable. . . . There is no absolute knowledge. . . . All information is imperfect. We have to treat it with humility. That is the human condition; and that is what quantum physics says. . . . The Principle of Uncertainty . . . fixed once and for all the realization that all knowledge is limited.*[18]

Like Darwin's theory of human origins, Freud's theory of human nature, and the transformation of classical space by modern artists, the modifications of the Newtonian picture by modern physicists have enlarged our understanding. At the same time they have contributed to the sense of uncertainty and disorientation that characterizes the twentieth century.

The Enlightenment Tradition in Disarray

Most nineteenth-century thinkers carried forward the spirit of the Enlightenment, particularly in its emphasis on science and its concern for individual liberty and social reform. In the tradition of the philosophes, nineteenth-century thinkers regarded science as humanity's greatest achievement and believed that through reason society could be reformed. The spread of parliamentary government and the extension of education, along with the many advances in science and technology, seemed to confirm the hopes of the philosophes in humanity's future progress.

But at the same time, the Enlightenment tradition was being undermined. In the early nineteenth century, the romantics revolted against the Enlightenment's rational-scientific spirit. In the closing decades of the century the Enlightenment tradition was challenged by Social Darwinists who glorified violence and saw conflict between individuals and between nations as a law of nature. A number of thinkers, rejecting the Enlightenment view of people as fundamentally rational, held that subconscious drives and impulses govern human behavior more than reason. These thinkers celebrated the irrational, which they regarded as the true essence of human beings.

Even theorists who studied the individual and society in a scientific way pointed out that below a surface of rationality lies a substratum of irrationality that constitutes a deeper reality. The conviction was growing that reason was a puny instrument in comparison to the volcanic strength of nonrational impulses, that these impulses pushed people toward destructive behavior and made political life precarious, and that the nonrational did not bend very much to education.

At the beginning of the twentieth century, the dominant mood remained that of confidence in Europe's future progress and in the values of European civilization. However, certain disquieting trends were evident that would grow to crisis proportions in succeeding decades. Although few people may have realized it, the Enlightenment tradition was in disarray.

The Enlightenment believed in an orderly, machine-like universe, in natural law and natural rights operating in the social world, in objective rules that gave form and structure to artistic productions, in the essential rationality and goodness of the individual, and in science and technology as instruments of progress. This coherent world-view, which had produced an attitude of certainty, security, and optimism, was in the process of dissolution by the early twentieth century. The common-sense Newtonian picture of the physical universe, with its inexorable laws of cause and effect, was altered; the belief in natural rights and objective standards governing morality was undermined; human rationality and goodness, the efficacy of science and technology, and the inevitability of human progress were being questioned. Rules and modes of expression that were at the very heart of Western aesthetics were abandoned.

By the early twentieth century, the universe no longer seemed an orderly system, an intelligible whole, but something fundamentally inexplicable. Human nature, too, seemed intrinsically unfathomable and problematic. To the question "Who is man?" Greek philosophers, medieval scholastics, Renaissance humanists, and eighteenth-century philosophes had provided a coherent and intelligible answer. By the early twentieth century, Western intellectuals no longer possessed a clear idea of the human being, and life seemed devoid of an overriding purpose, as Nietzsche sensed:

> *Disintegration characterizes this time, and thus uncertainty: nothing stands firmly on its feet or on a hard faith in itself; one lives for tomorrow as the day after tomorrow is dubious. Everything on our way is slippery and dangerous, and the ice that still supports us has become thin: all of us feel the warm, uncanny breath of the thawing wind; where we still walk, soon no one will be able to walk.*[19]

This radical new disorientation led some intellectuals to feel alienated from and even hostile toward Western civilization.

When the new century began, most Europeans were optimistic about the future, some even holding that European civilization was on the threshold of a golden age. Few suspected that European civilization would soon be gripped by a crisis that threatened its very survival. The powerful forces of irrationalism that had been hailed by Nietzsche, analyzed by Freud, and creatively expressed in modernist culture would erupt with devastating fury in twentieth-century political life, particularly in the form of extreme nationalism and racism that extolled violence. Disoriented and disillusioned people searching for new certainties and values would turn to political ideologies that openly rejected reason, lauded war, and scorned the inviolability of the human person. These currents began to form at the end of the nineteenth century, but World War I brought them together into a tidal wave.

World War I accentuated the questioning of established norms and the dissolution of Enlightenment certainties and drove many people to view Western civilization as dying and beyond redemption. The war not only exacerbated the spiritual crisis of the preceding generation, it also shattered Europe's political and social order and gave birth to totalitarian ideologies that nearly obliterated the legacy of the Enlightenment.

Notes

1. Quoted in Ernst Cassirer, *The Problem of Knowledge,* trans. by William H. Woglom and Charles W. Hendel (New Haven: Yale University Press, 1950), p. 244.
2. Karl Pearson, *National Life from the Standpoint of Science* (London: Adam and Charles Black, 1905), p. 21.
3. Quoted in H. W. Koch, "Social Darwinism in the 'New Imperialism,'" in H. W. Koch, ed., *The Origins of the First World War* (New York: Taplinger, 1972), p. 341.
4. Ibid., p. 345.
5. Friedrich Nietzsche, *The Will to Power,* vol. 2, trans. by A. M. Ludovici (New York: Russell & Russell, 1964), sec. 861–862, pp. 297–298.
6. Friedrich Nietzsche, *The Will to Power,* trans. by Walter Kaufmann and R. J. Hollingdale, and ed. by Walter Kaufmann (New York: Vintage Books, 1968), pp. 383–384.
7. Quoted in R. J. Hollingdale, *Nietzsche* (London: Routledge and Kegan Paul, 1973), p. 82.
8. Ibid., p. 518.
9. Ibid., p. 386.
10. Sigmund Freud, *Civilization and Its Discontents* (New York: W. W. Norton, 1961), p. 62.
11. Quotes in this paragraph are from ibid., pp. 58, 59, 61, and 69.
12. Irving Howe, ed., *The Idea of the Modern in Literature and the Arts* (New York: Horizon Press, 1967), p. 16.
13. Quoted in ibid., p. 15.
14. Daniel Bell, *The Cultural Contradictions of Capitalism* (New York: Basic Books, 1976), p. 110.
15. Paul Klee, *On Modern Art,* trans. by Paul Findlay (London: Faber & Faber, 1948), p. 51.
16. John Canaday, *Mainstreams of Modern Art* (New York: Holt, 1961), p. 458.
17. Quoted in A. E. E. McKenzie, *The Major Achievements of Science,* vol. 1 (New York: Cambridge University Press, 1960), p. 310.
18. Jacob Bronowski, *The Ascent of Man* (Boston: Little, Brown, 1973), p. 353.
19. Nietzsche, *The Will to Power,* sec. 57, p. 40.

Suggested Reading

Baumer, Franklin, *Modern European Thought* (1977). A well-informed study of modern thought.

Bradbury, Malcolm, and James McFarlane, eds., *Modernism, 1890–1930* (1974). Essays on various phases of modernism; valuable bibliography.

Farrington, Benjamin, *What Darwin Really Said* (1966). A brief study of Darwin's work.

Grant, Damian, *Realism* (1970). A good short survey.

Greene, J. C., *The Death of Adam* (1961). The impact of evolution on Western thought.

Hamilton, G. H., *Painting and Sculpture in Europe, 1880–1940* (1967). An authoritative study.

Hemmings, F. W. J., ed., *The Age of Realism* (1978). A series of essays on realism in various countries.

Hollingdale, R. J., *Nietzsche* (1973). A lucid and insightful study.

Masur, Gerhard, *Prophets of Yesterday* (1961). Studies in European culture, 1890–1914.

McLellan, David, *Karl Marx: His Life and Thought* (1977). A highly regarded biography.

Nelson, Benjamin, ed., *Freud and the Twentieth Century* (1957). A valuable collection of essays.

Roazen, Paul, *Freud's Political and Social Thought* (1968). The wider implications of Freudian psychology.

Stromberg, Roland N., *An Intellectual History of Modern Europe* (1975). A fine text.

Tucker, Robert, *The Marxian Revolutionary Idea* (1969). Marxism as a radical social philosophy.

———, ed., *The Marx-Engels Reader* (1972). An anthology of Marx's essential writings.

Zeitlin, I. M., *Ideology and the Development of Sociological Theory* (1968). Examines in detail the thought of major shapers of sociological theory.

Review Questions

1. Realism and positivism coincided with an attitude of mind shaped by science, industrialism, and secularism. Discuss this statement.
2. The theory of evolution had revolutionary consequences in areas other than science. Discuss this statement.
3. What was the significance of Nietzsche's thought?
4. How did Bergson reflect the growing irrationalism of the age?
5. How did Sorel show the political potential of the nonrational?
6. In what way was Freud a child of the Enlightenment? How did he differ from the philosophes?
7. What were the standards of esthetics that had governed Western literature and art since the Renaissance? How did the modernist movement break with these standards?
8. For Durkheim, what constituted the crisis of modern society? How did he attempt to cope with crisis?
9. What do you think of Pareto's judgment that the masses in a democratic state are not really influenced by rational argument?
10. For Weber, what was the terrible paradox of reason?
11. Describe the view of the universe held by Westerners about 1880. How was this view altered by modern physics? What is the significance of this revolution to our perception of the universe?
12. In what ways was the Enlightenment tradition in disarray by the early years of the twentieth century?

Allied Soldiers in the Trenches During World War I. (*Imperial War Museum, London*)

V · Western Civilization in Crisis: World Wars and Totalitarianism

1914–1945

Chapter ✿ 17

World War I:
The West in Despair

Prior to 1914 the dominant mood in Europe was one of pride in the accomplishments of Western civilization and confidence in its future progress. Advances in science and technology, the rising standard of living, the spread of democratic institutions, the expansion of social reform, the increase in literacy for the masses, Europe's position of power in the world—all contributed to a sense of optimism. Other reasons for optimism were that since the defeat of Napoleon, Europe had avoided a general war, and since the Franco-Prussian War (1870–71), the Great Powers had not fought each other. Few people recognized that the West's outward achievements masked an inner turbulence that was propelling Western civilization toward a cataclysm. The European state system was failing.

By 1914, national states, answering to no higher power, were fueled by an explosive nationalism and were grouped into alliances that faced each other with ever-mounting hostility. Nationalist passions, overheated by the popular press and expansionist societies, poisoned international relations. Nationalist thinkers propagated pseudoscientific racial and Social Darwinist doctrines that glorified conflict and justified the subjugation of other peoples. Committed to enhancing national power, statesmen lost sight of Europe as a community of nations sharing a common civilization. Caution and restraint gave way to belligerency in foreign relations.

The failure of the European state system was paralleled by a cultural crisis. Some European intellectuals attacked the rational tradition of the Enlightenment and celebrated the primitive, the instinctual, and the irrational. Increasingly, young people grew attracted to philosophies of action that ridiculed liberal bourgeois values and viewed war as a purifying and ennobling experience. Colonial wars, colorfully portrayed in the popular press, ignited the imagination of bored factory workers and daydreaming students and reinforced a sense of duty and an urge for gallantry among soldiers and aristocrats. These "splendid" little colonial wars helped fashion an attitude that made war acceptable, if not laudable. Yearning to break loose from their ordinary lives and to embrace heroic values, many Europeans regarded violent conflict as the highest expression of individual and national life. Although technology was making warfare more brutal and dangerous, Europe retained a romantic illusion about combat.

While Europe was seemingly progressing in the art of civilization, the mythic power of nationalism and the primitive appeal of conflict were driving European civilization to the abyss. Few people recognized the potential crisis—certainly not the statesmen whose reckless blundering allowed the Continent to stumble into war. ✦

Aggravated Nationalist Tensions in Austria-Hungary

On June 28, 1914, a young terrorist with the support of the Black Hand, a secret Serbian nationalist society, murdered Archduke Francis Ferdinand, heir to the throne of Austria-Hungary. Six weeks later the armies of Europe were on the march; an incident in the Balkans had sparked a world war. An analysis of why Austria-Hungary felt compelled to attack Serbia, and why the other powers became enmeshed in the conflict, shows how explosive Europe was in 1914. And nowhere were conditions more volatile than in Austria-Hungary, the scene of the assassination.

With its several nationalities, each with its own national history and traditions and often conflicting aspirations, Austria-Hungary stood in opposition to nationalism, the most powerful spiritual force of the age. Perhaps the supranational Austro-Hungarian Empire was obsolete in a world of states based on the principle of nationality. Dominated by Germans and Hungarians, the empire remained unable either to satisfy the grievances or to contain the nationalist aims of its minorities, particularly the Czechs and South Slavs (Croats, Slovenes, Serbs).

Heightened agitation among the several nationalities, which worsened in the decade before 1914, created terrible anxieties among Austrian leaders. The fear that the empire would be torn apart by rebellion caused Austria to pursue a forceful policy against any nation that fanned the nationalist feelings of its

Slavic minorities. In particular, this policy meant worsening tensions between Austria and small Serbia, which had been independent of the Ottoman Empire since 1878.

Captivated by Western ideas of nationalism, the Serbs sought to create a Greater Serbia by uniting with their racial kin, the South Slavs who dwelt in Austria-Hungary. Since some 7 million South Slavs lived in the Hapsburg Empire, the dream of a Greater Serbia, shrilly expressed by Serbian nationalists, caused nightmares in Austria. Some Austrian leaders, fearing that continued Serbian agitation would encourage the South Slavs to press for secession, urged the destruction of the Serbian menace.

The tensions arising out of the multinational character of the Austro-Hungarian Empire in an age of heightened nationalist feeling set off the explosion in 1914. Unable to solve its minority problems and fearful of pan-Serbism, Austria-Hungary felt itself in a life-or-death situation. This sense of desperation led it to lash out at Serbia after the assassination of Archduke Francis Ferdinand.

The German System of Alliances

The war might have been avoided, however, or might have remained limited to Austria and Serbia, had Europe in 1914 not been divided into two hostile alliance systems. Such a situation contains inherent dangers. For example, knowing that it has the support of allies, a country might pursue a more provocative and reckless course and be less conciliatory during a crisis. Second, a conflict between two states might spark a chain reaction that can draw in the other powers, thereby transforming a limited war into a general war. This course is precisely what followed the assassination. The origins of this dangerous alliance system go back to Bismarck and the Franco-Prussian War.

The New German Empire

The unification of Germany in 1870–71 turned the new state into an international power of the first rank, upsetting the balance of power in Europe. For the first time since the wars of the French Revolution, a nation was in a position to dominate the European continent. To German nationalists, the unification of Germany was both the fulfillment of a national dream and the starting point for an even more ambitious goal—the extension of German power in Europe and the world.

As the nineteenth century drew to a close, German nationalism grew more extreme. Believing that Germany must either grow or die, nationalists pressed

Map 17.1 Ethnic Groups in Germany, Austria, and the Balkans Before World War I ▶

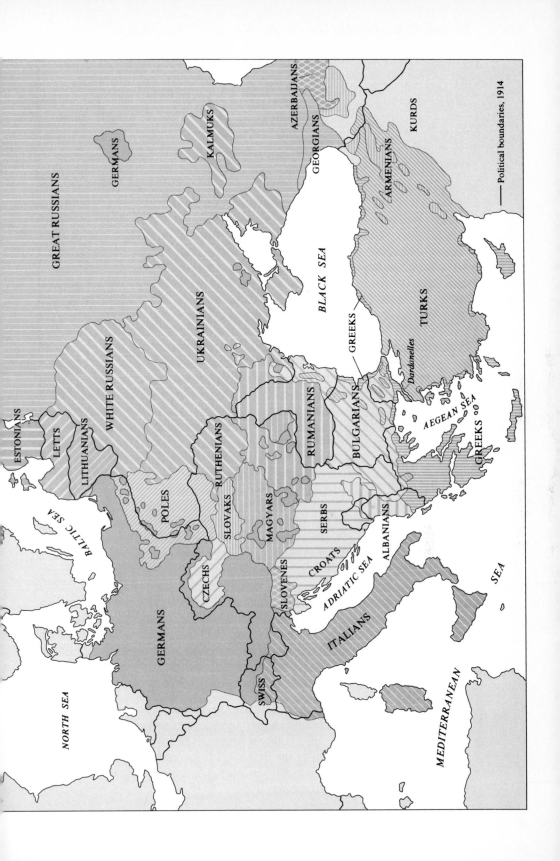

NORTH SEA

BALTIC SEA

ESTONIANS

LETTS

LITHUANIANS

GERMANS

GREAT RUSSIANS

GERMANS

WHITE RUSSIANS

KALMUKS

POLES

CZECHS

SWISS

SLOVAKS

RUTHENIANS

MAGYARS

UKRAINIANS

SLOVENES

CROATS

SERBS

RUMANIANS

BULGARIANS

BLACK SEA

GEORGIANS

AZERBAIJANS

ARMENIANS

KURDS

ITALIANS

ALBANIANS

ADRIATIC SEA

GREEKS

GREEKS

Dardanelles

AEGEAN SEA

TURKS

GREEKS

MEDITERRANEAN SEA

——— Political boundaries, 1914

the government to build a powerful navy, acquire colonies, gain a much greater share of the world's markets, and expand German interests and influence in Europe. Sometimes these goals were expressed in the language of Social Darwinism—nations are engaged in an eternal struggle for survival and domination. Decisive victories against Austria (1866) and France (1871), the formation of the German Reich, rapid industrialization, and the impressive achievements of German science and scholarship had molded a powerful and dynamic nation. Imbued with great expectations for the future, Germans became increasingly impatient to see the fatherland gain its "rightful" place in world affairs—an attitude that frightened non-Germans.

Bismarck's Goals

Under Bismarck, who did not seek additional territory but wanted only to preserve the recently achieved unification, Germany pursued a moderate and cautious foreign policy. One of Bismarck's principal goals was to keep France isolated and friendless. France had suffered deep humiliation as a result of its defeat in the Franco-Prussian War. Compounding French humiliation was the loss of Alsace and Lorraine to Germany. Although French nationalists yearned for a war of revenge against Germany, the government, aware of Germany's strength, was unlikely to initiate such a conflict. Still, the issue of Alsace-Lorraine increased tensions between France and Germany.

Bismarck also hoped to prevent a war between Russia and Austria-Hungary, for such a conflict could lead to German involvement, to the breakup of Austria-Hungary, and to Russian expansion in eastern Europe. To maintain peace and Germany's existing borders, Bismarck forged complex alliances. In the decade of the 1880s, he created the Triple Alliance—consisting of Germany, Austria-Hungary, and Italy—and an alliance with Russia.

Bismarck conducted foreign policy with restraint. He formed alliances not to conquer new lands but to protect Germany from aggression from either France or Russia, not to launch war but to preserve order and stability in Europe. In 1888, a new emperor ascended the German throne; when the young Kaiser William II (1888–1918) clashed with his aging prime minister, Bismarck was forced to resign (1890). Lacking Bismarck's diplomatic skills, his cool restraint, and his determination to keep peace in Europe, the new German leaders pursued a belligerent and imperialistic foreign policy in the following decades that frightened other states, particularly Britain. Whereas Bismarck considered Germany a satiated power, these men insisted that Germany must have its place in the sun.

The first act of the new leadership was to permit the treaty with Russia to lapse, thereby allowing Germany to give full support to Austria, which was considered a more reliable ally. Whereas Bismarck had warned Austria to act with moderation and caution in the Balkans, his successors not only failed to hold Austria in check but actually encouraged Austrian aggression. This proved fatal to the peace of Europe.

The Triple Entente

Fear of Germany

When Germany broke with Russia in 1890, France was quick to take advantage of the situation. Frightened by Germany's increasing military strength, expanding industries, growing population, and alliance with Austria and Italy, France eagerly coveted Russia as an ally. In 1894, France and Russia entered into an alliance; the isolation forced on France by Bismarck had ended.

Like France and Russia, Great Britain was alarmed by Germany's growing military might. Furthermore, because of its spectacular industrial growth, Germany had become a potent trade rival of England. Britain was also distressed by Germany's increased efforts to become a great colonial power—a goal demanded by German nationalists. But most alarming was Germany's decision to build a great navy, for it could interfere with British overseas trade or even blockade the British Isles. Germany's naval program was the single most important reason that Britain moved closer first to France and then to Russia. Germany's naval construction, designed to increase its stature as a Great Power but not really necessary for its security, was one indication that German leaders had abandoned Bismarck's policy of good sense. Eager to add the British as an ally and demonstrating superb diplomatic skill, France moved to end longstanding colonial disputes with Britain. The Entente Cordiale of 1904 accomplished this conciliation. England had emerged from its self-imposed splendid isolation.

Desiring to erect a strong alliance to counter Germany's Triple Alliance, French diplomats now sought to ease tensions between their Russian ally and their new British friend. Two events convinced Russia to adopt a more conciliatory attitude toward Britain: a disastrous and unexpected defeat in the Russo-Japanese War of 1904–1905 and a working-class revolution in 1905. Shocked by defeat, its army bordering on disintegration, its workers restive, Russia was now receptive to settling its imperial disputes with Britain over Persia, Tibet, and Afghanistan, a decision encouraged by France. In the Anglo-Russian Entente of 1907, as in the Anglo-French Entente Cordiale of 1904, the former rivals conducted themselves in a conciliatory if not friendly manner. In both instances, what engendered this spirit of cooperation was fear of Germany.

Europe was now broken into two hostile camps: the Triple Entente of France, Russia, and Britain; and the Triple Alliance of Germany, Austria-Hungary, and Italy. Serving to increase fear and suspicion between the alliances was the costly arms race and the maintenance of large standing armies by all the states except Britain.

German Reactions

Germany denounced the Triple Entente as a hostile anti-German coalition designed to encircle and crush Germany. If Germany were to survive, it must break this ring. Considering Austria-Hungary as its only reliable ally, Germany resolved to preserve the power and dignity of the Hapsburg Empire. If Austria-Hungary fell from the ranks of Great Powers, Germany would have to stand alone against its enemies. At all costs Austria-Hungary must not be weakened.

But this assessment suffered from dangerous miscalculations. First, Germany overstressed the hostile nature of the Triple Entente. In reality, France, Russia, and Britain drew closer together not to wage aggressive war against Germany but to protect themselves against burgeoning German military, industrial, and diplomatic power. Second, by linking German security to Austria, Germany greatly increased the chance of war. Becoming increasingly fearful of pan-Serbism, Austria might well decide that only a war could prevent its empire from disintegrating. Confident of German support, Austria would be more likely to resort to force; fearful of any diminution of Austrian power, Germany would be more likely to give Austria that support.

The Drift Toward War

The Bosnian Crisis

After 1908, several crises tested the competing alliances, pushing Europe closer to war. Particularly significant was the Bosnian affair, which involved Russia, Austria-Hungary, and Serbia. This incident contained many of the ingredients that eventually ignited the war in 1914. Russia's humiliating defeat by Japan in 1905 had diminished its stature as a Great Power. The new Russian foreign minister, Alexander Izvolsky, hoped to gain a diplomatic triumph by compelling Turkey to allow Russian warships to pass through the Dardanelles, fulfilling a centuries-old dream of extending Russian power into the Mediterranean.

Russia made a deal with Austria: Russia would permit Austrian annexation of the provinces of Bosnia and Herzegovina, and Austria would support Russia's move to open the Dardanelles. Officially a part of the Ottoman Empire, these provinces had been administered by Austria-Hungary since 1878. The population consisted mainly of ethnic cousins of the Serbs. A formal annexation would certainly infuriate the Serbs, who hoped one day to make the region part of a Greater Serbia.

In 1908, Austria proceeded to annex the provinces, but Russia met stiff resistance from England and France when it presented its case for opening the straits to Russian warships. Austria had gained a diplomatic victory, while Russia suffered another humiliation. Even more enraged than Russia was Serbia, which threatened to invade Bosnia to liberate its cousins from Austrian oppression. The Serbian press openly declared that Austria-Hungary must perish if the South Slavs were to achieve liberty and unity. A fiery attitude also prevailed in Vienna—Austria-Hungary could not survive unless Serbia was destroyed.

During this period of intense hostility between Austria-Hungary and Serbia, Germany supported its Austrian ally. To keep Austria strong, Germany would even agree to the dismemberment of Serbia and to its incorporation into the Hapsburg empire. Unlike Bismarck, who tried to hold Austria in check, German leadership now coolly envisioned an Austrian attack on Serbia, and just as coolly offered German support if Russia intervened.

Balkan Wars

The Bosnian crisis pushed Germany and Austria closer together, brought relations between Austria and Serbia to the breaking point, and inflicted another humiliation on Russia. The first Balkan War (1912) continued these trends. The Balkan states of Montenegro, Serbia, Bulgaria, and Greece attacked a dying Ottoman Empire. In a brief campaign, the Balkan armies captured the Turkish empire's European territory, with the exception of Constantinople. Because it was on the victorious side, landlocked Serbia gained the Albanian coast, which gave it a long-desired outlet to the sea. Austria was determined to keep its enemy from reaping this reward, and Germany, as in the Bosnian crisis, supported its ally. Unable to secure Russian support, an enraged Serbia was forced to surrender the territory, which became the state of Albania.

Incensed Serbian nationalists accelerated their campaign of propaganda and terrorism against Austria. Believing that another humiliation would irreparably damage its prestige, Russia vowed to back Serbia in its next confrontation with Austria. And Austria had reached the end of its patience with Serbia. Emboldened by German encouragement, Austria would end the Serbian threat once and for all. Thus the ingredients for war between Austria and Serbia, a war that might easily draw in Russia and Germany, were present. Another incident might well start a war; it came on June 28, 1914.

Assassination of Francis Ferdinand

On June 28, 1914, Francis Ferdinand was assassinated while making a state visit to Sarajevo, capital of Bosnia. Young Gavrilo Princip, part of a team of Bosnian terrorists linked to the Black Hand, a Serbian nationalist society, fired two shots at close range into the archduke's car. Francis Ferdinand and his wife died within fifteen minutes. By killing the archduke, the terrorists hoped to bring to a boiling point tensions within the Hapsburg Empire and to prepare the way for revolution.

For many years, leaders of Austria had yearned for war with Serbia in order to end the agitation for the union of the South Slavs. Now, they reasoned, the hour had struck. But war with Serbia would require the approval of Germany. Believing that Austria was Germany's only reliable ally and that a diminution of Austrian power and prestige threatened German security, German statesmen encouraged their ally to take up arms against Serbia. Germany and Austria wanted a quick strike to overwhelm Serbia before other countries were drawn in.

The Assassins of the Archduke Francis Ferdinand and His Wife Being Captured in Sarajevo, June 28, 1914.   The assassination of the archduke and his wife was the spark that ignited World War I. The adversaries looked forward to a short, decisive conflict. Emotions ran high with visions of gallantry. Only a few foresaw the collapse of a Western ideal: a world ruled by reason and morality. (*The Granger Collection, New York*)

Germany Encourages Austria

Confident of German backing, on July 23 Austria presented Serbia with an ultimatum and demanded a response within forty-eight hours. The terms of the ultimatum were so harsh that it was next to impossible for Serbia to accept them. This reaction was the one that Austria intended, as it sought a military solution to the crisis rather than a diplomatic one. But Russia would not remain indifferent to an Austro-German effort to liquidate Serbia. Russia feared that an Austrian conquest of Serbia was just the first step in an Austro-German plan to dominate the Balkans. Such an extension of German and Austrian power in a region bordering Russia was unthinkable to the tsar's government. Moreover, after suffering repeated reverses in foreign affairs, Russia would not tolerate another humiliation. As Germany had resolved to back its Austrian ally, Russia determined not to abandon Serbia.

Serbia responded to Austria's ultimatum in a conciliatory manner, agreeing to virtually all Austria's demands. But Serbia would not allow Austrian officials into Serbia to investigate the assassination. Having already decided against a peaceful settlement, Austria insisted that Serbia's failure to accept one provision meant that the entire ultimatum had been rejected and ordered mobilization of the Austrian army.

This was a crucial moment for Germany. Would it continue to support Austria, knowing that an Austrian attack on Serbia would probably bring Russia into the conflict? Determined not to desert Austria and believing that a showdown with Russia was inevitable anyway, the German war party continued to urge Austrian action against Serbia. They argued that it was better to fight Russia in 1914 than a few years later, when the tsar's empire would be stronger. Confident of the superiority of the German army, the war party held that Germany could defeat both Russia and France, and that Britain's army was too weak to make a difference.

On July 28, 1914, Austria declared war on Serbia; Russia, with the assurance of French support, proclaimed partial mobilization aimed at Austria alone. But the military warned that partial mobilization would throw the slow-moving Russian war machine into total confusion if the order had to be changed suddenly to full mobilization. Moreover, the only plans the Russian general staff had drawn up called for full mobilization, that is, for war against both Austria and Germany. The tsar, pressured by his generals, gave the order for full mobilization on July 30. Russian forces would be arrayed against Germany as well as Austria.

Because the country that struck first had the advantage of fighting according to its own plans rather than having to improvise in response to the enemy's attack, generals regarded mobilization by the enemy as an act of war. Therefore, when Russia refused a German warning to halt mobilization, Germany, on August 1, ordered a general mobilization and declared war on Russia. Two days later Germany also declared war on France, believing that France would support its Russian ally. Moreover, German battle plans were based on a war with both Russia and France. Thus a war between Germany and Russia automatically meant a German attack on France.

When Belgium refused to allow German troops to march through Belgian territory into France, Germany invaded the small nation, which brought Britain, pledged to guarantee Belgian neutrality, into the war. Britain could never tolerate German troops directly across the English-Channel in any case, nor could it brook German mastery of western Europe.

War as Celebration

When war was certain, an extraordinary phenomenon occurred. Crowds gathered in capital cities and expressed their loyalty to the fatherland and their readiness to fight. It seemed as if people wanted violence for its own sake. It was as if war provided an escape from the dull routine of classroom, job, and home; from the emptiness, drabness, mediocrity, and pointlessness of bourgeois society; from "a world grown old and cold and weary," said Rupert Brooke, a young British poet.[1] To some, war was a "beautiful . . . sacred moment" that satisfied an "ethical yearning."[2] But more significantly, the outpouring of patriotic sentiments demonstrated the immense power that nationalism exercised over the European mind. With extraordinary success, nationalism welded millions of people into a collectivity ready to devote body and soul to the nation, especially during its hour of need.

In Paris, men marched down the boulevards singing the stirring words of the French national anthem, the "Marseillaise," while women showered young soldiers with flowers. A participant in these days recalls: "Young and old, civilians and military men burned with the same excitement. . . . Beginning the next day, thousands of men eager to fight would jostle one another outside recruiting offices, waiting to join up. . . . The word 'duty' had a meaning for them, and the word 'country' had regained its splendor."[3] Similar scenes occurred in Berlin. "It is a joy to be alive," editorialized one newspaper. "We wished so much for this hour. . . . The sword which has been forced into our hand will not be sheathed until our aims are won and our territory extended as far as necessity demands."[4]

Soldiers bound for battle acted as if they were going off on a great adventure. "My dear ones, be proud that you live in such a time and in such a nation and that you . . . have the privilege of sending those you love into so glorious a battle," wrote a young German law student to his family.[5] The young warriors yearned to do something noble and altruistic, to win glory, and to experience life at its most intense moments.

Many of Europe's most distinguished intellectuals were also captivated by the martial mood, sharing Rupert Brooke's sentiments: "Now God be thanked Who has matched us with His hour,/And caught our youth, and wakened us from sleeping."[6] To the prominent German historian Friedrich Meinecke, August 1914 was "one of the great moments of my life which suddenly filled my soul with the deepest confidence in our people and the profoundest joy."[7] Besides being gripped by a thirst for excitement and a quest for the heroic, some intellectuals welcomed the war because it unified the nation in a spirit of fraternity and self-sacrifice. It was a return, some felt, to the organic roots of human existence, a way of overcoming a sense of individual isolation.

But it must be emphasized that the soldiers who went off to war singing and the statesmen and generals who welcomed war or did not try hard enough to prevent it, expected a short, decisive, gallant conflict. Virtually no one envisioned what the First World War turned out to be—four years of frightful, barbaric, indecisive, senseless bloodletting. But although their gloomy words were drowned out by the cheers of chauvinists and fools, there were prophets who realized that Europe was stumbling into darkness. "The lamps are going out all over Europe," said British Foreign Secretary Edward Grey. "We shall never see them lit again in our lifetime."

Map 17.2   World War I, 1914–1918 ▶

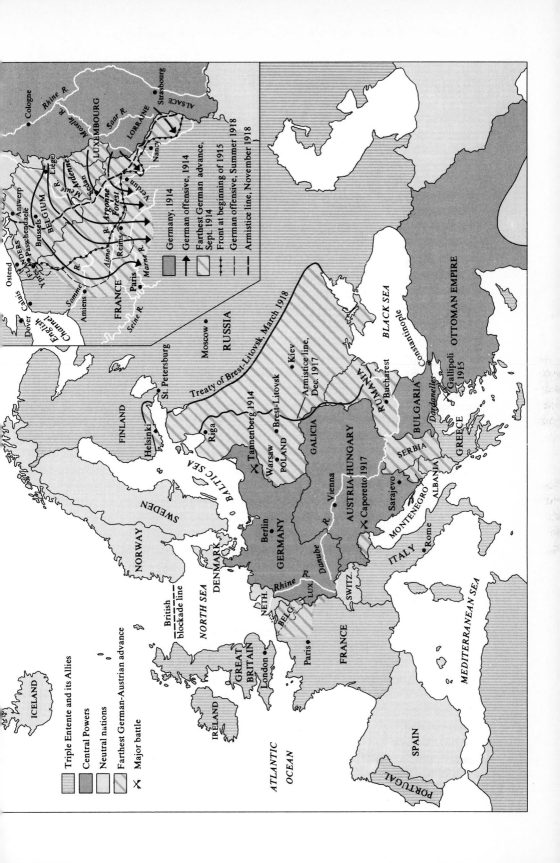

Germany, 1914

German offensive, 1914

Farthest German advance,
Sept. 1914

Front at beginning of 1915

German offensive, Summer 1918

Armistice line, November 1918

Triple Entente and its Allies

Central Powers

Neutral nations

Farthest German-Austrian advance

✕ Major battle

British
blockade line

Cologne
Rhine R.
Moselle R.
Saar R.
Strasbourg
ALSACE
LUXEMBOURG
LORRAINE
Nancy
Meuse R.
Ardennes
Liège
Argonne Forest
Sedan
Verdun
Antwerp
Brussels
BELGIUM
Passchendaele
FLANDERS
Aisne R.
Ypres
Reims
Ostend
Somme R.
Marne R.
Calais
Dover
Amiens
FRANCE
Paris
Seine R.
English Channel

RUSSIA
Moscow
St. Petersburg
Treaty of Brest-Litovsk, March 1918
Kiev
Armistice line, Dec. 1917
FINLAND
Helsinki
Riga
BALTIC SEA
✕ Tannenberg 1914
Warsaw
Brest-Litovsk
POLAND
GALICIA
RUMANIA
Bucharest
BLACK SEA
Constantinople
Dardanelles
Gallipoli 1915
OTTOMAN EMPIRE
SWEDEN
NORWAY
DENMARK
NORTH SEA
Berlin
GERMANY
Vienna
Danube R.
AUSTRIA-HUNGARY
✕ Caporetto 1917
Sarajevo
SERBIA
BULGARIA
GREECE
MONTENEGRO
ALBANIA
ITALY
Rome
Rhine R.
NETH.
BELG.
LUX.
SWITZ.
FRANCE
Paris
GREAT BRITAIN
London
IRELAND
ICELAND
ATLANTIC OCEAN
SPAIN
PORTUGAL
MEDITERRANEAN SEA

Stalemate in the West

On August 4, 1914, the German army invaded Belgium. German war plans, drawn up years earlier, principally by General Alfred von Schlieffen, called for the army to swing through Belgium to outflank French border defenses, envelop the French forces, and destroy the enemy by attacking their rear. With the French army smashed and Paris isolated, German railroads would rush the victorious troops to the eastern front to reinforce the small force that had been assigned to hold off the Russians. Everything depended on speed. France must be taken before the Russians could mobilize sufficient numbers to invade Germany. The Germans were confident that they would defeat France in two months or less.

But things did not turn out the way the German military had anticipated. Moving faster than the Germans expected, the Russians invaded East Prussia, which forced General Helmuth von Moltke to transfer troops from the French front, hampering the German advance. By early September the Germans had reached the Marne River, forty miles from Paris. With their capital at their backs, the regrouped French forces, aided by the British, fought with astounding courage. Moreover, in their rush toward Paris, the Germans had unknowingly exposed their flank, which the French attacked. The British then penetrated a gap that opened up between the German armies, forcing the Germans to retreat. The First Battle of the Marne had saved Paris. Now the war entered a new and unexpected phase—the deadlock of trench warfare.

For 400 miles across northern France, from the Alps to the North Sea, the opposing sides both constructed a vast network of trenches. These trenches had underground dugouts, and barbed wire stretched for yards before the front trenches as a barrier to attack. Behind the front trenches were other lines to which soldiers could retreat and from which support could be sent. Between the opposing armies lay "no man's land," a wasteland of mud, shattered trees, torn earth, and broken bodies. Trench warfare was a battle of nerves, endurance, and courage, waged to the constant thunder of heavy artillery. It was also butchery. As attacking troops climbed over their trenches and advanced bravely across no man's land, they were decimated by heavy artillery and chewed up by machine-gun fire. If they did penetrate the front-line trenches of the enemy, they would soon be thrown back by a counterattack.

Despite a frightful loss of life, little land changed hands. So much heroism, sacrifice, and death achieved nothing. The generals ordered still greater attacks to end the stalemate; this only increased the death toll, for the advantage was always with the defense, which possessed machine guns, magazine rifles, and barbed wire. Tanks could redress the balance, but the generals, committed to old concepts, did not make effective use of them. And whereas the technology of the machine gun had been perfected, the motorized tanks often broke down. Gains and losses of land were measured in yards, but the lives of Europe's youth were squandered by the hundreds of thousands. Against artillery, barbed wire, and machine guns, human courage had no chance; the generals—uncomprehending, unfeeling, and incompetent—persisted in their mass

British Munitions Workers.   With millions of men in the military, women took jobs
formerly held only by men. Women drove trucks and buses, operated cranes, and
worked in armament factories. Resistance to granting them equal rights diminished, as
politicians recognized the essential contribution of women to the war effort. (*Brown
Brothers*)

attacks. This futile effort at a breakthrough wasted untold lives to absolutely
no purpose.

In 1915, neither side could break the deadlock. Hoping to bleed the French
army dry and force its surrender, the Germans in February 1916 attacked the
town of Verdun. Knowing that the French could never permit a retreat from
this ancient fortress, they hoped that France would suffer such a loss of men
that it would be unable to continue the war. France and Germany suffered
more than a million casualties at Verdun, which one military historian calls
"the greatest battle in world history." When the British opened a major offensive on July 1, however, the Germans had to channel their reserves to the new
front, relieving the pressure on Verdun.

At the end of June 1916 the British, assisted by the French, attempted a
breakthrough at the Somme River. On July 1, after seven days of intense
bombardment intended to destroy German defenses, the British climbed out of
their trenches and ventured into no man's land. But German positions had not

been destroyed. Emerging from their deep dugouts, German machine gunners fired repeatedly at the British, who had been ordered to advance in rows. Marching into concentrated machine-gun fire, few British troops ever made it across no man's land. Out of 110,000 who attacked, 60,000 fell dead or wounded, "the heaviest loss ever suffered in a single day by a British army or by any army in the First World War."[8] When the battle of the Somme ended in mid-November, Britain and France had lost over 600,000 men, and the military situation remained essentially unchanged. The only victor was the war itself, which was devouring Europe's youth at an incredible rate.

In December 1916, General Robert Nivelle was appointed Commander-in-Chief of the French forces. Having learned little from past French failures to achieve a breakthrough, Nivelle ordered another mass attack for April 1917. The Germans discovered the battle plans on the body of a French officer and withdrew to a shorter line on high ground, constructing the strongest defense network of the war. Knowing that the French had lost the element of surprise and pushing aside the warnings of leading statesmen and military men, Nivelle went ahead with the attack. "The offensive alone gives victory; the defensive gives only defeat and shame," he told the president and the minister of war.[9]

The Nivelle offensive, which began on April 16, was another bloodbath. Sometimes the fire was so intense that the French could not make it out of their own trenches. Although French soldiers fought with courage, the situation was hopeless. Still Nivelle persisted with the attack; after ten days French casualties numbered 187,000. The disgraced Nivelle was soon relieved of his command.

Other Fronts

While the western front hardened into a stalemate, events moved more decisively on the eastern front. In August 1914, the Russians, with insufficient preparation, invaded East Prussia. After some initial successes, which sent a scare into the German general staff, the Russians were soundly defeated at the battle of Tannenberg (August 26–30, 1914) and forced to withdraw from German territory, which remained inviolate for the rest of the war.

Meanwhile Germany's ally Austria was having no success against Serbia and Russia. An invasion of Serbia was thrown back, and an ill-conceived offensive against Russia cost Austria its Galician provinces. Germany had to come to Austria's rescue. In the spring of 1915 the Germans made a breakthrough that forced the Russians to abandon Galicia and most of Poland. In June 1916 the Russians launched an offensive that opened a wide breach in the Austrian lines, but they could not maintain it. A German counteroffensive forced a retreat and cost the Russians over a million casualties.

In March 1917 food shortages and disgust with the great loss of life exploded into a spontaneous revolution; the tsar was forced to abdicate. The new government, dominated by liberals, opted to continue the war despite the weariness of the Russian masses. In November 1917 a second revolution brought the Bolsheviks or communists, who promised "Peace, Land, Bread," into power. In March 1918 the Bolsheviks signed the punitive Treaty of Brest-Litovsk, in which Russia surrendered Poland, the Ukraine, Finland, and the Baltic provinces. An insatiable Germany gained 34 percent of Russia's population, 32 percent of its farmland, 54 percent of its industrial enterprises, and 89 percent of its coal mines.

Several countries that were not belligerents in August 1914—among them, the Ottoman Empire and Italy—joined the war later. That autumn, the Ottoman Turks entered the conflict as allies of Germany. Prior to the war, Germany had cultivated the Ottoman Empire's friendship by training the Turkish army; on their part, the Turks wanted German help in case Russia attempted to seize the Dardanelles. Hoping to supply Russia and in turn to obtain badly needed Russian grain, the Allies did decide to capture the Dardanelles. In April 1915 a combined force of British, French, Australian, and New Zealander troops stormed the Gallipoli Peninsula on the European side of the Dardanelles. Ignorance of amphibious warfare, poor intelligence, and the fierce resistance of the Turks prevented the Allies from getting off the beaches and taking the heights. The Gallipoli campaign cost the Allies 252,000 casualties, and they had gained nothing.

Although a member of the Triple Alliance, Italy remained neutral when war broke out. In May 1915, on the promise of receiving Austrian territory, Italy entered the war on the side of the Allies. The Austrians repulsed a number of Italian offensives along the frontier and in 1916 took the offensive against Italy. A combined German and Austrian force finally broke through the Italian lines in the fall of 1917 at Caporetto, and the Italians retreated in disorder, leaving behind huge quantities of weapons. Germany and Austria took some 275,000 prisoners.

The Collapse of the Central Powers

American Entry

The year 1917 seemed disastrous for the Allies. The Nivelle offensive had failed, the French army had mutinied, a British attack at Passchendaele did not bring the expected breakthrough and added some 300,000 casualties to the list of butchery, and the Russians, torn by revolution and gripped by war weariness, were close to making a separate peace. But there was one encouraging development for the Allies. In April 1917 the United States declared war on Germany.

From the outset America's sympathies lay with the Allies. To most Americans, Britain and France were democracies, threatened by an autocratic and militaristic Germany. These sentiments were reinforced by British propaganda that depicted the Germans as cruel "Huns." Since most war news came to the United States from Britain, anti-German feeling gained momentum. What precipitated American entry was the German decision of January 1917 to launch a campaign of unrestricted submarine warfare. The Germans were determined to deprive Britain of war supplies and to starve it into submission. Their resolve meant that German U-boats would torpedo both enemy and neutral ships in the war zone around the British Isles. Since the United States was Britain's principal supplier, American ships became a target of German submarines.

Angered by American loss of life and materiel and by the violation of the doctrine of freedom of the seas, and fearful of a diminution of prestige if the United States took no action, President Woodrow Wilson (1856–1924) pressed for American entry. Also at stake was American security, which would be jeopardized by German domination of western Europe. Leading American statesmen and diplomats feared that such a radical change in the balance of power threatened American national interests. As German submarines continued to attack neutral shipping, President Wilson, on April 2, 1917, urged Congress to declare war on Germany, which it did on April 6.

Germany's Last Offensive

With Russia out of the war, General Erich Ludendorff prepared for a decisive offensive before the Americans could land sufficient troops in France to help the Allies. A war of attrition now favored the Allies, who could count on American supplies and manpower. Without an immediate and decisive victory, Germany could not win the war. On March 21, 1918, the Germans launched an offensive that was intended to bring victory in the west.

Suddenly the deadlock was broken; it was now a war of movement. Within two weeks the Germans had taken some 1,250 square miles. But British resistance was astonishing, and the Germans, exhausted and short of ammunition and food, called off the drive. A second offensive against the British in April also had to be called off, as the British contested every foot of ground. Both campaigns depleted German manpower while the Americans were arriving in great numbers to strengthen Allied lines and uplift morale. At the end of May Ludendorff resumed his offensive against the French. Attacking unexpectedly, the Germans broke through and advanced to within 56 miles of Paris by June 3. Reserves, braced the French lines, however, and in the battle of Belleau Wood (June 6–25, 1918), the Americans checked the Germans.

In mid-July the Germans tried again, crossing the Marne River in small boats. Although in one area they advanced nine miles, the offensive failed against determined American and French opposition. By August 3, the Second Battle of the Marne had come to an end. The Germans had thrown everything they had into their spring and summer offensive, but it was not enough. The Allies had bent, but reinforced and encouraged by American arms, they did not break. Now they began to counterattack, with great success.

Meanwhile German allies, deprived of support from a hard-pressed Germany, were unable to cope. An Allied army of French, Britons, Serbs, and Italians compelled Bulgaria to sign an armistice on September 29. Shortly afterward, British successes in the Middle East compelled Turkey to withdraw from the war. In the streets of Vienna people were shouting "Long live peace! Down with the monarchy!" The Austro-Hungarian Empire was rapidly disintegrating into separate states based on nationality.

By early October the last defensive position of the Germans had crumbled. Fearful that the Allies would invade the fatherland and shatter the reputation of the German army. Ludendorff wanted an immediate armistice. But he needed a way to obtain favorable armistice terms from President Wilson and to shift the blame for the lost war away from the military and the kaiser to the civilian leadership. Cynically, he urged the creation of a popular parliamentary government in Germany. But events in Germany went further than the general had anticipated. Whereas Ludendorff sought a limited monarchy, the shock of defeat and hunger sparked a revolution that forced the kaiser to abdicate. On November 11, the new German Republic signed an armistice ending the hostilities.

The Peace Conference

Wilson's Hope for a New World

In January 1919, representatives of the Allied Powers assembled in Paris to draw up peace terms; President Wilson was also there. The war-weary masses turned to Wilson as the prophet who would have the nations beat their swords into plowshares. For Wilson the war had been fought against autocracy. A peace settlement based on liberal-democratic ideals, he hoped, would sweep away the foundations of war. None of Wilson's principles seemed more just than the idea of self-determination—the right of a people to have its own state, free of foreign domination. In particular, this goal meant (or was interpreted to mean) the return of Alsace and Lorraine to France, the creation of an independent Poland, a readjustment of the frontiers of Italy to incorporate Austrian lands inhabited by Italians, and an opportunity for Slavs of the Austro-Hungarian Empire to form their own states.

Aware that a harshly treated Germany might well seek revenge, thereby engulfing the world in another cataclysm, Wilson insisted that there should be a "peace without victory." A just settlement would encourage a defeated Germany to work with the victorious Allies in building a new Europe. To preserve peace and to help remake the world. Wilson urged the formation of a League of Nations, an international parliament to settle disputes and discourage aggression. Wilson wanted a peace of justice to preserve Western civilization in its democratic and Christian form.

Problems of Peacemaking

Wilson's negotiating position was undermined by the Republican party's victory in the congressional elections of November 1918. Before the election, Wilson appealed to the American people to vote for Democrats as a vote of

Woodrow Wilson and the King of Italy Greeting Crowds in Italy After Signing the Peace Treaty.   Woodrow Wilson was greeted in Europe as the bringer of peace. His presence at the peace conference, where he had to haggle over points, and the Republican victory in the U.S. congressional election in November 1918, soon tarnished his image. (*Culver Pictures*)

confidence in his diplomacy. But Americans elected twenty-five Republicans and fifteen Democrats to the Senate. Whatever the motives of the American people in voting Republican—apparently their decision rested on local and national, not international, issues—the outcome diminished Wilson's prestige at the conference table. To his fellow negotiators, Wilson was trying to preach to Europe when he could not command the support of his own country. Since the Senate must ratify any American treaty, European diplomats had the terrible fear that what Wilson agreed to the Senate might reject—which is precisely what happened.

   Another obstacle to Wilson's peace program was France's demand for security and revenge. Nearly the entire war on the western front had been fought in French territory. Many French industries and farms had been ruined; the country mourned the loss of half its young men. Representing France at the conference table was George Clemenceau (1841–1929), nicknamed "the Ti-

Map 17.3   Post–World War I: Broken Empires and Changed Boundaries ▶

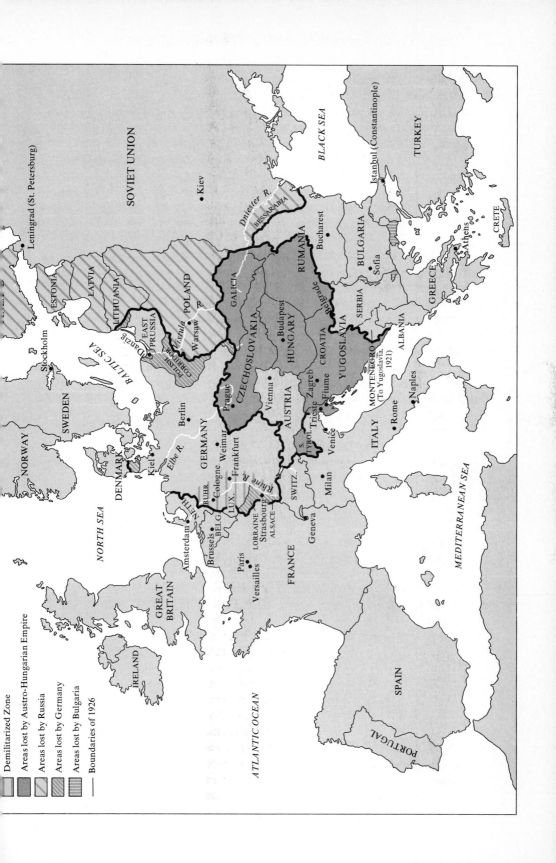

Demilitarized Zone

Areas lost by Austro-Hungarian Empire

Areas lost by Russia

Areas lost by Germany

Areas lost by Bulgaria

Boundaries of 1926

NORWAY

SWEDEN

Stockholm

BALTIC SEA

NORTH SEA

DENMARK

Kiel

Elbe R.

Berlin

GERMANY

Weimar

Cologne

Frankfurt

RUHR

Rhine R.

NETH.

Amsterdam

Brussels

BELG.

LUX.

LORRAINE

Strasbourg

ALSACE

SWITZ.

Geneva

Milan

FRANCE

Paris

Versailles

GREAT BRITAIN

IRELAND

ATLANTIC OCEAN

SPAIN

PORTUGAL

MEDITERRANEAN SEA

Leningrad (St. Petersburg)

SOVIET UNION

Kiev

ESTONIA

LATVIA

LITHUANIA

EAST PRUSSIA

Danzig

POLISH CORRIDOR

Vistula

POLAND

Warsaw

Prague

CZECHOSLOVAKIA

GALICIA

Dniester R.

BESSARABIA

RUMANIA

Bucharest

Budapest

HUNGARY

Vienna

AUSTRIA

S. TYROL

Venice

Trieste

Fiume

Zagreb

CROATIA

YUGOSLAVIA

SERBIA

Belgrade

BULGARIA

Sofia

MONTENEGRO
(To Yugoslavia,
1921)

ALBANIA

GREECE

Athens

CRETE

BLACK SEA

Istanbul (Constantinople)

TURKEY

ITALY

Rome

Naples

ger." Nobody loved France or hated Germany more. Cynical, suspicious of idealism, and not sharing Wilson's hope for a new world or his confidence in the future League of Nations, Clemenceau demanded that Germany be severely punished and its capacity to wage war destroyed.

Fearful of Germany's greater population and superior industrial strength, and of its military tradition that would not resign itself to defeat, Clemenceau wanted guarantees that the wars of 1870–1871 and 1914–1918 would not be repeated. The war had shown that without the help of Britain and the United States, France would have been at the mercy of Germany. Because there was no certainty that these states would again aid France, Clemenceau wanted to use his country's present advantage to cripple Germany.

The intermingling of European nationalities was another barrier to Wilson's program. Because in so many regions of central Europe there was a mixture of nationalities, no one could create a Europe completely free of minority problems; some nationalities would always feel that they had been treated shabbily. And the various nationalities were not willing to moderate their demands or lower their aspirations. For example, Wilson's Fourteen Points called for the creation of an independent Poland with secure access to the sea. But between Poland and the sea lay territory populated by Germans. Giving this land to Poland would violate German self-determination; denying it to Poland would mean that the new country had little chance of developing a sound economy. No matter what the decision, one people would regard it as unjust. Similarly, to provide the new Czechoslovakia with defensible borders, it would be necessary to give it territory inhabited principally by Germans. This too could be viewed as a denial of German self-determination, but not granting it to Czechoslovakia would mean that the new state would not be able to defend itself against Germany.

Also serving as a barrier to Wilson's program were the secret treaties drawn up by the Allies during the war. These agreements, dividing up German, Austrian, and Ottoman territory, did not square with the principle of self-determination. For example, to entice Italy into entering the war, the Allies had promised it Austrian lands that were inhabited predominantly by Germans and Slavs. Italy was not about to repudiate its prize because of Wilson's principles.

Finally, the war had aroused great bitterness that persisted after the guns had been silenced. Both the masses and their leaders demanded retribution and held exaggerated hopes for territory and reparations. In such an atmosphere of postwar enmity, the spirit of compromise and moderation could not overcome the desire for spoils and punishment.

The Settlement

After months of negotiations, punctuated often by acrimony, the peacemakers hammered out a settlement. Five treaties made up the Peace of Paris—one each with Germany, Austria, Hungary, Bulgaria, and Turkey. Of the five, the Treaty of Versailles, which Germany signed on June 28, 1919, was the most significant. France regained Alsace and Lorraine, lost to Germany in the Franco-Prussian War of 1870–71. The treaty barred Germany from placing fortifications in the Rhineland.

The French military had wanted to take the Rhineland from Germany and break it up into one or more republics under French suzerainty. The Rhine River was a natural defensive border; one had only to destroy the bridges to prevent a German invasion of France. With Germany deprived of this springboard for invasion, French security would be immensely improved. Recognizing that the German people would never permanently submit to the amputation of the Rhineland, which was inhabited by more than 5 million Germans and contained key industries, Wilson and British Prime Minister David Lloyd George (1863–1945) resisted these French demands.

Faced with the opposition of Wilson and Lloyd George, Clemenceau backed down and agreed instead to Allied occupation of the Rhineland for fifteen years, the demilitarization of the region, and an Anglo-American promise of assistance if Germany attacked France in the future. This last point, considered vital by France, proved useless. The alliance only went into effect if both the United States and Britain ratified it. Since the Security Treaty did not get past the United States Senate, Britain also refused to sign it. The French people felt that they had been duped and wronged. A related issue concerned French demands for annexation of the coal-rich Saar Basin, which adjoined Lorraine. By obtaining this region, France would weaken Germany's military potential and strengthen its own. France argued that this would be just compensation for the deliberate destruction of the French coal mines by the retreating German army at the end of the war. But here too France was disappointed. The final compromise called for a League of Nations commission to govern the Saar Basin for fifteen years, after which the inhabitants would decide whether their territory would be ceded to France or returned to Germany.

In eastern Germany, in certain districts of Silesia that had a large Polish population, a plebiscite determined the future of the region. As a result, part of Upper Silesia was ceded to Poland. The settlement also gave Poland a corridor cut through West Prussia and terminating in the Baltic port of Danzig, and Danzig itself was declared an international city, to be administered by a League of Nations commission. The Germans would never resign themselves to this loss of territory, which separated East Prussia from the rest of Germany.

The victorious nations were awarded control of German and Ottoman colonies. However, these nations held colonies not outright but as mandates under the supervision of the League, which would protect the interests of the native peoples. The mandate system implied the ultimate end of colonialism, for it clearly opposed the exploitation of colonial peoples and asserted independence as the rightful goal for subject nations.

Other issues revolved around the German military forces and reparations. To prevent a resurgence of militarism, the Germany army was limited to 100,000 volunteers and deprived of heavy artillery, tanks, and warplanes. The German navy was limited to a token force that did not include submarines. The issue of reparations (compensation) aroused terrible bitterness between

Wilson and his French and British adversaries. The American delegation wanted the treaty to fix a reasonable sum that Germany would have to pay and specify the period of years allotted for payment. But no such items were included; they were left for future consideration. The Treaty of Versailles left Germany with an open-ended bill that would probably take generations to pay. Moreover, Article 231, which preceded the reparation clauses, placed sole responsibility for the war on Germany and its allies. The Germans responded to this accusation with contempt.

In separate treaties the conference dealt with the dissolution of the Hapsburg empire. In the closing weeks of the war, the Austro-Hungarian Empire had crumbled as the various nationalities proclaimed their independence from Hapsburg rule. In most cases, the peacemakers ratified with treaties what the nationalities had already accomplished in fact. Serbia joined with Austrian lands inhabited by Croats and Slovenes to become Yugoslavia. Czechoslovakia arose from the predominantly Czech and Slovak regions of Austria. Hungary, which broke away from Austria to become a separate country, had to concede considerable land to Rumania and Yugoslavia. Austria had to turn over to Italy the South Tyrol, which was inhabited by 200,000 Austrian Germans. This clear violation of the principle of self-determination greatly offended liberal opinion. Deprived of its vast territories and prohibited from union with Germany, the new Austria was a third-rate power.

Assessment and Problems

The Germans unanimously denounced the Treaty of Versailles, for in their minds the war had ended not in German defeat but in a stalemate. They regarded the armistice as the prelude to a negotiated settlement among equals based on Wilson's call for a peace of justice. Instead the Germans were barred from participating in the negotiations. And they viewed the terms of the treaty as humiliating and vindictive—designed to keep Germany militarily and economically weak.

The Germans protested that when the United States entered the war, Wilson had stated that the enemy was not the German people but their government. Surely, the Germans now argued, the new German democracy should not be punished for the sins of the monarchy and the military. To the Germans, the Treaty of Versailles was not the dawning of the new world that Wilson had promised, but an abomination—a vile crime.

Critics in other lands also condemned the treaty as a punitive settlement in flagrant violation of Wilsonian idealism. The peacemakers, they argued, should have set aside past hatreds and, in cooperation with the new democratic German Republic, forged a just settlement that would serve as the foundation of a new world. Instead they burdened the fledgling German democracy with reparations that were impossible to pay, insulted it with the accusation of war guilt, and deprived it of territory in violation of the principle of self-determination. All these provisions, said the critics, would only exacerbate old hatreds and fan the flames of German nationalism. This was a poor beginning for democracy in Germany and for Wilson's new world.

Defenders of the peace settlement insisted that if Germany had won the war it would have imposed a far harsher settlement on the Allies. They pointed to German war aims, which called for the annexation of parts of France and Poland, the reduction of Belgium and Rumania to satellites, and German expansion in central Africa. They pointed also to the treaty of Brest-Litovsk, which Germany compelled Russia to sign in 1918, as an example of Germany's ruthless appetite. Moreover, they insisted that the peace settlement was by no means a repudiation of Wilson's principles. The new map of Europe was the closest approximation of the ethnic distribution of its peoples that Europe had ever known.

What is most significant about the Treaty of Versailles is that it did not solve the German problem. Germany was left weak but unbroken—its industrial and military power only temporarily contained, its nationalist fervor undimmed. The real danger in Europe was German unwillingness to accept defeat or surrender the dream of expansion.

Would France, Britain, and the United States enforce the treaty against a resurgent Germany? The war had demonstrated that an Allied victory depended on American intervention. But in 1920 the U.S. Senate, angry that Wilson had not taken Republicans with him to Paris and fearing that membership in the League of Nations would involve America in future wars, refused to ratify the Treaty of Versailles. Britain, feeling guilty over the treatment of Germany, lacked the will for enforcement and even came to favor treaty revision. The responsibility for preserving the settlement therefore rested primarily with France, which was not encouraging. The Paris peace settlement left Germany resentful but potentially powerful, and to the east lay small and weak states, some of them with sizable German minorities, that could not check a rearmed Germany.

The War and European Consciousness

"There will be wars as never before on earth," predicted Nietzsche. World War I bore him out. Modern technology enabled the combatants to kill with unprecedented efficiency; modern nationalism infused both civilians and soldiers with the determination to fight until the enemy was totally beaten. The modern state, exercising wide control over its citizens, mobilized its human, material, and spiritual resources to wage total war. As the war hardened into a savage and grueling fight, the statesmen did not press for a compromise peace, but demanded ever more mobilization, ever more escalation, and ever more sacrifices. The Great War profoundly altered the course of Western civilization, deepening the spiritual crisis that had produced it. How could one speak of the inviolability of the individual when Europe had become a slaughterhouse? Or of the primacy of reason when nations permitted slaughter to go unabated for four years? Western civilization had entered an age of violence, anxiety, and doubt that still persists.

The war left many with the gnawing feeling that Western civilization had lost its vitality and was caught in a rhythm of breakdown and disintegration. It seemed that Western civilization was fragile and perishable, that Western people, despite their extraordinary accomplishments, were never more than a step or two away from barbarism. Surely any civilization that could allow such senseless slaughter to last four years had entered its decline and could look forward to only the darkest of futures.

European intellectuals were demoralized and disillusioned. The orderly, peaceful, rational world of their youth had been destroyed. The Enlightenment world-view, weakened in the nineteenth century by the assault of romantics, Social Darwinists, extreme nationalists, race mystics, and glorifiers of the irrational, was now disintegrating. The enormity of the war had shattered faith in the capacity of reason to deal with crucial social and political questions. It appeared that civilization was fighting an unending and seemingly hopeless battle against the irrational elements in human nature and that war would be a recurring phenomenon in the twentieth century.

Confidence in the future gave way to doubt. The old beliefs in the perfectibility of humanity, the blessings of science, and ongoing progress now seemed an expression of naive optimism. A. J. P. Taylor concludes:

> The First World War was difficult to fit into the picture of a rational civilization advancing by ordered stages. The civilized men of the twentieth century had outdone in savagery the barbarians of all preceding ages, and their civilized virtues—organization, mechanical skill, self-sacrifice—had made war's savagery all the more terrible. Modern man had developed powers which he was not fit to use. European civilization had been weighed in the balance and found wanting.[10]

This disillusionment heralded a loss of faith in liberal-democratic values that contributed to the widespread popularity of fascist ideologies in the postwar world. Having lost confidence in the power of reason to solve the problems of the human community, in liberal doctrines of individual freedom, and in the institutions of parliamentary democracy, many people turned to fascism as a simple saving faith. Far from making the world safe for democracy as Wilson and other liberals had hoped, World War I gave rise to totalitarian movements that would nearly destroy democracy.

The war produced a generation of young people who had reached their maturity in combat. Violence had become a way of life for millions of soldiers hardened by battle and for millions of civilians aroused by four years of propaganda. The astronomical casualty figures—some 10 million dead and 21 million wounded—had a brutalizing effect. Violence, cruelty, suffering, and even wholesale death seemed to be natural and acceptable components of

Käthe Kollwitz: The Survivors.   With an estimated 10 million dead and 21 million wounded, World War I shattered the hope that western Europe had been making continuous progress toward universal peace and a rational and enlightened civilization. (*National Gallery of Art, Washington, D.C., Rosenwald Collection*)

human existence; the sanctity of the individual seemed to be liberal and Christian claptrap.

The fascination for violence and contempt for life lived on in the postwar world. Many returned veterans yearned for the excitement of battle and the fellowship of the trenches. They made ideal recruits for extremist political movements that glorified action and promised to rescue society from a decadent liberalism. Both Hitler and Mussolini, themselves ex-soldiers imbued with the ferocity of the front, knew how to appeal to veterans. The lovers of violence and the harbingers of hate who became the leaders of fascist parties would come within a hairsbreadth of destroying Western civilization. The intensified nationalist hatreds following World War I also helped to fuel the fires of World War II. The Germans swore to regain lands lost to the Poles; some Germans dreamed of a war of revenge. Italy, too, felt aggrieved because it had not received more territory from the dismembered Austro-Hungarian Empire.

However, while the experience of the trenches led some veterans to embrace an aggressive militarism, others were determined that the horror should never

Chronology 17.1 ❧ World War I

1882	Formation of the Triple Alliance of Germany, Austria-Hungary, and Italy
1894	Alliance between Russia and France
1904	Anglo-French Entente
1907	Anglo-Russian Entente
1908	Bosnian Crisis
June 28, 1914	Archduke Ferdinand of Austria is assassinated at Sarajevo
August 4, 1914	The Germans invade Belgium
September 1914	The first battle of the Marne saves Paris
May 1915	Italy enters the war on the Allies' side
1915	Germany forces Russia to abandon Galicia and most of Poland
February 1916	General Pétain leads French forces at Verdun; Germans fail to capture the fortress town
July–November 1916	The battle of the Somme—the Allies suffer 600,000 casualties
January 1917	Germany launches unrestricted submarine warfare
April 6, 1917	The United States declares war on Germany
November 1917	The Bolsheviks take power in Russia
March 1918	Russia signs the Treaty of Brest-Litovsk, losing territory to Germany and withdrawing from the war
March 21, 1918	The Germans launch a great offensive to end the war
June 3, 1918	The Germans advance to within 56 miles of Paris
August 8, 1918	The British win the battle of Amiens
October 1918	Turkey is forced to withdraw from the war after several British successes
November 3, 1918	Austria-Hungary signs an armistice with the Allies
November 11, 1918	Germany signs an armistice with the Allies, ending World War I
January 1919	Paris Peace Conference
June 28, 1919	Germany signs the Treaty of Versailles

be repeated. Tortured by the memory of the Great War, European intellectuals wrote pacifist plays and novels and signed pacifist declarations. In the 1930s, an attitude of "peace at any price" discouraged resistance to Nazi Germany in its bid to dominate Europe.

World War I was total war—it encompassed the entire nation and was without limits. States demanded total victory and total commitment from their citizens. They regulated industrial production, developed sophisticated propaganda techniques to strengthen morale, and exercised ever greater control over the lives of their people, organizing and disciplining them like soldiers. This total mobilization of nations' human and material resources provided a model for future dictators. With ever greater effectiveness and ruthlessness, dictators would centralize power and manipulate thinking. The first indication that the world would never be the same again, and perhaps the most important consequence of the war, was the Russian Revolution in 1917 and the Bolshevik seizure of power.

Notes

1. From "Peace," in *Collected Poems of Rupert Brooke* (New York: Dodd, Mead, 1941), p. 111.
2. Quoted in Joachim C. Fest, *Hitler* (New York: Harcourt Brace Jovanovich, 1973), p. 66.
3. George A. Panichas, ed., *Promise of Greatness* (New York: John Day, 1968), pp. 14–15.
4. Quoted in Barbara Tuchman, *The Guns of August* (New York: Macmillan, 1962), p. 145.
5. Quoted in Robert G. L. Waite, *Vanguard of Nazism* (New York: W. W. Norton, 1969), p. 22.
6. From "Peace," in *Collected Poems of Rupert Brooke,* p. 111.
7. Quoted in James Joll, "The Unspoken Assumptions," in H. W. Koch, ed., *The Origins of the First World War* (New York: Taplinger, 1972), p. 318.
8. A. J. P. Taylor, *A History of the First World War* (New York: Berkeley, 1966), p. 84.
9. Quoted in Richard M. Watt, *Dare Call It Treason* (New York: Simon & Schuster, 1963), p. 169.
10. A. J. P. Taylor, *From Sarajevo to Potsdam* (New York: Harcourt, Brace and World, 1966), pp. 55–56.

Suggested Reading

Berghahn, V. R., *Germany and the Approach of War in 1914* (1975). Relates German foreign policy to domestic problems.

Fay, Sidney, *The Origins of the World War,* 2 vols. (1966). A comprehensive study of the underlying and immediate causes of the war; first published in 1928.

Fischer, Fritz, *Germany's Aims in the First World War* (1967). A controversial work, stressing Germany's responsibility for the war.

Lafore, Laurence, *The Long Fuse* (1971). A beautifully written study of the causes of the conflict.

Leed, Eric J., *No Man's Land: Combat and Identity in World War I* (1979). The impact of the war on the men who participated in it.

Marshall, S. L. A., *The American Heritage History of World War I* (1966).

Probably the best account available.

Panichas, George A., ed., *Promise of Greatness* (1968). Recollections of the war by people of prominence.

Stromberg, Roland N., *Redemption by War: The Intellectuals and 1914* (1982). A superb analysis of the reason why so many intellectuals welcomed the war.

Review Questions

1. How did the nationality problems in Austria-Hungary contribute to the outbreak of World War I?
2. What conditions led to the formation of the Triple Entente? How did Germany respond to it?
3. After the assassination of Archduke Francis Ferdinand, what policies were pursued by Austria-Hungary, Germany, Russia?
4. What battle plans did Germany and France implement in 1914? What prevented Germany from reaching Paris in 1914?
5. Identify and explain the historical significance of the battles of Verdun, the Somme, and Gallipoli.
6. Why did the United States enter the war?
7. What was Wilson's peace program? What obstacles did he face?
8. What were the provisions of the Treaty of Versailles regarding Germany?
9. Why was World War I a great turning point in the history of the West?

Chapter · 18

The Soviet Union: Modernization and Totalitarianism

A fateful consequence of World War I, even before its final battles were fought, was the Russian Revolution of 1917. The revolution occurred in two stages. In March, the tsarist regime was overthrown. The March revolution ushered in a period of liberal government and freedom, which soon led to a complete breakdown of law and order. Taking advantage of the chaos, the Bolsheviks, in a second stage of the revolution, seized power in November and established a communist dictatorship.* The roots of the Russian Revolution lie in the failure of tsarist autocracy. ✿

Tsarist Autocracy

In the middle of the nineteenth century, Russia differed fundamentally from western Europe. The great movements that had shaped the outlook of the modern West—Renaissance, Reformation, Scientific Revolution, Enlightenment, and Industrial Revolution—had barely penetrated Russia. Autocracy, buttressed by the Orthodox church, reigned supreme; the small and insignificant middle class did not possess the dynamic, critical, and individualistic spirit that characterized the Western bourgeoisie, and the vast majority of the people were illiterate serfs.

After Napoleon's defeat in 1814, many returning Russian officers, asking why Russia could not share the civilized life they had seen in western Europe, turned revolutionary. The unsuccessful Decembrist uprising in 1825, during the brief interlude between the death of Alexander I (1801–1825) and the

---

* Until March 1918, events in Russia were dated by the Julian calendar, thirteen days behind the Gregorian calendar used in the West.

accession of Nicholas I (1825–1855), was the effort of a small group of conspirators demanding a constitution. Fear of revolution determined the character of the reign of Nicholas I and of tsarist governments thereafter.

Aware of the subversive influence of foreign ideas and conditions, Nicholas decreed an ideology of Russian superiority, called *official nationality*. The Russian people were taught to believe that the Orthodox creed of the Russian church, the autocratic rule of the tsar, and Russia's Slavic culture made the Russian Empire superior to the West. To enforce this contrived invincibility, Nicholas I created the Third Section, a secret agency of police spies, and controlled access to his country from Europe, drawing toward the end of his reign a virtual iron curtain to keep out dangerous influences. His ideal was a monolithic country run, like an army, by a vigorous administration centered on the monarch; all Russians were to obey his wise and fatherly commands.

Nicholas's successor, Alexander II (1855–1881), was determined to preserve autocratic rule. However, he wanted Russia to achieve what had made western Europe strong—the energetic support and free enterprise of its citizens. Whether stimulating popular initiative was possible without undermining autocracy was the key puzzle for him and for his successors to the end of the tsarist regime.

Alexander's boldest reforms included the emancipation of the serfs in 1861. They were liberated from bondage to the nobility and given land of their own, but not individual freedom. They remained tied to their village and to their households, which owned the land collectively. Emancipation did not transform the peasants into enterprising and loyal citizens. For the nonpeasant minority, a package of other reforms brought new opportunities: limited self-government for selected rural areas and urban settlements, an independent judiciary, and the rule of law. Trial by jury was introduced, as well as a profession novel to Russians—the practice of law.

Meanwhile, Alexander reopened the borders, allowing closer ties with Europe and westernizing Russian society. The rising class of businesspeople and professional experts looked west and conformed to Western middle-class standards. There was some relaxation in the repression of non-Russian minorities. Railroads were constructed, which facilitated agricultural exports and permitted the import of Western goods and capital. For some years the economy boomed.

More significant in the long run was the flowering of Russian thought and literature among the intelligentsia. These were educated Russians whose minds were shaped by Western schooling and travel, yet who still were prompted by the "Russian soul." They quarreled with fierce sincerity over whether Russia should pursue superiority by imitating the West or by cultivating its own Slavic genius, possibly through a pan-Slavic movement. Pan-Slavism, which glorified the solidarity of Russians with other Slavic peoples of eastern Europe, was a popular cause. Even more than the tsars, the intelligentsia hoped for a glorious Russia that would outshine the West.

Yet tsarist autocracy undercut their hopes. The tsar would not permit open discussion likely to provoke rebellion. Liberals advocating gradual change were thwarted by censorship and the police. The 1860s saw the rise of self-righteous fanatics ready to match the chicanery of the police and foment social revolution. By the late 1870s, they organized themselves into a secret terrorist organization. In 1881, they assassinated the tsar. The era of reforms ended.

The next tsar, Alexander III (1881–1894), a firm if unimaginative ruler, returned to the principles of Nicholas I. In defense against the revolutionaries, he perfected the police state, even enlisting anti-Semitism in its cause. He updated autocracy and stifled dissent, but he also promoted the economy. Russia had relied too heavily on foreign loans and goods; it had to build up its own resources. It also needed more railroads to bind its huge empire together. So in 1891 the tsar ordered construction of the Trans-Siberian Railroad. Soon afterward, Minister of Finance Sergei Witte used railroad expansion to boost heavy industry and industrialization generally.

In 1900, Witte addressed a far-sighted memorandum to the young Nicholas II (1894–1917), who, hopelessly unprepared and out of tune with the times, had succeeded his father in 1894:

> *Russia more than any other country needs a proper economic founda-*
> *tion for its national policy and culture. . . . If we do not take energetic*
> *and decisive measures so that in the course of the next decade our*
> *industry will be able to satisfy the needs of Russia, . . . then the rapidly*
> *growing foreign industries will . . . establish themselves in our father-*
> *land. . . . Our economic backwardness may lead to political and*
> *cultural backwardness as well. . . .*[1]

Yet forced industrialization also brought perils. It propelled the country into alien and often hated ways of life; it created a discontented new class of workers and it impoverished agriculture; it promoted mobility, literacy, and contact with western Europe, thereby increasing political agitation among the professional classes, intelligentsia, workers, peasants, and subject nationalities. Indispensable for national self-assertion and survival, industrialization strained the country's fragile unity.

The first jolt, the Revolution of 1905, followed Russia's defeat by Japan in the Russo-Japanese War. Fortunately for the tsar, his soldiers stayed loyal. The autocracy survived, although now saddled with a parliament called the Imperial Duma, a concession to the revolution. The new regime, inwardly rejected by Nicholas II, started auspiciously. Under its freedoms, Russian art and literature flourished and the economy progressed. Agrarian reforms introduced the incentives of private property and individual enterprise in the villages. The supporters of the new constitutional experiment hoped for a liberal Russia at last, but in vain.

The Russian Revolution of 1917

The Collapse of Autocracy

Among all classes, increased contact with "the West," as Russians called Europe, raised expectations and deepened dissatisfaction with the country's poverty and backwardness. Fears of revolution troubled foresighted Russians. During World War I, the volcano came to life. The ill-equipped and poorly led Russian armies suffered huge losses, and by 1916 the home front began to fall apart. Shops were empty, money was valueless, and hunger and cold stalked the working quarters of cities and towns. But Tsar Nicholas II (1868–1918), who was determined to preserve autocracy, resisted any suggestion that he liberalize the regime for the sake of the war effort.

The people of Russia had initially responded to the war with a show of patriotic fervor. But by January 1917, virtually all Russians, and foremost the soldiers, despaired of autocracy: it had failed to protect the country from the enemy, and economic conditions had deteriorated. Autocracy was ready to collapse at the slightest adversity. In early March (February 23 by the Russian calendar then in use) a strike, riots in the food lines, and street demonstrations in Petrograd (formerly St. Petersburg) flared into sudden, unpremeditated revolution. The soldiers, who in 1905 had stood by the tsar, now rushed to support the striking workers. The Romanov dynasty, after three hundred years of rule (1613–1917), came to an end. The Provisional Government—provisional until a representative Constituent Assembly, to be elected as soon as possible, could establish a permanent regime—was set up.

The Problems of the Provisional Government

The collapse of autocracy was followed by what supporters in Russia and the West hoped would be a liberal-democratic regime pledged to give Russia a constitution. In reality, however, the course of events from March to November 1917 resembled a free-for-all, no-holds-barred fight for the succession to autocracy, with only the fittest surviving. Events also demonstrated, under conditions of exceptional popular agitation and mobility, the desperate state of the Russian Empire, its internal disunity, and the furies of the accumulated resentments. Both Germany and national minorities in Russia took advantage of the anarchy to dismember the country.

Among the potential successors to the tsars, the liberals of various shades seemed at first to enjoy the best chances. They represented the educated and forward-looking elements in Russian society that had arisen after the reforms of the 1860s—lawyers, doctors, professional people of all kinds, intellectuals, businesspeople and industrialists, many landowners, and even some bureaucrats. Liberals had opposed autocracy and earned a reputation for leadership.

The liberals had joined the March revolution only reluctantly, for they were afraid of the masses and the violence of the streets; they dreaded social revolution that could result in the seizure of factories, dispossession of landowners, and tampering with property rights. Although most leaders of the Provisional Government had only modest means, they were "capitalists," believing in private enterprise as the means of promoting economic progress. Their ideal was a constitutional monarchy, its leadership entrusted to the educated and propertied elite familiar with the essentials of statecraft.

Unfortunately, the liberals misunderstood the mood of the people at home and abroad. Looking to the Western democracies—including, after April 1917, the United States—for political and financial support, the liberals were eager to continue the war on the side of the Allies, but found themselves discredited along with the Russian soldiers, almost two million of whom had deserted. At home, the liberals antagonized the Russian peasants by not giving them the landlords' lands free of charge. As Russian nationalists who wanted their country to remain undivided, the liberals opposed national minorities who sought self-determination, and lost their support.

The peasants began to divide the landlords' land among themselves, which encouraged more soldiers to desert in order to claim a share of the land. The breakdown of the railways stopped factory production; enraged workers ousted factory managers and owners. Consumer goods grew scarce and prices soared, and the peasants could see no reason to sell their crops if they could buy nothing in return. Thus the specter of famine in the cities arose. Hardships, and anger, mounted. Adding to the disorder were the demands of the non-Russian nationalities—Finns, Ukrainians, Georgians, and others—for self-determination and even secession.

Freedom in Russia was leading to dissolution and chaos. The largely illiterate peasant masses had no experience with or understanding of a free society. Without their cooperation, Russian liberalism collapsed. This outcome demonstrated the difficulty of establishing Western liberal-democratic forms of government in countries lacking a sense of unity, a strong middle class, and a tradition of responsible participation in public affairs.

By July 1917 when Aleksandr Kerensky (1881–1970), a radical lawyer of great eloquence, became the leader of the Provisional Government, it had become clear that law and order could be upheld only by brute force. In late August and early September, a conspiracy led by an energetic young general, Lavr Kornilov, aimed at setting up a military dictatorship. Kornilov had the support not only of the officer corps and the tsarist officials, but also of many liberals fed up with anarchy. What stopped the general was not Kerensky's government (which had no troops), but the workers of Petrograd. Their agitators demoralized Kornilov's soldiers, thereby proving that a dictatorship of the right had no mass support. The workers also repudiated Kerensky and the Provisional Government as well as their own moderate leaders; henceforth they supported the Bolsheviks.

The Bolshevik Revolution
Lenin and the Rise of Bolshevism

Revolutionary movements had a long history, going back to the early nineteenth century, when educated Russians began to compare their country unfavorably with western Europe. They too wanted constitutional liberty and free speech in order to make their country modern. Prohibited from speaking out in public, they went underground, giving up their liberalism as ineffective.

They saw revolutionary socialism, with its idealistic vision and compassion for the multitude, as a better ideology in the harsh struggle with the tsar's police. By the 1870s many socialists had evolved into austere and self-denying professional revolutionaries who, in the service of the cause, had no moral scruples, just as the police had no scruples in the defense of the tsars. Bank robbery, murder, assassination, treachery, and terror were not immoral if they served the revolutionary cause.

In the 1880s and 1890s, revolutionaries learned industrial economics and sociology from Marx; from Marxism they also acquired a vision of a universal and inevitable progression toward socialism and communism, which satisfied their semireligious craving for salvation in this world, not the next. Marxism also allied them with socialist movements in other lands, giving them an internationalist outlook. History, they believed, was on their side, as it was for all the proletarians and oppressed peoples in the world.

By 1900 a number of able young Russians had rallied to revolutionary Marxism, almost all of them from privileged families or favored by education. The most promising was Vladimir Ilyich Ulyanov, known as Lenin (1870– 1924), the son of a teacher and school administrator who had attained the rank of a nobleman. Lenin was trained as a lawyer, but devoted himself to revolution instead. His first contribution to the revolution lay in adapting Marxism to Russian conditions, taking considerable liberties with Marx's teaching. His second followed from the first: outlining the organization of an underground party capable of surviving against the tsarist police. It was to be a tightly knit conspiratorial elite of professional revolutionaries; its headquarters would be safely located abroad, and it would have close ties to the masses, that is, to the workers and other potentially revolutionary elements.

Two prominent Marxists close to Lenin were Leon Trotsky (1879–1940) and Joseph Stalin (1879–1953). Trotsky, whose original name was Lev Bronstein, was the son of a prosperous Jewish farmer from southern Russia and was soon known for his brilliant pen. Stalin (the man of steel), was originally named Iosif Dzhugashvili; he was from Georgia, beyond the Caucasus mountains. Bright enough to be sent to the best school in the area, he dropped out for a revolutionary career. While they were still young, Lenin, Trotsky, and Stalin were all hardened by arrest, lengthy imprisonments, and exile to Siberia. Lenin and Trotsky later lived abroad, while Stalin, following a harsher course, stayed in Russia; for four years before 1917 he was banished to bleakest northern Siberia, conditioned to ruthlessness for life.

In 1903 the Russian Marxists split into two factions, the moderate Mensheviks, so named after finding themselves in a minority (*menshinstvo*) at a rather unrepresentative vote at the Second Party Congress, and the extremist Bolsheviks, who at that moment were in the majority (*bolshinstvo*). They might more accurately have been called the "softs" and the "hards." The "softs" (Mensheviks) preserved basic moral scruples; they would not stoop to crime or undemocratic methods for the sake of political success. For that the "hards" (Bolsheviks) ridiculed them, noting that a dead, imprisoned, or unsuccessful revolutionary was of little use.

Lenin with Stalin, 1922.   This faked photograph was arranged by Stalin to show his close association with Lenin. Lenin, the architect of the Russian Revolution, is shown two years before his death. He was a visionary with intelligence, discipline, and dedication to his goals. Stalin, although often idealized in patriotic posters, was ruthless. He was determined to reshape the Soviet people's consciousness through the revolution of totalitarianism, laying the foundation for Soviet Russia's emergence as a superpower. (*The Mansell Collection*)

    Meanwhile, Lenin perfected Bolshevik revolutionary theory. He violated Marxist tradition by paying close attention to the revolutionary potential of peasants (thereby anticipating Mao Zedong). Lenin also looked closely at the numerous peoples in Asia who had recently fallen under Western imperialist domination. These people, he sensed, constituted a potential revolutionary force. In alliance with the Western—and Russian—proletariat, they might overthrow the worldwide capitalist order. The Bolsheviks, the most militant of all revolutionary socialists, were ready to assist in that gigantic struggle.

    Lenin was a Russian nationalist as well as a socialist internationalist; he had a vision of a modern and powerful Russian state destined to be a model in world affairs. Russian communism was thus nationalist communism; the Bolsheviks saw the abolition of income-producing property by the dictatorship of the proletariat as the most effective way of mobilizing the country's resources. Yet the Bolshevik mission was also internationalist. The Russian Revolution was to set off a world revolution, liberating all oppressed classes and peoples around the world, thereby achieving a higher stage of civilization.

Lenin's Opportunity

On April 16, 1917, Lenin, with German help, arrived in Petrograd from exile in Switzerland. The Provisional Government, he said, could not possibly preserve Russia from disintegration. The bulk of the soldiers, workers, and peasants would repudiate the Provisional Government's cautious liberalism in favor of a regime expressing their demand for peace and land. Nothing would stop them from avenging themselves for centuries of oppression. Lenin also felt that only complete state control of the economy could rescue the country from disaster. The sole way out, he insisted, was the "dictatorship of the proletariat" backed by *soviets* (councils) of soldiers, workers, and peasants, particularly the poorer peasants.

Lenin prepared his party for the second stage of the revolution of 1917—the seizure of power by the Bolsheviks. Conditions favored him, as he had predicted. The Bolsheviks obtained majorities in the soviets. The peasants were in active revolt, seizing the land themselves. The Provisional Government lost all control over the course of events. On November 6, Lenin urged immediate action: "The government is tottering. It must be *given the death-blow* at all costs." On the following day the Bolsheviks, meeting little resistance, seized power. Lenin permitted elections for the Constituent Assembly that had been scheduled by the Provisional Government. In the freest election in Russian history, the Bolsheviks received 24 percent of the vote. After meeting once in January 1918, however, the Constituent Assembly was disbanded by the Bolsheviks.

The Bolsheviks Survive

Civil War

Lenin contended that he was guiding the Russian proletariat and all humanity toward a higher social order, symbolizing—in Russia and much of the world—the rebellion of the disadvantaged against Western (or "capitalist") superiority. That is why, in 1918, he changed the name of his party from Bolshevik to Communist. For Lenin, as for Marx, a world without exploitation was humanity's noblest ideal.

But staggering adversity confronted Lenin after his seizure of power. In the prevailing anarchy, Russia lay open to the German armies. Under the Treaty of Brest-Litovsk, signed in March 1918, the lowest point in Russian history for over two hundred years, Russia lost Finland, Poland, the Baltic provinces—

Map 18.1   Russian Civil War, 1918–1920   ▶

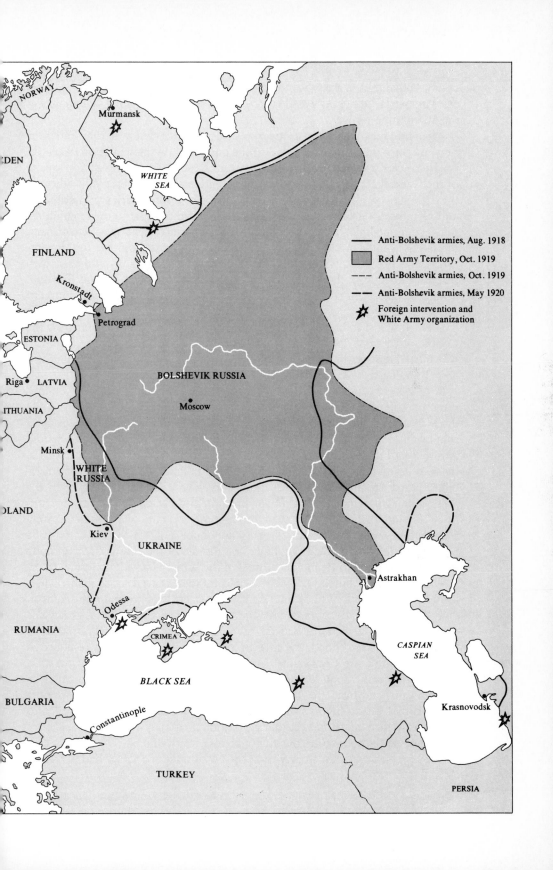

NORWAY

Murmansk

*WHITE
SEA*

FINLAND

Kronstadt

Petrograd

ESTONIA

Riga • LATVIA

LITHUANIA

Minsk •

WHITE
RUSSIA

POLAND

Kiev •

UKRAINE

RUMANIA

Odessa

CRIMEA

BULGARIA

Constantinople

BLACK SEA

TURKEY

BOLSHEVIK RUSSIA

Moscow •

Astrakhan

*CASPIAN
SEA*

Krasnovodsk

PERSIA

——— Anti-Bolshevik armies, Aug. 1918

▨ Red Army Territory, Oct. 1919

- - - Anti-Bolshevik armies, Oct. 1919

– – – Anti-Bolshevik armies, May 1920

✦ Foreign intervention and
White Army organization

regions inhabited largely by non-Russians—plus the rebellious Ukraine, its chief industrial base and breadbasket. Yet Lenin had no choice but to accept the humiliating terms.

After the Treaty of Brest-Litovsk was signed, the civil war that had been brewing since the summer of 1917 broke out in full. In the winter of 1917–18, tsarist officers had been gathering troops in the south, counting on the loyalty of the Cossacks*; other anti-Communist centers rose in Siberia, still others in the extreme north and along the Baltic coast. The political orientation of these anti-Communist groups, generally called Whites in contrast to the Communist Reds, combined all shades of opinion from moderate socialist to reactionary, the latter usually predominating. All received support from foreign governments that freely intervened in Russia's agony. The Germans, until their own revolution in November 1918, occupied much of southern Russia. England, France, and the United States sent troops to points in northern and southern European Russia; England, Japan, and the United States also sent troops to Siberia. At first they hoped to offset German expansion, later to overthrow the Communist regime. In May and June 1918, Czech prisoners of war, about to be evacuated, precipitated anti-Communist uprisings along the Siberian railway, bringing the civil war to fever pitch.

In July 1918, Nicholas II and his entire family were murdered by Communists. In August, a non-Communist socialist nearly assassinated Lenin, while the White forces in the south moved to cut off central Russia from its food supply. In response, the Communists speeded the buildup of their own Red Army. Recruited from the remnants of the tsarist army and its officer corps, the Red Army was reinforced by compulsory military service and strict discipline; Trotsky reintroduced the death penalty, which had been outlawed by the Provisional Government. Patriotism prompted many tsarist officers to continue serving their country, even though their loyalty was often severely strained. As a check on them, Trotsky appointed political commissars to be responsible for the political reliability and morale of the troops. Despite these measures, the Red Army, like the armies of the Whites, lacked discipline. In the civil war, soldiers butchered their own comrades as well as civilians. Their leaders, among both Whites and Reds, spared no lives to maintain control. Only the most ruthless commanders, including Trotsky and Stalin, prevailed.

In 1919, thanks to the Allied victory and the American contribution to it, the German menace ended. Yet foreign intervention stepped up in response to the formation of the Communist International (Comintern), an organization founded by Lenin to guide the international revolutionary movement that he expected to issue from the World War. Lenin sought revolutionary support from abroad for strengthening his hand at home; his enemies reached into Russia to defeat at its source the revolution that they feared in their own countries. At the same time the civil war rose to its climax.

Hard-pressed as Lenin's party was, by the autumn of 1920 it had prevailed

---

*Originating in southern and eastern Russia, the Cossacks became an elite corps in the tsars' armies and were used to quell uprisings.

Starving Children in a Famine Region of Russia, 1921.   The privations suffered by the Russian people in the years immediately following World War I and the Bolshevik Revolution were incalculable. The first four years of the new Communist regime, 1917–1921, were marked by civil war and foreign invasion. Cities faced starvation and food was taken from peasants at gunpoint. Several million lives were lost. (*Historical Pictures Service, Chicago*)

over its enemies. The Whites were divided among themselves and discredited by their association with the tsarist regime; the Bolsheviks had greater popular support, the advantage of interior communications, and superior political skills. The war-weary foreign interventionists called off their efforts to overthrow the Bolshevik regime by force.

The Communist victory in the civil war had exacted a staggering price. Reds and Whites alike had carried the tsarist tradition of political violence to a new pitch of horror (some of it described in famous novels by Pasternak and Sholokhov). The entire population, including the Communist party and its leaders, suffered in the war, which was followed in 1921–22 by a famine that took still more millions of lives.

War Communism and the New Economic Policy

World war and civil war had brought terrible suffering to the Russian people. Adding to their misery was the policy known as war communism, introduced in 1918 to deal with plummeting agricultural and economic production, rampant inflation, and desperate hunger in the cities. Under war communism, the state took over the means of production and greatly limited the sphere of private ownership; it conscripted labor and in effect confiscated grain from the peasants. War communism devastated the economy even further and alienated workers and peasants. Factories were mismanaged, workers stayed away from their jobs or performed poorly, and peasants resisted the food requisition detachments that seized their grain. Sometimes there were rebellions. In March 1921, an uprising of sailors at the Kronstadt naval base and of workers in nearby Petrograd indicated the need for a change of course. The people who in 1917 had been ready to give their lives for the revolution now rose against the repression that had been introduced during the civil war; they called for the establishment of socialist democracy. Trotsky ruthlessly suppressed that uprising, but the lesson was clear: the Communist regime had to retreat from war communism and to restore a measure of stability to the country.

In 1921 the Communist party adopted the New Economic Policy, generally called NEP, which lasted until 1928. Under a system that Lenin characterized as "state socialism," the government retained control of finance, industry, and transportation—"the commanding heights" of the economy—but allowed the rest of the economy to return to private enterprise. The peasants, after giving part of their crops to the government, were free to sell the rest in the open market; traders could buy and sell as they pleased. With the resumption of small-scale capitalism, an air of normal life returned.

One-Party Dictatorship

While the Communists were waging a fierce struggle against the Whites, they instituted a militant dictatorship run by their party. Numbering about 500,000 in 1921, the Communist party was controlled by a small, close-knit core of professional political leaders, the best of them unusually disciplined in personal dedication. This new elite's organizational skills permitted them to preserve their revolutionary drive in the face of both failure and success. From the start, those who did not pull their weight were purged.

Under its constitution, the "Russian Communist Party (Bolshevik)," as its formal title read, was a democratic body. Its members elected delegates to periodic party congresses, which in turn elected the membership of the central committee, where leadership originally centered. However, power soon shifted to a smaller and more intimate group, the *politburo* (political bureau), which assumed a dictatorial role. The key leaders—Lenin, Trotsky, Stalin, and a few others—determined policy, assigned tasks, and appointed important officials. The party dominated all public agencies; its leaders held the chief positions in government. No other political parties were tolerated, and trade unions became agents of the regime. Never before had the people of Russia come to depend so abjectly on their government.

Impatient with unending disputes among righteous and strong-willed old revolutionaries, Lenin, in agreement with other top leaders, demanded unconditional submission to his decisions. He even ordered that dissidents be disciplined and political enemies be terrorized. No price was too high to achieve monolithic party unity. As former victims of tsarist repression, the Communists felt no moral objection to the use of force or even of stark terror. As Lenin admonished his followers: "cleanse the land of Russia of all sorts of harmful insects, of crook-fleas, and bedbugs," by which he meant "the rich, the rogues, and the idlers." He even suggested that "one out of every ten idlers be shot on the spot."[2] Those not shot found themselves, with Lenin's blessings, in forced-labor camps directed by a ruthless security force, the dreaded *Cheka*. Staffed with hardened revolutionaries, it indulged in extreme terror not only against enemies of the regime but against the population at large. The Cheka established the forced-labor camps that became notorious under Stalin's regime. The means Lenin employed for ruling his backward country denied the human values that Marx had taken from the Enlightenment and put into his vision of socialist society.

The Communists abolished the power of the Orthodox church, the traditional ally of tsarism and the enemy of innovation. They were militant atheists, believing with Marx that religion was "opium for the people"; God had no place in their vision for a better society. Yet the Orthodox church and other religions survived, much reduced in influence and closely watched, an enduring target for atheist propaganda.

The Communists also simplified the alphabet, changed the calendar to the Gregorian system prevailing in the capitalist West, and brought theater and all arts, hitherto reserved for the elite, to the masses. Above all, they wiped out— by expropriation of property and discrimination, expulsion, and execution— the educated upper class of bureaucrats, landowners, professional people, and industrialists.

The party promised "to liberate woman from all the burdens of antiquated methods of housekeeping, by replacing them by house-communes, public kitchens, central laundries, nurseries, etc."[3] Traditional values, particularly in the Asian parts of the Soviet Union, hardly favored equality between the sexes, especially in political work. The practical necessity of combining work with family responsibility, moreover, tended to keep women out of managerial positions in the party and the organizations of the state, but the ideal remained alive.

The Bolsheviks never ceased to stress that they worked strenuously for the welfare of the vast majority of the population. They derived much acclaim for their emphasis on redistributing housing, food, and clothing and making education available to the masses. They were not opposed to some private property; they allowed items for personal use, provided they were in keeping with the standards of the common people. But they outlawed income-producing private property that enabled capitalists to employ (or exploit, as the Communists said) others for their own profit. With the disappearance of private enterprise—Stalin would soon eliminate the limited free enterprise permitted under NEP—the state gradually became the sole employer, thereby forcefully integrating the individual into the reconstruction of the country.

For Lenin, socialism meant reeducating the masses to a higher standard of individual conduct and economic productivity that would be superior even to capitalism. In the spring of 1918, he argued that the Russian workers had not yet matched capitalist performance: "The Russian worker is a bad worker compared with the workers of the advanced, i.e., western countries." To overcome this fatal handicap, Lenin urged competition—socialist competition—and relentlessly hammered home the need for "iron discipline at work" and "unquestioning obedience" to a single will—that of the Communist party. There was no alternative: "Large-scale machinery calls for absolute and strict unity of will, which directs the joint labors of hundreds and thousands and tens of thousands of people. A thousand wills are subordinated to one will. . . ."[4]

In these words lay the essence of subsequent Soviet industrialization. The entire economy was to be monolithic, rationally planned in its complex interdependence, and pursuing a single goal: overcoming the weaknesses of Russia so disastrously demonstrated in the war. Leaving the workers to their own spontaneity, Lenin held, would merely perpetuate Russian backwardness. Instead he called for a new "consciousness," a hard-driving work ethic expressed in the Russian Marxist revolutionary vocabulary.

In attempting to transform their Soviet Russia into a modern industrialized state that would serve as a model for the world, the Bolsheviks imposed a new autocracy even more authoritarian than the old. Russia must be rebuilt against the people's will, if necessary. In the view of the party leaders, the masses always needed firm guidance. The minds of the people therefore came under unprecedented government control. In education, from the kindergarten through the university, in press and radio, and in literature and the arts, the Communist party tried to fashion people's thoughts to create the proper "consciousness."

The party made Marxism-Leninism the sole source of truth, eliminating as best it could all rival creeds, whether religious, political, or philosophical. Minds were to be as reliably uniform as machine processes and totally committed to the party. Moreover, they were to be protected against all subversive capitalist influences. Soviet Russia, so the party boasted, had risen to a superior plane of social existence; it would attract other revolutionary states to its federal union, until eventually it covered the entire world. Lest Soviet citizens doubt their new superiority, the party prohibited all uncontrolled comparison with other countries.

Lenin made the Soviet Union an international revolutionary force, the champion of anticapitalism and of the liberation of colonial peoples. The Russian Revolution inspired nationalistic ambitions for political self-determination and cultural self-assertion among a growing number of peoples around the world, especially in Asia. It appealed particularly to intellectuals educated in the West (or in westernized schools) yet identifying themselves with their downtrodden compatriots.

As a political tool for world revolution, the International Comintern was created. The most radical successor to earlier socialist international associations, it helped organize small Communist parties in western Europe, which in time became dependable, although rather powerless, agents of Soviet Russia. In Asia, where no proletariat existed, Lenin tried to work closely with incipient nationalist movements. Lenin and the Bolshevik Revolution gained the admiration and instinctive loyalty of colonial and semicolonial peoples in what would come to be called the *Third World*.

riculture, for the peasants had to be forcibly integrated into the planned economy through collectivization. Agriculture—the peasants, their animals, their fields—had to submit to the same rational control as industry. Collectivization meant the pooling of farmlands, animals, and equipment for the sake of more efficient large-scale production. The Bolshevik solution for the backwardness of Russian argiculture had long been that the peasants should become like workers. But knowing the peasants' distaste for the factory, their attachment to their own land, and their stubbornness, the party had hesitated to carry out its ambition. In 1929, however, Stalin believed that for the sake of industrialization he had no choice. If the Five-Year Plan were to succeed, the government had to receive planned crops of planned size and quality at planned times. With collectivization, the ascendancy of the party over the people of Russia became almost complete.

For the peasants, the price was horrible. Stalin declared war on the Russian countryside. He ordered that the *kulaks,* the most enterprising and well-to-do peasants, be "liquidated as a class." Many were killed outright, and millions were deported to forced-labor camps in the far north. Their poorer and less efficient neighbors were herded onto collective farms at the point of a bayonet.

The peasants struck back, sometimes in pitched battles. The horror of forced collectivization broke the spirit even of hardened officials. "I am an old Bolshevik," sobbed a secret police colonel to a fellow passenger on a train; "I worked in the underground against the Tsar and then I fought in the civil war. Did I do all that in order that I should now surround villages with machine-guns and order my men to fire indiscriminately into crowds of peasants? Oh, no, no!"[5]

Defeated but unwilling to surrender their livestock, the peasants slaughtered their animals, gorging themselves in drunken orgies against the days of inevitable famine. The country's cattle herds declined by one-half, inflicting irreparable secondary losses as well. The number of horses, crucial for rural transport and farm work, fell by one-third. Crops were not planted or not harvested, the Five-Year Plan was disrupted, and in 1931–1933 untold millions starved to death.

The suffering was most cruel in the Ukraine, where famine killed approximately 7 million helpless people, many after extreme abuse and persecution. For the sake of buying industrial equipment abroad so that industrialization could proceed on target, the Soviet Union had to export food, as much of it as possible and for prices disastrously lowered by the Great Depression. Let the peasants in the Ukrainian breadbasket perish so that the country could grow strong! Moreover, Stalin relished the opportunity to punish the Ukrainians for their disloyalty during the civil war and their resistance to collectivization. Typically, the local officials and activists who stripped the peasants of their possessions and searched for hidden grain viewed themselves as idealists building a new society; they infused their own ruthlessness into the official orders. Their dedication to the triumph of communism overcame all doubts caused by the sight of starving people and the sounds of wailing women and children.

By 1935, practically all farming in Russia was collectivized. The kulaks had been wiped out as a class, and the peasants, ever rebellious under the tsars, had been cowed into permanent submission. In theory, the collective farms were run democratically, under an elected chairman; in practice, they followed as best they could the directives handed down from the nearest party office. People grumbled about the rise of a new serfdom; agricultural development had been stifled.

Total Control

To quash resistance and mold a new type of suitably motivated and disciplined citizen, Stalin unleashed a third revolution, the revolution of totalitarianism. It aimed at a total reconstruction of state and society, down to the innermost recesses of human consciousness. It called for "a new man" suited to the needs of Soviet industrialism.

The revolution of totalitarianism encompassed all cultural activity. All media of communications—literature, the arts, music, the stage—were forced into subservience to the Five-Year Plan and Soviet ideology. In literature, as in all art, an official style was promulgated. Called socialist realism, it aimed at describing the world as the party saw it or hoped to shape it. Novels in the social realist manner told how the romances of tractor drivers and milkmaids, or of lathe operators and office secretaries, led to new victories of production under the Five-Year Plan. Composers found their music examined for remnants of bourgeois spirit; they were to write simple tunes suitable for heroic times. Everywhere, huge high-color posters showed men and women hard at work with radiant faces, calling others to join them; often Stalin, the wise father and leader, was shown among them. In this manner artistic creativity was locked into a dull, utilitarian straitjacket of official cheerfulness; creativity was allowed only to boost industrial productivity. Behind the scenes, all artists were disciplined to conform to the will of the party or be crushed.

Education, from nursery school to university, was likewise harnessed to train dutiful and loyal citizens, and Soviet propaganda made a cult of Stalin that bordered on deification. Thus a writer declared in 1935:

> *Centuries will pass and the generations still to come will regard us as the happiest of mortals, as the most fortunate of men, because we . . . were privileged to see Stalin, our inspired leader. Yes, and we regard ourselves as the happiest of mortals because we are the contemporaries of a man who never had an equal in world history. The men of all ages will call on thy name, which is strong, beautiful, wise, and marvellous. Thy name is engraven on every factory, every machine, every place on the earth, and in the hearts of all men.*[6]

But still the Russian masses resisted the enforced change to the large-scale, rigidly restrictive cooperation of modern industrialism. Against that stubborn resistance, Stalin unleashed raw terror to break stubborn wills and compel conformity. Terror had been used as a tool of government ever since the Revolution (and the tsars had also used it, moderately and intermittently).

After the start of the first Five-Year Plan, show trials were staged that denounced as saboteurs the engineers who disagreed with Stalin's production timetable. The terror used to herd the peasants onto collective farms was of a larger scale. Stalin also used terror to crush opposition and to instill an abject fear not only in the ranks of the party but also in Russian society at large.

Purges had long been used to rid the party of weaklings. After 1934, however, they became an instrument of Stalin's drive for unchallenged personal power. In 1936 his vindictive terror broke into the open. The first batch of victims, including many founders of the Communist party, were accused of conspiring with the exiled Trotsky to set up a "terrorist center" and of scheming to terrorize the party. After being sentenced to death, they were immediately executed. In 1937 the next group, including prominent Communists of Lenin's day, were charged with cooperating with foreign intelligence agencies and wrecking "socialist reconstruction," the term for Stalin's revolution; they too were executed. Shortly afterward, a secret purge wiped out the military high command, leaving the Soviet army without leadership for years.

In 1938 the last and biggest show trial advanced the most bizarre accusation of all: sabotage, espionage, and attempting to dismember the Soviet Union and kill all its leaders (including Lenin in 1918). In the public hearings some defendants refuted the public prosecutor, but in the end all confessed before being executed. Western observers were aghast at the cynical charges and the tortures used to obtain the confessions.

The great trials, however, involved only a small minority of Stalin's victims; many more perished in silence. The terror hit first of all members of the party, especially the Old Bolsheviks, who had joined before the Revolution; they were the most independent-minded members and therefore the most dangerous to Stalin. But Stalin also diminished the cultural elite that had survived the Lenin revolution. Thousands of engineers, scientists, industrial managers, scholars, and artists disappeared; they were shot or sent to forced-labor camps, where most of them perished. No one was safe. To frighten the common people in all walks of life, men, women, and even children were dragged into the net of Stalin's secret police—a soul-killing reminder to the survivors: submit or else. The toll of the purges is reckoned in many millions; it included Trotsky, who in 1940 was murdered in Mexico. The blood-letting was ghastly, as Stalin's purge officials themselves followed each other into death and ignominy.

Stalin, who had passed through the hands of the tsarist police and had participated in the carnage of the civil war, was untroubled by the waste of life. He believed that without the total obedience of the Russian people, the Soviet economy could not be effectively and quickly mobilized, and that terror was necessary to compel compliance. By showing party officials and the Russian masses how vulnerable they were, how dependent they were on his will, Stalin frightened them into servility. No doubt the terror was also an expression of his craving for personal power and his sick, suspicious, and vengeful nature. He saw enemies everywhere, took pleasure in selecting victims, and reveled in his omnipotence.

Chronology 18.1 ❧ The Rise of the Soviet Union

March 1917	The tsarist regime is overthrown
November 1917	The Bolsheviks, led by Lenin, seize power
1918–1920	Civil war and foreign intervention
January 1918	The Bolsheviks disband the Constituent Assembly
November 1920	The remnants of the White Army are evacuated from the Crimean peninsula
1921–1928	The New Economic Policy
1922	Stalin becomes general secretary of the Communist party
January 1924	Lenin dies
1928	The first Five-Year Plan starts rapid industrialization
1929	Stalin in sole command; collectivization of agriculture starts
1936–1938	Stalin's terror purges

Stalin's Legacy

Stalin modernized his country and laid the foundations for the rise of Soviet Russia into a superpower, more secure and respected in the world than any previous Russian regime. For this achievement he could claim the same justification by which Western statesmen had sent millions of people to their deaths in World War I—the survival of the state. In 1931, he said:

> *Those who fall behind get beaten. But we do not want to be beaten. No, we refuse to be beaten. One feature of the history of old Russia was the continual beatings she suffered for falling behind, for her backwardness. All beat her—for her backwardness, for military backwardness, cultural backwardness, political backwardness, for industrial backwardness, for agricultural backwardness. She was beaten because to do so was profitable and could be done with impunity. . . . You are backward, you are weak—therefore you are wrong, hence you can be beaten and enslaved. You are mighty, therefore you are right, hence we must be wary of you. Such is the law of the exploiters. . . . That is why we must no longer lag behind.*[7]

Stalin set forth the stark reckoning of Russian history: the cost of foreign enslavement against the costs of a terror-driven mobilization. Only communist totalitarianism, he believed, could liberate Russia from its historic inferiority.

Moreover, the totalitarian state accorded with his desire to exercise total control over the party and the nation. For good reason, Stalin has been called a twentieth-century Ivan the Terrible. Like the sixteenth-century tsar, for whom he expressed admiration, Stalin stopped at no brutality in order to establish personal autocracy.

Notes

1. Theodore H. Von Laue, *Sergei Witte and the Industrialization of Russia* (New York: Columbia University Press, 1963), p. 3.
2. V. I. Lenin, "On Revolutionary Violence and Terror," *The Lenin Anthology,* ed. by R. C. Tucker (New York: W. W. Norton, 1975), p. 432.
3. All-Russian Communist Party (Bolsheviks), 1919, in *Soviet Communism: Programs and Rules. Officials Texts of 1919, 1952, (1956), 1961,* ed. Jan F. Triska (San Francisco: Chandler, 1962), p. 23.
4. V. I. Lenin, "The Immediate Tasks of the Soviet Government," *The Lenin Anthology,* pp. 448ff.
5. Quoted in Isaac Deutscher, *Stalin: A Political Biography* (New York: Oxford University Press, 1966), p. 325.
6. Excerpted in T. H. Rigby, ed., *Stalin* (Englewood Cliffs, N.J.: Prentice-Hall, 1966), p. 111.
7. J. V. Stalin, "Speech to Business Executives" (1931), in *A Documentary History of Communism from Lenin to Mao,* vol. 2, ed. by Robert V. Daniels (New York: Random House, 1960), p. 22.

Suggested Reading

Antonov-Ovseenko, Anton, *The Time of Stalin: Portrait of a Tyranny* (1981). A recent anti-Stalinist treatment by a Soviet author.

Carr, E. H., *The Russian Revolution from Lenin to Stalin* (1970). A brief summary based on the author's multivolume study of the years 1917–1929.

Conquest, Robert, *The Harvest of Sorrow: Soviet Collectivization and the Terror-Famine* (1986). The human consequences of collectivization.

Ginzburg, Eugenia, *Journey into the Whirlwind* (1967). A woman's experiences under the terror.

Koestler, Arthur, *Darkness at Noon* (1941). A revealing novel about the fate of an Old Bolshevik in the terror purge.

Lewin, Moshe, *The Making of the Soviet System: Essays in the Social History of Interwar Russia* (1985). A thoughtful analysis by a noted scholar.

Scott, John, *Behind the Urals: An American Worker in Russia's City of Steel* (1942, reprint 1973). A firsthand account of life under the first Five-Year Plan.

Sholokhov, Mikhail, *And Quiet Flows the Don; The Don Flows Home to the Sea,* 2 vols. (1934, 1940). A Nobel Prize-winning novel about the brutalizing effects of war, revolution, and civil war.

Solzhenitsyn, Aleksandr I., *One Day in the Life of Ivan Denisovich* (1963). The first account of life in one of Stalin's forced-labor camps to reach the public.

Tucker, Robert C., ed., *Stalinism: Essays in Historical Interpretation* (1977). Essays on Stalin by prominent scholars.

Ulam, Adam B., *The Bolsheviks: The Intellectual and Political History of the Triumph of Communism in Russia* (1965). A full account built around Lenin.

Von Laue, Theodore H., *Why Lenin? Why Stalin?* (1970). A readable survey emphasizing the global contexts.

Review Questions

1. Why did the tsarist regime collapse in March 1917?
2. Why did the Provisional Government and liberal democracy fail in 1917?
3. Why, by contrast, were the Bolsheviks successful in seizing and holding power from 1917 to 1921?
4. What was the purpose and the effects of the Five-Year Plans?
5. How did the Soviet leaders view the position of Russia in the world? What were their aims and ambitions? How did their goals compare with those of other states?
6. What were Stalin's motives and justifications for the terror purge?

Chapter ◈ 19

The Era of Fascism:
The Attack on
Reason and Freedom

In the immediate aftermath of World War I, it seemed that liberalism would continue to advance as it had in the nineteenth century. The collapse of the autocratic German and Austrian empires had led to the formation of parliamentary governments throughout eastern and central Europe. Yet within two decades, in an extraordinary turn of events, democracy seemed in its death throes. In Spain, Portugal, Italy, and Germany, and in all the newly created states of central and eastern Europe except Czechoslovakia, democracy collapsed and various forms of authoritarian governments arose. The defeat of democracy and the surge of authoritarianism were best exemplified by the triumph of totalitarian fascist movements in Italy and Germany. Fascist movements in more than twenty European lands after World War I signified that liberal society was in a state of disorientation and dissolution. Fascism was one response to a postwar society afflicted by spiritual disintegration, economic dislocation, political instability, and thwarted nationalist hopes. It was an expression of fear that the Bolshevik Revolution would spread westward. It was also an expression of hostility to democratic values and a reaction to the failure of liberal institutions to solve crushing problems of modern industrial society. To fascists and their sympathizers, democracy seemed an ineffective, spiritless, and enfeebled old regime ready to topple.

In their struggle to bring down the liberal state, fascist leaders aroused primitive impulses, resurrected ancient folkways and tribal loyalties, and made use of myths and rituals to mobilize and manipulate the masses. Organizing propaganda campaigns with the thoroughness of a military operation, fascists aroused and dominated the masses and confused and undermined their democratic opposition, breaking its will to resist. Fascists were most successful in countries with weak democratic traditions. When parliamentary government faltered, it had few staunch defenders, and many yearned to dance at its death.

The proliferation of fascist movements demonstrated that the habits of democracy are not quickly learned or easily retained. Particularly during times of crisis, people lose patience with parliamentary discussion and constitutional procedures, sink into nonrational modes of thought and behavior, and are easily manipulated by unscrupulous politicians. For the sake of economic or emotional security and national grandeur, people will often willingly sacrifice political freedom. Fascism starkly manifested the immense power of the irrational; it humbled liberals, making them permanently aware of the limitations of reason and the fragility of freedom.

The fascist goal of maximum centralization of power was furthered by developments during World War I—the expansion of bureaucracy, the concentration of industry into giant monopolies, and the close cooperation between industry and the state. The instruments of modern technology—radio, motion pictures, public address systems, telephone, teletype—made it possible for the state to indoctrinate, manipulate, and dominate its subjects. ✐

Elements of Fascism

Fascist movements were marked by an extreme nationalism and a determination to eradicate liberalism and Marxism—to undo the legacy of the French Revolution of 1789 and the Bolshevik Revolution of 1917. Fascists believed that theirs was a spiritual revolution, that they were initiating a new era in history, that they were building a new civilization on the ruins of liberal democracy. "We stand for a new principle in the world," said Mussolini. "We stand for the sheer, categorical, definitive antithesis to the world of democracy

... to the world which still abides by the fundamental principles laid down in 1789."[1]

Fascists regarded Marxism as another enemy, for class conflict divided the nation. To fascists, the Marxist call for workers of the world to unite meant the death of the national community. Fascism, in contrast, would reintegrate the proletariat into the nation and end class hostilities that divide and weaken the state and its people. By making people of all classes feel that they were a needed part of the nation, fascism offered a solution to the problem of insecurity and isolation in modern industrial society.

In contrast to liberalism and Marxism, fascism attacked the rational tradition of the Enlightenment and exalted will, blood, feeling, and instinct. Intellectual discussion and critical analysis, said fascists, cause national divisiveness; reason promotes doubt, enfeebles the will, and hinders instinctive, aggressive action. Glorifying action for its own sake, fascists aroused and manipulated brutal and primitive impulses and carried into politics the combative spirit of the trenches. They formed private armies that attracted veterans —many of them rootless, brutal, and maladjusted men who sought to preserve the loyalty, camaraderie, and violence of the front.

Fascism exalted the leader, who intuitively grasped what was best for the nation, and called for rule by an elite of dedicated party members. The leader and the party would relieve the individual of the need to make decisions. Holding that the liberal stress on individual freedom promoted competition and conflict that shattered national unity, fascists pressed for monolithic unity—one leader, one party, and one national will.

Fascism drew its mass support from the lower middle class—small merchants, artisans, white-collar workers, civil servants, peasants of moderate means—who were frightened by both big capitalism and socialism. They hoped that fascism would protect them from the competition of big business and prevent the hated working class from establishing a Marxist state that would threaten their property. The lower middle class saw in fascism a noncommunist way of overcoming economic crises and restoring traditional respect for family, native soil, and nation. Having no patience for parliamentary procedures or sympathy for democratic principles, they were drawn to demagogues who exuded confidence and promised direct action.

Although a radicalized middle class gave fascist movements their mass support, the fascists could not have captured the state without the aid of existing ruling elites—landed aristocrats, industrialists, and army leaders. In Russia, the Bolsheviks had to fight their way into power; in Italy and Germany the old ruling order virtually handed power to the fascists. In both countries fascist leaders succeeded in reassuring the conservative elite that they would not institute widespread social reforms or interfere with private property and would protect the nation from communism. The old elite abhorred the violent activism and demagoguery of fascism and had contempt for fascist leaders, who were often brutal men without breeding or culture. Yet to protect their interests, the old ruling class entered into an alliance with the fascists.

The Rise of Fascism in Italy

Postwar Unrest

Although Italy had been on the winning side in World War I, it had the appearance of a defeated nation. Food shortages, rising prices, massive unemployment, violent strikes, workers occupying factories, and peasants squatting on the uncultivated periphery of large estates created a climate of crisis. Italy required effective leadership and a reform program, but the liberal government was paralyzed by party disputes; with several competing parties, the liberals could not organize a solid majority that could cope with the domestic crisis.

The middle class was severely stressed. To meet its accelerating expenses, the government had increased taxes, but the burden fell unevenly on small landowners, small-business owners, civil-service workers, and professionals. Large landowners and industrialists feared that their nation was on the verge of a Bolshevik-style revolution. In truth, Italian socialists had no master plan to seize power. Peasant squatters and urban strikers were responding to the distress in their own regions and did not significantly coordinate their efforts with those in other localities. Moreover, when the workers realized that they could not keep the factories operating, their revolutionary zeal waned and they started to abandon the plants. The workers' and peasants' poorly led and futile struggles did not portend a Red Revolution. Nevertheless, the industrialists and landlords, with the Bolshevik Revolution still vivid in their minds, were taking no chances.

Adding to the unrest was national outrage at the terms of the World War I peace settlement. Italians felt that despite their sacrifices—500,000 dead and one million wounded—they had been robbed of the fruits of victory. Italy had been denied the Dalmatian coast, the Adriatic port of Fiume, and territory in Africa and the Middle East. Nationalists blamed the liberal government for what they called a "mutilated victory." In 1919, a force of war veterans led by the poet and adventurer Gabriele D'Annunzio (1863–1938) seized Fiume, to the delirious joy of Italian nationalists and the embarrassment of the government. D'Annunzio's occupation of the port lasted more than a year, adding fuel to the flames of Italian nationalism and demonstrating the weakness of the liberal regime in imposing its authority on rightist opponents.

Mussolini's Seizure of Power

Benito Mussolini (1883–1945), a former socialist and World War I veteran, exploited the unrest in postwar Italy in order to capture control of the state. In 1919 he organized the Fascist party, which attracted converts from the discontented, disillusioned, and uprooted. Many Italians viewed Mussolini as the leader who would gain Fiume, Dalmatia, and colonies and win Italy's rightful place of honor in international affairs. Hardened battle veterans joined the Fascist movement to escape the boredom and idleness of civilian life. They welcomed an opportunity to wear the uniforms of the Fascist militia (Black Shirts), parade in the streets, and do battle with socialist and labor-union

Mussolini at Rome, Celebrating the Tenth Anniversary of the Fascist Gathering in Milan for the March on Rome.   Initially, Mussolini was able to bluff his way to power because an indecisive liberal regime did not counter force with force. Although Mussolini established a one-party state and manipulated mass organizations and the mass media, he was less successful than Hitler or Stalin in creating a totalitarian regime. (*AP/Wide World Photos*)

opponents. Squads of Fascist Black Shirts (*squadristi*) raided socialist and trade-union offices, destroying property and beating the occupants. It soon appeared that Italy was drifting toward civil war, as socialist Red Shirts responded in kind.

Industrialists and landowners, hoping that Mussolini would rescue Italy from Bolshevism, contributed large sums to the Fascist party. The lower middle class, fearful that the growing power of labor unions and the Socialist party threatened their property and social prestige, viewed Mussolini as a protector. Middle-class university students, searching for adventure and an ideal, and army officers, dreaming of an Italian empire and hating parliamentary government, also were receptive to Mussolini's party. Intellectuals disenchanted with liberal politics and parliamentary democracy were intrigued by Mussolini's philosophy of action. Mussolini's nationalism, activism, and anticommunism gradually seduced elements of the power structure—capitalists, aristocrats, army officers, the royal family, the church. Regarding liberalism as bankrupt and parliamentary government as futile, many of these people yearned for a military dictatorship.

In 1922 Mussolini made his bid for power. Speaking at a giant rally of his followers in late October, he declared: "Either they will give us the government or we shall take it by descending on Rome. It is now a matter of days, perhaps hours." A few days later thousands of Fascists began the March on Rome. It would have been a relatively simple matter to crush the 20,000 Fascist marchers armed with little more than pistols and rifles, but King Victor Emmanuel III (1869–1947) refused to act. The king's advisers, some of them sympathetic to Mussolini, exaggerated the strength of the Fascists. Believing that he was rescuing Italy from terrible violence, the king appointed Mussolini prime minister.

Mussolini had bluffed his way into power. Fascism had triumphed not because of its own strength—the Fascists had only 35 of 535 seats in parliament—but because the liberal regime, irresolute and indecisive, did not counter force with force. In the past, the liberal state had not challenged Fascist acts of terror; now it feebly surrendered to Fascist blustering and threats. No doubt liberals hoped that once in power, the Fascists would forsake terror, pursue moderate aims, and act within the constitution. But the liberals were wrong; they had completely misjudged the antidemocratic character of Fascism.

The Fascist State in Italy

Mussolini gradually moved to establish a dictatorship. In 1925–26 he eliminated non-Fascists from his cabinet, dissolved opposition parties, smashed the independent trade unions, suppressed opposition newspapers, replaced local mayors with Fascist officials, and organized a secret police to round up troublemakers. Many anti-Fascists fled the country or were deported.

Mussolini was less successful than Hitler and Stalin in fashioning a totalitarian state. The industrialists, the large landowners, the church, and to some extent even the army never fell under the complete domination of the party. Nor did the regime possess the mind of its subjects with the same thoroughness as the Nazis did in Germany. Life in Italy was less regimented and the individual less fearful than in Nazi Germany or Communist Russia.

Like Communist Russia and Nazi Germany, however, Fascist Italy used mass organizations and mass media to control minds and regulate behavior. As in the Soviet Union and the Third Reich, the Fascist regime created a cult of the leader. "Mussolini goes forward with confidence, in a halo of myth, almost chosen by God, indefatigable and infallible, the instrument employed by Providence for the creation of a new civilization," wrote the philosopher Giovanni Gentile.[2] To convey the image of a virile leader, Mussolini had himself photographed bare-chested or in a uniform and a steel helmet. Elementary school textbooks depicted him as the savior of the nation, a modern-day Julius Caesar.

Fascist propaganda inculcated habits of discipline and obedience: "Mussolini is always right." "Believe! Obey! Fight!" Propaganda also glorified war: "A minute on the battlefield is worth a lifetime of peace." The press, radio, and cinema idealized life under Fascism, implying that Fascism had eradicated crime, poverty, and social tensions. Schoolteachers and university professors were compelled to swear allegiance to the Fascist government and to propagate Fascist ideals, while students were urged to criticize instructors who harbored liberal attitudes. Millions of youths belonged to Fascist organizations in which they participated in patriotic ceremonies and social functions, sang Fascist hymns, and wore Fascist uniforms. They submerged their own identities into the group.

Fascists denounced economic liberalism for promoting individual self-interest, and socialism for instigating conflicts between workers and capitalists that divided and weakened the nation. The Fascist way of resolving tensions between workers and employers was to abolish independent labor unions, prohibit strikes, and establish associations or corporations that included both the workers and employers within a given industry. In theory, representatives of labor and capital would cooperatively solve labor problems in a particular industry. In practice, the representatives of labor turned out to be Fascists who protected the interests of the industrialists. Although the Fascists lauded the corporative system as a creative approach to modern economic problems, in reality it played a minor role in Italian economic life. Big business continued to make its own decisions, paying scant attention to the corporations.

Nor did the Fascist government solve Italy's longstanding economic problems. To curtail the export of capital and to reduce the nation's dependency on imports in case of war, Mussolini sought to make Italy self-sufficient. To win the "battle of grain," the Fascist regime brought marginal lands under cultivation and urged farmers to concentrate on wheat rather than other crops. While wheat production increased substantially, total agricultural output declined, because wheat had been planted on land more suited to animal husbandry and fruit cultivation. To make Italy industrially self-sufficient, the regime limited imports of foreign goods, with the result that Italian consumers paid higher prices for Italian-manufactured goods. Mussolini posed as the protector of the little people, but under his regime the power and profits of big business grew and the standard of living of small farmers and urban workers declined.

Although anticlerical since his youth, Mussolini was also expedient. He recognized that coming to terms with the church would improve his image with Catholic public opinion. The Vatican regarded Mussolini's regime as a barrier against communism and as less hostile to church interests and more amenable to church direction than a liberal government. Pope Pius XI (1922–1939) was an ultraconservative whose hatred of liberalism and secularism led him to believe that the Fascists would increase the influence of the church in the nation.

In 1929 the Lateran Accords recognized the independence of Vatican City, repealed many of the anticlerical laws passed under the liberal government, and made religious instruction compulsory in all secondary schools. Relations between the Vatican and the Fascist government remained fairly good throughout the decade of the 1930s. When Mussolini invaded Ethiopia and intervened in the Spanish Civil War, the church supported him. Although the papacy criticized Mussolini for drawing closer to Hitler and introducing anti-Jewish legislation, it never broke with the Fascist regime.

The New German Republic

In the last days of World War I, a revolution brought down the German imperial government and led to the creation of a democratic republic. The new government, headed by Chancellor Friedrich Ebert (1871–1925), a Social Democrat, signed an armistice agreement ending the war. Many Germans blamed the new democratic leadership for the defeat—a baseless accusation—for the German generals, knowing that the war was lost, had sought an armistice. In February 1919 the recently elected National Assembly met at Weimar and proceeded to draw up a constitution for the new state. The Weimar Republic—born in revolution, which most Germans detested, and military defeat, which many attributed to the new government—faced an uncertain future.

Threats from Left and Right

The infant republic, dominated by moderate socialists, faced internal threats from both the radical left and the radical right. In January 1919 the newly established German Communist party, or Spartacists, disregarding the advice of their leaders Rosa Luxemburg and Karl Liebknecht, took to the streets of Berlin and declared the government of Ebert deposed. To crush the revolution, Ebert turned to the Free Corps—volunteer brigades of ex-soldiers and adventurers, led by officers loyal to the emperor, who had been fighting to protect the eastern borders from encroachments by the new states of Poland, Estonia, and Latvia. The men of the Free Corps relished action and despised Bolshevism. They suppressed the revolution and murdered Luxemburg and Liebknecht on January 15.

The Spartacist revolt and the short-lived Soviet Republic in Munich (and others in Baden and Brunswick) had profound effects on the German psyche. The Communists had been easily subdued, but fear of a communist insurrection remained deeply embedded in the middle and upper classes, a fear that drove many of them into the ranks of the Weimar Republic's right-wing opponents.

Refusing to disband as the government ordered, detachments of the right-wing Free Corps marched into Berlin and declared a new government headed by Wolfgang Kapp, a staunch nationalist. Insisting that it could not fire on fellow soldiers, the German army, the Reichswehr, made no move to defend the republic. A general strike called by the labor unions prevented Kapp from governing, and the coup collapsed. However, the Kapp Putsch demonstrated that the loyalty of the army to the republic was doubtful.

Economic Crisis

In addition to uprisings by the left and right, the republic was burdened by economic crisis. Unable to meet the deficit in the national budget, the government simply printed more money, causing the value of the German mark to decline precipitously. In 1919, the mark stood at 8.9 to the dollar; in November 1923, a dollar could be exchanged for 4 billion marks! Bank savings, war bonds, and pensions, representing years of toil and thrift, became worthless. Blaming the government for this disaster, the ruined middle class became more receptive to rightist movements that aimed to bring down the republic.

With the economy in shambles, the republic defaulted on reparation payments. Premier Raymond Poincaré (1860–1934) of France took a hard line and in January 1923 ordered French troops into the Ruhr—the nerve center of German industry. Responding to the republic's call for passive resistance, factory workers, miners, and railway workers in the Ruhr refused to work for the French.

Gustav Stresemann, who became chancellor in August 1923, skillfully placed the republic on the path to recovery. He declared Germany's willingness to make reparation payments and issued a new currency backed by a mortgage on German real estate. To protect the value of the new currency, the government did not print another issue. Inflation receded and confidence was restored.

A new arrangement regarding reparations also contributed to the economic recovery. In 1924 the parties accepted the Dawes Plan, which reduced reparations and based them on Germany's economic capacity. During the negotiations, France agreed to withdraw its troops from the Ruhr, another step toward easing tensions for the republic.

From 1924 to 1929 economic conditions improved. Foreign capitalists, particularly Americans, were attracted by high interest rates and the low cost of labor. Their investments in German businesses stimulated the economy. By 1929, iron, steel, coal, and chemical production exceeded prewar levels. The value of German exports also surpassed that of 1913. Real wages were higher than before the war, and improved unemployment benefits also made life better for the workers. It appeared that Germany had also achieved political stability, as threats from the extremist parties of the left and the right subsided. Given time and economic stability, democracy might have taken firmer root in Germany. But then came the Great Depression. The global economic crisis that began in October 1929 starkly revealed how weak the Weimar Republic was.

Fundamental Weaknesses of the Weimar Republic

German political experience provided poor soil for transplanting an Anglo-Saxon democratic parliamentary system. Before World War I, Germany had been a semiautocratic state ruled by an emperor who commanded the armed forces, controlled foreign policy, appointed the chancellor, and called and dismissed parliament. This authoritarian system blocked the German people from acquiring democratic habits and attitudes; still accustomed to rule from above, still adoring the power-state, many Germans sought the destruction of the Weimar Republic.

Traditional conservatives—the upper echelons of the civil service, judges, industrialists, large landowners, army leaders—were contemptuous of democracy and were avowed enemies of the republic. Nor did the middle class feel a commitment to the liberal-democratic principles on which the republic rested. The traditionally nationalistic middle class identified the republic with the defeat in war and the humiliation of the Versailles Treaty; rabidly antisocialist, this class saw the leaders of the republic as Marxists who would impose on Germany a working-class state. Right-wing intellectuals often attacked democracy as a barrier to the true unity of the German nation. In the tradition of nineteenth-century Volkish thinkers, they had contempt for reason and political freedom and glorified instincts, blood, and action. In doing so, they turned many Germans against the republic, thereby eroding the popular support on which democracy depends.

The Weimar Republic also showed the weaknesses of the multiparty system. With the vote spread over a number of parties, no one party held a majority of seats in the parliament (Reichstag), so the republic was governed by a coalition of several parties. But because of ideological differences, the coalition was always unstable and in danger of failing to function. This is precisely what happened during the Great Depression. When effective leadership was imperative, the government could not act. Political deadlock caused Germans to lose what little confidence they had in the democratic system. Support for the parties that wanted to preserve democracy dwindled, and extremist parties that aimed to topple the republic gained strength. Seeking to bring down the republic were the Communists, on the left, and two rightist parties—the Nationalists and the National Socialist German Workers party, led by Adolf Hitler.

The Rise of Hitler

Adolf Hitler (1889–1945) was born in Austria on April 20, 1889, the fourth child of a minor civil servant. A poor student at secondary school, although by no means unintelligent, Hitler left high school and lived idly for more than two years. In 1907 and again in 1908, the Vienna Academy of Fine Arts rejected his application for admission. Hitler did not seek to learn a trade or to work steadily, but earned some money by painting picture postcards. He read a lot, especially in art, history, and military affairs. He also read the racial, nationalist, anti-Semitic, and pan-German literature that abounded in multinational Vienna. The racist treatises preached the danger posed by mixing races, called for the liquidation of racial inferiors, and marked the Jew as the embodiment of evil and the source of all misfortune.

In Vienna, Hitler came into contact with Georg von Schönerer's pan-German movement. For Schönerer, the Jews were evil not because of their religion, not because they rejected Christ, but because they possessed evil racial qualities. Schönerer's followers wore watch chains etched with pictures of hanged Jews. Hitler was particularly impressed with Karl Lueger, the mayor of Vienna, a clever demagogue who skillfully manipulated the anti-Semitic feelings of the Viennese for his own political advantage. In Vienna, Hitler also acquired a hatred for Marxism and democracy and the conviction that the struggle for existence and the survival of the fittest are the essential facts of the social world.

When World War I began, Hitler was in Munich. He welcomed the war as a relief from his daily life, which had been devoid of purpose and excitement. Volunteering for the German army, Hitler found battle exhilarating, and he fought bravely, twice receiving the Iron Cross. The experience of battle taught Hitler to value discipline, regimentation, leadership, authority, struggle, ruthlessness—values that he carried with him into the politics of the postwar world.

The shock of Germany's defeat and revolution intensified his commitment to racial nationalism. To lead Germany to total victory over its racial enemies became his obsession. Germany's defeat and shame, he said, was due to the creators of the republic—the "November criminals"; and behind them was a Jewish-Bolshevik world conspiracy.

The Nazi Party

In 1919, Hitler joined a small, right-wing extremist group. Displaying fantastic energy and extraordinary ability as a demagogic orator, propagandist, and organizer, Hitler quickly became the leader of the party, whose name was changed to National Socialist German Workers' party (commonly called *Nazi*). As leader, Hitler insisted on absolute authority and total allegiance—a demand that coincided with the postwar longing for a strong leader who would set right a shattered nation.

Like Mussolini, Hitler incorporated military attitudes and techniques into politics. Uniforms, salutes, emblems, flags, and other symbols infused party members with a sense of solidarity and camaraderie. At mass meetings, Hitler was a spellbinder who gave stunning performances. His pounding fists, throbbing body, wild gesticulations, hypnotic eyes, rage-swollen face, and repeated, frenzied denunciations of the Versailles Treaty, Marxism, the republic, and Jews inflamed and mesmerized the audience. Hitler instinctively grasped the innermost feelings of his audience—their resentments and longings. "The intense will of the man, the passion of his sincerity seemed to flow from him into me. I experienced an exaltation that could be likened only to religious conversion," said one early admirer.[3]

In November 1923, Hitler attempted to seize power (the Munich or "Beer Hall" Putsch) in the state of Bavaria as a prelude to toppling the republic. The putsch failed, but, ironically, Hitler's prestige increased, for when he was put on trial, he used it as an opportunity to denounce the republic and the Versailles Treaty and to proclaim his philosophy of racial nationalism. His impassioned speeches, publicized by the press, earned Hitler a nationwide reputation and a light sentence—five years' imprisonment with the promise of quick parole. While in prison, Hitler dictated *Mein Kampf,* a rambling and turgid work that contained the essence of his world-view. The unsuccessful Munich Putsch taught Hitler a valuable lesson: armed insurrection against superior might fails. He would gain power not by force, but by exploiting the instruments of democracy—elections and party politics. He would use apparently legal means to destroy the Weimar Republic and impose a dictatorship.

Hitler's World-View

Racial Nationalism   Hitler's thought comprised a patchwork of nineteenth-century anti-Semitic, Volkish, Social Darwinist, antidemocratic, and anti-Marxist ideas. From these ideas, many of which enjoyed wide popularity, Hitler constructed a world-view rooted in myth and ritual. Nazism rejected both the Judeo-Christian and the Enlightenment traditions and sought to found a new world order based on racial nationalism. For Hitler, race was the key to understanding world history. He believed that a reawakened, racially united Germany, led by men of iron will, would carve out a vast European empire and would deal a decadent liberal civilization its deathblow. It would conquer Russia, eradicate communism, and reduce to serfdom the subhuman Slavs, "a mass of born slaves who feel the need of a master."[4]

In the tradition of Volkish thinkers and Social Darwinists, Hitler divided the world into superior and inferior races and pitted them against each other in a struggle for survival. This fight for life was a law of nature and of history. As a higher race, the Germans were entitled to conquer and subjugate other races. Germany must acquire *Lebensraum* ("living space") by expanding eastward at the expense of the racially inferior Slavs.

The Jew as Devil   An obsessive and virulent anti-Semitism dominated Hitler's mental outlook. In waging war against the Jews, Hitler believed that he was defending Germany from its worst enemy. In Hitler's mental picture, the Aryan was the originator and carrier of civilization. As descendants of the Aryans, the Germans embodied creativity, bravery, and loyalty. As the opposite of the Aryan, the Jew personified the vilest qualities. "Two worlds face one another," said Hitler, "the men of God and the men of Satan! The Jew is the anti-man, the creature of another god. He must have come from another root of the human race. I set the Aryan and the Jew over and against each other."[5] Everything Hitler despised—liberalism, intellectualism, pacifism, parliamentarism, internationalism, Marxism, modern art, individualism—he attributed to the Jew.

Hitler's anti-Semitism also served a functional purpose. By concentrating all evil in one enemy, "the conspirator and demonic" Jew, Hitler provided the masses with a simple, consistent, and emotionally satisfying explanation for all their misery. By defining themselves as the racial and spiritual opposites of Jews, Germans of all classes felt joined together in a Volkish union.

The surrender to myth served to disorient the German intellect and to unify the nation. When the mind accepts an image such as Hitler's image of Jews as vermin, germs, and satanic conspirators, it has lost all sense of balance and objectivity. Such a disoriented mind is ready to believe and to obey, to be manipulated and led, to brutalize and to tolerate brutality; it is ready to be absorbed into the will of the collective community.

The Importance of Propaganda   Hitler understood that in an age of political parties, universal suffrage, and a popular press—the legacies of the French and Industrial revolutions—the successful leader must win the support of the masses. This could be achieved best with propaganda. To be effective, said Hitler, propaganda must be aimed principally at the emotions. The masses are not moved by scientific ideas or by objective and abstract knowledge, but by primitive feelings, terror, force, discipline. Propaganda must reduce everything to simple slogans incessantly repeated and must concentrate on one enemy. The masses are aroused by the spoken, not the written, word—by a storm of hot passion erupting from the speaker "which like hammer blows can open the gates to the heart of the people."[6]

Hitler Gains Power

After serving only nine months, Hitler left prison in December 1924. He continued to build his party and waited for a crisis that would rock the republic and make his movement a force in national politics. The Great Depression, which began in the United States at the end of 1929, provided that crisis. As Germany's economic plight worsened, the German people became more amenable to Hitler's radicalism. His propaganda techniques worked. The Nazi party went from 810,000 votes in 1928 to 6,400,000 in 1930, and its representation in the Reichstag soared from 12 to 107.

To the lower middle class, the Nazis promised effective leadership and a solution to the economic crisis. But Nazism was more than a class movement. It appealed to the discontented and disillusioned from all segments of the population—embittered veterans; romantic nationalists; idealistic intellectuals; industrialists and large landowners frightened by communism and social democracy; rootless and resentful people who felt they had no place in the existing society; the unemployed; lovers of violence; and newly enfranchised youth yearning for a cause. And always there was the immense attraction of Hitler. Many Germans were won over by his fanatic sincerity, his iron will, and his conviction that he was chosen by fate to rescue Germany.

In the election of July 31, 1932, the Nazis received 37.3 percent of the vote and won 230 seats, far more than any other party but still not a majority. The recently resigned chancellor, Franz von Papen, persuaded the aging President Paul von Hindenburg (1847–1934) to appoint Hitler as chancellor. In this decision Papen had the support of German industrialists and aristocratic land-

Nazi Magazine Cover of Mother and Son. Nazi propaganda proclaimed the strength of the German Aryans through symbols easily grasped and guaranteed to strike proud nationalistic chords. (*Institut für Zeitgeschichte, München*)

owners, who regarded Hitler as a useful instrument to fight communism, block social reform, break the backs of organized labor, and rebuild the armament industry.

Never intending to rule within the spirit of the constitution, Hitler quickly moved to assume dictatorial powers. In February 1933 a Dutch drifter with communist leanings set a fire in the Reichstag. Hitler persuaded Hindenburg to sign an emergency decree suspending civil rights on the pretext that the state was threatened by internal subversion. The chancellor then used these emergency powers to arrest, without due process, Communist and Social Democratic deputies.

In the elections of March 1933, the German people elected 288 Nazi deputies in a Reichstag of 647 seats. With the support of 52 deputies of the Nationalist party and in the absence of Communist deputies, who were under arrest, the Nazis now had a secure majority. Hitler then bullied the Reichstag into passing the Enabling Act (in March 1933), which permitted the chancellor to enact legislation independently of the Reichstag. With astonishing passivity, the political parties had allowed the Nazis to dismantle the government and make Hitler a dictator with unlimited power. Hitler had used the instruments of democracy to destroy the republic and create a dictatorship. And he did it far more thoroughly and quickly than Mussolini had.

Nazi Germany

The Nazis moved to subjugate all political and economic institutions and all culture to the will of the party. There could be no separation between the private life and politics; ideology must pervade every phase of daily life; all organizations must come under party control; there could be no rights of the individual that must be respected by the state. The party became the state, its teachings the soul of the German nation.

Unlike absolute monarchies of the past, a totalitarian regime requires more than outward obedience to its commands; it seeks to control the inner person, to shape thoughts, feelings, and attitudes in accordance with the party ideology. It demands total allegiance and submission.

The Leader-State

The Third Reich was organized as a leader-state in which Hitler, the *Fuehrer* (leader), embodied and expressed the real will of the German people, commanded the supreme loyalty of the nation, and held omnipotent power. As a Nazi political theorist stated: "The authority of the Fuehrer is total and all-embracing . . . it is subject to no checks or controls; it is circumscribed by no . . . individual rights; it is . . . overriding and unfettered."[7]

In June 1933, the Social Democratic party was outlawed, and within a few weeks the other political parties simply disbanded on their own. In May 1933, the Nazis seized the property of the trade unions, arrested the leaders, and ended collective bargaining and strikes. The newly established German Labor Front, an instrument of the party, became the official organization of the working class.

Unlike the Bolsheviks, the Nazis did not destroy the upper classes of the Old Regime. Hitler made no war against the industrialists. From them he wanted loyalty, obedience, and a war machine. German businessmen prospered but exercised no influence on political decisions. The profits of industry rose, but the real wages of German workers did not improve. Nevertheless, workers lauded the regime for ending the unemployment crisis.

Nazism conflicted with the core values of Christianity. "The heaviest blow that ever struck humanity was the coming of Christianity," said Hitler to intimates during World War II.[8] Because Nazism could tolerate no other faith alongside itself and recognizing that Christianity was a rival claimant for the German soul, the Nazis moved to repress the Protestant and Catholic churches. In the public schools, religious instruction was cut back and the syllabus changed to omit the Jewish origins of Christianity. Christ was depicted not as a Jew, heir to the prophetic tradition of Hebrew monotheism, but as an Aryan hero. The *Gestapo* (secret state police) censored church newspapers, scrutinized sermons and church activities, forbade some clergymen to preach, dismissed the opponents of Nazism from theological schools, and arrested some clerical critics of the regime.

The clergy were well represented among those Germans who resisted Nazism; some were sent to concentration camps or were executed. But these courageous clergy were not representative of the German churches, which, as organized institutions, capitulated to and cooperated with the Nazi regime. Both the German Evangelical and German Catholic churches demanded that their faithful render loyalty to Hitler; both turned a blind eye to Nazi persecution of Jews; both condemned resistance and found much in the Third Reich to admire; both supported Hitler's war. The prominent Lutheran theologian who "welcomed that change that came to Germany in 1933 as a divine gift and miracle"[9] voiced the sentiments of many members of the clergy.

The Nazis instituted many anti-Jewish measures, designed to make outcasts of the Jews. Thousands of Jewish doctors, lawyers, musicians, artists, and professors were barred from practicing their professions, and Jewish members of the civil service were dismissed. A series of laws tightened the screws of humiliation and persecution. Marriage or sexual encounters between Germans and Jews were forbidden. Universities, schools, restaurants, pharmacies, hospitals, theaters, museums, and athletic fields were gradually closed to Jews.

In November 1938, using the assassination of a German diplomat by a Jewish youth as a pretext, the Nazis organized an extensive pogrom. Nazi gangs murdered scores of Jews and burned and looted thousands of Jewish homes and synagogues. The Reich then imposed on the Jewish community a fine of one billion marks. These measures were a mere prelude, however; the physical extermination of European Jewry became a cardinal Nazi objective during World War II.

Shaping the "New Man"

The Ministry of Popular Enlightenment, headed by Dr. Joseph Goebbels (1897–1945), controlled the press, book publishing, the radio, the theater, and the cinema. Nazi propaganda sought to condition the mind to revere the Fuehrer and to obey the new regime; it intended to deprive individuals of their capacity for independent thought. By concentrating on the myth of race and the infallibility of the Fuehrer, Nazi propaganda tried to disorient the rational mind and to give the individual new standards to believe in and obey. Propaganda aimed to mold the entire nation to think and respond as the leader-state directed.

The regime made a special effort to reach young people. All youths between the ages of ten and eighteen were urged to join the Hitler Youth, and all other youth organizations were dissolved. At camps and rallies, young people paraded, sang, saluted, and chanted: "we were slaves; we were outsiders in our own country. So were we before Hitler united us. Now we would fight against Hell itself for our leader."[10] The schools, long breeding grounds of nationalism, militarism, antiliberalism, and anti-Semitism, now indoctrinated the young in Nazi ideology. The Nazis instructed teachers how certain subjects

Art as History
1600 to the Present

The visual arts are a particularly rich source of information for historians of the modern West. Revolutionary changes in art styles reflect the stages and complexities of the modern age. What insights into modern history can be derived from examining these works of art?

Jan Vermeer (1632–1675): View of Delft, 1660. By the seventeenth century, tiny Holland, which had enterprising merchants, sailors, and fast ships, was wealthy. Its sea ports flourished. Well-to-do bourgeoisie built substantial homes and furnished them with oriental rugs and handsome pictures. What does this painting convey about the Dutch town, its people, and its culture? (*Mauritshuis, The Hague*)

Rembrandt van Ryn (1606–1669): The Anatomy Lesson, c. 1632.
A revolution occurred in the sciences when discoveries began to be drawn from experiments and direct observation. An early Rembrandt presents a physician explaining the anatomical features of the arm to students, who observe the dissection with intensity. Rembrandt uses dark and shade to heighten the drama. What does the picture suggest about Dutch science? (*Rijksmuseum, Amsterdam*)

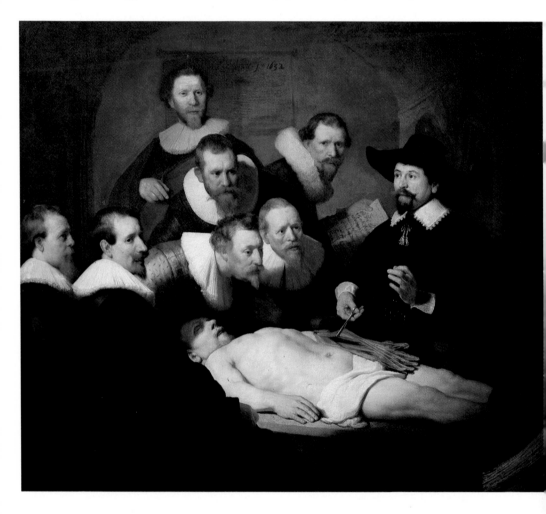

Jacques-Louis David (1748–1825): Napoleon in His Study, 1812 (opposite). David, the founder of the Neoclassic style, painted several portraits of Napoleon. Yet, despite David's skill, Napoleon's greatness as general and emperor was not conveyed. Here, the Code Napoléon manuscript lies on the desk and Plutarch's *Lives* is under the table. The candles and clock show that Napoleon has worked all night. Why are these details included and what image of Napoleon do they convey? (*National Gallery of Art, Washington; Samuel H. Kress Collection*)

J. M. W. Turner (1775–1851): Burning of the Houses of Parliament, c. 1835. Turner was preoccupied with shimmering light. Though he often used literary themes for his paintings, in accord with Romantic taste, the people, buildings, and ships were often obscured. What does this painting reveal about his temperament and perception of the world? (*Oil on canvas. H. 36¼" W. 48½" Philadelphia Museum of Art: The John H. McFadden Collection*)

Paul Cézanne (1839–1906): Still Life with Apples and Peaches, c. 1905 (opposite). Cézanne did not share the French impressionists' interest in showing a "slice of life." He searched for harmony of form and color; his forms are simplified and outlined, and the different objects are seen from varying viewpoints and eyelevels and do not conform to the laws of perspective. How does this picture reveal a movement away from reality in art in the late 1800s? (*National Gallery of Art, Washington; Gift of Eugene and Agnes Meyer*)

Auguste Rodin (1840–1917): The Thinker, 1888. Rodin redefined sculpture at the time that his countrymen Manet and Monet were redefining painting. Rather than working with bronze, Rodin modeled in wax or clay, so that the shapes "grew" and were built. When the bronzes were cast, the rough surfaces reflected light in different patterns and the works looked unfinished, not mechanical. *The Thinker* (bronze, H. 78″) is anonymous—part Adam, part Prometheus, part brute; he shows tension and action-in-repose. What elements in this statue evoke past cultures and/or France at the turn of the twentieth century? *(Baltimore Museum of Art; Jacob Epstein Collection, BMA 1930.25.1)*

Pablo Picasso (1881–1973): Les Demoiselles d'Avignon, 1907. The cubists took the distortion of perspective farther, to give viewers the feeling of seeing objects and people "in the round" and over time. In this picture, Picasso painted the female nude in the strong cubist style to express the forces of nature; he goes beyond the conscious level. Can a correlation be made between some twentieth-century art and the scientific examination of the unconscious? (*Oil on canvas. 8' × 7' 8". Collection, The Museum of Modern Art, New York. Acquired through the Lillie P. Bliss Bequest*)

Pierre Auguste Renoir (1841–1919): Le Bal à Bougival, 1883 (opposite). Joy and beauty shine in the impressionist paintings of Renoir. The impressionists in France broke with the Academy's classic themes and depicted scenes from daily life. They adopted a palette of luminous colors, as in this painting of young love dancing. What does the emphasis on ordinary human beings as fit subjects for art disclose about French —and Western—thinking of the late 1900s? (*Oil on canvas. Museum of Fine Arts, Boston. Anna Mitchell Richards Fund, 37.375*)

Frank Stella (b. 1936): Hiraqla, 1968. An abstract painting communicates with the viewer through its colors, textures, and shapes. Geometric abstract painting appeared in the years following the development of cubism, and continues to be developed by artists like Frank Stella. His canvases are often quite large, with great impact; *Hiraqla* is 120″ high by 240″ wide. What ideas and sensations does this painting impart? (© *Frank Stella/Collection of Mr. and Mrs. Graham Gund*)

Umberto Boccioni (1882–1916): Unique Forms of Continuity in Space, 1913 (cast 1931). This bronze figure (H. 43⅞″ × 34⅞″ × 15¾″) is by an Italian sculptor of the Futurist school. Boccioni depicts not the body, but its imprint as it moves through the air, creating turbulence. In comparing this sculpture with Rodin's *Thinker*, what differences in the sculptures' subjects and styles tell something about their eras? (*Collection, The Museum of Modern Art, New York. Acquired through the Lillie P. Bliss Bequest*)

Adolf Hitler at Nuremberg, Germany, September 1938.   Taken the month of the Munich Agreement, the photograph shows Hitler saluting before a huge crowd, including the labor army. (*UPI/Bettmann Newsphotos*)

were to be taught, and to insure obedience, members of the Hitler Youth were asked to report teachers who did not conform.

In May 1933, professors and students proudly burned books considered a threat to Nazi ideology. Many academics praised Hitler and the new regime. Some 10 percent of the university faculty, principally Jews, Social Democrats, and liberals, were dismissed, and their colleagues often approved. "From now on it will not be your job to determine whether something is true but whether it is in the spirit of the National Socialist revolution," the new minister of culture told university professors.[11] Numerous courses on "racial science" and Nazi ideology were introduced into the curriculum.

Symbolic of the Nazi regime were the monster rallies staged at Nuremberg. Scores of thousands roared, marched, and worshiped at their leader's feet. These true believers, the end product of Nazi indoctrination, celebrated Hitler's achievements and demonstrated their loyalty to their savior. Everything was brilliantly orchestrated to impress Germans and the world with the irresistible power, determination, and unity of the Nazi movement and the greatness of the Fuehrer. Armies of youths waving flags, stormtroopers bearing weapons, and workers shouldering long-handled spades paraded past Hitler, who stood at attention, his arm extended in the Nazi salute. The endless columns of marchers, the stirring martial music played by huge bands, the forest of flags, the chanting and cheering of spectators, and the burning torches and beaming spotlights united the participants into a racial community. "Wherever Hitler leads we follow," thundered thousands of Germans in a giant chorus.

Terror was another means of insuring compliance and obedience. The instrument of terror was the SS, which was organized in 1925 to protect Hitler and other party leaders and to stand guard at party meetings. Under the leadership of Heinrich Himmler (1900–1945), a fanatic believer in Hitler's racial theories, the SS was molded into an elite force of disciplined, dedicated, and utterly ruthless men.

Mass Support

The Nazi regime became a police state symbolized by mass arrests, the persecution of Jews, and concentration camps that institutionalized terror. Yet fewer heads had rolled than people expected, and in many ways life seemed normal. The Nazis skillfully established the totalitarian state without upsetting the daily life of the great majority of the population. Moreover, Hitler, like Mussolini, was careful to maintain the appearance of legality. By not abolishing parliament or repealing the constitution, he could claim that his was a legitimate government.

To people concerned with little but family, job, and friends—and this includes most people in any country—life in the first few years of the Third Reich seemed quite satisfying. People believed that the new government was trying to solve Germany's problems in a vigorous and sensible manner, in contrast to the ineffective Weimar leadership. By 1936, the invigoration of the economy, stimulated in part by rearmament, had virtually eliminated unemployment, which had reached six million when Hitler took power. An equally astounding achievement in the eyes of the German people was the rebuilding of the German war machine and the restoration of German power in international affairs. It seemed to most Germans that Hitler had awakened a sense of self-sacrifice and national dedication among a people dispirited by defeat and depression.

There was some opposition and resistance to the Hitler regime. Social Democrats and communists in particular organized small cells. Some conservatives, who considered Hitler a threat to traditional German values, and some clergy, who saw Nazism as a pagan religion in conflict with Christian morality, also formed small opposition groups. But only resistance from the army could have toppled Hitler. Some generals, even before World War II, urged such resistance, but the overwhelming majority of German officers either preferred the new regime, were too concerned about their careers to do anything, or considered it dishonorable to break their oath of loyalty to Hitler. These officers would remain loyal until the bitter end. Very few Germans realized that their country was passing through a long night of barbarism, and still fewer considered resistance.

Liberalism and Authoritarianism in Other Lands

The Spread of Authoritarianism

After World War I, in country after country, parliamentary democracy collapsed and authoritarian leaders came to power. In most of these countries, liberal ideals had not penetrated deeply. Proponents of liberalism met resistance from conservative elites.

Spain and Portugal   In both Spain and Portugal, parliamentary regimes faced strong opposition from the church, the army, and large landowners. In 1926, army officers overthrew the Portuguese Republic that had been created in 1910, and gradually Antonio de Oliveira Salazar (1889–1970), a professor of economics, emerged as dictator. In Spain, after antimonarchist forces won the election of 1931, King Alfonso XIII (1902–1931) left the country and Spain was proclaimed a republic. But the new government, led by socialists and liberals, faced the determined opposition of the ruling elite. The reforms introduced by the republic—expropriation of large estates, reduction of the number of army officers, dissolution of the Jesuit order, and the closing of church schools—only intensified the old order's hatred.

The difficulties of the Spanish Republic mounted: workers, near starvation, rioted and engaged in violent strikes; the military attempted a coup; Catalonia, with its long tradition of separatism, tried to establish its autonomy. Imitating the example of France, the parties of the left, including the Communists, united in the Popular Front, which came to power in February 1936. In July 1936, General Francisco Franco (1892–1975), stationed in Spanish Morocco, led a revolt against the republic. He was supported by army leaders, the church, monarchists, landlords, industrialists, and the Falange, a newly formed fascist party. Spain was torn by a bloody civil war. Aided by Fascist Italy and Nazi Germany, Franco won in 1939 and established a dictatorship.

Eastern and Central Europe   Parliamentary government in eastern Europe rested on weak foundations. Predominantly rural, these countries lacked the sizable professional and commercial classes that had promoted liberalism in western Europe. Only Czechoslovakia had a substantial native middle class with a strong liberal tradition. The rural masses of eastern Europe, traditionally subjected to monarchical and aristocratic authority, were not used to political thinking or civic responsibility. Students and intellectuals, often gripped by a romantic nationalism, were drawn to antidemocratic movements.

Right-wing leaders also played on the fear of communism. When parliamentary government failed to solve internal problems, the opponents of the liberal state seized the helm. Fascist movements, however, had little success in eastern Europe. It was authoritarian regimes headed by traditional ruling elites—army leaders or kings—that put an end to democracy there.

The Western Democracies

While liberal governments were everywhere failing, the great Western democracies—the United States, Britain, and France—continued to preserve democratic institutions. In Britain and the United States, fascist movements were no more than a nuisance. In France, fascism was more of a threat, because it exploited a deeply ingrained hostility in some quarters to the liberal ideals of the French Revolution.

The United States   The central problem faced by the Western democracies was the Great Depression, which started in the United States. In the 1920s, hundreds of thousands of Americans had bought stock on credit; this buying spree sent stock prices soaring well beyond what the stocks were actually worth. In late October 1929, the stock market was hit by a wave of panic selling; prices plummeted. Within a few weeks, the value of stocks listed on the New York Stock Exchange fell by some 26 billion dollars. A terrible chain reaction followed over the next few years. Businesses cut production and unemployment soared; farmers unable to meet mortgage payments lost their land; banks that had made poor investments closed down. American investors withdrew the capital they had invested in Europe, causing European banks and businesses to fail. Throughout the world, trade declined and unemployment rose.

When President Franklin Delano Roosevelt (1882–1945) took office in 1933, over 13 million Americans—one-quarter of the labor force—were out of work. Hunger and despair showed on the faces of the American people. Moving away from laissez-faire, Roosevelt instituted a comprehensive program of national planning, economic experimentation, and reform known as the New Deal. Although the American political and economic system faced a severe test, few Americans turned to fascism or communism, and the government, while engaging in national planning, did not break with democratic values and procedures.

Britain   Even before the Great Depression, Britain faced severe economic problems. Loss of markets to foreign competitors hurt British manufacturing, mining, and shipbuilding; rapid development of water and oil power reduced the demand for British coal, and outdated mining equipment put Britain in a poor competitive position. To reduce costs, mine owners in 1926 called for salary cuts; the coal miners countered with a strike and were joined by workers in other industries. To many Britons, the workers were leftist radicals trying to overthrow the government. Many wanted the state to break the strike. After nine days, industrial workers called it off, but the miners held out for another six months; they returned to work with longer hours and lower pay. Although the General Strike had failed, it did improve relations between the classes, for the workers had not called for revolution and they had refrained from violence. The fear that British workers would follow the Bolshevik path abated.

The Great Depression cast a pall of gloom over Britain. The Conservative party leadership tried to stimulate exports by devaluing the pound and to encourage industry by providing loans at lower interest rates, but in the main, it left the task of recovery to industry itself. Not until Britain began to rearm did unemployment decline significantly. Despite the economic slump of the 1920s and the Great Depression, Britain remained politically stable, a testament to the strength of its parliamentary tradition. Neither the communists nor the newly formed British Fascist party gained mass support.

France   In the early 1920s, France was concerned with restoring villages, railroads, mines, and forests that had been ruined by the war. From 1926 to 1929 France was relatively prosperous; industrial and agricultural production expanded, tourism increased, and the currency was stable. Although France did not feel the Great Depression as painfully as the United States and Germany did, the nation was hurt by the decline in trade and production and the rise in unemployment. The political instability that had beset the Third Republic virtually since its inception continued, and hostility to the republic mounted. As the leading parties failed to solve the nation's problems, a number of fascist-type groups gained strength.

Fear of growing fascist strength at home and in Italy and Germany led the parties of the left to form the Popular Front. In 1936 Léon Blum (1872–1950), a socialist and a Jew, became premier. Blum's Popular Front government instituted more reforms than any other ministry in the history of the Third Republic. To end a wave of strikes that tied up production, Blum gave workers a forty-hour week and holidays with pay and guaranteed them the right to collective bargaining. He took steps to nationalize the armaments and aircraft industries. To reduce the influence of the wealthiest families, he put the Bank of France under government control. By raising prices and buying wheat, he aided farmers. Conservatives and fascists denounced Blum as a Jewish socialist who was converting the fatherland into a communist state. "Better Hitler than Blum," grumbled French rightists.

Despite significant reforms, the Popular Front could not revitalize the economy. In 1937 the Blum ministry was overthrown and the Popular Front, always a tenuous alliance, fell apart. Through democratic means the Blum government had tried to give France its own New Deal, but the social reforms passed by the Popular Front only intensified hatred between the working classes and the rest of the nation. France had preserved democracy against the onslaught of domestic fascists, but it was a demoralized and divided nation that confronted a united and dynamic Nazi Germany.

Intellectuals and Artists in Troubled Times

Postwar Pessimism

After the Great War, Europeans looked at themselves and their civilization differently. It seemed that in science and technology Europeans had unleashed powers they could not control and that belief in the stability and security of European civilization was an illusion. Also illusory was the expectation that reason would banish surviving signs of darkness, ignorance, and injustice and usher in an age of continual progress. European intellectuals felt that they were living in a "broken world." In an age of heightened brutality and mobilized irrationality, the values of old Europe seemed beyond recovery. "All the great words," wrote D. H. Lawrence "were cancelled out for that generation."[12] The fissures discernible in European civilization prior to 1914 had grown wider and deeper. To be sure, Europe also had its optimists—those who found reason for hope in the League of Nations and in the easing of international tensions and improved economic conditions in the mid-1920s. However, the Great Depression and the triumph of totalitarianism intensified feelings of doubt and disillusionment.

Expressions of pessimism abounded after World War I. In 1919, Paul Valéry stated: "We modern civilizations have learned to recognize that we are mortal like the others. We feel that a civilization is as fragile as life."[13] "We are living today under the sign of the collapse of civilization,"[14] declared humanitarian Albert Schweitzer in 1923. "There is a growing awareness of imminent ruin tantamount to a dread of the approaching end of all that makes life worthwhile," said German philosopher Karl Jaspers in 1932.[15]

T. S. Eliot's "The Waste Land" (1922) is pervaded by the image of a collapsing European civilization. Eliot creates a macabre scenario. Hooded hordes, modern-day barbarians, swarm over plains and lay waste cities. Jerusalem, Athens, Alexandria, Vienna, and London—each once a great spiritual or cultural center—are now "falling towers." Amid this destruction, one hears "high in the air/Murmur of maternal lamentation."[16]

Carl Gustav Jung, a Swiss psychologist, said in *Modern Man in Search of a Soul* (1933):

> *I believe I am not exaggerating when I say that modern man has suffered an almost fatal shock, psychologically speaking, and as a result has fallen into profound uncertainty. . . . The revolution in our conscious outlook, brought about by the catastrophic results of the World War, shows itself in our inner life by the shattering of our faith in ourselves and our own worth. . . . I realize only too well that I am losing my faith in the possibility of a rational organization of the world, the old dream of the millennium, in which peace and harmony should rule, has grown pale.*[17]

In 1936, Dutch historian Johan Huizinga wrote in a chapter entitled "Apprehension of Doom":

We are living in a demented world. And we know it. . . . Everywhere there are doubts as to the solidity of our social structure, vague fears of the imminent future, a feeling that our civilization is on the way to ruin. . . . almost all things which once seemed sacred and immutable have now become unsettled, truth and humanity, justice and reason. . . . The sense of living in the midst of a violent crisis of civilization, threatening complete collapse, has spread far and wide.[18]

The most influential expression of pessimism was Oswald Spengler's *The Decline of the West*. The first volume was published in July 1918 as the Great War was drawing to a close, and the second volume in 1922. The work achieved instant notoriety, particularly in Spengler's native Germany, shattered by defeat. Spengler viewed history as an assemblage of many different cultures which, like living organisms, experience birth, youth, maturity, and death. What contemporaries pondered most was Spengler's insistence that Western civilization had entered its final stage and that its death could not be averted.

To an already troubled Western world, Spengler offered no solace. The West, like other cultures and like any living organism, is destined to die; its decline is irreversible, its death inevitable, and the symptoms of degeneration are already evident. Spengler's gloomy prognostication buttressed the fascists, who claimed that they were creating a new civilization on the ruins of a dying European civilization.

Literature and Art: Innovation, Disillusionment, and Social Commentary

Postwar pessimism did not prevent writers and artists from perpetuating the cultural innovations initiated before the war. In the works of D. H. Lawrence, Marcel Proust, André Gide, James Joyce, Franz Kafka, T. S. Eliot, and Thomas Mann the modernist movement achieved a brilliant flowering. Often these writers gave expression to the troubles and uncertainties of the postwar period.

Franz Kafka (1883–1924), a Czech Jew, perhaps better than any other novelist of his generation grasped the dilemma of the modern age. In Kafka's world, human beings are caught in a bureaucratic web that they cannot control; they live in a nightmare society dominated by oppressive, cruel, and corrupt officials and amoral torturers—a world where power is exercised without limits and traditional values and ordinary logic do not operate. In *The Trial*, for example, the hero is arrested and eventually executed without knowing why. In these observations, Kafka proved a prophet of the emerging totalitarian state. (Kafka's three sisters perished in the Holocaust.)

Kafka expressed the feelings of alienation and isolation that characterize the modern individual; he explored life's dreads and absurdities, offering no solutions or consolation. In Kafka's works people are defeated and unable to comprehend the irrational forces that contribute to their destruction. The mind yearns for coherence but, Kafka tells us, uncertainty, if not chaos, governs human relationships. We can neither be certain of our own identities or of the world we encounter, for human beings are the playthings of forces too unfathomable to comprehend, too irrational to master.

Before World War I, German writer Thomas Mann (1875–1955) had earned a reputation for his short stories and novels, particularly *Buddenbrooks* (1901), which portrayed the decline of a prosperous bourgeois family. In the *Magic Mountain* (1924), Mann reflected on the decomposition of bourgeois European civilization. The setting for the story is a Swiss sanitarium, whose patients, drawn from several European lands, suffer from tuberculosis. The sanitarium symbolizes Europe, and it is the European psyche that is diseased. The *Magic Mountain* raised, but did not resolve, crucial questions. Was the epoch of rational-humanist culture drawing to a close? Did Europeans welcome their spiritual illness in the same way that some of the patients in the sanitarium had a will-to-illness? How could Europe rescue itself from decadence?

Many writers, shattered by World War I, disgusted by fascism's growing strength, and moved by the terrible suffering of the Depression, became committed to social and political causes. Erich Maria Remarque's *All Quiet on the Western Front* (1929) was one of many antiwar novels. In *The Grapes of Wrath* (1939), John Steinbeck captured the suffering of American farmers driven from their land by the Dust Bowl and foreclosure during the Depression. George Orwell's *Road to Wigan Pier* (1937) recorded the bleak lives of English coal miners. Few issues stirred the conscience of intellectuals as did the Spanish Civil War, and many of them volunteered to fight with the Spanish Republicans against the fascists. Ernest Hemingway's *For Whom the Bell Tolls* (1940) expressed the sentiments of these thinkers. In *Mario and the Magician* (1930), Thomas Mann explicitly attacked fascism, and implied that it would have to be resisted by arms.

The new directions taken in art before World War I—abstractionism and expressionism—continued in the postwar decades. Picasso, Mondrian, Kandinsky, Matisse, Rouault, Braque, Modigliani, and other masters continued to refine their styles. In addition, new art trends emerged that mirrored the trauma of a generation that had experienced the war and lost its faith in Europe's moral and intellectual values.

In 1915 in Zurich, artists and writers founded a movement called Dada to express their revulsion against the war and the civilization that spawned it. From neutral Switzerland, the movement spread to Germany and Paris. Dada shared in the postwar mood of disorientation and despair. Dadaists viewed life as essentially absurd (Dada is a nonsense term) and cultivated indifference. "The acts of life have no beginning or end. Everything happens in a completely idiotic way,"[19] declared the poet Tristan Tzara, one of Dada's founders and its chief spokesman. Dadaists expressed contempt for artistic and literary standards and rejected both God and reason. "Through reason man becomes a tragic and ugly figure," said one Dadaist; "beauty is dead," said another. Tzara declared:

Salvador Dali (1904–1989): The Persistence of Memory, 1931.   Famous for his explorations of subconscious imagery, this Spanish surrealist painter brought images from his subconscious mind by inducing hallucinatory states through a process he called "paranoiac critical." Oil on canvas, 9½ × 13 in. (*Collection, The Museum of Modern Art, New York. Given anonymously.*)

> *What good did the theories of the philosophers do us? Did they help us to take a single step forward or backward? . . . We have had enough of the intelligent movements that have stretched beyond measure our credulity in the benefits of science. What we want now is spontaneity because everything that issues freely from ourselves, without the intervention of speculative ideas, represents us.*[20]

For Dadaists the world was nonsensical and reality disordered; hence they offered no solutions to anything. "Like everything in life, Dada is useless,"[21] said Tzara. Despite their nihilistic aims and "calculated irrationality," however, Dadaist artists, such as Marcel Duchamp, were innovative and creative.

Dada ended as a formal movement in 1924 and was succeeded by surrealism. Surrealists inherited from Dada a contempt for reason; they stressed fantasy and made use of Freudian insights and symbols in their art to reproduce the raw state of the unconscious and to arrive at truths beyond reason's grasp. In their attempt to break through the constraints of rationality in order to reach a higher reality—that is, a "Surreality"—leading surrealists like Max Ernst (1891–1976), Salvador Dali (1904–1989), and Joan Miró (1893–1983) produced works of undeniable artistic merit.

Artists, like writers, expressed a social conscience. George Grosz combined a Dadaist sense of life's meaninglessness with a new realism to depict the moral degeneration of middle-class German society. In *After the Questioning* (1935), Grosz, then living in the United States, dramatized Nazi brutality; in *The End of the World* (1936) he expressed his fear of another impending world war. Still another German artist, Käthe Kollwitz, showed a deep compassion for the sufferer—the unemployed, the hungry, the ill, the politically oppressed. William Gropper's *Migration* (1932) dramatized the suffering of the same dispossessed farmers described in Steinbeck's novel *The Grapes of Wrath*. Philip Evergood, in *Don't Cry Mother* (1938–1944), portrayed the apathy of starving children and their mother's terrible helplessness.

In his etchings of maimed, dying, and dead soldiers, German artist Otto Dix produced a powerful visual indictment of the Great War's cruelty and suffering. In *Guernica* (1937), Picasso memorialized the Spanish village decimated by saturation bombing during the Spanish Civil War. In the *White Crucifixion* (1938), Marc Chagall, a Russian-born Jew who had settled in Paris, depicted the terror and flight of Jews in Nazi Germany.

Communism: "The God That Failed"

The economic misery of the Depression and the rise of fascist barbarism led many intellectuals to find a new hope, even a secular faith, in communism. They praised the Soviet Union for supplanting capitalist greed with socialist cooperation, for replacing a haphazard economic system marred by repeated depressions with one based on planned production, and for providing employment for everyone when joblessness was endemic in capitalist lands. American literary critic Edmund Wilson said that in the Soviet Union, one felt at the "moral top of the world where the light never really goes out." To these intellectuals, it seemed that in the Soviet Union a vigorous and healthy civilization was emerging and that only communism could stem the tide of fascism. For many, however, the attraction was short-lived. Sickened by Stalin's purges and terror, the denial of individual freedom, and the suppression of truth, they came to view the Soviet Union as another totalitarian state and communism as another "god that failed."

One such intellectual was Arthur Koestler (1905–1983). Born in Budapest of Jewish ancestry and educated in Vienna, Koestler worked as a correspondent for a leading Berlin newspaper chain. He joined the Communist party at the very end of 1931 because he "lived in a disintegrating society thirsting for faith," was moved by the Depression, and saw communism as the "only force capable of resisting the onrush of the primitive [Nazi] horde."[22] Koestler visited the Soviet Union in 1933, experiencing firsthand both the starvation brought on by forced collectivization and the propaganda that grotesquely misrepresented life in Western lands. While his faith was shaken, he did not break with the party until 1938, in response to Stalin's liquidations.

In *Darkness at Noon* (1941), Koestler explored the attitudes of the Old Bolsheviks who were imprisoned, tortured, and executed by Stalin. These dedicated Communists had served the party faithfully, but Stalin, fearful of opposition, hating intellectuals, and driven by megalomania, denounced them as enemies of the people. In *Darkness at Noon,* the leading character, the imprisoned Rubashov, is a composite of the Old Bolsheviks. Although innocent, and without being tortured, Rubashov publicly confesses to political crimes that he never committed.

Rubashov is aware of the suffering that the party has brought to the Russian people:

> . . . *in the interests of a just distribution of land we deliberately let die of starvation about five million farmers and their families in one year. . . . [to liberate] human beings from the shackles of industrial exploitation . . . we sent about ten million people to do forced labour in the Arctic regions . . . under conditions similar to those of antique galley slaves. . . .*[23]

Nevertheless Rubashov remains the party's faithful servant; true believers do not easily break with their faith. By confessing, Rubashov performs his last service for the revolution: for the true believer, everything—truth, justice, and the sanctity of the individual—are properly sacrificed to the party.

Reaffirming the Christian Philosophy of History

By calling into question core liberal beliefs—the essential goodness of human nature, the primacy of reason, the efficacy of science, and the inevitability of progress—the Great War led some thinkers to find in Christianity an alternative view of the human experience and the crisis of the twentieth century. Christian thinkers, including Karl Barth, Paul Tillich, Reinhold Niebuhr, and T. S. Eliot, asserted the reality of evil in human nature and assailed liberals and Marxists for postulating a purely rational and secular philosophy of history and for anticipating an ideal society within the realm of historical time. In the Christian conception of history as a clash between human will and God's will, these thinkers found an intelligible explanation for the tragedies of the twentieth century. In 1933, Christopher Dawson, an English Catholic thinker, wrote: "If our civilization is to recover its vitality, or even to survive, it must cease to neglect its spiritual roots and must realize that religion is not a matter of personal sentiment which has nothing to do with the objective realities of society, but is, on the contrary, the very heart of social life and the root of every living culture."[24]

Reaffirming the Ideals of Reason and Freedom

Several thinkers tried to reaffirm the ideals of rationality and freedom that had been trampled on by totalitarian movements. In *The Treason of the Intel-*

lectuals (1927), Julien Benda (1867–1956), a French cultural critic of Jewish background, castigated intellectuals for intensifying hatred between nations, classes, and political factions. "Our age is indeed the age of the *intellectual organization of political hatreds*,"[25] he wrote. These intellectuals, said Benda, do not pursue justice or truth, but proclaim that "even if our country is wrong, we must think of it in the right." They scorn outsiders, extol harshness and action, and proclaim the superiority of instinct and will to intelligence; or they "assert that the intelligence to be venerated is that which limits its activities within the bounds of national interest." The logical end of this xenophobia, said Benda, "is the organized slaughter of nations and classes."[26]

José Ortega y Gasset (1883–1955), descendant of a noble Spanish family and a professor of philosophy, gained international recognition with the publication of *Revolt of the Masses* (1930). Ortega held that European civilization, the product of a creative elite, was degenerating into barbarism because of the growing power of the masses, who lack the mental discipline and commitment to reason to preserve Europe's intellectual and cultural traditions. Ortega did not equate the masses with the working class and the elite with the nobility; it was an attitude of mind, not a class affiliation, that distinguished the "mass-man" from the elite. The mass-man, said Ortega, has a commonplace mind and does not set high standards for himself. Faced with a problem, he "is satisfied with thinking the first thing he finds in his head," and "crushes . . . everything that is different, everything that is excellent, individual, qualified, and select. Anybody who is not like everybody, who does not think like everybody, runs the risk of being eliminated."[27] Such intellectually vulgar people, declared Ortega, cannot understand or preserve the processes of civilization. The fascists exemplify this revolt of the masses:

> *Under fascism there appears for the first time in Europe a type of man who does not want to give reasons or to be right, but simply shows himself resolved to impose his opinions. This is the new thing: the right not to be reasonable, the "reason of unreason." Hence I see the most palpable manifestation of the new mentality of the masses, due to their having decided to rule society without the capacity for doing so.*[28]

The mass-man, said Ortega, does not respect the tradition of reason; he does not enter into rational dialogue with others or defend his opinions logically. The mass-man rejects reason and glorifies violence—the ultimate expression of barbarism. If European civilization is to be rescued from fascism and communism, said Ortega, the elite must sustain civilized values and provide leadership for the masses.

Ernst Cassirer (1874–1945), a German philosopher of Jewish lineage, emigrated after Hitler came to power, eventually settling in the United States. A staunch defender of the Enlightenment tradition, Cassirer in 1932, just prior to Hitler's triumph, wrote: "More than ever before, it seems to me, the time is again ripe for applying . . . self-criticism to the present age, for holding up to it that bright clear mirror fashioned by the Enlightenment. . . . The age which venerated reason and science as man's highest faculty cannot and must not be lost even for us."[29]

In his last work, *The Myth of the State* (1946), Cassirer described Nazism as the triumph of mythical thinking over reason. The Nazis, said Cassirer, cleverly manufactured myths—of the race, the leader, the party, the state—that disoriented the intellect. Germans who embraced these myths surrendered their capacity for independent judgment, leaving themselves vulnerable to manipulation by the Nazi leadership. To contain the destructive powers of political myths, Cassirer urged strengthening the rational-humanist tradition, and called for the critical study of political myths, for "in order to fight an enemy you must know him. . . . We should carefully study the origin, the structure, the methods, and the technique of the political myths. We should see the adversary face to face in order to know how to combat him."[30]

Existentialism

The philosophic movement that best exemplified the anxiety and uncertainty of Europe in an era of world wars was existentialism. Like writers and artists, existentialist philosophers were responding to a European civilization that seemed to be in the throes of dissolution. What route should people take in a world where old values and certainties had dissolved, where universal truth was rejected and God's existence was denied? How could people cope in a society where they were menaced by technology, manipulated by impersonal bureaucracies, and overwhelmed by feelings of anxiety? If the universe is devoid of any overarching meaning, what meaning could one give to one's own life? These questions were at the crux of existentialist philosophy.

Existentialism does not lend itself to a single definition, for its principal theorists did not adhere to a common body of doctrines. For example, some existentialists were atheists, like Jean Paul Sartre, or omitted God from their thought, like Martin Heidegger; others, like Karl Jaspers, believed in God but not in Christian doctrines; still others, like Gabriel Marcel and Nikolai Berdyaev, were Christians, and Martin Buber was a believing Jew. Perhaps the essence of existentialism appears in the following principles, although not all existentialists would subscribe to each point or agree with the way it is expressed.

1. Reality defies ultimate comprehension; there are no timeless truths that exist independently of and prior to the individual human being.
2. Reason alone is an inadequate guide to living, for people are more than thinking subjects who approach the world through critical analysis. They are also feeling and willing beings who must participate fully in life, who must experience existence directly, actively, passionately. Only in this way does one live wholly and authentically.
3. Thought must not merely be abstract speculation, but must have a bearing on life; it must be translated into deeds.

Jean Paul Sartre and Simone de Beauvoir, 1956. The major philosophical movement in the twentieth century is existentialism. Sartre and de Beauvoir were two of its first exponents. (*AP/Wide World Photos*)

4. Human nature is problematic and paradoxical, not fixed or constant; each person is like no other. Self-realization comes when one affirms one's own uniqueness; one becomes less than human when one permits one's life to be determined by a mental outlook—a set of rules and values—imposed by others.

5. We are alone. The universe is indifferent to our expectations and needs, and death is ever stalking us.

6. We are free. It is in the act of choosing freely from among different possibilities that the individual shapes an authentic existence. There is a dynamic quality to human existence; the individual has the potential to become more than he or she is.

The Modern Predicament

The process of fragmentation that had showed itself in European thought and the arts at the end of the nineteenth century accelerated after World War I.

Increasingly, philosophers, writers, and artists expressed disillusionment with the rational-humanist tradition of the Enlightenment. They no longer shared the Enlightenment's confidence in either reason's capabilities or human goodness, and they viewed perpetual progress as an illusion.

For some thinkers the crucial problem was the great change in the European understanding of truth. Since the rise of philosophy in ancient Greece, Western thinkers had believed in the existence of objective, universal truths—truths that were inherent in nature and applied to all peoples at all times. (Christianity, of course, also taught the reality of truth as revealed by God.) It was held that such truths—the natural rights of the individual, for example—could be apprehended by the intellect and could serve as a standard for individual aspirations and social life. The recognition of these universal principles, it was believed, compels people to measure the world of the here and now in the light of rational and universal norms and to institute appropriate reforms. It was the task of philosophy to reconcile human existence with the objective order.

During the nineteenth century, the existence of universal truth came into doubt. A growing historical consciousness led some thinkers to maintain that what people considered truth was merely a reflection of their culture at a given stage in history, their perception of things at a specific point in the evolution of human consciousness. These thinkers, called historicists, held that universal truths were not woven into the fabric of nature. There were no natural rights of life, liberty, and property that constituted the individual's birthright; there were no standards of justice or equality inherent in nature and ascertainable by reason. It was people, said historicists, who elevated the beliefs and values of an age to the status of objective truth. This radical break with the traditional attitude toward truth contributed substantially to the crisis of European consciousness that marked the first half of the twentieth century. Traditional values and beliefs, either those inherited from the Enlightenment or those taught by Christianity, no longer gave Europeans a sense of certainty and security; people were left without a normative order to serve as a guide to living.

By the early twentieth century, the attitude of Westerners toward reason had undergone a radical transformation. Some thinkers who placed their hopes in the rational tradition of the Enlightenment were distressed by reason's inability to resolve the tensions and conflicts of modern industrial society. Moreover, the growing recognition of the nonrational—of human actions determined by hidden impulses—led people to doubt that reason plays the dominant role in human behavior. Other thinkers viewed the problem of reason differently. They reviled an attitude of mind that found no room for Christianity because its teachings did not pass the test of reason and science. Or they attacked reason for fashioning a technological and bureaucratic society that devalued and crushed human passions and stifled individuality; these thinkers insisted that human beings cannot fulfill their potential, cannot live wholly, if their feelings are denied. They agreed with D. H. Lawrence's critique of rationalism: "The attribution of rationality to human nature, instead of enriching it, now seems to me to have impoverished it. It ignored certain powerful and valuable springs of feeling. Some of the spontaneous, irrational outbursts of human nature can have a sort of value from which our schematism was cut off."[31]

While many thinkers focused on reason's limitations, others, particularly existentialists, pointed out that reason was a double-edged sword; it could demean as well as ennoble the individual. These thinkers attacked all theories that subordinated the individual to a rigid system. They denounced positivism for reducing human personality to psychological laws, and Marxism for making social class a higher reality than the individual. They rebelled against political collectivization that regulated individuals lives according to the needs of the corporate state, and they assailed modern technology and bureaucracy, creations of the rational mind, for fashioning a social order that devalued and depersonalized the individual, denying people an opportunity for independent growth and a richer existence. These thinkers held that modern industrial society, in its drive for efficiency and uniformity, deprived people of their uniqueness and reduced flesh-and-blood human beings to cogs in a mechanical system.

Responding to these critiques of reason, others maintained that it was necessary to reaffirm the rational tradition first proclaimed by the Greeks and given its modern expression by the Enlightenment. Reason, they said, was indispensable to civilization. What these thinkers advocated was broadening the scope of reason in order to accommodate the insights into human nature advanced by the romantics, Nietzsche, Freud, modernist writers and artists, and others who explored the world of feelings, will, and the unconscious.

In the decades shaped by world wars and totalitarianism, intellectuals raised questions that went to the heart of the dilemma of modern life. How can civilized life be safeguarded against human irrationality, particularly when it is channeled into political ideologies that idolize the state, the leader, the party, or the race? How can individual human personality be rescued from a relentless rationalism that organizes the individual as it would any material object? Do the values associated with the Enlightenment provide a sound basis around which to integrate society? Can the individual find meaning in what many now regarded as a meaningless universe? World War II gave these questions a special poignancy.

Notes

1. Quoted in Zeev Sternhill, "Fascist Ideology," in Walter Laqueur, *Fascism: A Reader's Guide* (Berkeley: University of California Press, 1976), p. 338.

2. Quoted in Max Gallo, *Mussolini's Italy* (New York: Macmillan, 1973), p. 218.

3. Quoted in Joachim C. Fest, *Hitler,* trans. by Richard and Clara Winston (New York: Harcourt Brace Jovanovich, 1974), p. 162.

4. *Hitler's Secret Conversations, 1941–1944,* with an introductory essay by H. R. Trevor Roper (New York: Farrar, Straus & Young, 1953), p. 28.

5. Quoted in Lucy S. Dawidowicz, *The War Against the Jews 1933–1945* (New York: Holt, Rinehart and Winston, 1975), p. 21.

6. Adolf Hitler, *Mein Kampf* (Boston: Houghton Mifflin, 1962), p. 107.
7. Quoted in Helmut Krausnick, et al., *Anatomy of the SS State* (London: Collins, 1968), p. 128.
8. *Hitler's Secret Conversations,* p. 6.
9. Quoted in Hermann Graml, et al., *The German Resistance to Hitler* (Berkeley: University of California Press, 1970), p. 206.
10. Quoted in T. L. Jarman, *The Rise and Fall of Nazi Germany* (New York: New York University Press, 1956), p. 182.
11. Quoted in Karl Dietrich Bracher, *The German Dictatorship,* trans. by Jean Steinberg (New York: Praeger, 1970), p. 268.
12. Quoted in Fest, *Hitler,* p. 532.
13. Quoted in Hans Kohn, "The Crisis in European Thought and Culture," in Jack J. Roth, ed., *World War I: A Turning Point in Modern History* (New York: Knopf, 1967), p. 28.
14. Quoted in Franklin L. Baumer, "Twentieth-Century Version of the Apocalypse," *Cahiers d'Histoire Mondiale* (*Journal of World History*) 1, no. 3 (January 1954): 624.
15. Ibid.
16. T. S. Eliot, "The Wasteland," *Collected Poems, 1909–1962* (New York: Harcourt, Brace, 1970), p. 67.
17. Carl Gustav Jung, *Modern Man in Search of a Soul,* trans. by W. S. Dell and Cary F. Baynes (New York: Harcourt, Brace, 1933), pp. 231, 234–235.
18. Johan Huizinga, *In the Shadow of*

Tomorrow (London: Heinemann, 1936), pp. 1–3.
19. Tristan Tzara, "Lecture on Dada (1922)," trans. by Ralph Mannheim, in Robert Motherwell, ed., *The Dada Painters and Poets* (New York: Witterborn, Schultz, 1951), p. 250.
20. Ibid., p. 248.
21. Ibid., p. 251.
22. Richard Crossman, ed., *The God That Failed* (New York: Bantam Books, 1951), pp. 15, 21.
23. Arthur Koestler, *Darkness at Noon* (New York: Macmillan, 1941), pp. 158–159.
24. Quoted in C. T. McIntire, ed., *God, History, and Historians* (New York: Oxford University Press, 1977), p. 9.
25. Julien Benda, *The Betrayal of the Intellectuals,* trans. Richard Aldington (Boston: Beacon Press, 1955), p. 21.
26. Quotes in this paragraph are from ibid., pp. 38, 122, and 162.
27. José Ortega y Gasset, *The Revolt of the Masses* (New York: W. W. Norton, 1957), pp. 63, 18.
28. Ibid., p. 73.
29. Ernst Cassirer, *The Philosophy of the Enlightenment,* trans. by Fritz C. A. Koelln and James P. Pettegrove (Boston: Beacon Press, 1955), pp. xi–xii.
30. Ernst Cassirer, *The Myth of the State* (New Haven: Yale University Press, 1946), p. 296.
31. Quoted in Anthony Arblaster, *The Rise and Decline of Western Liberalism* (Oxford: Basil Blackwell, 1984), p. 81.

Suggested Reading

Allen, William Sheridan, *The Nazi Seizure of Power* (1965). An illuminating study of how the people of a small German town reacted to Nazism during the years 1930–1935.
Bissel, Richard, ed., *Life in the Third Reich* (1987). Essays dealing with various aspects of life in Hitler's Germany; good overviews.
Blackham, H. J., *Six Existentialist Thinkers* (1952). Useful analyses of Kier-

kegaard, Nietzsche, Jaspers, Marcel, Heidegger, and Jean Paul Sartre.
———, ed., *Reality, Man and Existence* (1965). Essential works of existentialism.
Bracher, Karl Dietrich, *The German Dictatorship* (1970). A highly regarded analysis of all phases of the Nazi state.
Bullock, Alan, *Hitler: A Study in Tyranny* (1964). An excellent biography.

Cassels, Alan, *Fascist Italy* (1968). A clearly written introduction.

Fest, Joachim C., *Hitler* (1974). An excellent biography.

Jackel, Eberhard, *Hitler's Weltanschauung* (1972). An analysis of Hitler's world-view.

Laqueur, Walter, ed., *Fascism: A Reader's Guide* (1976). A superb collection of essays.

Mack Smith, Denis, *Mussolini* (1982). By a leading historian of modern Italy.

Macquarrie, John, *Existentialism* (1972). A lucid discussion of existentialism.

Paxton, Robert O., *Europe in the Twentieth Century* (1975). A first-rate text with an excellent bibliography.

Spielvogel, Jackson J., *Hitler and Nazi Germany* (1988). Clearly written, up-to-date survey.

Wagar, W. Warren, ed., *European Thought Since 1914* (1968). A valuable collection of sources.

Review Questions

1. How did fascist principles "stand for the sheer, categorical, definitive antithesis to the world of democracy . . . to the world which still abides by the fundamental principles laid down in 1789"?
2. Why did some Italians support Benito Mussolini? In what ways was Mussolini less effective than Adolf Hitler in establishing a totalitarian state?
3. How was Hitler's outlook shaped by his experiences in Vienna, and what were his attitudes toward democracy, the masses, war, the Jews, propaganda?
4. How did the Nazis extend their control over Germany?
5. How did Nazism conflict with the core values of Christianity? What was the general policy of the Nazis toward the churches? Why did the German churches generally fail to take a stand against the Nazi regime?
6. By 1939, most Germans were enthusiastic about the Nazi regime. Explain this statement.
7. After World War I, in country after country, parliamentary democracy collapsed and authoritarian leaders came to power. Explain.
8. How did the United States, Britain, and France try to cope with the Great Depression?
9. What factors contributed to a mood of pessimism in the period after World War I?
10. Better than any other novelist of his time, Franz Kafka grasped the dilemma of the modern age. Discuss this statement. Do his insights still apply today?
11. In *The Magic Mountain,* Thomas Mann reflected on the decomposition of bourgeois European civilization. Discuss this statement.
12. In what ways were both Dada and surrealism an expression of the times?
13. Why were many intellectuals attracted to communism in the 1930s?
14. What did Ortega y Gasset mean by the "mass-man"? What dangers were presented by the mass-man?
15. Why did Julien Benda entitle his book *The Treason of the Intellectuals?*
16. What was Ernst Cassirer's attitude toward the Enlightenment? How did he interpret Nazism?
17. What were some of the conditions that gave rise to existentialism? What are the basic principles of existentialism?

Chapter ✿ 20

World War II:
Western Civilization
in the Balance

From the early days of his political career, Hitler dreamed of forging a vast German empire in central and eastern Europe. He believed that only by waging a war of conquest against Russia could the German nation gain the living space and security it required and, as a superior race, deserved. War was an essential component of National Socialist ideology, and it accorded with Hitler's temperament. For the former corporal from the trenches, the Great War had never ended. Hitler aspired to political power because he wanted to mobilize the material and human resources of the German nation for war and conquest. Although historians may debate the question of responsibility for World War I, few would deny that World War II was Hitler's war: "It appears to be an almost incontrovertible fact that the Second World War was brought on by the actions of the Hitler government, that these actions were the expression of a policy laid down well in advance in *Mein Kampf*, and that this war could have been averted up until the last moment if the German government had so wished."[1] Western statesmen had sufficient warnings that Hitler was a threat to peace and the essential values of Western civilization, but they failed to rally their people and take a stand until Germany had greatly increased its capacity to wage aggressive war. ✿

The Road to War

Hitler's Foreign Policy Aims

After consolidating his power and mobilizing the nation, Hitler moved to implement his foreign-policy objectives: the destruction of the Versailles Treaty, the conquest and colonization of eastern Europe, and the domination and exploitation of racial inferiors. In foreign affairs, Hitler demonstrated that same blend of opportunism and singleness of purpose that had brought him to power. Here, too, he made use of propaganda to undermine his opponents' will to resist. The Nazi propaganda machine, which had effectively won the minds of the German people, became an instrument of foreign policy. To promote social and political disorientation in other lands, the Nazis propagated anti-Semitism on a worldwide basis; Nazi propagandists also tried to draw international support for Hitler as Europe's best defense against the Soviet Union and Bolshevism.

As Hitler anticipated, the British and the French backed down when faced with his violations of the Versailles Treaty and threats of war. Haunted by the memory of World War I, Britain and France went to great lengths to avoid another catastrophe—a policy that had the overwhelming support of public opinion. Because Britain believed that Germany had been treated too severely by the Versailles Treaty and knew that its own military forces were woefully unprepared for war, from 1933 to 1939 the British were amenable to making concessions to Hitler. Although France had the strongest army on the Continent, it was prepared to fight only a defensive war—the reverse of its World War I strategy. France built immense fortifications, called the Maginot Line, to protect its borders from a German invasion, but it lacked a mobile striking force that could punish an aggressive Germany. The United States, concerned with the problems of the Great Depression and standing aloof from Europe's troubles, did nothing to strengthen the resolve of France and Britain. Since both France and Britain feared and mistrusted the Soviet Union, the grand alliance of World War I was not renewed. There was an added factor: suffering from a failure of leadership and a political and economic unrest that eroded national unity, France was experiencing a decline in morale and a loss of nerve. It consistently turned to Britain for direction.

British statesmen championed a policy of appeasement—giving in to Germany in the hope that a satisfied Hitler would not drag Europe through another world war. British policy rested on the disastrous illusion that Hitler, like his Weimar predecessors, sought peaceful revision of the Versailles Treaty and that he could be contained through concessions. Some British appeasers, accepting the view that Nazi propaganda cleverly propagated and exploited, also regarded Hitler as a defender of European civilization and the capitalist economic order against Soviet communism. Appeasement, which in the end was capitulation to blackmail, failed. Germany grew stronger and the German people more devoted to the Fuehrer. Hitler did not moderate his ambitions, and the appeasers did not avert war.

Breakdown of Peace

To realize his foreign-policy aims, Hitler required a formidable military machine; Germany had to rearm, despite the hindrances of the Treaty of Versailles. It had limited the size of the German army to 100,000 volunteers; had restricted the navy's size; had forbidden the production of military aircraft, heavy artillery, and tanks; and had disbanded the general staff. In March 1935, Hitler declared that Germany was no longer bound by the Versailles Treaty. Germany would restore conscription, build an air force (which it had been doing secretly), and strengthen its navy. France and Britain offered no resistance.

A decisive event in the breakdown of peace was Italy's invasion of Ethiopia in October 1935. The League of Nations called for economic sanctions against Italy, and most League members restricted trade with the aggressor. But Italy continued to receive oil, particularly from American suppliers, and neither Britain nor France sought to restrain Italy. Mussolini's subjugation of Ethiopia discredited the League of Nations, which had already been weakened by its failure to deal effectively with Japan's invasion of the mineral-rich Chinese province of Manchuria in 1931. The fall of Ethiopia, like that of Manchuria, showed that the League was reluctant to use force to resist aggression.

On March 7, 1936, Hitler marched troops into the Rhineland, violating the Versailles Treaty, which called for the demilitarization of these German border lands. German generals had cautioned Hitler that such a move would provoke a French invasion of Germany, which the German army could not repulse. But Hitler gambled that France and Britain, lacking the will to fight, would take no action.

Hitler had correctly assessed the Anglo-French mood. Britain was not greatly alarmed by the remilitarization of the Rhineland. Hitler, after all, was not expanding the borders of Germany, but was only sending soldiers to Germany's frontier. Such a move, reasoned British officials, did not warrant risking a war, and France would not act alone. Moreover, the French general staff overestimated German military strength and thought only of defending French soil from a German attack, not of initiating a strike against Germany.

The Spanish Civil War of 1936–1939 was another victory for fascism. Nazi Germany and Fascist Italy aided Franco; the Soviet Union supplied the Spanish Republic. By October 1937, some 60,000 Italian "volunteers" were fighting in Spain. Hitler sent from 5,000 to 6,000 men and hundreds of planes, which proved decisive in winning the war. By comparison, the Soviet Union's aid was meager.

Without considerable help from France, the Spanish Republic was doomed, but Prime Minister Léon Blum feared that French intervention might lead to war with Germany. Moreover, supplying the republic would have dangerous consequences at home, because French rightists were sympathetic to Franco's conservative-clerical authoritarianism. In 1939 the republic fell, and Franco established a dictatorship. The Spanish Civil War provided Germany with an opportunity to test weapons and pilots and demonstrated again that France and Britain lacked the determination to fight fascism.

One of Hitler's aims was incorporation of Austria into the Third Reich, but the Treaty of Versailles had expressly prohibited the union of the two German-speaking countries. In March 1938, under the pretext of preventing violence, Hitler ordered his troops into Austria, which—with the enthusiastic support of the Austrians—was made a province of the German Reich.

Hitler obtained Austria merely by threatening force. Another threat would give him the Sudetenland of Czechoslovakia. Of the 3.5 million people living in the Sudetenland, some 2.8 million were ethnic Germans. Encouraged and instructed by Germany, the Sudeten Germans, led by Konrad Henlein, shrilly denounced the Czech government for "persecuting" its German minority and depriving it of its right to self-determination. The Sudeten Germans agitated for local autonomy and the right to profess the National Socialist ideology. Behind this demand was the goal of German annexation of the Sudetenland.

While negotiations between the Sudeten Germans and the Czech government proceeded, Hitler's propaganda machine accused the Czechs of hideous crimes against the German minority and warned of retribution. Hitler also ordered his generals to prepare for an invasion of Czechoslovakia. Fighting between Czechs and Sudeten Germans heightened the tensions. Seeking to preserve peace, Prime Minister Neville Chamberlain (1869–1940) of Britain offered to confer with Hitler, who then extended an invitation.

Britain and France held somewhat different positions toward Czechoslovakia—the only democracy in eastern Europe. In 1924, France and Czechoslovakia had concluded an agreement of mutual assistance in the event either was attacked by Germany. Czechoslovakia had a similar agreement with Russia, but with the provision that Russian assistance depended on France's first fulfilling the terms of its agreement. Britain had no commitment to Czechoslovakia. Some of the British officials, swallowing Hitler's propaganda, believed that the Sudeten Germans were indeed a suppressed minority entitled to self-determination, and that the Sudetenland, like Austria, was not worth a war that could destroy Western civilization. Hitler, they said, only wanted to incorporate Germans living outside of Germany; he was only carrying the principle of self-determination to its logical conclusion. Once these Germans lived under the German flag, argued these British officials, Hitler would be satisfied. In any case, Britain's failure to rearm between 1933 and 1938 weakened its position. The British chiefs of staff believed that the nation was not prepared to fight, that it was necessary to sacrifice Czechoslovakia to buy time.

Czechoslovakia's fate was decided at the Munich Conference (September 1938), attended by Chamberlain, Hitler, Mussolini, and Prime Minister Édouard Daladier (1884–1970) of France. The Munich Agreement gave the Sudetenland to Germany. Both Chamberlain and Daladier were showered with praise by the people of Britain and France for keeping the peace.

Map 20.1   World War II: The European Theater   ▶

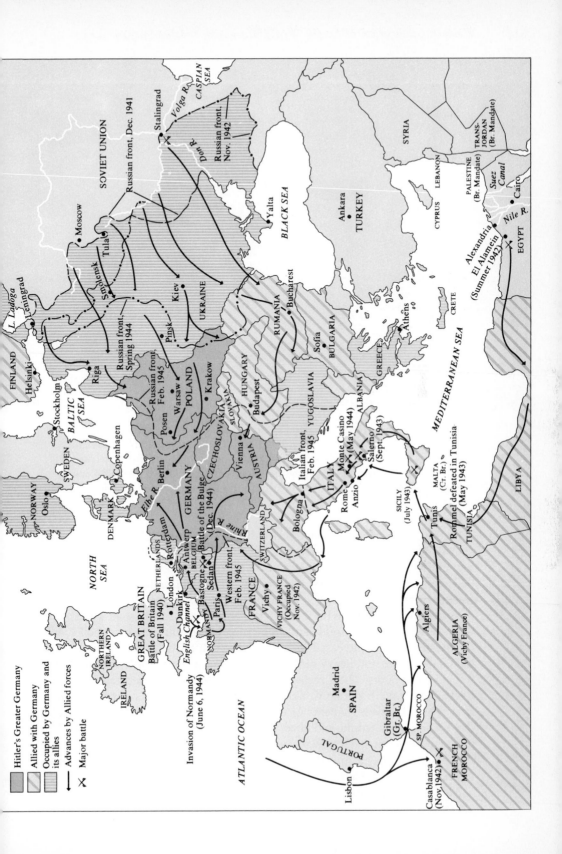

Legend (top left):

- Hitler's Greater Germany
- Allied with Germany
- Occupied by Germany and its allies
- ↓ Advances by Allied forces
- ✕ Major battle

Map labels:

ATLANTIC OCEAN

NORTH SEA

SOVIET UNION

L. Ladoga
FINLAND
Leningrad
Helsinki
SWEDEN
Stockholm
NORWAY
Oslo
BALTIC SEA
Riga

Moscow
Tula
Smolensk
Kiev
UKRAINE
Pinsk

Volga R.
CASPIAN SEA
Stalingrad ✕
Don R.
Russian front, Dec. 1941
Russian front, Nov. 1942

Russian front, Spring 1944
Russian front, Feb. 1945

BLACK SEA
Yalta
Ankara
TURKEY
CYPRUS
SYRIA
LEBANON
PALESTINE (Br. Mandate)
TRANS-JORDAN (Br. Mandate)
Suez Canal
Cairo
Nile R.
EGYPT
Alexandria
El Alamein (Summer 1942) ✕

Copenhagen
DENMARK
Elbe R.
Berlin
GERMANY
CZECHOSLOVAKIA
Posen
Warsaw
POLAND
Krakow
SLOVAKIA
Vienna
AUSTRIA
HUNGARY
Budapest
RUMANIA
Bucharest
BULGARIA
Sofia
YUGOSLAVIA
ALBANIA
GREECE
Athens
CRETE

Rotterdam
NETHERLANDS
Antwerp
BELGIUM
London
GREAT BRITAIN
Battle of Britain (Fall 1940)
Dunkirk
English Channel
NORTHERN IRELAND
IRELAND
NORMANDY
Invasion of Normandy (June 6, 1944)
Bastogne ✕
Battle of the Bulge (Dec. 1944)
Sedan
Paris
FRANCE
Western front, Feb. 1945
Rhine R.
SWITZERLAND
Vichy
VICHY FRANCE (Occupied Nov. 1942)

Italian front, Feb. 1945
ITALY
Monte Casino ✕ (May 1944)
Rome
Anzio
Salerno (Sept. 1943) ✕
Bologna
MEDITERRANEAN SEA
MALTA (Gr. Br.)
SICILY (July 1943)
Tunis ✕
Rommel defeated in Tunisia (May 1943)
TUNISIA
LIBYA
Algiers
ALGERIA (Vichy France)
SP. MOROCCO
FRENCH MOROCCO
Casablanca (Nov. 1942) ✕

Madrid
SPAIN
PORTUGAL
Lisbon
Gibraltar (Gr. Br.)

Munich Conference, 1938. England's Prime Minister Neville Chamberlain (left) was lauded as a keeper of the peace after the Munich Conference; the praise was short-lived. Adolf Hitler (middle) used the following months to undermine the territorial integrity of Czechoslovakia. With the end of Czech independence, Hitler's plans for European domination could not be denied. (*Imperial War Museum, London*)

Critics of Chamberlain have insisted that the Munich Agreement was an enormous blunder and tragedy. Chamberlain, they say, was a fool to believe that Hitler, who sought domination over Europe, could be bought off with the Sudetenland. Hitler regarded concessions by Britain and France as signs of weakness; they only increased his appetite for more territory. Second, argue the critics, it would have been better to fight Hitler in 1938 than a year later when war actually did break out. To be sure, in the year following the Munich Agreement, Britain increased its military arsenal, but so did Germany, which built submarines and heavy tanks, strengthened western border defenses, and trained more pilots. The Czechs had a sizable number of good tanks, and the Czech people were willing to fight to preserve their nation's territorial integrity. While the main elements of the German army were battling the Czechs, the French, who could mobilize a hundred divisions, could have broken through the German West Wall, which was defended by only five regular and four reserve divisions, invaded the Rhineland, and devastated German industrial centers in the Ruhr.

After the annexation of the Sudetenland, the Fuehrer plotted to extinguish Czechoslovakia's existence. He encouraged the Slovak minority in Czechoslovakia, led by a fascist priest, Josef Tiso, to demand complete separation. On the pretext of protecting the Slovak people's right of self-determination, Hitler ordered his troops to enter Prague. In March 1939, Czech independence came to an end.

The destruction of Czechoslovakia was of a different character from the remilitarization of the Rhineland, the Anschluss with Austria, and the annexation of the Sudetenland. In all these previous cases, Hitler could claim the right of self-determination, Woodrow Wilson's grand principle. The occupation of Prague and the end of Czech independence, though, showed that Hitler really sought European hegemony. Outraged statesmen now demanded that the Fuehrer be deterred from further aggression.

On May 22, 1939, Hitler and Mussolini entered into the Pact of Steel, promising mutual aid in the event of war. The following day, Hitler told his officers that Germany's real goal was the destruction of Poland. "Danzig is not the objective. It is a matter of expanding our living space in the east, of making our food supplies secure. . . . There is therefore no question of sparing Poland, and the decision remains to attack Poland at the first suitable opportunity."[2]

Britain, France, and the Soviet Union had been engaged in negotiations since April. The Soviet Union wanted a mutual assistance pact including joint military planning, and demanded bases in Poland and Rumania in preparation for a German attack. Britain was reluctant to endorse these demands, fearing that a mutual assistance pact with Russia might cause Hitler to embark on a mad adventure that would drag Britain into war. Moreover, Poland would not allow Russian troops on its soil, fearing Russian expansion.

At the same time, Russia was conducting secret talks with Nazi Germany. Unlike the Allies, Stalin could be tempted with territory that would serve as a buffer between Germany and Russia. Moreover, a treaty with Germany would give Russia time to strengthen its armed forces. On August 23, 1939, the two totalitarian states signed a nonaggression pact that stunned the world. A secret section of the pact called for the partition of Poland between the two parties and Russian control over Latvia and Estonia. By signing such an agreement with his enemy, Hitler had pulled off an extraordinary diplomatic coup: he blocked the Soviet Union, Britain, and France from duplicating their World War I grand alliance against Germany. The Nazi-Soviet Pact was the green light for an invasion of Poland, and at dawn on September 1, 1939, German troops crossed the frontier. When Germany did not respond to their demand for a halt to the invasion, Britain and France declared war.

The Nazi Blitzkrieg

Germany struck at Poland with speed and power. The German air force, the *Luftwaffe,* destroyed Polish planes on the ground, attacked tanks, pounded defense networks, and bombed Warsaw, terrorizing the population. Tanks opened up breaches in the Polish defenses, and mechanized columns overran the foot-marching Polish army, trapping large numbers of soldiers. The Polish high command could not cope with the incredible speed and coordination of German air and ground attacks. By September 8, the Germans had advanced to the outskirts of Warsaw. On September 17, Soviet troops invaded Poland from the east. On September 27, Poland surrendered. In less than a month the Nazi *blitzkrieg* (lightning war) had vanquished Poland.

The Fall of France

For Hitler the conquest of Poland was only the prelude to a German empire stretching from the Atlantic to the Urals. When weather conditions were right, he would unleash a great offensive in the west. In early April 1940, the Germans struck at Denmark and Norway. Denmark surrendered within hours. A British-French force tried to assist the Norwegians, but the landings, badly coordinated and lacking in air support, failed.

On May 10, 1940, Hitler launched his offensive in the west with an invasion of neutral Belgium, Holland, and Luxembourg. On May 14, after the Luftwaffe bombed Rotterdam, destroying the center of the city and killing many people, the Dutch surrendered. Meeting almost no resistance, German Panzer divisions had moved through the narrow mountain passes of Luxembourg and the dense Forest of Ardennes in southern Belgium. On May 12, German units were on French soil near Sedan. Thinking that the Forest of Ardennes could not be penetrated by a major German force, the French had only lightly fortified the western extension of the Maginot Line. The Germans were racing across northern France to the sea, which they reached on May 20, cutting the Anglo-French forces in two.

The Germans now sought to surround and annihilate the Allied forces converging on the French seaport of Dunkirk, the last port of escape. But inexplicably Hitler called off his tanks just as they prepared to take Dunkirk; instead he ordered the Luftwaffe to finish off the Allied troops, but fog and rain prevented German planes from operating at full strength. While the Luftwaffe bombed the beaches, some 338,000 British and French troops were ferried across the English Channel by destroyers, merchant ships, motorboats, fishing boats, tugboats, and private yachts. Hitler's personal decision to hold back his tanks made the miracle of Dunkirk possible.

Meanwhile, the battle for France was turning into a rout. With authority breaking down, demoralization spreading, and resistance dying, the French cabinet appealed for an armistice, which was signed on June 22 in the same railway car in which Germany had agreed to the armistice ending World War I.

How can the collapse of France be explained? The French had as many planes and tanks as the Germans, but their military leaders, unlike the German command, had not mastered the psychology and technology of motorized warfare. One senses also a loss of will among the French people—a product of internal political disputes that divided the nation, poor leadership, the years of appeasement and lost opportunities, and German propaganda, which depicted

St. Paul's Cathedral During the London Blitz.   More than 30,000 Londoners were killed and over 50,000 wounded during the World War II bombings, and most public buildings, including St. Paul's, were damaged. (*Associated Newspapers/Pictorial Parade*)

Nazism as irresistible and the Fuehrer as a man of destiny. It was France's darkest hour. According to the terms of the armistice, Germany occupied northern France and the coast. The French military was demobilized, and the French government, now located at Vichy in the south, would collaborate with the German authorities in occupied France. Refusing to recognize defeat, General Charles de Gaulle (1890–1970) escaped to London and organized the Free French forces. The Germans gloried in their revenge; the French wept in their humiliation; the British gathered their courage, for they now stood alone.

The Battle of Britain

Hitler expected that after his stunning victories in the west, Britain would make peace. The British, however, continued to reject Hitler's peace overtures, for they envisioned only a bleak future if Hitler dominated the Continent. After the German victory in Norway, Chamberlain's support in the House of Commons had eroded and he had been replaced by Winston Churchill, who had opposed appeasement. Dynamic, courageous, and eloquent, Churchill had the capacity to stir and lead his people in the struggle against Nazism. "The Battle of Britain is about to begin," Churchill told them. "Upon this battle depends the survival of Christian civilization. . . . if we fail, then . . . all we have known and cared for will sink into the abyss of a new Dark Age."[3]

With Britain unwilling to come to terms, Hitler proceeded in earnest with invasion plans. But a successful crossing of the English Channel and the establishment of beachheads on the English coast depended on control of the skies. Marshal Hermann Goering assured Hitler that his Luftwaffe could destroy the British Royal Air Force (RAF), and in early August 1940 the Luftwaffe began massive attacks on British air and naval installations. Virtually every day during the "Battle of Britain," weather permitting, hundreds of planes battled in the sky above Britain. Convinced that Goering could not fulfill his promise to destroy British air defenses, Hitler called off the invasion. The development of radar by British scientists, the skill and courage of British fighter pilots, and the inability of Germany to make up its losses in planes saved Britain in its struggle for survival.

The Invasion of Russia

The obliteration of Bolshevism and the conquest, exploitation, and colonization of Russia by the German master race were cardinal elements of Hitler's ideology. To prevent any interference with the forthcoming invasion of Russia, the Balkan flank had to be secured. On April 6, 1941, the Germans struck at both Greece, where an Italian attack had failed, and Yugoslavia. Yugoslavia was quickly overrun, and Greece, although aided by 50,000 British, New Zealander, and Australian troops, fell at the end of April.

For the war against Russia, Hitler had assembled a massive force—some 4 million men, 3,300 tanks, and 5,000 planes. In the early hours of June 22, 1941, the Germans launched their offensive over a wide front. Raiding Russian airfields, the Luftwaffe destroyed 1,200 aircraft on the first day. The Germans drove deeply into Russia, cutting up and surrounding the disorganized and unprepared Russian forces. The Russians suffered terrible losses. In a little more than three months, 2.5 million Russian soldiers had been killed, wounded, or captured and 14,000 tanks destroyed. Describing the war as a crusade to save Europe from "Jewish Bolshevism," German propaganda claimed that victory had been assured.

But there were also disquieting signs for the Nazi invaders. The Russians, who had a proven capacity to endure hardships, fought doggedly and courageously, and the government would not consider capitulation. Russian reserve strength was far greater than the Germans had estimated. The *Wehrmacht* (German army), far from its supply lines, was running short of fuel, and trucks and cars had to contend with primitive roads that turned into seas of mud when the autumn rains came. Early and bitter cold weather hampered the German attempt to capture Moscow. The Germans advanced to within twenty miles of Moscow, but on December 6 a Red Army counterattack forced them to postpone the assault on the Russian capital.

By the end of 1941, Germany had conquered vast regions of Russia but had failed to bring the country to its knees. There would be no repetition of the collapse of France. The Russian campaign demonstrated that the Russian people would make incredible sacrifices for their land and that the Nazis were not invincible.

The New Order

By 1942, Germany ruled virtually all of Europe from the Atlantic to deep into Russia. Some conquered territory was annexed outright; other lands were administered by German officials; in still other countries, the Germans ruled through local officials sympathetic to Nazism or willing to collaborate with the Germans. Over this vast empire, Hitler and his henchmen imposed a New Order.

Exploitation and Terror

The Germans systematically looted the lands they conquered, taking gold, art treasures, machinery, and food supplies back to Germany and exploiting the industrial and agricultural potential of non-German lands to aid the German war economy. The Nazis also made slave laborers of conquered peoples. Some 7 million people from all over Europe were wrested from their homes and transported to Germany. These forced laborers, particularly the Russians and Poles, whom Nazi ideology classified as subhumans, lived in wretched, unheated barracks and were poorly fed and overworked; many died of disease, hunger, and exhaustion.

The Nazis ruled by force and terror. The prison cell, the torture chamber, the firing squad, and the concentration camp symbolized the New Order. In the Polish province annexed to Germany, the Nazis jailed and executed intellectuals and priests, closed all schools and most churches, and forbade Poles to hold professional positions. In the region of Poland administered by German officials, most schools above the fourth grade were shut down. The Germans were particularly ruthless toward the Russians, whom they regarded as an especially low form of humanity. Soviet political officials were immediately executed; many prisoners of war were herded into camps and deliberately starved to death. In all, the Germans took some 5.5 million Russian prisoners, of whom more than 3.5 million perished.

Extermination

Against the Jews of Europe, the Germans waged a war of extermination. The task of imposing the "Final Solution of the Jewish Problem" was given to Himmler's SS; Himmler fulfilled his grisly duties with fanaticism and bureaucratic efficiency. Himmler and the SS believed that they had a holy mission to rid the world of worthless life—a satanic foe that was plotting to destroy Germany. Regarding themselves as idealists who were writing a glorious chapter in the history of Germany, the SS tortured and murdered with immense dedication. Special squads of SS—the *Einsatzgruppen,* trained for mass murder—followed on the heels of the German army into Russia. Entering captured villages and cities, they rounded up Jewish men, women, and children, herded them to execution grounds, and slaughtered them with machine gun and rifle fire. Aided by Ukrainian, Lithuanian, and Latvian auxiliaries, the Einsatzgruppen massacred some 2 million Russian Jews.

To speed up the Final Solution, concentration camps, originally established for political prisoners, were transformed into killing centers, and new ones were built for that purpose. Jews from all over Europe were rounded up, jammed into sealed cattle cars, and shipped to Treblinka, Auschwitz, and other death camps, where they entered another world:

> *Corpses were strewn all over the road; bodies were hanging from the barbed-wire fence; the sound of shots rang in the air continuously. Blazing flames shot into the sky; a giant smoke cloud ascended about them. Starving, emaciated human skeletons stumbled forward toward us, uttering incoherent sounds. They fell down right in front of our eyes gasping out their last breath.*
>
> *Here and there a hand tried to reach up, but when this happened an SS man came right away and stepped on it. Those who were merely exhausted were simply thrown on the dead pile. . . . Every night a truck came by, and all of them, dead or not, were thrown on it and taken to the crematory.*[4]

SS doctors quickly inspected the new arrivals—"the freight," as they referred to them. Those unfit for work, including children, were immediately exterminated in gas chambers. When Auschwitz's gas chambers were in full operation, 20,000 people a day were murdered. To economize on gas, or because no more people could be squeezed into the chambers, orders were given to throw children into the crematoria alive. Those not immediately exterminated faced a living death in the camp, which also included non-Jewish inmates. The SS took sadistic pleasure in humiliating and brutalizing their Jewish victims. When exhausted, starved, diseased, and beaten prisoners became unfit for work, generally within a few months, they were sent to the gas chambers.

There have been many massacres during the course of world history. And the Nazis murdered many non-Jews in concentration camps and in reprisal for acts of resistance. What is unique about the Holocaust—the systematic extermination of European Jewry—was the Nazis' determination to murder without exception every single Jew who came within their grasp, and the fanaticism, ingenuity, and cruelty with which they pursued this goal. Despite the protests of the army, the SS murdered Jews whose labor was needed for the war effort, and when Germany's military position was desperate, the SS still diverted military personnel and railway cars to deport Jews to the death camps.

The Holocaust was the terrible fulfillment of Nazi racial theories. Believing that they were cleansing Europe of a lower and dangerous race that threatened the German people, Nazi executioners performed their evil work with dedication and resourcefulness, with precision and moral indifference—a terrible testament to human irrationality and wickedness. Using the technology and bureaucracy of a modern state, the Germans killed approximately 6 million Jews—*two-thirds* of the Jewish population of Europe. Some 1.5 million of the murdered were children. Tens of thousands of entire families were wiped out without a trace. Centuries-old Jewish community life vanished, never to be restored. Burned into the soul of the Jewish people was a wound that could never entirely heal. Written into the history of Western civilization was an episode that would forever cast doubt on the Enlightenment conception of human goodness, rationality, and the progress of civilization.

Resistance

Each occupied country had its collaborators, who welcomed the demise of democracy, saw Hitler as Europe's best defense against communism, and profited from the sale of war material. Each country also produced a resistance movement that grew stronger as Nazi barbarism became more visible and prospects of a German defeat more likely. The Nazis retaliated by torturing and executing captured resistance fighters and killing hostages—generally fifty for every German killed.

In western Europe the resistance rescued downed Allied airmen, radioed military intelligence to Britain, and sabotaged German installations. Norwegians blew up the German stock of heavy water needed for atomic research. The Danish underground sabotaged railways and smuggled into neutral Sweden almost all of Denmark's 8,000 Jews just before they were to be deported to the death camps. After the Allies landed on the coast of France in June 1944, the French resistance delayed the movement of German reinforcements and liberated sections of the country.

In eastern Europe, resistance took the form of guerrilla warfare as well as sabotage. In August 1944, with Soviet forces approaching Warsaw, the Poles staged a full-scale revolt against the German occupiers. The Poles appealed to the Soviets, camped ten miles away, for help. Thinking about a future Russian-dominated Poland, the Soviets did not move. After sixty-three days of street fighting, remnants of the Polish underground surrendered and the Germans destroyed what was left of Warsaw. Russian partisans numbered several hundred thousand men and women. Operating behind the German lines, they sabotaged railways, destroyed trucks, and killed scores of thousands of German soldiers in hit-and-run attacks. The mountains and forests of Yugoslavia provided excellent terrain for guerrilla warfare. The leading Yugoslav resistance army was headed by Josip Broz (1892–1980), better known as Tito.

Moscow-trained, intelligent, and courageous, Tito organized the partisans into a disciplined fighting force that tied down a huge German army and ultimately liberated the country from German rule.

Italy and Germany also had resistance movements. After the Allies landed in Italy in 1943, bands of Italian partisans helped to liberate Italy from fascism and the German occupation. In Germany, army officers plotted to assassinate the Fuehrer. On July 20, 1944, Colonel Claus von Stauffenberg planted a bomb at a staff conference attended by Hitler, but the Fuehrer escaped serious injury. In retaliation, some 5,000 suspected anti-Nazis were tortured and executed in exceptionally barbarous fashion.

The Turn of the Tide

The Japanese Offensive

At the same time that Germany was subduing Europe, its ally, Japan, was extending its dominion over areas of Asia. Seeking raw materials and secure markets for Japanese goods, and driven by a xenophobic nationalism, Japan in 1931 had attacked Manchuria in northern China. Quickly overrunning the province, the Japanese established the puppet state of Manchukuo in 1932. After a period of truce, the war against China was renewed in July 1937. Japan captured leading cities, including China's principal seaports, and inflicted heavy casualties on the poorly organized Chinese forces, forcing the government of Chiang Kai-shek (1887–1975) to withdraw to Chungking in the interior.

In 1940, after the defeat of France and with Britain standing alone against Nazi Germany, Japan eyed southeast Asia—French Indochina, British Burma and Malaya, and the Dutch East Indies. From these lands Japan planned to obtain the oil, rubber, and tin vitally needed by Japanese industry and enough rice to feed the nation. Japan hoped that a quick strike against the American fleet in the Pacific would give it time to enlarge and consolidate its empire. On December 7, 1941, the Japanese struck with carrier-based planes at Pearl Harbor in Hawaii. Taken by surprise, the Americans suffered a total defeat: the attackers sank seventeen ships, including seven of eight battleships; destroyed 188 airplanes and damaged 159 others; and killed 2,403 men. The Japanese lost only 29 planes. After the attack on Pearl Harbor, Germany declared war on the United States. Now the immense American industrial capacity could be put to work against the Axis powers—Germany, Italy, and Japan.

By the spring of 1942, the Axis powers held the upper hand. The Japanese empire included the coast of China, Indochina, Thailand, Burma, Malaya, the Dutch East Indies, the Philippines, and other islands in the Pacific. Germany

Map 20.2   World War II: The Pacific Theater ▶

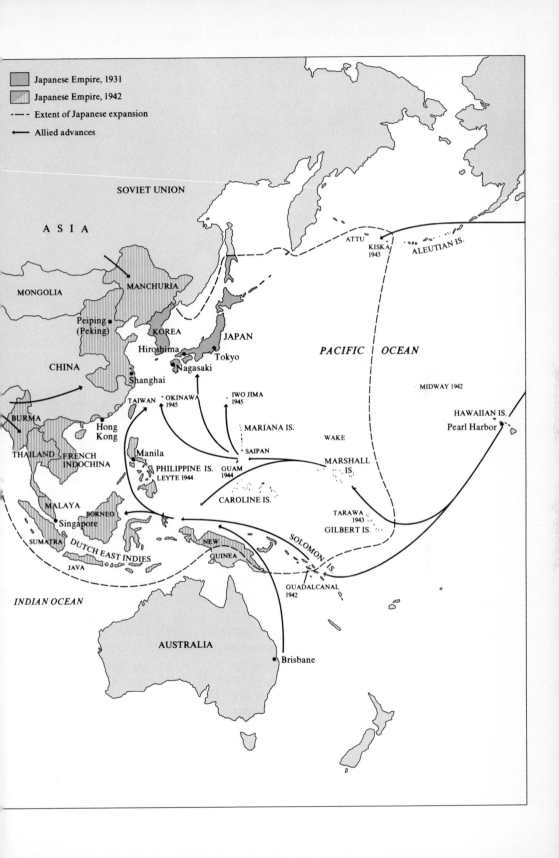

Japanese Empire, 1931
Japanese Empire, 1942
- - - Extent of Japanese expansion
⟶ Allied advances

SOVIET UNION

ASIA

MONGOLIA

MANCHURIA

Peiping
(Peking)

KOREA

Hiroshima

JAPAN

Tokyo

Nagasaki

CHINA

Shanghai

ATTU

KISKA
1943

ALEUTIAN IS.

PACIFIC   OCEAN

MIDWAY 1942

TAIWAN

OKINAWA
1945

IWO JIMA
1945

HAWAIIAN IS.

Pearl Harbor

BURMA

Hong
Kong

MARIANA IS.

WAKE

THAILAND   FRENCH
INDOCHINA

Manila

PHILIPPINE IS.

LEYTE 1944

GUAM
1944

SAIPAN

MARSHALL
IS.

CAROLINE IS.

MALAYA

BORNEO

Singapore

SUMATRA

DUTCH EAST INDIES

JAVA

NEW

GUINEA

SOLOMON IS.

TARAWA
1943

GILBERT IS.

GUADALCANAL
1942

INDIAN OCEAN

AUSTRALIA

Brisbane

Kamikaze Attack on the *Hornet*, Painted from Combat Experience by Lt. Dwight C. Chepler, U.S.N.R.   With the bombing of Pearl Harbor, Japan had destroyed much of the American fleet and expected a quick, easy victory. The U.S. triumph at the Battle of Midway on June 4, 1942, however, broke Japan's initiative. (*Popperfoto*)

controlled Europe almost to Moscow. When the year ended, however, the Allies seemed assured of victory. Three decisive battles—Midway, Stalingrad, and El Alamein—reversed the tide of war.

In June 1942, the main body of the Japanese fleet headed for Midway, 1,100 miles northwest of Pearl Harbor; another section sailed toward the Aleutian Islands in an attempt to divide the American fleet. But the Americans had broken the Japanese naval code and were aware of the Japanese plan. On June 4, 1942, the two navies fought a strange naval battle; it was waged entirely by carrier-based planes, for the two fleets were too far from each other to use their big guns. Demonstrating marked superiority over their opponents and extraordinary courage, American pilots destroyed 4 aircraft carriers and downed 322 Japanese planes. The battle of Midway cost Japan the initiative. With American industrial production accelerating, the opportunity for a Japanese victory had passed.

Defeat of the Axis Powers

After being stymied at the outskirts of Moscow in December 1941, the Germans renewed their offensive in the spring and summer of 1942. Hitler's goal was Stalingrad, the great industrial center located on the Volga River; control of Stalingrad would give Germany command of vital rail transportation. The battle of Stalingrad was an epic struggle in which Russian soldiers and civilians contested for every building and street. The remnants of the German Sixth Army surrendered in February 1943. Some 260,000 German soldiers had perished in the battle of Stalingrad, and another 110,000 were taken prisoner.

In January 1941, the British were routing the Italians in northern Africa. Hitler assigned General Erwin Rommel (1891–1944) to halt the British advance. Rommel drove the British out of Libya and with strong reinforcements might have taken Egypt and the Suez Canal. But Hitler's concern was with seizing Yugoslavia and Greece and preparing for the invasion of Russia. In the beginning of 1942, Rommel resumed his advance, intending to conquer Egypt. The British Eighth Army, commanded by General Bernard L. Montgomery, stopped him at the battle of El Alamein in October 1942. The victory of El Alamein was followed by an Anglo-American invasion of northwest Africa in November 1942. By May 1943, the Germans and Italians were defeated in North Africa.

After securing North Africa, the Allies, seeking complete control of the Mediterranean, invaded Sicily in July 1943 and quickly conquered the island. Mussolini's fellow Fascist leaders turned against the Duce (leader) and the king dismissed him as prime minister. In September the new government surrendered to the Allies, and in the following month Italy declared war on Germany. Italian partisans, whose number would grow to 300,000, resisted the occupying German troops, who were determined to hold on to central and northern Italy. At the same time, the Allies fought their way up the Italian peninsula. Captured by partisans, Mussolini was executed (April 28, 1945), and his dead body, hanging upside-down, was publicly displayed.

On June 6, 1944—D-Day—the Allies landed on the beaches of Normandy in France. They had assembled a massive force for the invasion—2 million men and 5,000 vessels. The success of D-Day depended on securing the beaches and marching inland, which the Allies did despite stubborn German resistance on some beaches. By the end of July, the Allies had built up their strength in France to a million and a half. In the middle of August, Paris rose up against the German occupiers and was soon liberated.

As winter approached, the situation looked hopeless for Germany. Brussels and Antwerp fell to the Allies; Allied bombers were striking German factories and mass-bombing German cities in terror raids that took a terrible toll of life. The desperate Hitler made one last gamble. In mid-December 1944 he launched an offensive to split the Allied forces and regain the vital port of Antwerp. The Allies were taken by surprise in the battle of the Bulge, but a heroic defense by the Americans at Bastogne helped stop the German offensive. While their allies were advancing in the west, the Russians were continuing their drive in the east, advancing into the Baltic states, Poland, and Hungary. By February 1945, they stood within one hundred miles of Berlin.

By April 1945, British, American, and Russian troops were penetrating into Germany from east and west. From his underground bunker near the chancellery in Berlin, Hitler, physically exhausted and emotionally unhinged, engaged in wild fantasies about new German victories. On April 30, 1945, with the Russians only blocks away, the Fuehrer took his own life. On May 7, 1945, a demoralized and devastated Germany surrendered unconditionally.

In the Pacific war, after the victory at Midway in June 1942, American forces attacked strategic islands held by Japan. American troops had to battle their way up beaches and through jungles tenaciously defended by Japanese soldiers, who believed that death was preferable to the disgrace of surrender. In March 1945, 21,000 Japanese perished on Iwo Jima; another 100,000 died on Okinawa in April 1945 as they contested for every inch of the island.

On August 6, 1945, the United States dropped an atomic bomb on Hiroshima, killing more than 78,000 people and demolishing 60 percent of the city. President Harry S Truman said that he ordered the atomic attack to avoid an American invasion of the Japanese homeland that would have cost hundreds of thousands of lives. Truman's decision has aroused considerable debate. Some analysts say that dropping the bomb was unnecessary, that Japan, deprived of oil, rice, and other essentials by an American naval blockade and defenseless against unrelenting aerial bombardments, was close to surrender and had indicated as much. It has been suggested that with the Soviet Union about to enter the conflict against Japan, Truman wanted to end the war immediately, thereby depriving the USSR of an opportunity to extend its influence in East Asia. On August 8, Russia entered the war against Japan, invading Manchuria. After a second atomic bomb was dropped on Nagasaki on August 9, the Japanese asked for peace.

The Legacy of World War II

World War II was the most destructive war in history. Estimates of the number of dead range as high as 50 million, including 20 million Russians, who sacrificed more than the other participants in both population and material resources. The war produced a vast migration of peoples unparalleled in modern European history. The Soviet Union annexed the Baltic lands of Latvia, Lithuania, and Estonia, forcibly deporting many of the native inhabitants into central Russia. The bulk of East Prussia was taken over by Poland, and Russia annexed the northeastern portion. Millions of Germans fled or were forced out of Prussia and regions of Czechoslovakia, Rumania, Yugoslavia, and Hungary, places where their ancestors had lived for centuries. Material costs were staggering. Everywhere cities were in rubble; bridges, railway systems, waterways, and harbors destroyed; farmlands laid waste; livestock killed; coal mines wrecked. Homeless and hungry people wandered the streets and roads. Europe faced the gigantic task of rebuilding. Yet Europe did recover from this material blight, and with astonishing speed.

World War II produced a shift in power arrangements. The United States and the Soviet Union emerged as the two most powerful states in the world; the traditional Great Powers—Britain, France, Germany—were now dwarfed by these *superpowers*. The United States had the atomic bomb and immense industrial might; the Soviet Union had the largest army in the world and was extending its dominion over eastern Europe. With Germany prostrate and occupied, the principal incentive for Soviet-American cooperation had evaporated. Whereas World War I was followed by an intensification of nationalist passions, after World War II western Europeans progressed toward cooperation and unity. The Hitler years had convinced many Europeans of the dangers inherent in extreme nationalism, and fear of the Soviet Union fortified the need for greater cooperation.

World War II accelerated the disintegration of Europe's overseas empires. The European states could hardly justify ruling over Africans and Asians after they had fought to liberate European lands from German imperialism. Nor could they ask their peoples, exhausted by the Hitler years and concentrating all their energies on reconstruction, to fight new wars against Africans and Asians pressing for independence. In the years just after the war, Great Britain surrendered India, France lost Lebanon and Syria, and the Dutch departed from Indonesia. In the 1950s and 1960s, virtually every colonial territory gained independence. In those instances where the colonial power resisted independence for the colony, the price was bloodshed.

The consciousness of Europe, already profoundly damaged by World War I, was again grievously wounded. Nazi racial theories showed that in an age of sophisticated science, the mind has not forsaken irrational beliefs and mythical imagery; Nazi atrocities demonstrated that people will torture and kill with religious zeal and machinelike indifference. The Nazi onslaught against reason and freedom demonstrated anew the fragility of Western civilization. Both the Christian and Enlightenment traditions had failed the West. Some intellectuals, shocked by the horrors of the Hitler era, drifted into despair. To these thinkers, life was absurd, without meaning; human beings could neither comprehend nor control it. In 1945 only the naive could have faith in continuous progress or believe in the essential goodness of human beings. The future envisioned by the philosophes seemed further away than ever.

World War II ushered in the atomic age. At the end of the war, only the United States had the atomic bomb, but soon the Soviet Union and other states acquired an arsenal of atomic weapons. That people now possess the weapons to destroy themselves and their planet is the ever-present, ever-terrifying, and ultimately most significant legacy of World War II.

Chronology 20.1 ❧ World War II

1931	Japan invades Manchuria
March 1935	Hitler announces German rearmament
October 1935	Italy invades Ethiopia
1936–1939	The Spanish Civil War
March 7, 1936	Germany remilitarizes the Rhineland
July 1937	Japan invades China
March 13, 1938	Anschluss with Austria, which becomes a German province
September 1938	The Munich Agreement—Germany's annexation of Sudetenland is approved by Britain and France
March 1939	Germany invades Czechoslovakia
April 1939	Italy invades Albania
August 23, 1939	Nonaggression pact between Germany and Russia
September 1 & 3, 1939	Germany invades Poland; Britain and France declare war
September 27, 1939	Poland surrenders
April 1940	Germany attacks Denmark and Norway
May 10, 1940	Germany invades Belgium, Holland, and Luxembourg
June 22, 1940	France surrenders
August–September 1940	The battle of Britain
June 22, 1941	Germany launches offensive against Russia
December 7, 1941	Japan attacks Pearl Harbor; United States enters the war against Japan and Germany
1942	The tide of battle turns in the Allies' favor: Midway (Pacific Ocean), Stalingrad (Soviet Union), and El Alamein (North Africa)
September 1943	Italy surrenders to Allies, following invasion
June 6, 1944	D-Day—Allies land in Normandy, France
May 7, 1945	Germany surrenders unconditionally
August 1945	United States drops atomic bombs on Hiroshima and Nagasaki; Soviet Union invades Manchuria; Japan surrenders

Notes

1. Pierre Renouvin, *World War II and Its Origins* (New York: Harper & Row, 1969), p. 167.
2. *Documents on German Foreign Policy, 1918–1945,* vol. 6 (London: Her Majesty's Stationery Office, 1956), series D, no. 433.
3. Winston S. Churchill, *The Second World War: Their Finest Hour,* vol. 2 (Boston: Houghton Mifflin, 1949), pp. 225–226.
4. Judith Sternberg Newman, *In the Hell of Auschwitz* (New York: Exposition, 1964), p. 18.

Suggested Reading

Bauer, Yehuda, *A History of the Holocaust* (1982). An authoritative study.
Baumont, Maurice, *The Origins of the Second World War* (1978). A brief work by a distinguished French scholar.
Calvocoressi, Peter, and Guy Wint, *Total War* (1972). A good account of World War II.
Hildebrand, Klaus, *The Foreign Policy of the Third Reich* (1973). A brief assessment of Nazi foreign policy.
Marrus, Michael R., *The Holocaust in History* (1987). An excellent summary of key issues and problems.
Michel, Henri, *The Second World War,* 2 vols. (1975). Translation of an important study by a prominent French historian.
Remak, Joachim, *The Origins of the Second World War* (1976). A useful essay, followed by documents.
Wiesel, Elie, *Night* (1960). A moving personal record of the Holocaust.

Review Questions

1. What were Adolf Hitler's foreign-policy aims?
2. Why did Britain and France practice a policy of appeasement?
3. Discuss the significance of each of the following: Italy's invasion of Ethiopia (1935), Germany's remilitarization of the Rhineland (1936), the Spanish Civil War (1936–1939), Germany's union with Austria (1938), the occupation of Prague (1939), and the Nazi-Soviet Pact (1939).
4. What factors made possible the quick fall of France?
5. Describe the New Order the Nazis established in Europe.
6. In your opinion, what is the meaning of the Holocaust for Western civilization? For Jews? For Christians? For Germans?
7. Discuss the significance of each of the following battles: Midway (1942), Stalingrad (1942–1943), El Alamein (1942), and D-Day (1944).
8. What was the legacy of World War II?

A street scene in Shenzen, China, with a Marlboro billboard.
(Robert Wallis, J. B. Pictures)

VI ⚚ The Contemporary World: The Global Age

Since 1945

Chapter ✦ 21

Europe After 1945:
Recovery, Realignment, Division

At the end of World War II, Winston Churchill described Europe as "a rubble heap, a charnel house, a breeding ground for pestilence and hate." Millions had perished. Industry, transportation, and communication had come to a virtual standstill; bridges, canals, dikes, and farmlands were ruined. Ragged, worn people picked among the rubble and bartered their valuables for food.

Europe was politically cut in half. The division arose because in pursuing Hitler's armies, the Soviet troops had overrun Eastern Europe and penetrated into the heart of Germany. The Yalta agreement of February 1945, signed by Roosevelt, Churchill, and Stalin on Stalin's home ground in the Crimean peninsula, turned the prevailing military balance of power into a political settlement, with Soviet promises (not kept) for free elections in Soviet-dominated Eastern Europe. The American bargaining position at Yalta was weakened by the expectation that Soviet help would be needed for victory over Japan.

Europe's future now depended on two countries, the United States and the Soviet Union, which soon became embroiled in an embittered cold war. The Soviet Union, exhausted by World War II and fearful for its security, imposed its grim tradition of dictatorship on Eastern Europe, while the United States, virtually unharmed by the war, brought the boons of its wealth and power to help rebuild Western Europe. Henceforth, the United States stood out as the heir to and guardian of the Western tradition, a political giant come into its own. ✦

Marshall Plan Aid. Since much of Europe lay in rubble at the conclusion of World War II, the U.S. Congress approved the European Recovery Program (the official name of the Marshall Plan) in 1948. The funds were to be used to buy U.S. goods. The earliest aid, however, went toward food, agricultural assistance, and housing construction to alleviate malnutrition and homelessness. (*UPI/Bettmann Newsphotos*)

Western Europe

U.S. military power had liberated Western Europe from Hitler's tyranny. Thereafter, U.S. military presence and superiority in nuclear weapons protected Western Europe against the widely dreaded westward expansion of Soviet communism. Against that threat, the United States and the countries of Western Europe established the North Atlantic Treaty Organization (NATO) in 1949. NATO combined the armed forces of the United States, Canada, Portugal, Norway, Iceland, Denmark, Italy, Britain, France, and the Benelux countries (Belgium, Holland, and Luxemburg). Greece and ·Turkey soon joined; West Germany was included in 1955, and Spain in 1982. The postwar rebuilding of Western Europe proceeded under the protection of U.S. military power.

Even before committing itself to a military presence, the United States had begun an extensive program of financial assistance for the economic recovery of Western Europe. In June 1947, Secretary of State George C. Marshall announced an impressive scheme of economic aid formally called the European Recovery Program, but widely known as the Marshall Plan. By December 1959, the Marshall Plan had supplied Europe with a total of over $74 billion in aid, a modest pump-priming for the subsequent record upswing in U.S., Western European, and even global prosperity. Western Europe recovered, and the United States gained economically strong allies and trading partners.

U.S. military and economic pre-eminence after the war also prepared the way for the influx of American ways of life and culture abroad. The languages of Western Europe became permeated with American words and phrases. Young people especially favored American popular music as well as fashions. More generally, Western Europeans adopted the casual American lifestyle.

European Unity

Although Europeans share a common cultural heritage, the diversity of their history and national temperaments has burdened them in the past with incessant warfare. After two ruinous world wars, many people at last began to feel that the price of violent conflict had become excessive; war no longer served any national interest. The extension of Soviet power made some form of Western European unity attractive.

Western European economic cooperation began rather modestly with the creation of the European Coal and Steel Community (ECSC) in 1951. It drew together the chief Continental consumers and producers of coal and steel, the two items most essential for the rebuilding of Western Europe. Its members were France, West Germany, the three Benelux countries, and Italy; these six countries thus became the core countries of Western European unity. Their design was to put the Ruhr industrial complex, the heart of German industrial power, under international control, thereby promoting cooperation and reconciliation as well as economic strength.

Emboldened by the success of the ECSC, in 1957 the six countries established the European Economic Community (EEC)—also known as the Common Market—a customs union that created a free market among the member states and sought to improve living conditions in them. In 1973 the original members were joined by Great Britain and Denmark in what was now called the European Community (EC); in 1986, Spain, Portugal, and Greece became members. All told, the EC carries much weight in the world. It constitutes the largest single trading entity, conducting over one-fifth of the world's commerce.

Economic and Political Developments

The most striking fact of recent history in the West, as in the world generally, is the unprecedented economic advance. Between the early 1950s and the late 1970s, production in Western Europe and the United States surpassed all previous records. The rapid postwar economic boom was not, however, destined to last. It had been fed by abundant and exceptionally cheap supplies of oil, but after 1973 the Organization of Petroleum Exporting Countries (OPEC) drastically raised the price of that essential source of energy. OPEC's action aggravated adverse worldwide economic trends that had been evident since the late 1960s (and were caused in part by the U.S. war in Vietnam). Inflation,

Map 21.1 Western Europe After 1945

unemployment, falling productivity, competition (from Japan especially) in automobiles and electronics, and a worldwide economic recession plagued all the governments of Western Europe. After another oil crisis in 1979, the economy recovered, and prosperity has continued through the 1980s. Unemployment in Western Europe, however, remained high, even in West Germany, the strongest country economically.

Stimulated by the expansion of U.S. multinational corporations into Western Europe and by the opportunities offered by the European Community, many European companies have become multinational and grown bigger than any nationalized industry. The Western European economy is now dominated by gigantic private and public enterprises that are tied to other parts of the world.

Boosted by rising standards of living and by U.S. power, the overall trend of political life in the West since World War II has been toward constitutional democracy. Although Spain and Portugal retained their prewar dictatorships until the mid-1970s and Greece for a time wavered between democracy and dictatorship, by the late 1970s even these countries had conformed to the common pattern.

Problems and Tensions

Western Europe did not escape serious problems and tensions after World War II. With the rise of the public sector and the increase in social services, government and bureaucracy grew huge and more impersonal. Individuals felt dwarfed by the state and lost in a complex, interdependent society. The massive spurt of affluence had unsettling effects on European culture. Although prosperity provided more people with more material goods, it also encouraged a hedonistic self-indulgence that ran contrary to the puritan strain in Western tradition.

Young people especially were in ferment, tending to repudiate the new affluence and the complexity on which it was based. They also emphasized its drawbacks: stark inequality in the world, social callousness at home, the breakdown of human intimacy and community, and the mounting strain on human energy and integrity. In their protest, some of the young sided with a romantic counterculture, disdaining traditional middle-class restraints, above all in sex, and proclaiming their solidarity with all oppressed peoples around the world.

In 1968, youthful frustration broke into politics—angrily and sometimes destructively—foremost in France and slightly less drastically throughout Western Europe (as it did, more mildly, in the anti–Vietnam War agitation in the United States). During May 1968, a spontaneous and embittered demonstration of students and workers in Paris set off a massive general strike such as France had not seen since 1936. Yet no revolution followed, no sudden social change, only a conservative backlash at the next national election.

Some impatient young protesters meanwhile turned to outright terrorism, especially in West Germany and Italy. In their eyes, the entire system of state and society was inhumane and deserved destruction by any means available. The targets of their attacks were leading representatives of "the system": politicians, industrialists, judges, and the police. Terrorists of all kinds established links with their counterparts in other troubled areas of the world, creating a sort of international terrorist movement. Raw violence offered young idealists the opportunity for politically aware and self-denying heroism, but it provided no answer to the intricate problems of modern society. After a few spectacular assassinations, public opinion began to favor more effective countermeasures, thus curtailing terrorist violence.

Meanwhile, youthful protest had turned to environmental issues and nuclear disarmament. Both young and old gathered in mass demonstrations. They agitated against the pollution of water and air, dramatized the plight of dying forests, opposed nuclear power plants, and called attention to the threat of nuclear war.

The Leading Western European States
France

After 1945, France, reorganized under its fourth republican constitution, quickly laid the foundation for its subsequent rapid economic advance. Under the leadership of Jean Monnet, an able group of economists and planners mapped out strategies and institutions that have become models of state guidance in a mixed economy of public and private enterprise. During the 1950s, the French economy grew at a very respectable rate.

In national politics the sense of common purpose was less evident. In 1946, the new constitution creating the Fourth Republic followed the pattern of the Third. The twenty-six short-lived governments of the Fourth Republic valiantly coped with a number of grave problems, including communist-led strikes in 1947 and 1948 and colonial liberation movements in Indochina and Algeria. In 1954 the French army suffered a resounding defeat in Indochina. In Algeria, administratively a part of France proper, French settlers and soldiers were determined to thwart demands for independence.

The long and bloody Algerian conflict had serious repercussions for French political life. In 1958, the insubordination of army leaders brought down the Fourth Republic with a resounding call for the return of General Charles de Gaulle, the leader of the Free French forces in World War II. De Gaulle then wrote the constitution of the Fifth Republic, which gave considerable powers to the presidency.

De Gaulle's grand design was simple enough: to restore France to its rightful place in Europe and the world. He insisted that France have its own nuclear force, pulled France out of the NATO high command, and consented to Algerian independence, over the protest of the army. But his France, a mere middle-sized state in the global world, was too small for De Gaulle's ambition; his grand style in foreign policy did not survive him. His successors, Georges Pompidou (1969–1974) and Valéry Giscard D'Estaing (1974–1981), did emphasize, however, that France was "the third nuclear power" after the United States and the Soviet Union and was determined to assert its independence.

In the elections of 1981, the French communists agreed to a coalition government dominated by the socialists led by François Mitterrand, who became

The Berlin Wall.   Although an open city since the end of World War II, Berlin was physically divided overnight in 1961 when the East German government erected the wall that still separates the city. The Berlin Wall and the Cuban missile crisis of 1962 brought the U.S. and Soviet superpowers to two of the most dangerous crises in the long history of the cold war. (*UPI/Bettmann Newsphotos*)

president. The new president shifted course to the left with a program to nationalize industries and banks and increase government jobs. The socialist remedies applied by Mitterrand failed, forcing the government into a course of unpopular austerity. Not surprisingly, the socialists lost to the conservatives in the parliamentary elections of March 1986, forcing President Mitterrand to appoint a conservative prime minister, Jacques Chirac. Despite the political differences between the president and the prime minister, the government has been effective. In 1988, Mitterrand was re-elected for a second seven-year term.

West Germany

In 1945, its cities in ruins, Germany had been defeated, occupied, and branded as a moral outcast for the horrors that Nazi rule had brought to Europe. Divided among four occupying powers, the German nation was politically extinct. The state of Prussia was declared dissolved; extensive eastern lands were handed to Poland and the Soviet Union. The dream of national glory that had provided the chief momentum in German life for more than a century was over.

By 1949, two new and chastened Germanys had emerged. The Federal Republic of Germany, formed from the three western zones of occupation, faced a hostile, Soviet-dominated German Democratic Republic in the east. The partition of Germany signified not only the destruction of Germany's traditional political identity but also a personal tragedy for almost all Germans: families were split as the division interrupted communication between the two Germanys. The national trauma reached a peak in August 1961 when the East German government suddenly threw up a wall dividing the city of Berlin and for years tightly sealing off East from West Germany.

The cold war proved a boon to West Germany; feared and despised though they were, the West Germans were needed. Located next door to the Red Army, they were in a strategic position for the defense of Western Europe. Even more important, German industry and expertise were indispensable for the success of the Marshall Plan. Finally, a democratic West Germany would aid the course of Western European unity.

On this basis, the Federal Republic of Germany (far larger than its communist counterpart to the east and the most populous of all Western European countries) began to build a political identity of its own. Konrad Adenauer, chancellor from 1949 to 1963, was the founding hero of the Federal Republic of Germany. A vigorous old-timer (he was seventy-five when appointed chancellor), known as a courageous anti-Nazi in the Hitler years, he represented the pro-Western, liberal-democratic tradition of the Weimar Republic. His aim was simple: restore respect for Germany in cooperation with the United States and the leading states of Western Europe. As a patriot, he rebuilt a cautious continuity with the German past, shouldering responsibility for the crimes of the Nazi regime. Given the opportunity, West Germans threw themselves into rebuilding their economy and their country, quickly creating a citadel of economic strength. The whole world admired the West German "economic miracle." Adenauer's policy paid off within a few years; West Germany regained its sovereignty. In 1955, a cautiously remilitarized West Germany became a member of NATO, and in 1957 the country was a founding member of the European Economic Community, of which it soon became the linchpin.

German minds, however, were hardly at peace. The Nazi era remained a moral embarrassment. After the war, the Nuremberg trials of the major war criminals had been followed by de-Nazification under West German courts. Members of Nazi elite organizations were barred from public office and higher education. Many people guilty of atrocities were prosecuted; others went into hiding in Germany or abroad. The search and the trials still continue, the West German Parliament having consistently refused to enact a statute of limitations on crimes committed under the Nazis. In an effort at restitution, the government also has paid damages to Israel and to survivors among Nazi victims and their kin. "We are all responsible for the unspeakable sorrow that occurred in the name of Germany," said Richard von Weizsäcker, president of West Germany in 1985, in attempting to make Germans face up to their past.

Great Britain

World War II compounded Britain's long-standing economic woes, leaving the country impoverished and highly vulnerable in its dependence on imported food and raw materials. The British Empire was gradually and peaceably dismantled. Unlike the French, the English fought no last-ditch wars for retaining colonial control. Confronted with the choice between maintaining a global military presence and building a welfare state at home, the British people clearly preferred the latter.

A Labour government under Clement Attlee (1883–1967), elected immediately after the war, carried out the wartime promises of increased social services. Health care for the British people, traditionally deficient by Western European standards, was particularly improved. For better control over the national economy, the Labour government also nationalized the Bank of England, public transport, and the coal mines; eventually even the iron and steel industries came under government ownership.

The Conservatives who came to power in 1951 favored private enterprise but continued the extension of the welfare state, most notably by an ambitious public construction program that greatly improved British housing. The Labour party, back in power from 1964 to 1970, promised to boost the ailing economy. That, however, proved a difficult task. British industry had not modernized itself as rapidly as its chief competitors. It was hampered by poor management and frequent strikes. British exports were lagging while imports soared; the value of the pound continued to decline. Costly imports and pressures for higher wages and welfare benefits contributed to high inflation.

In 1979, the voters elected a Conservative government under Margaret Thatcher, the first woman prime minister in British history. "Maggie" Thatcher soon proved herself an "Iron Lady." A vigorous partisan of private enterprise, she favored the return of nationalized industries to private hands. Aided by high unemployment she succeeded in breaking the power of the labor unions. She also fought inflation with rigorous austerity (although she never tried to eliminate unemployment benefits and other essentials of the welfare state); she has preferred to let adversity bestir British employers and workers into efficiency and innovation. She also electrified the raw nerve of patriotism, long dulled by a decline of imperial fortune, when British forces drove out an Argentine force that had just invaded the distant Falkland Islands; located off the coast of Argentina in the South Atlantic Ocean, they are one of Britain's remaining possessions. In her domestic and foreign policies, Thatcher has stressed her close ties to the U.S. government under Presidents Ronald Reagan and George Bush.

During the 1980s, the British economy improved; London regained some of its former glory as a powerful financial center. The south of England has prospered, while the old, outmoded industrial areas of the Midlands and the north have declined, causing widespread unemployment, poverty, and occasional violence. Everywhere in the country the influx of people from the former colonies in Asia, Africa, and the West Indies has provoked racial friction.

British society has lost its homogeneity—and some of its tolerance. The violent conflict in Northern Ireland between Protestants and the large Catholic minority remains a constant irritant.

Italy

World War II had a sobering effect on Italy. Fascism was refuted, its chief henchman punished. In 1946 the monarchy, discredited by its subservience to Mussolini, was rejected and Italy became a republic. Hopeful for the future, the new republic could not escape the past. Italy has always been divided by internal rifts, the chief of which is the contrast between north and south, each worlds apart from the other. A lively localism impeded national unity; so did an anarchical individualism. Far from forming an organic whole, the state and the individual were in continuous tension and conflict.

Divisiveness did not hamper the economy, however. Spurred by the new postwar opportunities, Italian enterprise produced a striking economic advance. Its rate of growth, culminating in the years 1958–1962, propelled it into the ranks of the ten leading industrial nations of the world. As a result, personal incomes, particularly in northern Italy, came to resemble those of the richer European countries.

Dissatisfaction with the government has at times exploded into terrorist violence. Terrorists (not counting the criminal elements) have come from the extremes at both ends of the political spectrum. The neofascists, however, have been less active than the left-wing Red Brigades. Trying to create conditions favoring the overthrow of the ineffectual democratic constitution, the terrorists have resorted to bombings, kidnapings, maimings, and political murders, including that in 1978 of the much-respected Aldo Moro, leader of the Christian Democratic party.

The Soviet Union
Stalin's Last Years

In Soviet experience, World War II was another cruel landmark in the long succession of wars, revolutions, and crises that had started in 1914; nothing basically changed even after its end. The liberation from terror and dictatorship, which many soldiers had hoped for as a reward for their heroism, never occurred.

Corrupted by unlimited power and unrestrained adulation, Stalin displayed in his last years an unrelenting ruthlessness and a suspiciousness raised to the pitch of paranoia. He saw no ground for relaxing control. The country still had immense problems: the large anti-Soviet populations in Eastern Europe; the destruction wrought by the war; the political unreliability of returning soldiers and prisoners of war; and the overwhelming strength of the United States. Stalin's indomitable ambition, undiminished by age (he was sixty-six years old in 1945), was to build up Soviet power in his lifetime, whatever the human cost. More Five-Year Plans, more terror were needed.

On this familiar note the Soviet Union slid from war into peace, staggering through the hardships and hunger of the war's aftermath, mourning its dead soldiers, desperately short of men. With planning, much selfless hard work, manpower released from the army, and resources requisitioned from all occupied territories, industrial production was back to prewar levels within three years—no mean achievement.

With the return to Five-Year Plans came a deliberate tightening of ideological control. The party boss of Leningrad, Andrei Zhdanov (1896–1948), lashed out against any form of Western influence. Thousands of returning soldiers and prisoners of war, who had seen too much in the West, were sent to forced-labor camps. The Soviet intelligentsia was again terrorized into compliance with the party line. And in 1948, the chief leaders of Leningrad's heroic struggle against the Nazi siege were arrested and shot. That same year Stalin brought Eastern Europe under tight rein.

Stalin continued to build Soviet power. By 1949, sooner than expected, Soviet Russia possessed the atomic bomb. By 1953, at the same time as the United States, it had the hydrogen bomb as well. Stalin also helped lay the foundation for *Sputnik I* (meaning "fellow traveler"—of the Earth), the first artificial satellite to orbit the globe.

In his last years Stalin withdrew into virtual isolation, surrounded by a few fawning and fearful subordinates, and his sickly suspicion worsened. Before he died, he "recognized" a plot among the doctors who treated him and personally issued orders for their torture (which killed one of them). When on March 5, 1953, the failing dictator died of a stroke, his advisers sighed with relief, but many people wept: to them Stalin was the godlike leader and savior of the nation.

Stalin's Successors

The most hated among Stalin's potential heirs was Lavrenti Beria, the head of the secret police and the vast empire of forced-labor camps. In December 1953, he was suddenly executed, together with his chief henchmen, for having been a "foreign spy." These cynical accusations and violent deaths were the last gasp of Stalinism; ever since, the rivals for supreme leadership have died of natural causes.

Gradually leadership was assumed by a team headed by Nikita Khrushchev (1894–1971), who breathed fresh air into Soviet life. Khrushchev was the driving force behind the "thaw" that emptied the forced-labor camps and allowed the return to their native regions of most nationalities that had been forcibly resettled during the war. In a speech at the Twentieth Party Congress in February 1956, Khrushchev even dared to attack Stalin himself. His audi-

Map 21.2   Eastern Europe After 1945 ▶

German territory to Poland
Acquired by Soviet Union, 1939-1945
Soviet satellites
Communist, nonsatellite nation
"Iron Curtain" after 1950

NORWAY

SWEDEN

FINLAND

Helsinki

Leningrad

Stockholm

G. of Finland

ESTONIA

BALTIC SEA

LATVIA

Moscow

DENMARK

Copenhagen

LITHUANIA

SOVIET UNION

Hamburg

Gdansk (Danzig)

Elbe R.

NETHERLANDS

Berlin

EAST GERMANY

Vistula R.

Warsaw

WHITE RUSSIA

Bonn

WEST GERMANY

POLAND

Rhine R.

Prague

Kiev

CZECHOSLOVAKIA

UKRAINE

Dnieper R.

Munich

Vienna

Dniester R.

SWITZERLAND

AUSTRIA

Budapest

BESSARABIA

HUNGARY

Po R.

RUMANIA

CRIMEA

ITALY

Belgrade

Bucharest

BLACK SEA

CORSICA

YUGOSLAVIA

Danube R.

Rome

BULGARIA

Sofia

Istanbul

Tirane

Ankara

SARDINIA

ALBANIA

ADRIATIC SEA

GREECE

AEGEAN SEA

TURKEY

SICILY

Athens

CYPRUS

MEDITERRANEAN SEA

ence gasped with horror as he recited the facts: "Of the 139 members and candidates of the Party Central Committee who were elected at the 17th congress, 98 persons, i.e., 70%, were arrested . . . and shot. . . ."[1] In this vein, Khrushchev cited example after example of Stalin's terror. Without criticizing the Soviet system, Khrushchev acknowledged and rejected the excesses of Stalinism.

Khrushchev's revelations created a profound stir around the world and promoted defection from communist ranks everywhere. Among the Soviet satellite countries, Poland was on the brink of rebellion by 1956; a workers' uprising forced a change of leadership. In Hungary in 1956, the entire communist regime was overthrown before the Red Army reoccupied the country.

In foreign policy Khrushchev professed to promote peace. But while trying to reduce the role of the army, he also made some provocative moves by threatening Western access to West Berlin and placing missiles in Cuba; U.S. pressure forced him to withdraw in both cases. Not wishing to help communist China build atomic weapons, he withdrew, after mutual recrimination, all Soviet advisers in 1960, causing a break between the two communist nations. Mao then charged him with "revisionism" as well as imperialism.

Eager to prod his country toward a higher level of Marxist-Leninist ideology, Khrushchev presented a new party program and impatiently pressed for reforms in industry, agriculture, and party organization. His ceaseless reorganizations and impatient manner antagonized wide sections of state and party administration. In October 1964, while he was on vacation, his comrades on the politburo unceremoniously ousted him for "ill health" or, as they later added, his "hare-brained schemes." He was retired and allowed to live out his years in peace.

Khrushchev was succeeded, as was Stalin, by a group of leaders acting in common. Among these men, Leonid Brezhnev (1906–1982) gradually rose to the fore. Under his leadership the government of the U.S.S.R. turned from a personal dictatorship into an oligarchy—the collective rule of a privileged minority. Brezhnev's style stressed reasoned agreement rather than command. Soviet officials breathed more easily, and Soviet society in turn grew less authoritarian.

In the 1970s, international relations entered a limited phase of peaceful cooperation called *détente* (see Chapter 22). At the same time, the Soviet Union achieved a rough parity in nuclear weapons with the United States; henceforth, it was protected by deterrence just like the United States. Never before in Soviet history had the country enjoyed such external security. As a result, the rigors of authoritarian rule could be relaxed and the country be opened, cautiously, to the outside world. Young people, for instance, were allowed access to Western styles of music and dress. More issues of state policy were opened to public debate and more latitude granted to artistic expression. Interest in religion revived.

The fate of Russian dissidents, however, remained uncertain. For example, Andrei Sakharov, who had helped to develop the Soviet H-bomb but subsequently defended human rights, was exiled from Moscow and placed under house arrest.* The most adamant critics, like Aleksandr Solzhenitsyn or Andrei Amalrik, were expelled (or allowed to emigrate). Other critics who stayed were declared insane and confined in mental hospitals, following a practice begun under Nicholas I. The secret police (KGB) remained as powerful as ever.

Gorbachev's Challenge

Brezhnev died in 1982; his immediate successors, chosen by agreement among top party officials, were old men who survived in office only for a short time. Former KGB chief Yuri Andropov (aged sixty-eight), in poor health from the start, died in early 1984. He was replaced by Konstantin Chernenko, a man of Brezhnev's generation likewise in poor health, who lasted until early 1985. In that year, Mikhail Gorbachev (b. 1931) took over, representing at last a younger and more sophisticated age group that had grown up in the calmer times after Stalin's death.

Self-confident, energetic, and articulate, Gorbachev was keenly aware of his country's problems and eager to confront them. He knew that the Soviet Union had to update its industrial and agricultural productivity to compete with Japan, South Korea, Taiwan, the countries of Western Europe, and the United States. In particular, the Soviet Union lagged in the design and production of computers. A sobering demonstration of inefficiency and mismanagement occurred in late April 1986 when, because of staff misjudgment, a reactor at the nuclear power plant at Chernobyl exploded, spewing dangerous radiation high into the atmosphere; poisonous fallout covered much of Europe. Wherever Gorbachev looked, the mismanagement caused by rigid, centralized planning stifled innovation.

Gorbachev demanded no less than a fundamental reorganization—a *perestroika*—of the Soviet system, with the party in charge but responding more readily to the plans and hopes of Soviet citizens. Even more than his predecessors, he advocated "the democratization of society," hoping to stimulate participation by ordinary citizens, especially at their place of work and in local administration. He called for multiple candidates for elected posts, a novel experience for Soviet voters. To loosen up administrative rigidity, he also granted greater freedom to local entrepreneurs in agriculture, industry, and consumer services, demanding that supply and demand be closely coordinated as in a free market.

Even more significantly, Gorbachev tried to overcome the widespread indifference and weariness with a new policy of openness (*glasnost*) in the discussion of public affairs. Let all the problems of Soviet society, hitherto kept under cover, be openly discussed: corruption, abuse of power, disregard for legality, and stifling of criticism. Domestic news began to depict Soviet reality more accurately. There was also a novel candor about the Soviet past. During the

---

* Sakharov's six-year internal exile ended in 1986, and in 1989 he took a seat in the new Soviet legislature.

Reagan and Gorbachev in Geneva, 1985.   After alternating periods of cold war and détente, the United States and the Soviet Union have attempted to curb the staggering costs of military expenditures by seeking more peaceful coexistence. In spite of the show of friendship, distrust still continues. (*AP/Wide World Photos*)

seventieth anniversary of the Bolshevik Revolution, Gorbachev asserted that "the guilt of Stalin . . . for the wholesale repressive measures and acts of lawlessness is enormous and unforgivable." Gorbachev then assured Soviet citizens that they should not hesitate to speak out freely. "We are for the diversity of public opinion, a richness of spiritual life. We need not fear openly raising and solving difficult problems of social development, criticizing and arguing. It is in such circumstances that the truth is born and that correct decisions take shape."[2]

Gorbachev also sought to ease international tensions. National security in the nuclear age, he urged, called for superpower cooperation for the sake of common survival. In the spirit of glasnost, he frankly admitted that the adverse prospects of his country's economy forced him to advocate not only "normal international relations" but also an end to the arms race. Setting an example, with a touch of Western sartorial elegance, he traveled abroad and cautiously lifted the restrictions barring access to the outside world. Jewish emigration was eased; foreign firms were invited to help stimulate the Soviet economy; high-level discussions between Russians and Americans became commonplace. Gorbachev promised to withdraw the Soviet army from Afghanistan by the end of 1988, admitting that the 1979 invasion of Afghanistan had been a mistake.

Stepping forward as an eloquent advocate of peace and disarmament, Gorbachev pleaded for international cooperation in solving the human problems on earth, especially among countries of the Third World. His initiatives bore fruit in summit meetings with President Reagan in Reykjavik, Iceland (1986), and most successfully in Washington, D.C., in December 1987. At the Washington summit, an agreement was signed to dismantle intermediate-range nuclear missiles in Western and Eastern Europe, a cautious beginning to a process that, according to Gorbachev, might eventually end the nuclear threat.

The Soviet Satellites

The Stalinization of Eastern Europe

As the Red Armies fought their way west in 1944–45, Eastern European communists, trained in the Soviet Union, followed behind them. The Baltic states (Lithuania, Latvia, Estonia), seized after the Nazi-Soviet Pact of 1939 and then lost to Hitler, were reincorporated into the Soviet Union as "soviet socialist republics." Elsewhere Stalin respected, outwardly at least, the national sovereignty of the occupied countries by ruling through returning native communists and whatever sympathizers he could find.

By the end of 1948, however, the countries of eastern and southeastern Europe had emerged as "people's democracies." The Soviet Union continued to claim the right, based on conquest, of intervening at will in the internal affairs of its satellites. Thus the pall of Stalinism hung over war-torn and impoverished Eastern Europe. The puppet regimes leveled the formerly privileged classes, curtailing or abolishing private enterprise. The economy was socialized and rigid, and hasty plans were implemented for industrialization and the collectivization of agriculture. Religion and the churches were repressed and political liberty and free speech stamped out. Even the "proletarian masses" derived few benefits from the artificial revolution engineered from Moscow, because Stalin drained Eastern Europe of its resources for the sake of rebuilding the Soviet Union. Contact with Western Europe or the United States was banned. Each satellite existed in isolation, surrounded by borders fortified with barbed wire and watch towers set along mined corridors cut through the landscape. Fear and terror reached deep into every house and individual soul as little Stalins copied their mentor's style in East Berlin, Warsaw, Prague, Budapest, Sofia, and Bucharest.

An exception to this trend emerged in Yugoslavia under the leadership of the pugnacious Marshal Tito (see page 551), who became a symbol of defiance to Stalin. During World War II, he had led the Yugoslav resistance movement against Nazi occupation. A convinced and hardened communist, Tito was also a Yugoslav patriot committed to rebuilding and unifying his country. Thus

Yugoslavia escaped Soviet occupation. Backed by his party and his people, Tito guided his country on an independent course.

Elsewhere in Eastern Europe, Soviet control continued. All communist parties (by whatever name) were guided by Moscow; Soviet troops remained strategically stationed in the area. Created in 1955, the Warsaw Pact—or Warsaw Treaty Organization (WTO)—coordinated the armies of the satellite countries with the Red Army as a military instrument for preserving the ideological and political unity of the bloc and for counterbalancing NATO.

A New Era: Permissiveness and Reprisals

Stalin's successors, realizing that continued repression among the satellites would provoke trouble, began to relax their controls. A new era began for eastern and southeastern Europe. The Soviet satellites began to move toward greater national self-determination, searching for their own forms of industrialization, collectivization of agriculture, and communist dictatorship. The history of the region since 1953 was thus a series of experiments to determine what deviations from Soviet practice in domestic politics and what measure of self-assertion in foreign policy the Kremlin would tolerate.

No event proved more crucial than Khrushchev's attack on Stalin in 1956. It set off a political earthquake throughout the bloc, discrediting Stalinists and encouraging moderates in the parties, reviving cautious discussions among intellectuals, and even arousing visions of national self-determination.

The first tremors of protest rumbled in June 1956 in Poland—the largest and most troublesome of the satellite countries. The crisis came to a head in October: would Poland revolt, inviting invasion by the Red Army, or would Khrushchev ease Soviet control? The Soviet boss yielded in return for a Polish pledge of continued loyalty to the Soviet Union. Thereafter, Poland breathed more freely, clinging to its Catholicism as a cornerstone of its national identity.

Although the "Polish October" ended peacefully, events moved to a brutal showdown in Hungary. The Stalinists had suppressed national pride in Hungary for too long. On October 20, 1956, an uprising in Budapest raised anti-Soviet feeling to a fever pitch and forced Soviet troops to withdraw from the country. Next, a moderate communist government, eager to capture popular sentiment, called for Western-style political democracy and Hungary's withdrawal from the Warsaw Pact. Thoroughly alarmed, and with the backing of Mao and even Tito, the Soviet leaders struck back. On November 4, 1956, Soviet troops re-entered the country and crushed all opposition. Yet the bold uprising had left its mark.

The new communist leader of Hungary, János Kádár, was a moderate, who with Khrushchev's approval built a pragmatic regime of consumer-oriented "goulash communism" that granted considerable opportunity to private enterprise. Kádár's regime also allowed noncommunists to participate extensively in public affairs. Relaxation and decentralization of planning made possible in the 1970s a remarkable increase in popular prosperity and individual freedom; the Hungarian experiment became the envy of all other Soviet-bloc countries.

After 1956, Soviet leaders grew more circumspect in their approach to the satellite countries' internal affairs, allowing increasing diversity of political development. The post-Stalin permissiveness was never without risks, even under the milder regime of Brezhnev, as was shown in Czechoslovakia in 1968. A new group of Czech communists led by Alexander Dubček sought to liberalize their regime to include noncommunists, allow greater freedom of speech, and rid the economy of the rigidities that for so long had prevented prosperity. Their goal was a "humanist democratic socialism," or "socialism with a human face"—a communist party supported by public good will rather than by the secret police.

This program panicked the governments of East Germany, Poland, and the Soviet Union. On August 21, East German, Polish, Hungarian, and Soviet troops, under the provisions of the Warsaw Pact, carried out a swift and well-prepared occupation of Czechoslovakia but failed to break the rebellious will of its reformers. While Soviet tanks rumbled through Prague, an extraordinary Czechoslovak party congress secretly met in choked fury. Never had the Soviet leaders encountered such united resistance by a communist party! Nonetheless, the revolt ended in failure. The party was purged; all reforms were cancelled; and the country was reduced to abject hopelessness. But the Soviet Union paid a high price: a cry of moral outrage resounded around the world; protests were heard even in Moscow.

Extraordinary events have occurred in Poland in recent years. Industrial workers, presumably the real masters in communist regimes, have embarrassed their government by taking the lead in pressing for freedom and a better standard of living. When a Polish cardinal became Pope John Paul II in 1978, patriotism surged. In 1980, workers under the leadership of an electrician named Lech Walesa succeeded, with the blessing of the church, in forming an independent labor union called Solidarity, which engaged in numerous strikes.

In 1981, matters came to a head: some of Solidarity's more radical members spoke of bringing free elections to Poland. In December, a military dictatorship, suddenly formed under General Wojciech Jaruzelski, imposed martial law. Walesa and other leaders of Solidarity were arrested, and protesting workers were dispersed by force. Faced with a deteriorating economy and recognizing Solidarity's popularity with the Polish masses, Jaruzelski legalized the union in 1989. Permitted to run against Communist party candidates in a free election, Solidarity won an overwhelming victory. The once-jailed Solidarity members now sit in the Polish parliament next to their former jailers, and Tadeusz Mazowiecki, a member of Solidarity, has become prime minister. However, burdened by a huge foreign debt, low productivity, acute shortages of materials, machinery, and capital, Poland remains a troubled country.

The German Democratic Republic (East Germany) at first shared the fate of all Soviet satellites. Under the leadership of German communists who spent the Nazi years in the Soviet Union, industry was nationalized, agriculture collectivized, and the people regimented under the Communist party (here called the Socialist Unity party). But protests against Stalinism appeared earlier here than

Solidarity Flag at a Papal Mass in Poland, 1983. The unevenness of economic advance and the deep-rooted nationalism in the Soviet satellite countries continue to breed dissent. In Poland the independent labor union called Solidarity erupted in 1980. Its advocacy of free elections led to the imposition of martial law in 1981. But, in 1989, Solidarity was legalized. (*Fabian/Sygma*)

elsewhere. In June 1953, the workers of Berlin staged an uprising, gaining some concessions. Then followed a steady exodus of skilled manpower to West Germany, mostly via West Berlin. More than 3 million people escaped before the East German government, in August 1961, suddenly threw up a wall—the famous "Berlin Wall"—and built equally deadly barriers along the entire border with West Germany. For a time, all contact between the two Germanys ceased.

With increased control over their people, the communist leaders—first Walter Ulbricht and, since the early 1970s, Erich Honecker—concentrated on advancing the economy, with marked success. Their people, numbering less than a quarter of the West German population, enjoy the highest standard of living in the entire Soviet bloc. In 1972, détente led to the establishment of diplomatic relations between the two Germanys and to closer economic ties, which made East Germany virtually a beneficiary of the European Community. Welcoming close economic relations with West Germany for their own good, the Soviet masters raised no objections. They are opposed, however, to any speculation about German reunification. East Germans are aware of their privileged position within the Soviet bloc; they recognize the futility of revolt and work hard at their jobs. Secretly some may hope to escape someday to the West, whose affluence and freedom they can see on West German television.

Chronology 21.1 ♦ Europe After 1945

1945	Eastern Europe occupied by Red Army
1947	The Marshall Plan inaugurated
1948	Czech coup; Stalinization of Eastern Europe; Tito's Yugoslavia breaks with the Soviet Union
1949	NATO formed
1953	Stalin dies
1956	Khrushchev's secret speech on Stalin's crimes; the Polish October; the Hungarian uprising crushed
1957	Sputnik launched—the space age begins; the EEC established
1961	Berlin Wall built, dividing the city of Berlin
1964	Khrushchev ousted; Brezhnev and Kosygin installed as leaders in U.S.S.R.
1968	Czechoslovakia's "Prague Spring"—Dubček's "Socialism with a human face"
1971	Détente in East-West relations
1979	Soviet Union invades Afghanistan
1980	Solidarity trade union in Poland
1982	Brezhnev dies, succeeded by Andropov (died 1984) and Chernenko (died 1985)
1985	Gorbachev becomes U.S.S.R. leader
1988	Soviet Union withdraws from Afghanistan

The Soviet Union in an Age of Globalism

In the seventy-odd years between the collapse of the Russian state at the end of World War I and Gorbachev's era, communist Russia has changed from a backward country of tradition-bound peasants to a modern superpower claiming equality with the United States. In its seven decades, the Soviet Union has tried to make its presence felt over the entire world—strengthening its borders, holding tightly onto its territorial gains, and advertising with imposing moral righteousness its achievements as an example for all peoples. The U.S.S.R. has been inspired by its long-range goal, hoping like the United States to reshape the world in its own image. National liberation movements directed against

Western nations have found a willing ally in Moscow. Always feeling humiliated by Western superiority, Moscow has endeavored to outdo the West on its own terms, whether in spectacular technological feats like space exploration, or in its military bases set up around the world, or in the ultimate promise of providing the best society.

Yet the Leninist dream of world revolution has vanished. The Kremlin now conducts its foreign affairs pragmatically, guided by a sober sense of self-interest. Cautiously trying to assert its power in competition with the United States, Soviet Russia has become dependent on the developed industrial countries in the widening network of global interdependence. It still needs to draw on Western know-how (along with Japan's) to satisfy the material wishes of its subjects, whom it can no longer insulate from the outside world.

At home, too, Soviet leaders have reason to worry. Revolutionary zeal has faded among their peoples, who crave freedom and prosperity but lack the knowledge and the self-discipline necessary for managing an innovative industrial economy. The peoples also lack a firm sense of unity. The ethnic and religious diversity of the Soviet Union continues to provide a source of disloyalty. More ominously, the rapid population growth of non-Russian nationalities in Soviet central Asia threatens the traditional preponderance of the Russian population in the Soviet Union.

Notes

1. Nikita S. Krushchev's speech (in translation) in *The Crimes of the Stalin Era: Special Report to the 20th Congress of the Communist Party of the Soviet Union*, annotated by Boris I. Nicolaevsky, *The New Leader* (New York), 1956.

2. Gorbachev's Speech at the 70th Anniversary of the Bolshevik Revolution, quoted in the *New York Times*, November 3, 1987, sec. A, p. 3.

Suggested Reading

Garrison, Mark, and Abbot Gleason, eds., *Shared Destiny: Fifty Years of Soviet-American Relations* (1985). Distinguished experts reflect on the blunders, misperceptions, and lost opportunities that have created the gulf between the two countries.

Gelb, Norman, *The Berlin Wall* (1987). An on-the-spot account of the building of the wall. Implications for the city, for the two Germanys, and for East-West relations are considered.

Schell, Jonathan, *The Fate of the Earth* (1982). The book everybody should read about the prospects for and the results of a nuclear war.

Ulam, Adam B., *Dangerous Relations: The Soviet Union in World Politics,* 1970–1982 (1983). Soviet foreign relations under Brezhnev.

Van Dusen, Henry P., *Dag Hammarskjöld: The Statesman and His Faith* (1967). An introduction to the work of the United Nations as reflected in the life of its most prominent official.

Wegg, Robert J., *Europe Since 1945* (1984). A concise history.

Weisberger, Bernard A., *Cold War, Cold Peace: The United States and Russia Since 1945* (1984). A history of four decades of tension, conflict, détente, and living with the nuclear threat.

Yergin, Daniel, *Shattered Peace: The Origins of the Cold War and the National Security State* (1977). The best book on the subject, written with verve and insight.

Review Questions

1. What do you consider the biggest changes to have taken place in Western Europe after World War II?
2. What have been the major problems of government in France and Britain since 1945?
3. What problems in the Soviet Union did Stalin face after the end of World War II? How did he try to cope with them?
4. What happened to Stalinism after Stalin's death? Under Khrushchev? Under Gorbachev?
5. What are the objectives of Gorbachev's policies? What are the obstacles? How would you rank Gorbachev among Stalin's successors?
6. How do Soviet leaders view their Eastern European satellites? How do these satellite countries view the Soviet Union?

Chapter ⚘ 22

The New Globalism: Problems and Prospects

World War II propelled the earth's inhabitants into an inescapable, tight, global interdependence. Whatever the differences between them, close neighbors as well as people in distant lands were thrust together in intense interaction, whether for cooperation or conflict, for peace or war. As the colonial empires of the Western European states dissolved, the liberated peoples in Asia and Africa formed sovereign countries, initially patterned after the Western European democracies. These new countries, too, plunged into the universal competition for wealth and power. They became involved in the rivalry between the superpowers, while also often bitterly feuding among themselves.

The new globalism was reflected in the United Nations (UN), established in April 1945 by the victorious wartime coalition led by the United States. The UN considered itself to be a peace-keeping organization, designed to "achieve international co-operation in solving international problems of an economic, social, cultural, or humanitarian character, and in promoting and encouraging respect for human rights and for fundamental human freedom for all without distinction of race, language, or religion." It aimed at "harmonizing the action of nations in the attainment of these common ends."[1] But by the last decade of this century, the global community has become an unruly association of some 160 sovereign states. Because of disunity among its members and cold war politics, the UN has been able neither to prevent the many small wars that have flared up in Asia, the Mideast, Africa, and Central America nor to reduce, let alone stop, the nuclear arms race. ⚘

The Origins of the Cold War

The cold war (the phrase was coined in 1947 by the American financier Bernard Baruch) stemmed from the divergent historical experiences and the incompatible political ambitions of the United States and the Soviet Union, which clashed head-on as the new global order began to take shape. During the war, the basic differences between the West and the U.S.S.R. had been glossed over. Once the common danger receded, the differences between political institutions and ideologies pushed again to the fore, aggravated by the flush of victory and postwar opportunity. Hostility soon escalated between the superpowers, propelled by mutual fear, aggressive self-protection, raised ambitions, and collective pride.

The Cold War in Europe

The incompatibility of objectives had become clear even before the end of hostilities. As the Red Army moved through Eastern Europe, the fate of the East European peoples hung in the balance. The Western allies, advancing from the Atlantic against Hitler's armies, were in no position to stop Stalin from doing as he wished. As the Red Army occupied Poland, Stalin installed a pro-Soviet governing regime. Other countries in Eastern Europe suffered the same fate. Ever worried about the security of his country's western boundaries, Stalin incorporated the East European countries into a buffer zone for protection against Western attack. The Soviet occupation of Eastern Europe was considered a dire calamity by the local populations and their sympathizers in Western European nations and the United States. But short of starting another war, the latter countries were powerless to intervene.

Germany remained divided. In the Soviet-occupied zone, Stalin arranged for the establishment of communist rule. This area became the German Democratic Republic, while the three other zones combined as the democratic Federal Republic of Germany.

Further afield, in the eastern Mediterranean, Stalin was suspected of aiding communist guerrillas in the Greek civil war of 1946–47. The guerrillas were supported by the neighboring Soviet-dominated countries of Albania, Bulgaria, and Yugoslavia; Stalin's influence on the course of the war was in fact minimal. He did, however, lay claim to the Straits of Constantinople, and he unduly prolonged the wartime Soviet occupation of northern Iran.

In March 1947, alarmed by the threat of Soviet penetration into the eastern Mediterranean and by British weakness in that area, President Harry S Truman proclaimed the Truman Doctrine: "It must be the policy of the United States to support free peoples who are resisting attempted subjugation by armed minorities or by outside pressures."[2] The Truman Doctrine was the centerpiece of the new policy of *containment*, of holding Soviet power within its then-current boundaries. U.S. military and economic support soon went to Greece and Turkey. Thus, a sharp reversal took place in American foreign

The United Nations Building in New York. The UN Declaration of Human Rights announced that "the recognition of the inherent dignity and of the equal and inalienable rights of all members of the human family is the foundation of freedom, justice and peace in the world." (*UN Photo*)

policy; prewar isolation gave way to worldwide vigilance against any Soviet effort at expansion. In June 1947 the United States took a further step toward strengthening the West. Secretary of State George C. Marshall announced an impressive scheme of economic aid to Europe (the European Recovery Program) for rebuilding prosperity and stability (see page 563).

These measures were accompanied by a massive ideological mobilization of American opinion against communism and a new apprehension about national security. As a result, the armed forces and the defense industries supporting them—the "military-industrial complex," in President Dwight D. Eisenhower's words—attained unprecedented political power in U.S. politics.

At the same time, Stalin brutally intensified ideological and political controls not only in his own country but also in Eastern Europe. In February 1948, with couplike suddenness, he replaced the mildly procommunist coalition government of Czechoslovakia with an outright Stalinist clique. Less dramatically, Soviet control was completed over Bulgaria, Romania, Hungary, Poland, and

East Germany. Only Marshal Tito, the wartime hero of Yugoslav resistance to Nazi rule, and now the country's leader, eluded Stalin's reach. Stalin also promoted a Communist Information Bureau (COMINFORM) to enforce tighter obedience among communist parties in Eastern and Western Europe. By these and similar actions he profoundly alarmed Western Europeans, who, three years after the end of the war, redoubled their search for military security.

The most spectacular test between the two superpowers took place from June 1948 to May 1949, after the Soviet authorities severed all overland access to the western sectors of Berlin. The Soviets aimed to starve into submission a half-city of about two million inhabitants who, because of their freedom, were "a bone in the communist throat" (as Khrushchev later put it). West Berlin was saved by an impressive airlift in which, under U.S. direction, the French, British, and Americans flew in supplies around the clock in all kinds of weather. In response to these conditions NATO was formed.

The year 1949 was a turning point in the cold war, which spread from Europe into the world at large, intensifying as it did so. The victory of the Chinese communists under Mao Zedong seemed more threatening to the United States than the Berlin blockade. Now another communist giant had joined the Soviet Union. Even more alarming was the fact that, sooner than expected, the Soviet Union had exploded its first atomic bomb, breaking the U.S. monopoly of that all-powerful weapon, which had inspired American self-confidence in the immediate postwar years. Now Americans felt that they also had to keep ahead of the Soviets in nuclear weapons.

The Growth of Military Alliances

In June 1950, war broke out in Korea, a country divided in 1945 between a pro-Soviet communist regime in the north and a pro-American regime in the south. Eager to restore Korean national unity and mistakenly assuming U.S. nonintervention, the North Korean army invaded South Korea, possibly with Stalin's approval. Immediately the Americans took countermeasures, gaining UN backing for their war against North Korea. Under the command of General Douglas MacArthur, South Korean and U.S. troops, assisted by a token force from other UN members, fought their way north toward the Chinese border. Fearing for his own security, Mao Zedong thereupon dispatched Chinese "volunteers" to drive back the approaching enemy in a surprise attack. Forced to retreat, General MacArthur's troops eventually withdrew from North Korea. Peace was restored in 1953, with the division of Korea reaffirmed; South Korea became an outpost of U.S. power.

The fear of Soviet global ambition redoubled Washington's resolve to contain Soviet power. Under President Eisenhower, the United States extended its military alliances into central and East Asia for reasons stated when he assumed office: "The freedom we cherish and defend in Europe and in the Americas is no different from the freedom that is imperiled in Asia." As a result, two more alliance systems were added to NATO. The Central Treaty

Organization (CENTO) united Turkey, Iraq, Iran, and Pakistan with Britain and the United States. Iran was at that time a loyal ally of the United States (and remained so until the overthrow of the shah in 1979). It was strategically important because a pro-Western Iran could prevent Soviet access to the crucial oil reserves of the Persian Gulf. The purpose of CENTO was to protect the southern neighbors of the Soviet Union from Soviet penetration.

The anti-Soviet alliance of lands further east was called the Southeast Asia Treaty Organization (SEATO). It contained, besides the United States, Britain, and France, the Asian countries of Pakistan and Thailand, and, in the Pacific Ocean, the Philippines, Australia, and New Zealand. In the Mideast, Israel constituted an additional reliable U.S. ally. Still closer to home, in the Western Hemisphere, the United States made sure, by economic pressure, subversion, or military intervention if necessary, that no pro-Soviet or even Marxist regime established itself.

The Cuban Missile Crisis

Confrontation between the superpowers rose to a terrifying climax in 1962 during the Cuban missile crisis. In 1959, the infamous dictatorship of Fulgencio Batista had been toppled by Fidel Castro (b. 1927), a left-wing revolutionary who turned Cuba into a totalitarian state. After an American attempt to overthrow him—the bungled Bay of Pigs operation—Castro was ready to turn his country into an outpost of Soviet power. Khrushchev planned to exploit this foothold within the Western Hemisphere by installing Soviet nuclear missiles in Cuba. The United States, admittedly, had for some time stationed nuclear weapons in Turkey within easy reach of Soviet targets. But the reverse situation—allowing a major Soviet threat close to home—was alarming. President John F. Kennedy demanded that Khrushchev withdraw the Soviet missiles from Cuba. For an awesome moment, the cold war confrontation threatened to turn into a very hot nuclear war. In the end, however, Khrushchev backed down, a move that contributed to his fall from power two years later. No Soviet missiles were stationed in Cuba.

The Vietnam War

The new countries in Asia and Africa, emerging from colonial rule offered seductive opportunities for Soviet global ambitions. From the U.S. perspective, the biggest challenge arose in Vietnam, where the communist regime in the north threatened to take over South Vietnam as well. The threat had started with the partition of the country in 1954. From the north, the authoritarian regime of Ho Chi Minh (1890–1969), backed by indigenous nationalism and Soviet aid, cast its shadow over a disorganized south. In the south, American sponsors, with the help of Ngo Dinh Diem, a Catholic anticommunist and long a resident in the United States, tried to create a democratic nation. Provid-

Bogged Down in Vietnam.   The domino theory, which predicted the fall of East
Asian countries to communist rule, led to American defense of South Vietnam against
a threatened takeover by communist North Vietnam. Between 1964 and 1973, U.S.
involvement in the unsuccessful Vietnam War cost tens of thousands of American and
Vietnamese lives, ruined South Vietnam, and polarized U.S. public opinion over the
morality of the war. (*AP/Wide World Photos*)

ing South Vietnam with the stability and strength needed to resist communist
infiltration required increasing U.S. aid, including troops to fight off the communist guerrillas, the Vietcong. If the communists prevailed, so the argument
ran, all the other countries in East and Southeast Asia emerging from colonial
rule would fall like dominoes under communist influence. Under President
Johnson, U.S. intervention in South Vietnam became the (undeclared) Vietnam
War.

The U.S. government shipped to Vietnam nearly half a million soldiers,
equipped with the most advanced chemical weapons and electronic equipment
available. Yet victory eluded the American forces. The North Vietnamese
government and its people withstood the cruelest punishment of bombs and
chemical weapons ever inflicted on human beings. Nor was South Vietnam
spared; virtually every South Vietnamese family saw relatives killed or
maimed, and their farms and livelihoods ruined.

In the face of rising domestic opposition and unbroken Vietcong resistance,
it was clear to President Richard M. Nixon, elected in 1968, that the war had

to be ended by "peace with honor." While he initiated negotiations with North Vietnam, U.S. forces put pressure on the enemy by attacking communist bases and supply routes in neighboring Cambodia and Laos. Civilians were bombed more fiercely than had been the case in World War II. In 1973, by agreement with North Vietnam, the United States withdrew its forces from the area. In 1975 the North Vietnamese swept aside the inept South Vietnamese army and unified the country under a communist dictatorship. Ho Chi Minh had triumphed against the mightiest nation in the world.

In the wake of the American withdrawal, Cambodian communists, called the Khmer Rouge, seized power under their leader, Pol Pot. He drove over two million people from the capital city of Phnom Penh and tried to establish a new order based on ideologically regimented rural communes. Hundreds of thousands of people died in the evacuation and more died later in the countryside. In 1979, the blood-stained and starving country, together with Laos, was occupied by Vietnamese troops, visiting further catastrophe on its people.

Détente—and More Cold War

The nuclear arms race was made even more deadly by ICBMs, each equipped with a multiple independently targeted re-entry vehicle (MIRV) capable of hitting up to ten widely scattered targets. In 1972 the Soviet Union and the United States agreed to limit antiballistic missiles (ABMs) designed to destroy incoming missiles. The ABM treaty reflected a new phase in U.S.–Soviet relations, soon known by the term *détente*. There were good reasons for a relaxation of tensions. The Vietnam War had made Americans more realistic. Feeling more secure, the Soviet leaders in turn softened the aggressive tone of their foreign policy. In addition, West Germany's chancellor, Willy Brandt, was eager to reduce the strain between West and East Germany. He concluded treaties with the Soviet Union, Poland, and East Germany, formally accepting the division of Germany and assuring continued Western contact with West Berlin. Tension was also eased by the admission of both West and East Germany to the United Nations.

Of broader significance were the Helsinki Agreements of 1975, signed in neutral Finland, amid considerable pomp, by all European governments plus Canada and the United States. The first of these agreements legitimized all borders drawn in central Europe at the end of the war; they took the place of the peace that had never been officially concluded. Another agreement, especially important to the Soviet Union, stipulated the free exchange of technical and scientific data. The final agreement, and subsequently the most troublesome, called for the free movement of peoples and ideas across what Churchill had called the "iron curtain." But the Soviet government could hardly

Map 22.1   Southeast Asia and the Vietnam War   ▶

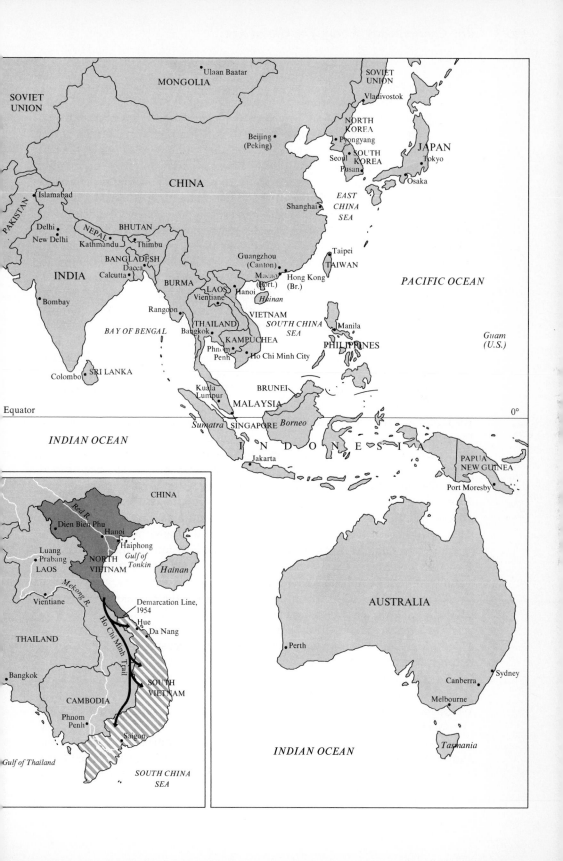

SOVIET
UNION

MONGOLIA

• Ulaan Baatar

SOVIET
UNION

• Vladivostok

NORTH
KOREA
• Pyongyang

Beijing •
(Peking)

Seoul •
• Pusan
SOUTH
KOREA

JAPAN
• Tokyo

• Osaka

CHINA

• Islamabad

EAST
CHINA
SEA

Shanghai •

PAKISTAN

Delhi •
New Delhi
NEPAL
Kathmandu •
BHUTAN
• Thimbu

BANGLADESH
Dacca
Calcutta •

INDIA

Guangzhou •
(Canton)
Macau
(Port.)
Hong Kong
(Br.)

Taipei •
TAIWAN

PACIFIC OCEAN

BURMA

LAOS
Vientiane •
Hanoi •
Hainan

• Bombay

Rangoon •

THAILAND
Bangkok •

VIETNAM
SOUTH CHINA
SEA

Manila •

Guam
(U.S.)

BAY OF BENGAL

KAMPUCHEA
Phnom
Penh •
• Ho Chi Minh City

PHILIPPINES

• Colombo
SRI LANKA

Kuala
Lumpur •

BRUNEI

MALAYSIA

Equator

0°

INDIAN OCEAN

Sumatra SINGAPORE
Borneo

I N D O N E S I A

PAPUA
NEW GUINEA

• Jakarta

• Port Moresby

AUSTRALIA

• Perth

Canberra •
• Sydney

• Melbourne

INDIAN OCEAN

Tasmania

CHINA

Red R.
• Dien Bien Phu
• Hanoi
• Haiphong

Luang
• Prabang
LAOS
NORTH
VIETNAM
Gulf of
Tonkin

Hainan

Mekong R.

• Vientiane

Demarcation Line,
1954
Hue
• Da Nang

THAILAND

Ho Chi Minh Trail

• Bangkok

SOUTH
VIETNAM

CAMBODIA

Phnom
Penh •

• Saigon

Gulf of Thailand

SOUTH CHINA
SEA

allow all those who wished to escape from oppression to leave the Soviet Union or its satellite countries.

Meanwhile, détente, combined with the fact that the Soviet Union had achieved parity in ICBMs and therefore felt more secure, favored further agreements for slowing down the arms race. Together with the ABM treaty, the first Strategic Arms Limitation Treaty (SALT I) was negotiated. It froze the number of strategic missile launchers at existing levels and stipulated that the construction of more ballistic missiles be offset by the dismantling of older equipment of the same type. Hopes ran high that even more stringent reductions of nuclear delivery systems and warheads might be negotiated. Yet SALT II, which spelled out these hopes in specific detail, fell victim to the collapse of détente in 1979. That treaty was not ratified by the United States, although its terms were voluntarily adhered to by both sides even after détente had faded.

In fact, détente had never been deeply rooted. There were the continuous violations of civil and human rights by the Soviet government. Additional friction arose subsequently over a pro-Soviet regime in Ethiopia, followed by the dispatch of Cuban soldiers and experts to Angola. Obviously, by U.S. judgment, the Soviet Union had not given up its expansionist ambitions. The traditional harassment of Jews in the Soviet Union especially soured U.S.–Soviet relations, leading on the eve of the Helsinki Agreements to discrimination against Soviet trade. American suspicion of Soviet motives never abated, breaking into full force again in 1979 when, after the overthrow of the pro-American shah of Iran by Islamic fundamentalists, the Soviet Union invaded Afghanistan to forestall a similar Islamic takeover.

In April 1978, Communists seized power in Afghanistan. The new leadership jailed and executed opponents and moved to establish a Marxist society. Worried about the Communists' ability to suppress a subsequent rebellion by Islamic traditionalists and tribal groups, the USSR under Brezhnev sent troops to Afghanistan in December 1979, and installed a new, more strongly pro-Soviet leadership. Afghans resisted the Soviet invasion, setting off a bitter civil war. For Americans, the Soviet invasion of Afghanistan constituted dramatic proof of Soviet expansionism. Stepping up its hostility against what President Ronald Reagan called "the evil empire," the U.S. government sent military aid to the Afghan insurgents, making it difficult for the Soviet government to extricate itself with honor from this Vietnam-like venture. Now the U.S.–Soviet confrontation was extended to a highly sensitive area on the Soviet southern border.

The resumption of the cold war also revived the arms race. In 1981 the United States introduced the neutron bomb, a weapon capable of killing people by massive doses of fatal radiation without destroying their cities. In 1983 President Reagan announced the Strategic Defense Initiative (SDI), nicknamed "Star Wars," designed to build a space shield of electronic equipment over the United States capable of destroying incoming weapons. Critics pointed to its exorbitant cost as well as its ineffectiveness. In any case, SDI propelled the arms race further into space.

After 1985 the new Soviet leader, Mikhail Gorbachev, undertook a major initiative for arms limitation. The high costs of the arms race seriously impeded the reforms in the Soviet economy that he was so urgently promoting. At the Washington summit conference in late 1987, the United States and the Soviet Union agreed to eliminate intermediate-range nuclear weapons (the INF treaty), which raised hopes for reducing long-range missiles as well. However, the basic causes of the arms race persist, for the long-range ambitions of both superpowers remain unchanged—the United States still perceives itself as the leader of a global mission for democracy, while the U.S.S.R. still believes in a communist course for humanity's future.

Decolonization and Worldwide Westernization

Below the surface of global politics, a profound and still unfinished process of cultural transformation is at work. No other civilization in history has managed to universalize itself to the extent of imposing its achievements and its spirit on all others the way Western civilization has. For better or worse, Europeans and people of European descent have taken the initiative in creating the irreversibly interdependent world with which the present and all future generations must cope. Penetrating all lands, the West has revamped a fragmented world of villages, loosely structured political communities, and a few effective nation-states into a quarrelsome global community.

In trying to adjust in the name of modernization to the institutions, machines, and human attitudes evolved by Western civilization, non-Westerners often find themselves in permanent conflict with their indigenous traditions. The agonizing task of fusing Western and non-Western ways in order to build a modern state and a modern economy started with the process of decolonization after the end of World War II.

After World War II, the rising militancy of nationalist movements bloomed amid the declining resources of the colonial empires. The political agitation of the war, in which many colonial soldiers loyally fought, fired the desire for political independence; after all, freedom and self-determination had been prominent Allied war slogans. Exhausted by the war, European colonial powers had no strength left for colonial rule.

In this setting, a mighty ground swell of decolonization after 1946 abolished all overseas empires and propelled their former subjects into independent statehood. At best, the colonial powers, under the threat of violence, relinquished their control quietly. At worst, they were driven out by bitter wars of liberation. Sometimes independence was followed by civil war.

Decolonization began when in 1946 the United States granted independence to the Philippines. In 1947, India and Pakistan attained sovereign statehood. In 1948, Burma and Ceylon (later renamed Sri Lanka) emerged. In 1949, it was the turn of the Dutch possessions in Indonesia. In 1954 the French quit Laos, Cambodia, and Vietnam (leaving the Americans to defend South Vietnam against the communist revolutionaries of North Vietnam until 1973). In 1956

France freed its northern African colonies, Morocco and Tunisia (but not Algeria, which attained independence in 1962 after a cruel revolutionary war).

To the cheers of black people everywhere, Ghana in 1957 declared its independence, the first sub-Saharan African country to do so. After 1959, virtually all French and English possessions in Africa were decolonized. In 1960 the Belgians reluctantly left the Congo (now called Zaire), which started independence amid a civil war. By 1975 even the Portuguese, determined to the last to keep their African colonies, were driven out. In 1980 white-ruled Rhodesia became the African state of Zimbabwe. Only in South Africa and Southwest Africa (renamed Namibia) did white settlers, including the long-established Afrikaners, continue to defy black majority rule.

In the Mideast, Egypt and Saudi Arabia, which had become independent before World War II, were joined between 1951 and 1971 by other free Arab states. By the mid-1970s, Western colonialism had formally come to an end. But the accumulated resentments of colonial rule and the struggle for independence remained a potent political legacy.

The newly independent states drew up enlightened democratic constitutions. The most Westernized and cosmopolitan elements in the population attained the seats of power. But disillusionment arrived swiftly. Often excruciatingly poor, composed of quarreling ethnic groups that felt no attachment to the new nation, and crowded with illiterate, disease-ridden, stubborn peasants, the new countries entered the race for power and prestige with severe handicaps.

These countries quickly learned that the competition for status is exceedingly keen; under the new globalism, the world is perceived as a pyramid of prestige and power. At the top—the "First World"—stand the advanced countries, representing essentially the states of Western Europe and North America; they were joined in the 1960s by Japan. The Soviet Union and its satellites occupy the "Second World," while the majority of humanity occupies the lower-level "Third World," where the "less developed" rank above the "least developed" countries.

"Backwardness," in any form and by any name, represents humiliation to be escaped as fast as possible by "development"—by catching up to the "advanced" countries. "Development" aims at a raised standard of living, at industrialization, at participation in scientific and technological progress, and foremost, at prestige in the world. In this sense, the struggle for development among non-Western peoples represents the culmination of westernization. All humanity strives to "modernize"—to master institutions and technologies originally developed by the West. But how? Unfortunately, the newcomers to modern statehood were, for the most part, entirely unprepared for managing the large-scale organizations required for statehood and global competition.

Perilous Experiments in Modernization

Each non-Western country has conducted its own experiments in modernization, limited by its own history and resources. Ranging from remarkable success to brutal failure, these efforts offer a panorama of a world in agonized transition.

Asia

Japan   The most spectacular model of triumphant modernization was Japan, which enjoyed the benefit of a headstart. Starting in 1867 under the Meiji emperor (see page 416), the Japanese government, with the full support of leading elements of Japanese society, deliberately copied those aspects of Western civilization that lay behind superior military power, including Western forms of government, law, education, science, and technology. At the same time Japan kept its own spiritual traditions. A unique case, the Japanese contributed from their own history the essentials of modern power: a high level of technical competence, a strict self-discipline needed for civic cooperation, and a tradition of readily absorbing foreign cultures into their own without giving up their own identity.

The fusion of Western and Japanese culture was not complete, however. In the 1930s the Japanese warrior heritage gained the upper hand; it encouraged an anti-Western orientation that led to World War II—and disaster. Defeated and utterly exhausted, Japan had to make a new start, laboring for seven years under U.S. occupation. The Americans imposed a Western democratic constitution and, while preserving the role of the emperor, abolished the traditional strongholds of power. Thus began Japan's miraculous rise to the position of economic superpower, rivaling and in some respects even outpacing the United States.

This miracle was possible, first of all, because the country started with a clean slate. Its own industrial capacity destroyed, it began reconstruction by humbly taking the best and the latest advances in technology and industrial science from the United States and Western Europe, gradually learning to improve the imported techniques, and concentrating on long-range goals. Second, undaunted by their misery after the war, the Japanese people were willing to work hard and live austerely, putting the welfare of the country ahead of their individual gain. Third, the tradition of selfless civic cooperation, unbroken by defeat and foreign occupation, permeated the political, economic, and social life of the country; little time was lost in social conflict, strikes, or work stoppages. Finally, national pride ran high, spurred by the desire to escape the humiliation of 1945, by the marked successes in industrial technology, and by the world's respect for the superior quality of Japanese products. In the 1970s, Japanese steel, ships, cameras, automobiles, and computers were rated among the best—if not *the* best—in the world; Japanese firms dominated world trade, entering into partnership with firms in the United States and other countries. By the 1980s, Japan's industrial and financial strength began to threaten the United States' economy. The Japanese standard of living rose, although not to the American level.

China   While postwar Japan rose from ashes to economic glory, events next door in China took a different and infinitely more tragic course. The Chinese

Chairman Mao with Teachers and Schoolchildren in 1959. Mao overestimated the creativity of the masses to conquer all obstacles, but he united China under his rule. With nuclear capability and a quarter of the world's population, China is a potential world force. (*UPI/Bettmann Newsphotos*)

experiment in modernization after World War II is known as Maoism, from the name of its leader, Mao Zedong (Mao Tse-tung, 1898–1976), chairman of the Chinese Communist party. Coming from a peasant family somewhat better off than most, Mao became a student of Western learning; he went into politics with the Chinese Communist party, risking his life and living under extreme hardships as he was pursued by the forces of Chiang Kai-shek. He tried to win the peasants over to the demanding routines of guerrilla warfare, political agitation, and more efficient agriculture. His success came because he stayed close to the people and, unlike other rulers of China, showed genuine concern for their needs.

Throughout World War II, the Chinese communists fought the Japanese invaders more vigorously than Chiang's forces did. In the civil war following World War II, the communists defeated Chiang's Kuomintang (Guomindong), and in 1949, with superior organization and purpose as well as with peasant support, they became masters of a new China.

Mao oversimplified the complexities of industrial society. This trait showed up disastrously when in 1958 he staked his leadership on a campaign to create giant communes engaged in agriculture, industry, education, defense, and administration. As his Soviet critics had predicted, this Great Leap Forward into communism proved a catastrophe; twenty-five to thirty million Chinese died of starvation. Mao for a while retired from the limelight. At the same time the Chinese communists, angered by Soviet arrogance and traditionally suspicious of Russian territorial ambition at China's expense, broke away from Moscow's leadership. The Sino-Soviet rift inflicted a serious blow on the unity of world communism. For the next two decades, until a lessening of hostilities in the 1980s, the two huge countries held each other in mutual distrust. The Chinese dreaded the Soviet troops and their missiles near their country's long boundaries. The Soviet government feared invasion by the Chinese masses.

China's isolation was greatest in 1966, when Mao, with the help of the army, staged the Great Proletarian Cultural Revolution. It was directed at entrenched and autocratic bureaucrats and experts, and at any lingering veneration of the Chinese past or foreign models. The agents of this new revolution were young zealots carrying a little red book called *Quotations from Chairman Mao*. In these years Chairman Mao was God; never was the cult of personality and revolutionary zeal carried to greater extremes. The revolution closed universities and institutes of scientific research for many years and carried the country to the verge of economic and civic chaos; it unleashed a wave of violence as brutal as Stalin's terror, discrediting in its aftermath the integrity of revolutionary idealism. The only experts spared were the scientists working on nuclear weapons, the most prestigious instruments of national security. Four years later, Mao, having purged potential rivals, returned to a calmer course.

At his death in 1976, at the age of eighty-three, Mao left to his successors a troubled country. Admitting that he had made mistakes, they cautiously reversed his policies, reinstating the victims of the Great Proletarian Cultural Revolution and setting a new course toward the "Four Modernizations"—in science and technology, in industry, in agriculture, and in national defense. Under the leadership of Deng Xiaoping (b. 1904), they allowed a measure of private enterprise and opened the country to the outside world. Though fearing the subversion of their Chinese ways and communist dedication, they still were eager to attract foreign enterprise from Europe, the United States, Japan, and even Taiwan and Hong Kong, to help them accomplish their goals.

Yet the pressure of a huge and growing population on the country's limited resources remains a baffling problem. China has attempted during the 1980s to curb its population growth, at first by coercive methods that attracted worldwide criticism and achieved only partial success. Official attempts to limit families to one child have been resisted. China's population, now 1.3 billion, is expected to rise to at least 1.5 billion early in the next century. Transforming the teeming masses of China, characterized early in the century as "a sheet of sand," into a national team as disciplined as their Japanese neighbors remains another unresolved challenge.

Hopes for a freer China dimmed in 1989 when troops in Beijing killed hundreds of students demonstrating for democracy. The massacre was followed by the detention or arrest of student leaders and dissident intellectuals, some of whom were executed.

In contrast with the experiment on the mainland, the Chinese offshore island of Taiwan, where the survivors of the Kuomintang fled, proved a remarkable success under far more favorable circumstances. Firmly ruled by a dictatorial regime under U.S. military protection, working with a small population open to the outside world, and benefiting from heavy American investment, prosperous Taiwan has been held up by Western traditionalists as proof that free enterprise is superior to Marxist collectivism as practiced on mainland China. Smallness combined with easy access to the world market and American help obviously facilitated economic modernization.

India   Yet another experiment was started in India, which, with its 785 million people, is the most populous nation in the world after China. British political tradition and the diversity of people helped to preserve a pluralist democratic order, protected by a federal constitution. Under the leadership of Jawaharlal Nehru (1889–1964), the country started its independence in 1947 with high hopes and Five-Year plans; industrialization was considered essential for overcoming poverty and unemployment.

India's industry and agriculture made remarkable progress; with assistance from Western countries and the Soviet Union, the country did manage to feed itself. But modernization created two Indias, existing side by side in stark contrast. Westernized India is capable even of exporting industrial equipment; it lives in reasonable comfort. Yet the other India persists—poor, traditional, caste-ridden, violent, and with little hope for improvement. Ancient customs long suppressed by the British, like widow-burning or banditry, have stealthily re-emerged. Tensions run high between the Westernized and traditional Indias. Nehru's hope for an organic combination of the best in Indian tradition with industrial modernism has not materialized.

The Middle East

Iran   A painful experiment in modernization took place in Iran. The shah of Iran, Mohammed Riza Pahlavi (1919–1980), pressed a precipitous revolution of westernization from above. With the help of his country's oil riches, Western investments, and American weapons, the shah attempted to build a modern state and economy, disregarding his country's religious leaders and savagely repressing all resistance. But the forces of tradition, threatened with extinction, struck back. Deeply stirred, Shiite Muslim fundamentalists, basing their creed on the Koran and moving the mass of people to acts of bravery and martyrdom, staged a revolution that drove out the shah in early 1979.

Then began a new experiment, as extreme as that of the shah, under Ayatollah (the highest rank of religious leader) Ruholla Khomeini (1902–1989). An aged, unbending, and puritanical Muslim, he decried all Western influences, trying to make his Iran—half modern and half traditional—conform to the simple teachings of the prophet Muhammad. Yet Muslim fundamentalists cannot escape modernity. They have proclaimed a constitution and held elections, and they continue to buy modern weapons. They must satisfy the expectations of their people for a better life, give jobs to the unemployed, conduct foreign relations, import food, and sell oil. Although they denounce the materialist immorality of the West and rage against the United States, they must come to terms with the complex Western instruments of power if their revolution is to survive.

In September 1980, President Saddam Hussein of Iraq sent his armies against Khomeini's Iran. The turmoil in Iran may have led him to expect an easy victory, but the Iran-Iraq war has continued inconclusively ever since, claiming over a million casualties. In 1987, it brought the United States fleet into the Persian Gulf to protect the oil shipments of its allies. In 1988, the weary belligerents at last began to prepare for peace.

Israel   Both superpowers are involved in the most protracted conflict in the Middle East, the wars between Arabs and the new state of Israel. War started in 1948–49, when, over the bitter opposition of the Palestinians and their Arab allies, the State of Israel was founded in part of Palestine, which had been a British mandate since 1920. Israel, which brought together Jews from many lands, faced an uncertain future amid relentless terror and counterterror.

In 1956, Egypt under Colonel Gamal Abdul Nasser (1918–1970), who had just started his own experiment in leading Egypt to glory, took over the Suez Canal (hitherto under British control), while threatening Israel. Israel victoriously struck back. Military mobilization for further wars continued, on Israel's side with generous U.S. help, on the Arab side with Soviet support. War broke out again in 1967, leading within six days to a resounding Israeli victory: Israel's warplanes destroyed the airpower of the surrounding Arab states of Egypt, Syria, Iraq, and Jordan in a surprise attack. Drastic Arab defeat, however, did not prevent a further attack by Egypt and Syria on an unprepared Israel in 1973, on Yom Kippur. Both Egypt attacking from the south and Syria from the Golan Heights in the north made impressive gains in the early days of the war, until a hurried mobilization by the Israeli army held and repulsed Arab attacks. Israel broke through on the Egyptian front and crossed to the west bank of the Suez Canal. In the north the Syrian lines were pushed back, although the war with Syria dragged on into 1974.

Neighboring Lebanon, which was being torn apart by civil war between Muslims and Christians, was invaded by Israel in 1982. Israel was determined to drive the displaced Palestinians, organized as a political and military force by the Palestine Liberation Organization (PLO), from that country. The PLO had built up a network of strongholds in Lebanon, subjecting northern Israel to shelling and terrorist infiltration. Meanwhile, the Lebanese conflict had attracted U.S. military intervention as part of a multinational peace-keeping force. Marines landed in Beirut in 1983 but were swiftly withdrawn after a suicide truck bomb destroyed the marine headquarters, leaving 241 dead. The attack was thought to be the work of a fundamentalist Shiite Moslem group with ties to Iran. Humiliating Arab defeats drove embittered Palestinians to increasing acts of terror against Israel and the United States, exporting the fury of Middle Eastern politics into other parts of the world.

Israel has great assets. It can count on the loyalty of its citizens, bound together by a common religion and life threatened daily by war. Israel also has access to American capital and power; in its desire for democratic government and civil liberties, it is part of the West. At the same time, Israel is a hazardous, long-range experiment. Can it prevent the bitter disputes between secular and ultra-orthodox Jews from dividing the country? Can it fuse together its heterogeneous Jewish peoples, many of them from non-Western lands? Above all, can it evolve a constructive relationship with its Arab neighbors, especially the Palestinians, many of whom were displaced from their homeland? Bitterness has escalated into bloodshed between Israelis and Palestinians, threatening to spill over into neighboring states and causing division and dismay among the American friends of Israel.

Africa

The African experience of decolonization is well illustrated by the example of Ghana. The hero of African liberation was Kwame Nkrumah (1909–1972), who transformed the small but comparatively advanced British colony of the Gold Coast into the independent country of Ghana, named after a fabled medieval empire in the western Sahel region of central Africa. From Ghana, Nkrumah hoped to advance the ideal of a powerful united Africa. He symbolized the promise of liberated Africa, preaching pan-Africanism.

Democratic at the outset, Nkrumah's regime soon turned into a personal dictatorship; his one-party state became an instrument for the personal enrichment of his lieutenants, despite its increasingly socialist ideology. Nkrumah took Ghana out of the British Commonwealth, spent the financial reserves left from British rule on hasty and overambitious ventures of economic development, and antagonized the leaders of other newly independent African states. He soon lost the confidence of even his own people and was exiled in 1966 by a military coup. His successors—military, civilian, and military again—have failed to restore the promise or even the prosperity with which Ghanaian independence began.

The tribulations of Ghana were shared by most of the other newly created African states. Starting with democratic constitutions, they changed into one-party states, military dictatorships, or personal regimes. Some of them were benevolent, like those of Jomo Kenyatta of Kenya or Julius Nyerere of Tanzania. All had to try desperately to hold their multiethnic states together, while also paying lip service to African unity. Throughout sub-Saharan Africa, loyalty still centers on family, lineage, and ethnic groups. Only the most uprooted, foreign-educated Africans put their country first.

Unity often was preserved by compulsion and repression, sometimes degenerating into genocidal violence. In a few lands, time-honored African forms of government were perverted by the demands of statehood into unbridled personal rule, rendered murderous by imported Western techniques, as in the case of Idi Amin Dada of Uganda. Some lands, like the former French colonies of Senegal and the Ivory Coast, remained closely associated with their ex-masters; there economic conditions improved and governments remained sta-

Food Relief in Ethiopia. Western nations, benefiting from their agricultural efficiency, try to help raise standards of living around the world. They also help feed people in countries haunted by famine, such as Ethiopia. (© *Sebastiao Salgado/Magnum Photos, Inc.*)

ble. Among the former English colonies, Nigeria was rent by a destructive civil war and barely prevented secession of a large section of the country. By 1979, the most powerful of the sub-Saharan states, its economy buoyed by large exports of oil, Nigeria changed from a military to a civilian regime, beginning a short-lived experiment of democratic rule. Immediately after the first election in early 1984, the army again took over under conditions of serious economic distress precipitated by the sudden decline in oil exports. It promised return to civilian rule in 1992.

In addition to economic underdevelopment and political instability, Africans face the problems of high birth-rates (highest in Kenya) and adverse climate. In 1984–85, sub-Saharan Africa suffered a prolonged drought in which over a million people died. Trapped in their poverty, decimated by disease (including AIDS), and deeply in debt to the leading industrial countries, most African states face a grim future.

At the southern tip of the continent, in the Republic of South Africa, the Africans' desire for self-determination is thwarted by a small minority of European settlers, who date their hold on the country back to the seventeenth century. Clinging to their cultural heritage, the Afrikaners (as they call themselves) also want to continue their advanced industrial economy, which benefits their nonwhite subjects and their African neighbors as well. They bitterly, and often brutally, resist all pressure to end their policy, called *apartheid,* of favoring whites and oppressing the black population.

Latin America

Africa's problems are familiar to the countries of Latin America. After gaining their independence in the early nineteenth century, they have failed to duplicate the progress of North America or Europe. These Latin American nations have been beset by many ills: poverty, rapid population increase, unemployment (or underemployment), malnutrition, ethnic tensions, political instability, and a deep sense of frustration. In the 1980s, after the worldwide economic upswing of the 1960s and 1970s, their fortunes sagged. In 1987, Latin America's foreign debt, a telling index of its economic crisis, exceeded $400 billion. Declining standards of living put a heavy burden on the new democratic regimes that replaced the military juntas previously in power.

In Argentina, the brutal rule of the generals, which began in 1976, collapsed in 1983 after their humiliation by Britain in the contest over the Falkland Islands (see Chapter 21), but the military continues to threaten the civilian government of President Raúl Alfonsín. In neighboring Chile, by contrast, military rule, instituted in 1973 with help from Washington, still reigns under General Augusto Pinochet, whose rule proceeds under a constitution sanctioning his election (and re-election) by plebiscite. In Brazil, the largest South American country, industrialization has advanced rapidly, following the example of Asian countries like South Korea, but its large, heterogeneous population (140 million) is not easily governed. In 1985, after twenty-one years of military rule, Brazil adopted a democratic constitution, although governmental inefficiency and corruption persist. Further north, Venezuela has enjoyed the most stable democratic government in Latin America, benefiting from its rich oil deposits, although suffering from the sharp decline in oil prices after 1979. Neighboring Colombia, meanwhile, struggles with drug producers and their agents, who terrorize both government and society. In Latin America, drug exports have proved to be the only reliable source of foreign exchange for countries with a chronic imbalance of trade and heavy foreign indebtedness, mostly to U.S. banks.

The Latin American country most significant to the United States is Mexico, its southern neighbor. A federal republic under its constitution of 1917, it has been ruled in recent years by the Institutional Revolutionary party (PRI), which follows a middle course between conservatives and Marxists, the latter eager to mobilize (without apparent success) the discontent of the poor. The election of 1988, however, has revived party pluralism. Political stability has been ensured in part by U.S. and foreign investments, but these also contribute to the country's heavy foreign debt and inflation. Even more alarming is the high birthrate among the 90 million Mexicans.

The small Central American countries south of Mexico, lacking (except for

Costa Rica) the preconditions for democratic government, are a battleground between Marxist revolutionaries siding with the poor and conservative dictatorships allied to the rich as well as to the United States. The Marxists look toward Cuba, where Fidel Castro follows the Soviet pattern of modernization while also extending his influence among anti-Western regimes, especially in Africa. Yet his experiment fares no better than its Soviet model.

More than developing countries elsewhere, Latin America—and especially Central America—manages its affairs under the shadow of the United States. Washington protects the interests of American firms operating in the area, and above all tries to keep Soviet influence out of this politically volatile part of the world. For both these reasons, all U.S. presidents since World War II have dispatched armed forces to squash, in President Johnson's words, "the specter of communism." In the 1980s, President Reagan supported the training and arming of the contra forces in his effort to overthrow the socialist Sandinista government in Nicaragua. In 1983, he ordered the invasion of the tiny island-state of Grenada to save it from a reputed Cuban takeover.

Development: Which Way?

As the foregoing cases show, the experiments of westernization and modernization, of adjustment to an interdependent, competitive world, have exacted an excruciating human toll from societies culturally unprepared for drastic changes. Unwilling and unable to break with their cultural heritage yet eager to reap the benefits of modernity, people still wonder: which way should they go, the capitalist way, or the socialist way?

Concluding Reflections: Optimism or Pessimism?

The world is inhabited by over 5 billion human beings; the figure is expected to be around 6 billion by the year 2000, and higher thereafter. Helping to sustain them is a vast array of originally Western achievements: the nation-state, industrialism, science and technology, and world-spanning organizations for business and international cooperation. Some non-Western peoples are now matching Western accomplishments; keeping up with the latest innovations has become an ardent desire—or even an outright necessity—among all people, no matter how attached to their past they feel. Survival depends on mastery of the skills of modernity—originally Western skills—in economic productivity, in scientific and technological progress, and in the development of the most advanced weapons; these capabilities are the keys that command power and prestige in the world. Thus, through westernization and economic interdependence, the new globalism has become an irresistible worldwide reality; it has ominously accelerated the pace of change. Has the transformation been for the better or worse?

Cause for Optimism

Many people dwell on the positive aspects. Global interdependence, they argue, has vastly increased worldwide cooperation. For the first time in all human experience, people from the entire world have a chance to work together for the common good. Look at the impressive results. The volume of world trade has vastly increased, providing new material security for human life—and resulting in a rapid increase in the world's population. People hitherto isolated have been exposed to new opportunities for personal development; they have become mobile in their search to improve their lot.

Global interdependence, furthermore, has stimulated minds over the entire world, recruiting talent from many countries. The advances in all fields of learning have been astounding. Science and technology, more closely linked than ever, have increased human control over nature beyond the wildest dreams of earlier ages. Physicists have explored the atom down to the smallest components of matter; biologists have laid bare the genetic structures of animate matter. Human beings have set foot on the moon. Rockets with sophisticated equipment have been sent to the distant reaches of the solar system. Advances in electronics have brought the whole world to remote villages in Asia and Africa through radio and television. Computers, indispensable to scientists and engineers, have invaded everyday life in finance and business, even in ordinary households.

In the arts and literature, the interaction of cultural influences from all parts of the world has been a creative stimulus. Even more significantly, concern for human dignity has spread. However spurned in practice, the United Nations Universal Declaration of Human Rights sets a worldwide standard as a guide for the future. Agencies like Amnesty International keep track of human rights violations; others send relief in case of famine, epidemic, and natural catastrophe. These developments have created a mood of optimism for some people, who perceive a chance for enlightened control of human destiny over the entire world. Postwar prosperity encouraged an international effort at cooperation to bring natural resources and world population into a steady equilibrium, to provide greater equality around the world, and to avoid devastating world wars. That mood is still alive in some quarters.

Cause for Concern

At the same time, however, there is a contrary mood of pessimism. Despite all the progress, the bulk of humanity is still miserable; more people means more poverty. Inadequate supplies of food, clean water, and medical help diminish the opportunities of about half the world's population. Underfed, diseased, and untrained people perpetuate or even increase the already widespread poverty. Also, the postwar rise in living standards experienced by some peoples is receding in many countries.

Map 22.2   World Population Densities ▶

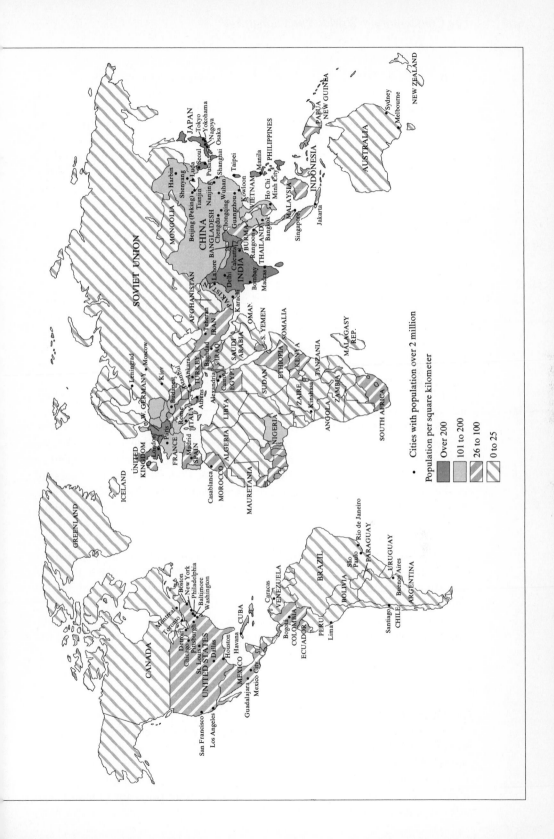

JAPAN
Tokyo
Seoul — Yokohama
Pusan Nagoya
Luda Osaka

Harbin
Shenyang

MONGOLIA

Beijing (Peking) Tianjin
Nanjing
CHINA
Chengdu Wuhan
Chongqing
BANGLADESH Guangzhou Taipei
Calcutta Kowloon PHILIPPINES Manila
Lahore Nanjing
INDIA Rangoon VIETNAM
Delhi BURMA Ho Chi Minh City
Bombay THAILAND
Karachi Madras Bangkok
PAKISTAN Jakarta
Singapore

PAPUA
NEW GUINEA

INDONESIA

MALAYSIA

AUSTRALIA

Sydney
Melbourne

NEW ZEALAND

SOVIET UNION

Leningrad Moscow
Kiev
Istanbul
Budapest
W. GERMANY Ankara
Rome TURKEY
ITALY Athens
Madrid SPAIN
Paris
FRANCE
UNITED
KINGDOM
London

AFGHANISTAN
Tehran
IRAN
Baghdad
IRAQ
SAUDI
ARABIA
S. YEMEN
OMAN

Alexandria
Cairo
EGYPT
LIBYA
SUDAN
ETHIOPIA
SOMALIA
KENYA
TANZANIA
ZAIRE
Kinshasa
ANGOLA ZAMBIA
MALAGASY
REP.

NIGERIA

ALGERIA

MOROCCO
Casablanca
MAURETANIA

SOUTH AFRICA

ICELAND

GREENLAND

CANADA

Montreal
Toronto Boston
Detroit New York
Chicago Pittsburgh Philadelphia
St. Louis Baltimore
Washington
UNITED STATES
Dallas
San Francisco Houston
Los Angeles CUBA
Havana
Guadalajara
Mexico City
MEXICO

Caracas
VENEZUELA
Bogotá
COLOMBIA
ECUADOR
PERU
Lima
BOLIVIA

BRAZIL
Rio de Janeiro
São Paulo
PARAGUAY
URUGUAY
Buenos Aires
Santiago ARGENTINA
CHILE

• Cities with population over 2 million

Population per square kilometer

Over 200

101 to 200

26 to 100

0 to 25

Since World War II, all efforts to bridge the gap between rich and poor nations have failed; in fact the gap has widened. Modern communications have raised the expectations of poor people around the globe, but their societies suffer from staggering burdens that impede development: soaring populations, widespread illiteracy, malnutrition, disease, and huge debts. Furthermore, global military expenditures exceed the combined gross national product of China, India, and sub-Saharan Africa. Third World military outlays grow even faster, as a percentage of their GNP, than those of the developed countries. More money is spent on trading weapons on the international market than on trading grains.

Added to this dismal picture is the pollution of the atmosphere, seas, and soil caused by industrialization and human greed and carelessness. Forests dwindle and soil erodes as people clear trees for fuel and farmland. And the basic resources—arable land, water, and fuel—needed to support ever-larger populations become scarcer with each passing year. The new globalism has raised, for the first time in human existence, alarm over the limited physical resources of Planet Earth. Anxiety also has risen over the migration of the poor from villages to the ever-expanding cities, and from overcrowded lands to richer opportunities in Western Europe or North America. Such migration has already heightened racial, religious, and cultural tensions.

Disabled by poverty, non-Western lands also have to struggle with cultural disorientation. In most non-Western parts of the world, traditional cultures have been subverted by Western influence. A generally Western-educated elite follows a Western lifestyle—sometimes with irresponsible extravagance—while still tied to native tradition. The bulk of the population is caught between tradition and Western ways. The old ways, with their moral obligations justified by tradition and religion, are discredited by the influx of modernity from the West. The moral vacuum, combined with the ordeals of modernizing, encourages corruption, violence, and, all too often, utter inhumanity.

Under these conditions, stable governments have little chance to emerge, and without stable governments, effective self-help seems impossible. The historical record of the past thirty years shows a rising level of violence within the new states created after World War II. The brutal communist and fascist regimes before World War II have their imitators in many parts of today's world. Terrorism born of desperation and fanaticism is rising around the world. And people worldwide suffer from an ever-present anxiety evoked by the existence of weapons that can wipe out the human race.

Coping with the Future

Optimists and pessimists, as well as pro-Western and anti-Western voices, clash furiously in the contemporary world. In the growing confusion, powerful groups of fundamentalists want to go back to the traditional past, to the old creeds. Others want to reorder the world according to such universal prescriptions as socialism or communism, which hold the past in contempt. Americans advertise their own democratic experience as a prescription for global peace and happiness. Meanwhile, many people, confused by the diverse views that

Chronology 22.1 ◊ International Relations in an Age of Superpowers

April 1945	United Nations established
1946–1947	Greek Civil War
1947	Truman Doctrine; Marshall Plan inaugurated
1948	Creation of Israel
1948–1949	Stalinization of Eastern Europe; Berlin airlift
1949	Federal Republic of Germany (West Germany) established; NATO formed; first Soviet atomic bomb exploded; People's Republic of China established under Mao Zedong
1950–1953	Korean War
1953	American and Soviet hydrogen bombs developed
1957	Sputnik launched—the space age begins
1959	Castro overthrows Batista regime in Cuba
1960	American Inter-Continental Ballistic Missile developed
1961	Berlin Wall built, dividing the city of Berlin
1962	Cuban missile crisis
1963–1973	Vietnam War
1972	Détente; Anti-Ballistic Missile Treaty
1975	Helsinki Agreements
1979	Shah of Persia ousted; Soviet Union invades Afghanistan
1987	Gorbachev-Reagan summit in Washington; INF Treaty agreed

impinge on them, tend to withdraw into themselves, concentrating on the work before them and seeking their own pleasures.

Looking back over the long evolution of Western civilization to its present culmination, we should take to heart, in case we grow too complacent about its accomplishments, the warning of the English statesman Walter Bagehot. He pointed out that the decline of the Roman and English nations lay in their failure to understand the institutions that they had created. Can the present generation of Western peoples, above all Americans, understand our greatest institution—the newly created global community—and shape its development according to the highest ideals of Western civilization—reason, freedom, and respect for human dignity?

Notes

1. "The Charter of the United Nations," *Yearbook of the United Nations,* 37 (New York: Department of Public Information, United Nations, 1983), p. 1325.

2. "The Truman Doctrine," *Major Problems in American Foreign Policy: Documents and Essays,* vol. 2, ed. by Thomas G. Paterson (Lexington, Mass.: D. C. Heath, 1978), p. 290.

Suggested Reading

Achebe, Chinua, *Man of the People* (1966). A great Nigerian novelist describes the ways of Nigerian politics after independence.

Barnet, Richard J., *The Lean Years: Politics in the Age of Scarcity* (1980). A useful survey of the relationship between population and world resources, with an eye to the politics involved.

Butterfield, Fox, *China, Alive in the Bitter Sea* (1982). An illuminating account of life in China by a *New York Times* correspondent.

LaFeber, Walter, *Inevitable Revolutions: The United States in Central America* (1983). The collision of U.S. national security and commercial interests with revolutionary aspirations and reform.

Liang Heng and Judith Shapiro, *Son of the Revolution* (1983). A personal account of life in Mao's China during the Cultural Revolution.

Mansfield, Peter, *The Arabs* (1985). A basic guide to the Arab world.

Naipaul, V. S., *A Bend in the River* (1977). Insights into culture conflict in central Africa.

———, *India: A Wounded Civilization* (1978). An account of India in the clash of cultures by one of the world's foremost contemporary writers, himself the product of several cultures.

North-South: A Program for Survival. The Report of the Independent Commission on International Development Issues under the Chairmanship of Willy Brandt (1980). A significant document on the needs for peace, justice, and jobs in the Third World.

Oz, Amos, *In the Land of Israel* (1983). An invaluable background book on the people and politics of Israel.

Sick, Gary, *All Fall Down: America's Tragic Encounter with Iran* (1985). An insider's account of the fall of the shah and the subsequent hostage crisis.

Vogel, Ezra, *Japan Number One* (1980). A challenging view of Japan's rapid advance.

Review Questions

1. How did the cold war affect the organization of Europe from 1947 to 1958?

2. What were the causes of détente? Was it a temporary phenomenon, or does it have a lasting basis?

3. Outline the effects of decolonization. What benefits were expected, and what were the actual consequences?

4. In what respect does the modern development of Japan differ from that of China, India, or the African countries?

5. What were the conditions and the problems facing Mao Zedong in his effort to modernize China? In what respects did he succeed? In what respects did he fail?

6. What would you say were the chief developments in the Indian subcontinent after World War II? What is the current news from that part of the world?

7. Which area of the world do you consider the most troublesome and dangerous from the point of view of U.S. national security?

8. Do you consider yourself an optimist or a pessimist? What do you see as the major problems confronting your generation?

Index

Student Evaluation of

Western Civilization: A Brief Survey

While a textbook is being written, the publisher works closely with the author(s) and with course instructors to be sure that the book is useful and interesting. Since the main reader of this textbook is you the student, we at Houghton Mifflin Company would also like to know what you think about the quality of this text.

Please answer the questions below, and mail this response sheet to

College Marketing Services
Houghton Mifflin Company, One Beacon Street
Boston, MA 02108

We will appreciate reading your comments on the textbook.

1. Does the textbook cover the information necessary to master your course? Circle the appropriate number.

1	2	3	4
No, none of the information is there	Yes, some of the information is there	Yes, most of the information is there	Yes, almost all of the information is there

2. Was the textbook excessively difficult to read?

1	2	3	4
Yes, I often had to consult a dictionary	No, although there were some unfamiliar words	No, the book was not too difficult to read and understand	No, the textbook was almost too easy to read

3. Did the textbook hold your interest?

1	2	3	4
No, I often had trouble concentrating	Yes, but a few parts are dull	Yes, the text held my attention	Yes, I enjoyed many parts of the book

4. Which three chapters are the best?　　　　　　　Why?

5. Which three chapters are least effective?　　　　　Why?

6. Do any parts of the book stand out in your mind? Please identify them by page number or topic, and please explain why you remember these sections.

7. Do you have any general suggestions for improving the text?

Thank you for giving your reactions to this textbook.

(Optional)

Course Title _____

Name _____

College _____

City _____*State* _____